Peer Programs on the College Campus

Theory, Training, and "Voice of the Peers"

Sherry L. Hatcher, PhD, Editor

Resource Publications, Inc.
San Jose, California

Editorial director: Kenneth Guentert
Managing editor: Elizabeth J. Asborno

© 1995 Resource Publications, Inc. All rights reserved. No part of this book may be reproduced without written permission from the publisher. For reprint permission, write to:

Reprint Department
Resource Publications, Inc.
160 E. Virginia Street #290
San Jose, CA 95112-5876

Library of Congress Cataloging in Publication Data
Peer programs on the college campus : theory, training,
   and "voice of the peers" / [edited by] Sherry L. Hatcher.
     p.   cm.
   Includes bibliographical references.
   ISBN 0-89390-349-3 (pbk.)
   1. Peer counseling—United States. 2. Counseling in higher education—United States. I. Hatcher, Sherry L.
   LB2343.P366 1995
   378.1'94—dc20   95-31772

Printed in the United States of America

99 98 97 96 95 | 5 4 3 2 1

*To Robert Hatcher, Jessamyn Anne, and Juliet Leslie—
whose natural empathy, wit, and love
inspire and support this project;
and to my parents,
who have shown courage in challenging times.*

Contents

Acknowledgments vii
About the Contributors xi

A College-Level Course on Peer Counseling

1. Why Peer Counseling on the College Campus? 3
   Sherry L. Hatcher, PhD

2. Rationale for an Academic Course in Peer Counseling 20
   *Sherry L. Hatcher, PhD, Lisa Walsh, MA,
   Meredith Reynolds, MA, and Jill Sullivan, BA*

3. The Peer Counseling Course for College Students 31
   *Sherry L. Hatcher, PhD, Lisa Walsh, MA,
   Meredith Reynolds, MA, and Jill Sullivan, BA*

Peer Counseling Practica

4. A Peer Counseling Phone Line 83
   Doreen Murasky, ACSW, and Todd Sevig, PhD

5. Resident Staff As Peer Mentors 134
   Robin Sarris MPH, MBA

6. A Peer Counseling Program for Older Persons 161
   Ruth Campbell, MSW

Peer Education Practica

7. Peer Education at University Health Services 183
   *Janet Zielasko, MPH, CHES, Polly Paulson, MPH, CHES,
   Robin Nwankwo, MS, MPH, RD, Gen Stewart, MPH,
   and Kristin Hoppe, MPH, CHES*

8. A Campus Peer Education and Counseling Line
   for Sexual Assault Prevention and Awareness 239
   Kata Issari, MSW

Academic Peer Advising Practicum

9. An Academic Peer Advising Program in Psychology 275
   Sherry Hatcher, PhD, and Kate Fodor, BA

Peer Teaching

10. Peer Writing Tutors 311
    *Phyllis Lassner, PhD, Helen Isaacson, PhD,
    and Susan Marie Harrington, PhD*

11. Peer Facilitation in the Feminist Classroom: A Model
    for Peer Teaching an Introductory Course in Women's Studies . . 327
    Jane Hassinger, MSW, Mildred Tirado, Phd, and Ruby Beale, PhD

12. Reactions to Peer Teaching Assistants
    in the College-Level Peer Counseling Course. 352
    Sherry Hatcher, PhD, and Brian Litzenberger, MA

Multicultural Peer Facilitation

13. Addressing Ethnicity within Peer Helping Programs 365
    Calvin Chin, BA, and Jena Baker, BA

14. Bridging Differences
    through Peer-Facilitated Intergroup Dialogues 378
    Biren A. Nagda, MSW, Ximena Zúñiga, PhD, and Todd Sevig, PhD

Discussion and Conclusions

15. Peer Helping for Prevention on the College Campus. 417
    Sherry Hatcher, PhD

Appendices

Appendix A. Presenting Concerns to College Peer Counselors:
  Roleplay Scenarios. 425
Appendix B. Sample Exercises to Practice Peer Counseling Skills. . . . 435
Appendix C. Interview Schedules for Research Protocol 443
Appendix D. Coding Schema for Analyzing the Data 447
Appendix E. Demographic and Survey Findings 452

Acknowledgments

This book was born from a course that I introduced at the University of Michigan in 1987 with the help of several gifted graduate students. It is not easy to initiate a new course at a large university, and this would not have been possible without the support of two successive Psychology Department Chairs: Professor Albert C. Cain and Professor Patricia Gurin. Professor Gurin further gave me the opportunity to help design and supervise the Psychology Peer Advising Program, and it was her idea to let the peer helpers speak in their own voices. I am deeply grateful to these two good mentors and friends.

The Office of the Vice President for Research at the University of Michigan awarded me a grant that allowed this research to go forward. It covered costs of equipment, supplies, transcription of the tapes, and some data analysis. For this generous help, which made it possible to conduct and code a large number of interviews, I am very grateful. Nancy Bates, Department of Psychology Manager, who graciously administered this grant for us, deserves our thanks as well.

Mr. Kenneth Guentert, Editorial Director of Resource Publications, Inc., has been supportive of our efforts to offer a creative new text at the college level on peer helping. Our profound thanks are due both to Mr. Guentert and to Resource Publications, Inc., for their faith in, and great help with, this volume. We appreciate also the encouragement and insightful suggestions of Ms. Elizabeth J. Asborno, managing editor of Resource Publications, Inc.

Acknowledgments

A number of teaching and research assistants have contributed enthusiastically to this text. One of them, Jill Sullivan, BA, has been with the project from its inception and has served as my chief research assistant. Her contributions to this work have been generous, multifaceted, and invaluable.

Graduate teaching assistants who helped me to initiate the peer counseling course were: Lisa Walsh, Missi Nadeau, and Ken Miller. Others who later taught for the course include Meredith Reynolds, Jerry Galea, Brian Litzenberger, Kate Porterfield, and Nikeea Copeland. Thanks also to Bettye Elkins for her wise counsel on this project and to Dr. Robert Hatcher, who did extraordinary repairs of all computer glitches.

I was fortunate to have many talented research assistants, who helped conduct the interviews and analyze the resulting data over a period of three years. They are (in alphabetical order): Sarah Bench, Laurie Berkwitz, Kathryn Foley, Alex Grossberg, Hilda Hall, Juliet Hatcher, Heather Heydens, Michael Hoexster, Brie Jeweler, Gregory Marion, Meredith Reynolds, Wendy Richman, Liat Riff, Jennifer Stevens, Brian Stull, Jill Sullivan, Renee Tikkanen, and Anne Vogel. I thank all of these students for their hard work and loyal dedication to this complex and demanding project.

Special words of appreciation must be offered in memory of Terry VanBrunt, whose untimely death interrupted her enthusiastic and beautiful work on this manuscript. Her contributions in support of this book were great and would have undoubtedly continued much longer. All who knew her miss her very much.

Finally, and quite importantly, thanks are due to the University of Michigan for offering such a plentiful range of high quality peer programs.[1] I am enormously grateful in particular to all of the authors who have faithfully contributed to our course and who wrote for this volume with so much

---

[1] The different programs included in this volume are administered by various units in the university: the College of Literature, Science, and the Arts (chapters 3, 9, 19, 11, 12, 14), the Office of the Vice President for Student Affairs (chapters 4, 5, 7, 8, 14), the Rackham School of Graduate Studies (chapter 13), and the medical school (chapter 6).

Acknowledgments

thoughtfulness and enthusiasm. Our profound gratitude goes also to their peer facilitators, who allowed us to "hear" their unique voices and moving stories about peer helping on a college campus. I expect that these interviews were maximally candid as they were told to "peer interviewers" on my research team.

Jill Sullivan and I inserted the interview material, "the voices of the peers," into the text of each chapter, and I have attempted to edit the entire work for consistency of style and spirit across chapters. I hope that this work will be of interest to all those who believe—not in "giving psychology away," as it is sometimes stated pejoratively, but rather in sharing it for the benefit of all who care about health and prevention.

Sherry Lynn Hatcher, Editor

About the Contributors

SHERRY L. HATCHER, PhD, editor, is an Adjunct Associate Professor of Psychology, Director of Peer Programs, and Clinical Area Associate Chair in the Department of Psychology at the University of Michigan. She is a licensed clinical psychologist who has published previously on such topics as adolescent development, the psychology of women, psychotherapy research, and peer counseling. Dr. Hatcher has twice won Excellence in Education Awards for teaching undergraduates at Michigan; she is also an Associate Research Scholar at the Center for the Education of Women at the University of Michigan.

JENA BAKER, BA, received her BA in sociology from the University of Michigan and is currently a graduate student in the School of Public Health at UM. Her area of specialty is public health policy and administration with a concentration in child and family health.

RUBY BEALE, PhD, is an Adjunct Assistant Professor of Business Administration and Organizational Psychology and former lecturer in women's studies at the University of Michigan. Dr. Beale also works as a consultant to an organization on problems of leadership, diversity, and group cohesion.

RUTH CAMPBELL, MSW, is the Associate Director for Social Work and Community Programs at the University of Michigan Geriatrics Center, a faculty associate of the Institute of Gerontology, and Director of the Social Work program at Turner Geriatric Clinic. In addition, she is a research associate of the UM's Center for Japanese Studies and has been awarded an ABE Fellowship for 1995-6 to write a book on aging in Japan.

CALVIN CHIN, BA, is a graduate of the University of Michigan and a graduate student in the Department of Clinical Psychology at

About the Contributors

New York University, where he hopes to continue his work on underrepresented populations.

KATE FODOR, BA, is a graduate of Oberlin College and has taught in Baltimore with the *Teach for America* program. During the summer of 1992, she was a visiting scholar and research assistant for Dr. Hatcher at the University of Michigan.

SUSAN MARIE HARRINGTON, PhD, a graduate of Dartmouth College with a MA and PhD from the University of Michigan, is currently an Assistant Professor of English and Director of Placement and Assessment at Indiana University-Purdue University at Indianapolis and teaches a variety of courses. Her current research interest is the ways students and teachers communicate about the quality of student work, course goals, and grades.

JANE HASSINGER, MSW, is a lecturer in psychology, the School of Social Work, and women's studies at the University of Michigan and is in private practice as a psychotherapist. She also co-directs the Interdisciplinary Program in Feminist Practice, which organizes seminars and bibliographic materials on feminist scholarship for faculty and graduate students. She was a staff member at Counseling Services for many years, where she supervised several peer programs.

KRISTIN HOPPE, MPH, CHES, is a health educator who oversaw the Stress and Time Management Peer Program at University Health Service. She was also a coordinator of the HIV testing program and a patient-relations representative at UHS.

HELEN ISAACSON, PhD, has been at the University of Michigan since 1976 teaching courses such as "Writing about Psychology" and "Writing about Art." For the past four years she has trained and supervised the peer tutors who work for the English Composition Board at the University of Michigan.

KATA ISSARI, MSW, served as the Senior Counselor and acting Director of the University of Michigan's Sexual Assault Prevention and Awareness Center. She currently serves as Development Specialist at the Center for the Prevention of Sexual and Domestic Violence and as President of the National Coalition Against Sexual Assault.

PHYLLIS LASSNER, PhD, teaches writing and women's studies at Northwestern University, a position she held for many years at the University of Michigan. She is the author of two books on the Anglo-Irish author Elizabeth Bowen and articles on feminist theory

About the Contributors

and composition as well as on British fiction of the Second World War.

BRIAN LITZENBERGER, MA, a graduate of Yale College, is a doctoral student in clinical psychology at the University of Michigan. He studied peer counseling with Peter Salovey at Yale and is writing his dissertation on psychosexual development, which he plans to continue in an academic career.

DOREEN MURASKY, ACSW, is a clinical social worker in private practice in Ann Arbor. She obtained her MSW from the University of Michigan School of Social Work. She worked at the University of Michigan Counseling Services and coordinated the 76-GUIDE program for six years.

BIREN NAGDA, MSW, is a doctoral student in the joint program in social work and psychology at the University of Michigan. He works as an instructor, trainer, and consultant with the Program on Intergroup Relations and Conflict. He has taught courses in intergroup relations and conflict and multicultural group processes. His teaching and research interests are in multicultural education, educational equality, and multicultural organization development.

ROBIN NWANKWO, MS, MPH, RD, is a staff dietician and health educator at the University of Michigan Health Services. She has overseen "The Body Image, Healthy and Disordered Eating Program" there.

POLLY PAULSON, MPH, CHES, is a health educator and certified HIV counselor who works with the University of Michigan Health Services in designing and implementing sexual health education programs and the anonymous HIV Counseling and Testing Program. She is also an HIV instructor for the American Red Cross and a certified sex educator with the American Association of Sex Educators, Counselors, and Therapists.

MEREDITH REYNOLDS, MA, is a doctoral student in clinical psychology at the University of Michigan. She plans an academic career in researching developmental issues in human sexuality.

ROBIN SARRIS, MPH, MSW, is formerly the Assistant Director of Housing and Residence Education at the University of Michigan. Currently she is the Administrative Manager of the Department of English Language and Literature at the University of Michigan.

TODD SEVIG, PhD, is a staff psychologist at Counseling Services and program associate of the Program on Intergroup Relations and Conflict at the University of Michigan. He obtained his PhD from

Ohio State University in counseling psychology. His interests are peer approaches to counseling/programming and working with multicultural approaches to training, teaching, counseling, and research. He coordinated the 76-GUIDE program for three years.

GEN STEWART, MPH, received her degree from the University of Michigan with a specialization in health education. She is a Certified Health Education Specialist who specializes in drug prevention/education and stress and time management.

JILL SULLIVAN, BA, a graduate of the University of Michigan, is currently a doctoral student in clinical psychology at the University of Minnesota, where she is studying resiliency in the children of alcoholics and doing research with the Minnesota Twin Families study.

MILDRED TIRADO, PhD, is a lecturer in psychology and women's studies and staff psychologist at Counseling Services at the University of Michigan. Dr. Tirado consults extensively on issues of diversity in groups and gender equality.

LISA WALSH, MA, is a doctoral student in clinical psychology at the University of Michigan. Her dissertation is on eating disorders in college women. In the future, she plans to work with children, adolescents, and their families.

JANET ZIELASKO, MS, CHES, is Director of the Health Promotion and Community Relations Department at the University of Michigan Health Service. She has developed, implemented, evaluated, and supervised all of the health education programs and materials for the UM community, including support staff, interns, and peer health educators. Ms. Zielasko also coordinates the Contraceptive Peer Education Program through the Health Service. She has worked in this field for sixteen years.

XIMENA ZÚÑIGA, PhD, has been Director of the Program on Intergroup Relations and Conflict at the University of Michigan. She obtained her PhD in education at the University of Michigan and MA at the Universidad Católica de Chile. She teaches courses on multicultural group processes, intergroup relations, and women working across differences. Her research interests include education equality, multiculturalism, and participatory approaches to research and social action.

A College-Level Peer Counseling Course

Chapter 1

Why Peer Counseling on the College Campus?

Sherry L. Hatcher, PhD

The Myths Surrounding Peer Counseling

Not long ago, we were invited to introduce peer counseling to a high school parent association meeting—the students in this college preparatory institution had requested such a program. They thought that it might be useful to learn listening skills and to mentor their peers, both agemates and younger students alike.

When the subject was introduced, a number of parents were exercised at the very mention of peer counseling. The misconception they clearly held was that peer counseling meant unsupervised and immature adolescents conducting "psychotherapy." As we attempted to intervene—to explain that responsible peer counseling is always supervised by a qualified professional counselor; that student peer counselors are intensively trained, then screened for successful training; that they are taught to make referrals to professionals when indicated and that peer "helping"[1] deals with "problems in everyday living"—we were shouted down by one parent who said: "Everyone knows what peer counseling is."

---

[1] "Peer helping" is the term preferred by the National Peer Helpers Association so as to avoid the connotations of "professional counseling"; peer counseling, peer education, peer advising, and peer teaching are sub-categories of peer helping.

Unfortunately this parent's sentiment is widely shared, yet unfounded. Even among professional social workers, psychologists, and psychiatrists, we have discovered a widespread mythology regarding peer counseling—about what it is and what it is not. A number of professionals with whom I have worked for over twenty years in my capacity as a clinical psychologist have alluded to the idea that this peer work (which many in the field view as prevention) is somehow unseemly—i.e., that it is less than a serious endeavor to train paraprofessionals to listen to the concerns of others. Still more discouraging, a few clinicians have openly worried that if this prevention movement were to accelerate, it might affect their economic security. Indeed, it seems to be the case that even many highly educated mental health professionals harbor misconceptions similar to those of laypersons about "peer counseling"—what it is and what it is not.

Add to this confusion the various distinctions among *peer counseling, peer education, (academic) peer advising, peer teaching,* and *group peer facilitation* and one gets responses of increased perplexity. This is exemplified in a survey conducted by two students (Foley & Shafer, 1992), in which misconceptions and myths about peer facilitative work were convincingly documented. A number of subjects, drawn from a variety of college classes and who had not taken peer counseling training, when asked to differentiate between peer helping and professional counseling, simply wrote on their questionnaires: "What's the difference?" When further asked to describe the likely services of a peer counseling, academic peer advising, or peer education program as contrasted with analogous professional services, still more confusion resulted. Almost one third of the respondents surveyed could not differentiate among the types of peer helping nor could they effectively contrast the functions of professional interventions from peer paraprofessional services. Typical misconceptions suggested that peer counseling is viewed simply as peers offering psychotherapy or peers giving advice to others, both of which are specifically countermanded by peer helping guidelines. Such inexact responses are not so very different from those offered by our professional colleagues. Clearly there is a problem in educating both the lay public and professionals about the purposes, scope, ethics, and supervisory backup inherent in responsible peer counseling programs.

It is the intention of this volume to address some of this mythology, to define and clarify the types and purposes of peer helping, and, most specifically, to illustrate its many natural and successful applications on a college campus. To accomplish this, we offer this and another introductory chapter which address the teaching of peer helping to post-secondary students; these are followed by chapters authored by those who have helped to organize peer programs in a university setting. Thus, distinctions among the variety of peer helping services cited above will be defined and illustrated with model programs in the chapters that follow. Throughout the text you will find "the voices of the peers," the words of those college students who took our class and those young women and men who participated in the wide range of peer programs on campus.

Peer Programs and the College Student

The college years present a stage in which the developmental advances of cognition, moral sensibility, and introspection are blossoming (Piaget, 1972; Kohlberg, 1964; Hatcher, R., et al., 1990). It is a stage in which prevention and paraprofessional training are particularly well utilized (Hatcher, S., et al., 1994) and it would be a shame to have this movement which has burgeoned so extensively at the high school level (Myrick & Erney, 1978; Carr & Saunders, 1980; Tindall, 1989; Sturkie & Gibson, 1989; Varenhorst, 1984) be less accessible to the age group for which it may be most particularly well utilized. It is hoped that this collection of chapters by experts in the field may serve as a useful text at the college level, where such literature is in very short supply and where classes and applied programs for peer work may be enormously useful. It is also hoped that its usefulness will transcend the classroom and lead to the development of peer programs in a wide variety of settings.

In their introduction to *Peer Counseling: Skills and Perspectives*, the primary existing text exclusively for college level peer counselors, D'Andrea and Salovey (1983) conclude the following from their evaluation of peer programs at Yale:

1. There is a broad student interest in peer counselor training.

2. University and college counseling centers should encourage interested students to develop peer counseling services to supplement the existing professional counseling services.

3. A peer counseling service should be operated and evaluated with the same care as a professional clinical service.

4. A peer counseling service is a valuable addition to a campus clinical service but does not replace the existing professional service (xvii).

This volume is offered with the spirit of the above mandate. As is clearly stated by de Rosenroll (1989), to initiate a peer program and/or peer counseling training class requires the support of relevant community members, administrators, and professional counterparts to the paraprofessional or peer counselors. Such support as noted at the outset of this volume is not often garnered without some healthy debate. The good news is that most responsibly run peer programs tend to be greatly esteemed, once having proven their effectiveness and utility. Thus, program evaluation is an essential component for all peer programs.

In the chapters that follow, the authors were asked to describe their training, program designs, the ethical issues that impact their work, including their provision for professional supervision and how their peer programs are evaluated. Our research project enabled us to interview 110 peer helpers and to contribute their "voices" to each chapter (chapters 3 through 14).

What Is Peer Counseling?

D'Andrea and Salovey define peer counseling as follows:

...the use of active listening and problem-solving skills, along with knowledge about human growth and mental health, to counsel people who are our peers....The basic premise is that people are capable of solving most of their own problems of daily living if given the chance. The role of the counselor in peer counseling is not to solve people's problems for them but rather to assist them in finding their own solutions....By using active listening and counseling skills...the peer counselor helps the counselee clarify his or her thoughts and feelings and explore various options and solutions (3).

If this definition has a Rogerian ring, it is no accident. It was indeed reassuring to us, as clinical psychologists in search of prevention techniques, to access a body of work largely present in the education and counseling literatures but fathered by clinical psychologist Carl Rogers (Rogers, 1951, 1969, 1980; Kirschenbaum & Henderson, 1989).

The tenets cited above by D'Andrea and Salovey are all aspects of client-centered or "person-centered" psychotherapy, in which the emphasis, unlike for psychodynamic therapies, is most often on the present rather than on the past. Rogerian-based work stresses that it is the client who solves his or her own problems in an atmosphere of non-judgmentalness, empathic listening, and the clarification of affective expressions of the counselee by the peer counselor—in sum, what Rogers (1951) called "unconditional positive regard" for the client.

The first paraprofessional adaptation of Rogerian work was published in 1969 in the *Personnel and Guidance Journal*; it was a program for high school students to help peers in an academic setting. While the client-centered heritage of peer counseling is occasionally cited in the peer helping literature, it is oddly omitted in an otherwise excellent and comprehensive history of the field of peer helping (Varenhorst, 1984). While Carl Rogers' last work (1983) was very much oriented to societal applications of client-centered work, Rogers did not live to see the full range of prevention applications of the client-centered movement. Interestingly, in 1987, Rogers was posthumously awarded the Nobel Peace Prize for his work in the prevention of individual and societal aggression. One imagines that it would have afforded him great pleasure to learn of the burgeoning and far-reaching applications of his work in the peer helping movement.

Applications of Peer Counseling

Peer counseling may be applied in a wide variety of settings. Many of these prototypes will be illustrated in this text in the example of one college campus and its particularly rich array of peer helping programs.[2] This range of peer programs is representative of those on many large campuses throughout the United States and Canada. While each peer program described here offers a model of peer helping with a specific focus, all relate to work with college students. At the same time, many of these programs are translatable to non-college settings such as medicine, business, politics, and a variety of other educational milieu.

We focus on college students in this volume because we believe it is a particularly appropriate stage of life for peer work. College students are developmentally interested in and capable of self-observation and empathy in ways that have not been possible earlier for either the immature child or the budding adolescent. The maturing identity consolidation of the college student (Erikson, 1968) forms an essential backdrop for peer counselor training and is benefited by the relatively stable ego capacities of cognition, engagement with introspection, empathic concern, and solid reality testing, which generally appear at this time of life.

While still relatively sparse, there is an increasing research literature which addresses the success of peer work at the college level for "problems in everyday living." Studies by Zunker and Brown (1966) and Botvin et al. (1990) report that college students can be at least as effective as professionals in helping peers with everyday problems, academic advising, and peer education issues. In conjunction with *but never instead of* professional services on the campus, peer helping

---

[2] All programs and classes presented in this book are from the University of Michigan.

is therefore a very appropriate medium for student community service.

From preadolescence onward, youth gravitate to their peers for comfort and advice as developmentally appropriate stand-ins for grownups, from whom they are striving for psychological and physical independence (Blos, 1962). The fact that our society fosters adolescent peer relationships as a way-station between childhood and adulthood (Adelson, 1980; Hatcher, S., et al., 1994) makes it all the more compelling that peers should be well trained in skills of listening to and helping their agemates to effectively solve their own problems. At the same time, it should be noted that the very definition of adolescence—the origin of the term itself (Hall, 1905)—is somewhat culturally specific. More efforts must be made to translate peer helping service into its potentially culturally sensitive variations (see chapters 13 and 14).

Because peers often have more available time than busy professionals, because they tend to be enthusiastic, flexible, and accessible, and because of their similar life space and experience, they can be especially empathic to their agemates when properly trained and supervised. The peer aspect of a counseling relationship often creates a sense of comfort for the counselee, an initial positive alliance so important in all aspects of counseling work. Such empathic connections may not be as readily experienced by the student with a counselor who is the age of the student's parents. This sentiment is quite clear in the many voices of the peers you will read throughout this volume.

Finally, the services of peer counselors are cost effective and can potentiate the financial resources and capabilities of existing professional agencies on a campus. Usually there is more than enough business to go around for both professional and peer counselors.

The Voice of the Peers in the Classroom

As we present various peer programs ranging from a counseling hotline to peer education programs at the health services to multiculturally oriented workshops, you will notice varied training techniques and different modes of supervisory input. But there will be commonalties, too: in the emphasis on high ethical standards, in the professional "backup" provided to peer helpers, and in the quality of program-specific content. In collecting a variety of program structures, content areas, and philosophies of college level peer helping, we hope to give you a sense of the breadth of this field. For those who are considering the implementation of a peer program at the post-secondary level, we hope to offer a menu of options which can be combined and tailored to individual institutional needs.

Relationship between the Course on Peer Counseling and the Applied Programs on Campus

A few college campuses have one or more courses from which peer counselors are trained, tested, and subsequently "certified." Since basic peer counseling skills are offered in a course we teach in the Department of Psychology (Peer Counseling for College Students), many of the peer helping programs on our campus recruit peer helpers, at least in part, from our class. In addition, most campus programs offer their own training specific to the content of their work. This will become clear as the text evolves.

Students in our peer counseling course have the opportunity to exercise in a practical setting the skills they have learned by volunteering to work in one or more of these related programs. Such a mutual exchange between the classroom and campus agencies is reflected in the format of this text. The thread that weaves together the chapters, each on different programs, is the "voice of the peers."

"Voice of the Peers" in the Course on Peer Counseling

We will begin with "the voice of the peers" in our classroom, essentially working backward from the feedback students gave us on the peer counseling course to the nature of the content we have taught in this class (see chapters 2 and 3) and how we have taught it so as to address college-level issues and techniques.

Why Peer Counseling on the College Campus?

Many of the peers who have taken our course have given important feedback in the journals and evaluations they write. At the end of the course they offer a perspective on what they have gained and what they still wish to learn. It is from some of these "reports" that we cull a humanistic summary of many of the principles of peer counseling, summarized by D'Andrea and Salovey as "The Eight Commandments for Peer Counselors" (2):

1. Be nonjudgmental

2. Be empathic

3. Don't give personal advice

4. Don't ask questions that begin with "why"

5. Don't take responsibility for the other person's problems

6. Don't interpret (when paraphrase will do)

7. Stick with the here and now

8. Deal with feelings first

Much of the feedback we have received from students who completed the course addresses their experience of these commandments. Students' feedback alludes to their developing skills of empathic listening, the roleplays they invent in order to practice these skills,[3] the discussions they have in which they frequently reflect on the value of what they have learned, and all of the above as it applies to their everyday lives.

An increasingly prolific literature suggests that peer counselor training and practice benefit not only the intended counselees but also the counselors themselves (Frisz, 1984; Hahn & Le Capitaine, 1990; Hatcher, S., et al., 1994). Peer counselors' self-esteem, capacity for empathy, self-awareness, and non-judgmental acceptance of a wide variety of people and values are apparently ameliorated by peer facilitation training.

---

[3] See Appendix A for many roleplays specifically relevant to college student life.

In the spirit of introducing "the voice of the peers," here is a sample of the feedback from our peer counseling course participants:[4]

> *Student B*: I have always been known as the advice giver among my circle of friends. I never suggested that they look into solving a problem for themselves. Since the start of this class, I have noticed that I am less judgmental or at least more conscious of my own value systems. I have begun to concentrate more on feelings than on content, which is a hard thing to do. Yet, I have noticed that conversations go a lot further when the focus is on feelings. Specific exercises that we did in class have helped me to confront issues that I had pushed aside. It gave me a boost in feeling comfortable about disclosing my feelings. It gave me an effective tool to address issues I have with my family and with my friends.

> *Student D*: The techniques of peer counseling should be learned by everybody engaging in any type of relationship—which would cover just about everyone in the world. These strategies for talking to and helping others help themselves are useful for everyday situations. If everybody could use these skills, many relationships would be at higher levels of communication, and many failing friendships could certainly be saved. I have already found and will in the future find many uses for the skills acquired in this class.

> *Student E*: In the future I hope to apply these techniques to teaching. I plan to get a teaching certificate for elementary education. Hopefully I'll teach early middle school. This can be a very hard time for a child. They are moving

---

[4] The "voices of the peers" were originally tape recorded then transcribed and edited for publication in this book.

into adolescence. With my skills I can listen better and be more in tune with my students' needs. I can also, if one doesn't already exist, help implement a peer counseling program into the school system. I am surprised that all schools don't already have such a program. Peer counseling is so helpful. It can help individuals feel better about problems they are having and help them to help themselves.

Not all undergraduates in the class are young. We have returning, "non-traditional" students, some of whom are already professional teachers and counselors. Indeed, we have recently helped organize a peer program for non-traditional students at a women's center on campus (Hatcher, S., & Soellner Younce, 1994). One such non-traditional student writes:

Student F: The communication skills taught in the peer counseling class are important in many aspects of life. I can avoid many misunderstandings because I am practicing a better approach to communication and helping others. Eliminating communication roadblocks encourages honest interaction and understanding. I did not think I had a problem with empathy, but I did have a tendency to analyze and sympathize. I was always telling my husband and son, "You don't mean that," without really listening to the possibilities of why it was said. I think I might be belittling my son's problems when I tell him not to worry about something that I see as a minor, but he may see as a major, event. I have found it is easier to concentrate on listening and observing when I am not responsible for advice or sympathy. It forces me to concentrate on the other person's feelings and interpretation of the situation, instead of my own values/issues. If the matter is not clear, I can use a few relevant open questions to help gather information instead of being curious about facts. The quality of almost all my relationships is better using the skills and techniques from this class. Avoiding phrases that stifle honesty and listening attentively make it easier to use summaries and give feedback for validation and understanding. I know when I feel understood, I have a more positive outlook and feel more comfortable in my surroundings. Helping others feel that way—and perhaps showing them skills through these interactions—deepens our relationships and fosters human growth.

Looking at the Content of these Reactions

If we were able to do a content analysis of typical reactions to the peer counseling course, we would basically have an outline of the course material presented in chapter 3: empathic listening, learning to avoid "roadblocks to communication," learning the difference between open- and closed-ended questions, knowing how to give positive and "constructive" feedback, mastering methods for decision making and, of the most overriding importance, learning how to suspend one's own value system in order to really listen to someone who may have a quite different perspective and/or socio-cultural background from one's own. The curriculum we use, based on a combination of existing materials and our own additions, will be presented in the next chapter. But first we will highlight how these materials, adapted for a college population, are crafted differently than for younger peer helping trainees.

Clearly there are issues, as alluded to above, particular to the concerns and lives of college students. For example, how does a student walk the fine line between being a peer counselor and a classmate? How does a college peer counselor negotiate impulses to be "counselor-like" with a friend? Such questions arise frequently in our classroom discussions because for college students—as for young adolescents—the issue of friendship with peers is crucial to the process of identity consolidation. The difference between secondary and post-secondary students is that the more sophisticated cognition and self-observational attitude of college students brings such debates into clear focus. Our college students do not want to be easily identified, they sometimes joke, as someone taking the peer counseling course because their "empathic leads" are showing. They want to make their peer counseling skills a more "natural" part of their communication repertoire and at the same time effectively assume the role of "peer counselor" when it is appropriate to do so.

The very factors which make peer work so natural for college life are the same ones that create a dilemma when the need arises to be "professional" with one's peers. A strong impulse to bond with a counselee because of natural empathy or because one may have experienced similar issues makes it imperative that college peer helpers keep clear boundaries. They need to be mindful that a problem similar to one they have encountered may be quite differently experienced by others; i.e., the solution they find for themselves may not be the one that works well for someone else. Carl Rogers' description of "empathy"—to "be in the life of the other" and to be non-judgmental—is something of which college student peer helpers need constant reminder. When mastered, such Rogerian concepts generate much excitement, interest, and gratification for the college-aged peer counselor.

Empathy or Sympathy?
The Discussion of Complex Issues

At the beginning of the class, students often experience much confusion between the concepts of empathy and sympathy. As time goes on, students come to understand that empathy is to put oneself "as if" in the place of the other, to feel what "the other" feels, to get "a taste" of what it is like to be that other person, then to step back and be oneself, the (para)professional counselor. On the other hand, students discover, sympathy connotes pity, a kind of overidentification, which—as a childhood precursor of empathy—has less place in a mature counseling situation. When one "sympathizes," one's ego boundaries are fluid so that what happens to another person feels like it is happening to oneself. Among the developmental milestones that most college-age students achieve is the ability to feel empathy more often than sympathy.

Discussions on this and other issues take place consistently, semester upon semester. Our college students tell us that for them this new knowledge is like an "aha" experience since many of them were not raised in families that were nonjudgmental or where relatives knew how to listen with "the third ear" (Reik 1948). The heart of the preventive effort of the peer counseling course is to turn students on to a way of listening in which they truly hear what the other person is saying and in which they can "put themselves in the shoes of another person" (Myrick & Erney, 1978) while still preserving their own emerging identities.

As one might imagine, there are times when the excitement in discovering empathic and psychologically minded ways of observing both others and oneself is so powerful that college student trainees forget to "turn off" their counseling alter-egos. Some students report how their friends sometimes remind them that they are "peer counseling" in the friendship. This is the case partly because newly acquired listening skills are not yet "natural" for many students; partly because student trainees need to learn when not to utilize their new-found professional personae; and partly because they experience the same phenomena that affects professional psychologists when at a party where others, upon learning they are counselors, invariably query, "Are you going to analyze me?"

For the most part, however, and as evidenced by the testimonials above, the greater number of students find their relationships with others significantly improved by their budding counseling skills. Many speak of how the insights they gain in this training bring to light communication problems in their own families. Students debate endlessly about how and whether to implement their new-found skills for the betterment of their personal relationships.

Although our research (Hatcher, S., et. al., 1994) demonstrates that college students are developmentally more adept at empathic listening than their younger counterparts, and even though there is less pressure to be "cool" and "tough" than in the middle and high school years, college students struggle with the issue of becoming comfortable as peer counselors. They search to find their natural styles of interacting in counseling with others. How one takes the basic skills learned in the course and integrates these in an effective manner that feels like "one's own"—i.e., not the voice of the professor or supervisor—is a formidable challenge.

Another great challenge for college-age peer counselors is to recognize their own limits. In our course, we emphasize the ethical standards of both the National Peer Helpers Association (NPHA) and the American Psychological Association (APA). Among the most crucial standards in this regard is that peer counselors be able to recognize when the issues presented are "over their heads" and thus require referral. The college student peer counselor is well equipped with referral lists composed of professionals both on campus and in the community.

Correct use of referral resources requires that the peer counselors understand the limits of their role as a paraprofessional and that they summon available backup supervision as any questions may arise. Sometimes it is difficult for college students to want to access supervisory input as they struggle at the doorstep of adulthood. Reluctance to call on the wisdom of a more experienced person exemplifies the kinds of "rescue fantasies" that plague many helping professionals. This type of conflict is successfully worked through both in the classroom and in the applied programs; the supervisory relationship with the college student allows for much stimulating debate and discussion.

In the next two chapters we will offer an elaborated explication of our course, emphasizing the advanced concepts that college adults are capable of learning. The capacity to deal with complex theoretical and practical concepts distinguishes college students from their younger peer helping counterparts.

REFERENCES

Adelson, J. (1980). *Handbook of adolescent psychology*. New York: Wiley.

Blos, P. (1962). *On adolescence.* Glencoe, Illinois: Free Press.

Botvin, G. J., Baker, E., Filazzola, A. D., & Botvin, E. M. (1990). A cognitive-behavioral approach to substance abuse prevention. *Addictive Behaviors, 15,* 47-63.

Carr, R., & Saunders, G. (1980). *Peer counseling starter kit.* Victoria, British Columbia: University of Victoria Peer Counselling Project.

D'Andrea, V., & Salovey, P. (1983). *Peer counseling: Skills and perspectives.* Palo Alto: Science and Behavior Books.

de Rosenroll, D. (1988). *Peer counselling implementation, maintenance, and research.* Victoria, British Columbia: University of Victoria Peer Counselling Project.

Erikson, E. (1968). *Identity, youth, and crisis.* New York: Norton.

Foley, K., & Shafer, K. L. (1992). Perceptions of peer helping programs: Misconception, awareness, and utilization. Unpublished manuscript, University of Michigan.

Frisz, R. (1984). The perceived influence of a peer advisement program on a group of former peer advisors. *Personnel and Guidance Journal, 62* (10), 616-19.

Hahn, J. A., & Le Capitaine, J. E. (1990). The impact of peer counseling upon the emotional development, ego development, and self concepts of peer counselors. *College Student Journal, 24,* 410-420.

Hall, G. S. (1905). *Adolescence: Its psychology and its relations to physiology, anthropology, sociology, sex, crime, religion, and education* (Vol. 1). New York: Appleton.

Hatcher, R., Hatcher, S., Berlin, M., Okla, K., & Richards, J. (1990). Psychological mindedness and abstract reasoning in late childhood and adolescence: An exploration using new instruments. *Journal of Youth and Adolescence, 19* (4), 307-326.

Hatcher, S., Nadeau, M., Walsh, L., Reynolds, M., Galea, J., & Marz, K. (1994). The teaching of empathy for high school and college students: Testing Rogerian methods with the Interpersonal Reactivity Index. *Adolescence, 29* (116), 961-974.

Hatcher, S., & Soellner Younce, P. A peer counseling program for non-traditional women college students. *Peer Facilitator Quarterly, 12* (2), 30-33.

Kirschenbaum, H., & Henderson, V. L. (1984). *The Carl Rogers reader.* Boston: Houghton Mifflin Co.

Kohlberg, L. (1964). Development of moral character and moral ideology. In M. C. Hoffman & L. V. Hoffman (Eds.), *Review of child development research*, Vol. 1 (383-431). New York: Russell Sage Foundation.

Myrick, R. D., & Erney, T. (1978). *Caring and sharing: Becoming a peer facilitator*. Minneapolis: Educational Media Corp.

Piaget, J. (1972). Intellectual evolution from adolescence to adulthood. *Human Development, 15*, 1-12.

Reik, T. (1948). *Listening with the third ear*. New York: Farrar, Straus, and Giroux.

Rogers, C. R. (1951). *Client-centered therapy: its current practice, implications, and theory*. Boston: Houghton Mifflin.

Rogers, C. R. (1969). *Freedom to learn: a view of what education might become*. Columbus, Ohio: Charles Merrill.

Rogers, C. R. (1980). *A way of being*. Boston: Houghton Mifflin.

Sturkie, J., & Gibson, V. (1989). *The peer counselor's pocket book*. San Jose: Resource Publications, Inc.

Varenhorst, B. (1984). Peer counseling: past promises, current status, and future directions. In *Handbook of counseling psychology* (716-751). New York: Wiley and Sons.

Vrrend, T. J. (1969). High-performing inner-city adolescents assist low-performing peers in counseling groups. *Personnel and Guidance Journal, 49*, 897-904.

Zunker, V. G., & Brown, W. F. (1966). Comparative effectiveness of student and professional counselors. *Personnel and Guidance Journal, 66*, 738-743.

Chapter 2

Rationale for an Academic Course in Peer Counseling

*Sherry L. Hatcher, PhD, Lisa Walsh, MA,
Meredith Reynolds, MA, and Jill Sullivan, BA*

Recently at a conference for peer helping, our group presented a paper and a training video based on our course.[1] We were one of only three college presentations among several hundred offered. Similarly, at the conference booksellers' display, we could only find one or two books among hundreds offered that specifically addressed the needs of college students. Since many of the techniques younger people can use in peer work—empathic listening, decision making models, giving feedback, and so on—can also be utilized by college students, why is the dearth of college-focused material such a problem?

This question may be answered in two ways: first, the developmental capabilities of college youth yield great advances over younger adolescents; second, many of the contextual concerns of college students are different from those of their younger counterparts.

---

[1] Presenters at the National Peer Helpers Association conference, June 1991, were Sherry L. Hatcher, PhD, Missi Nadeau, MA, Lisa Walsh, MA, Meredith Reynolds, MA, and Jerry Galea, BA, producer of the video.

Developmental Differences in High School and College Youth

Whereas younger students in middle school and high school are at the apex of peer pressure vulnerabilities, college students are beginning to become more "inner directed"; this increase in self-directedness in turn enhances their potential for learning and utilizing peer counseling skills. Whereas the capacity for abstract thought in middle and high school students is developing (Keating, 1980), logical reasoning is not yet solidified and does not reach its peak until late in the college years.

Similarly, although the capacity for moral sensibility increases during early and middle adolescence, higher levels of morality, which in turn depend on solid abstract thought, are similarly not attained until late in the college years (Hoffman, 1980). This developmental schema is particularly important in considering the aptitude of peer counselors because they are asked to suspend their own value systems in order to objectively listen to the backgrounds and views of others. For dramatic and frequently opinionated early adolescents, whose identity formations are still fragile and developing, such requisite non-judgmentalness is likely to be too tall an order.

Issues involving peer acceptance are so very poignant for high school students, even those who become peer counselors, that they often have a difficult time separating their values from those of their counselees. The combination of solid abstract thought, mature moral judgment, and the ability to be self-directed and to resist peer pressure gives the college student special potential to become an optimal peer counselor.

Our own study has indicated that the trainability of empathy in adolescence is maximized for both genders during the college years (Hatcher, et al., 1994). While younger teens are becoming able to think about their own thoughts for the first time in their development, the process of introspection is far more stable for most college-aged youth.[2]

---

[2] Exceptions to this developmental rule are of course possible; some high school students may be precocious in this skill while some college students may not be as advanced.

Peer helpers in both high school and college are generally selected in their junior and senior years. Upper-class college students are particularly appropriate for peer facilitation training and can readily serve as role models for those just arriving at school. The college environment, with its milieu of autonomy and individuality encouraged by living away from home (often for the first time), fosters a mindset of introspective reflectiveness. The intellectual stimulation of cognitive abilities in the context of advanced course offerings further allows college students to understand the dynamics of interpersonal influence; this, in turn, leaves them far less susceptible to peer pressures.

Some Advanced Concepts, Which College Students Can Master

Because of these newly emerging aptitudes, we are able to teach our college students not to practice psychotherapy but rather to understand useful concepts from the professional counseling literatures, which would be outside the realm of mastery for most younger students. While not ever interpreting such psychodynamics as "transference," "countertransference," or "resistance" to the counseling process, the college student can profitably be taught about the existence of these important and ubiquitous phenomena. So, for example, when in the process of their work a client has a strong transferential reaction—i.e., the counselee reacts to the peer counselor on the basis of old relationships—the peer counselor will have been educated to recognize it as such. In addition, the peer counselor must be aware of how events in his/her own life might affect a counselee; that is, to understand the nature of a countertransference phenomenon.

Since frequently such reactions occur outside the conscious awareness of the peer counselor and/or the counselee, it is helpful if the college peer counselor can identify what has occurred. An example of a peer counselor's countertransference was offered by one of our students who noticed that when he was bereaved over the recent death of his dog, he felt less emotionally attuned to a peer counselee whose presenting issue concerned the loss of a loved one. Recognition of such a "countertransference reaction" is important both for the sake of the "client" and for the quality of the counselor's self-observational efforts. This particular self-reflection, shared in a group supervisory meeting, need only have been noted by the peer counselor himself; it would not have been appropriate or necessary for the peer counselor to share this insight with his counselee. Having understood this "countertransference reaction" for himself, the peer counselor with his supervisor was able to improve his empathic responsiveness to his counselee.

Similarly, pulls from the counselees' pasts—perhaps an overly strong identification with the peer counselor as a favorite or even less-favored sibling are useful "transference phenomena" for the peer counselor to recognize. Once again, we must emphasize that no such material will be "interpreted" to the counselee but rather used solely by the peer counselor in the service of helping and not overreacting to the client. We find that college students are quite capable of understanding such concepts as transference and countertransference without misusing them; in this way they enter into what is the province of the professional therapist—but only as a cognitive and intellectual exercise, solely for the purpose of better understanding the counseling process.

We also teach our students about the psychotherapeutic concept of "resistance" to change. Like professional therapists, and indeed all of us, peer counselors regularly encounter such phenomena. Most of us tend to preserve, even treasure, what is familiar in ourselves, even at those times when it is counterproductive to do so. When peer counselors understand that "resistance to change" is a natural aspect of all counseling situations, this aids the empathic process. Furthermore, understanding this phenomenon helps the college peer counselor to be less judgmental and to be able to introspect with regard to the supervisory process so as to observe their own resistance to change. Many of the peer interviews which follow make quite clear this valiant struggle with change—and how it often precedes progress for peer counselees and peer counselors alike.

The Milieu of the College Student

In addition to the maturation of college students' intellect, morality, and self-observational skills, it is important to note that real life issues of college youth are quite different from those of their younger counterparts. The content of roleplays and some of the training techniques and exercises suggested in such fine high school texts as Tindall (1989) often feel infantalizing to the college student. Their concerns are no longer the curfew, the post-high school vocational or educational choice, daily acute peer pressure, or questions about whether they can borrow the car. Rather, concerns of college life include roommate conflicts, homesickness, academic anxieties, choosing a major, negotiating a balance of work and social activity, financing a college education, and one's incipient identity commitments (Hatcher, 1994; see also Appendix A).

In college, one begins to think about interpersonal commitments and solidifying sexual identity issues. On top of this are oncoming career choices: What will one do afterward? Get a job? Go to graduate school? If so, can one be self-supporting for these ventures?

Separation from the family of origin for college students may bring into clear focus concerns within the family which before were not as visible. The college student must renegotiate the relationship with his/her parents or family of origin; this a mutually challenging endeavor, to be sure (Coburn & Treager, 1988).

Diversity and Identity

Since today's college students do not normally have a curfew and since colleges no longer act in *loco parentis* (see chapter 5), college students have to find their own balance between work and leisure, between their "psychosocial moratorium" (Erikson, 1968) and adult responsibilities. At the same time, the world of college students is much wider than that inhabited by high school youth. College students live and work together with people from all over the country, from all over the world; their roommates or dormmates may be from a different socioeconomic group or even from a different culture (see chapter 14). College students need diversity not just in the political sense but to understand their own complex identities. They wonder who their friends will be, their significant others. Their listening ears need to hear deeper and wider than most of their high school counterparts'.

Then there are the political issues of the college campus—this too involves considerably more latitude than is possible in most high schools. College campuses are forums for free speech; one needs to make decisions about how to socialize oneself in the midst of a political smorgasbord. Similarly, the college student must make choices about his/her social politics. If there are sororities and fraternities on campus, does one join, or does one eschew these? How does one decide about the possibility of sexual activity, sexual safety, and contraception? (See chapter 7.) How does one deal with substance abuse on campus and sexual assault prevention? (See chapters 7 and 8, respectively.) How should the college student address mental health concerns when one needs guidelines in order to assist roommates, classmates, and dormmates with problems, or in dealing with one's own concerns and crises? (See chapters 4, 5, and 7). In general, the college student must learn to deal with the everyday stressors of college life exacerbated by independent living and the "sudden," multiple responsibilities that accrue with autonomy. For many, going to college brings with it joyful anticipation, but there is inevitably an accumulation of much new responsibility which can also feel like "culture shock" (Hatcher, 1994).

Clearly, few if any of the above concerns occur before the college years or, if they do, certainly without the intensity created by college life. Professors and college counselors, while of tremendous assistance, are often busy and overworked; economics do not often permit a sufficiently attentive staff-to-student ratio. Trained peers are capable of helping to fill this gap by dealing with issues that do not require professional intervention alone. The value of peer helping is obvious as we consider the multiple life questions that are posed for each college student. The need for a curriculum to train competent peer counselors for college-level work is also clear.

Roleplays for Experiential Learning

Roleplays are one of the most valuable teaching tools for peer counselor training across all ages. However, the scenarios that are developed need to be based on the situations, issues, and conflicts pertinent to the developmental stage of the peer counselor—in this case, the college student. When we first began to train college-aged peer counselors, we used some roleplay situations suggested in high school texts; we were quickly told by our students that these were "babyish" to them. Developmentally inappropriate content was not helpful to their sense of maturation and may have been denigrated all the more for its regressive valence.

In the next chapter we offer a proven curriculum for peer counselor training on a college campus. In Appendix A we present specific roleplay scenarios suggested by the college students themselves on those issues that particularly affected them during their college years.

As you can see from this compilation of roleplays, it is possible for college students to be quite creative in practicing counseling scenarios with their peers. The roleplay scenarios constructed for this population are limited only by the imaginations of the participants themselves. In general, the concerns of college students are very different from those of high school students, both because the context of their respective environments differs and because college students think differently about issues even when the topic is similar; for example, while peer relationships concern both high school and college students, the maturity of these relationships and the ways they are conceptualized by each age group are vastly different.

Not only is the content of college-level roleplays necessarily more advanced, but we have found that, likely because of their prodigious cognitive-, moral-, and psychological-mindedness, most college students need less time in instruction and can use more time in the practice of peer counseling skills. Thus, a novel marriage between a peer counseling curriculum and applied programs such as those described in the following chapters is particularly appropriate in a college setting. It has been our experience that on many college campuses, and on ours until recently, a course on peer counseling and related practica opportunities for peer work were quite discrete and separate.

Teaching Counseling Skills for College Peer Helping Programs

We hope that this volume offers a useful model for the integration of peer services on campus, for the establishment of lines of intercommunication that allow and encourage exchange in the training of basic peer counseling skills, and for the development of applied settings for the implementation of such skills. It should be noted that even when practica do not stress basic peer counseling skills (e.g., as in some peer education and peer teaching programs), it is our strong belief that such training is very helpful because counseling issues inevitably arise even in peer education and peer teaching settings, which are not explicitly designed for personal counseling issues.

For example, the stated purpose of a peer advising practicum, described in chapter 9, is academic peer advising. Students can speak with a trained peer in order to plan their concentration, discuss their major, access suitable courses, work on their career plans, and prepare for graduate school admission. While some of the several hundred student clients served by this program each year bring routine questions concerning their academic concentration, at least as many others come to talk about "underlying issues." For instance, a student may tell the peer advisor: "I want to be a psychologist but my parents want me to be an engineer" or "I want to go to graduate school in psychology but I'm not sure if I'd like the work." Without the use of well-honed peer counseling skills, a very different—and in our view less helpful—service would be provided to student clientele. This program offers a particularly good example of a peer program in which students are dually trained in counseling skills and the content of academic advising by a specialist in each area. Several of the other programs use similar two-faceted training so that their peer helpers will know the relevant "facts" of their service in combination with solid counseling skills. In that way the peer counselor can communicate essential information but also know how to listen to the full range of concerns that may be brought by the peer counselee, including the possible need for referral to a professional counselor.

Student Feedback on the Philosophy of the Course

As will become abundantly clear in the chapters that follow, our college students tell us that learning and practicing good communication skills affect all of their interactions and relationships in positive ways; with practice, such skills become firmly rooted in habitual modes of communication with friends, family, professors, employers, and—of course—their peers.

Through their peer counseling training, students notice that they learn to identify and become sensitive to differences among people; they learn to relate to and respect those who have values and backgrounds different from their own. That advice-giving is not usually recommended in the context of peer counseling is often a new idea for college students, especially for those who have not been a part of a peer helping program in their secondary schools. Ultimately, most students find that letting others develop their own solutions to a problem pays off both in the working relationship with their counselees and in their own lives as well.

Since college life occurs at a time when many important commitments are incipient, decision-making skills and models are especially helpful to peer counselors as well as to their clients. A college-level course in basic peer counseling skills often helps students decide whether or not to pursue a career in one of the helping professions. Many college students seek out the peer counseling course because they are entertaining the possibility of becoming a counselor in their careers. For most, this career interest is confirmed by the work of the class; others may decide that they are not patient enough, that it is too difficult to suspend their own strong opinions to really hear those of another. This self-knowledge can be just as valuable for those who learn that they are not well suited to empathic listening and helping others to problem-solve as it is for those who learn that they are "natural" for the helping professions.

RESOURCES

Coburn, K., & Treager, M. (1988). *Letting go.* Bethesda, Maryland: Alder and Alder.

Erikson, E. (1968). *Identity, youth, and crisis.* New York: Norton.

Damon, W., & Hart, D. (1982). The development of self understanding from infancy through adolescence. *Child Development, 53,* 841-64.

Galea, J. (1991). *The basics of peer counseling.* [Videotape.] Ann Arbor: University of Michigan, Department of Psychology.

Greenson, R. (1960). The vicissitudes of empathy. *International Journal of Psychoanalysis, 41,* 417-24.

Hatcher, S. (1989). Aspects of turmoil and self-containment in the adolescent psychotherapy patient. In E. M. Stern (Ed.), *Psychotherapy and the self-contained patient* (73-83). New York: Haworth Press, Inc.

Hatcher, S. Personal rites of passage: stories of college youth. In A. Leiblich & R. Josselson (Eds.), *The narrative study of lives Vol. 2* (169-94). Thousand Oaks, California: Sage.

Hatcher, S., Nadeau, M., Walsh, L., Reynolds, M., Galea, J., & Marz, K. (1994). The teaching of empathy for high school and college students: Testing Rogerian methods with the Interpersonal Reactivity Index. Adolescence, 29 (116), 961-74.

Hoffman, M. (1980). Moral development in adolescence. In J. Adelson (Ed.), *Handbook of adolescent psychology* (295-343). New York: Wiley & Sons.

Ivey, A. E., & Authier, J. (1978). *Microcounseling.* Springfield, Illinois: Charles C. Thomas.

Keating, D. (1980). Thinking processes in adolescence. In J. Adelson (Ed.), *Handbook of adolescent psychology* (211-47). New York: Wiley & Sons.

Rogers, C. R. (1965). Client-centered therapy [Film no. 1]. In E. Shostrom (Ed.), *Three approaches to psychotherapy* [Three 16-mm. color films]. Orange, California: Psychological Films, Inc.

Schoem, D., Frankel, L., Zuñiga, X., & Lewis, E. (Eds.). (1993). *Multicultural teaching in the university*. Westport, Connecticut: Praeger.

Sheir-Younis, L. F., & Weingarten, H. (1992). Social identity groups exercise. Ann Arbor, Michigan: FAIRteach Workshop.

Simon, S., Howe, L., & Kirschebaum, H. (1972). *Values clarification: A handbook of practical strategies for teachers and students*. New York: Hart Publishing.

Talmers, P. (1991). Countertransference in peer advising. Unpublished manuscript, University of Michigan.

Thorne, B. (1992). *Carl Rogers*. Thousand Oaks, California: Sage.

Truax, C. B., & Carkhuff, R. R. (1967). *Toward effective counseling and psychotherapy*. Chicago: Aldine.

Chapter 3

The Peer Counseling Course for College Students

Sherry L. Hatcher, PhD, Lisa Walsh, MA,
Meredith Reynolds, MA, and Jill Sullivan, BA

We now present our peer counseling curriculum for college students. While it includes many elements of established peer counselor training in communication skills (D'Andrea & Salovey, 1983; Carr & Saunders, 1980), some of the format of our class is original, adapted for the needs of the college classroom. For example, most of the authors whose chapters follow this one (chapters 4 through 14) regularly present guest lectures to our class, in which they offer examples of peer helping practica opportunities for our students who want to apply what they have learned in the classroom. In turn, our course helps train many of their peer helpers in the basics of counseling and communication skills.

What Is "New"

Peer Counseling for College Students[1] is staffed by a professor, a paid graduate student, and six to eight undergraduate peer teaching assistants, whom we fondly called "UGTAs." These are students who have previously taken the class with successful outcomes and who now help us to teach

---

[1] Psychology 412 was introduced by Dr. Sherry Hatcher in 1989 as the first academic course on peer counseling at the University of Michigan.

it (Hatcher & Litzenberger, 1994; see chapter 12). This novel administrative structure allows for additional "person power" for implementing extensive videotaping, discussion, and analysis of roleplays. Such filmed roleplays are viewed as an optimal pedagogical means for teaching and mastering peer counseling skills. Playing back roleplays for students permits them to receive feedback from the professor, the teaching assistants, and their peers and to observe for themselves how they appear as counselors. More frequently than not, a student will say: "Oh, I had no idea that I tap my foot as I speak" or "I didn't realize that my voice was so quiet" or "I didn't know I could do this work but I really think that I sounded empathic with the counselee."

Other innovative elements in our course include the teaching of concepts from the counseling and psychotherapy literatures as described in the previous chapter. In addition, the use of extensive journaling and the midterm roleplay assignment—soon to be described—as well as a final paper in which students are asked to design a peer program for a population of particular interest to them—are all novel and valuable training tools particularly suitable for aptitudes of the college student.

It is the blending of "old" and "new" in our peer counseling curriculum that is, in our view, one of its richest assets. It is also important that we are able to keep the class size small, with four sections of fifteen students each semester. This allows students to learn in an atmosphere of augmented trust and emotional intimacy—a rare opportunity at most large colleges and universities.

Structure of the Course

Our college peer counseling course offers students a combination of academic readings, writings, subjective weekly journals, the instruction and demonstration of applied peer counseling skills, and experiential practice. Emphasized strongly in the course are ethical standards including a signed contract of confidentiality and the essential provision of ongoing and backup supervision for all peer helping practica experiences. In addition, there are the weekly guest lectures by those who run peer services on campus and whose work is represented in this volume in many of the subsequent chapters. "The voices of the peers," of the students who work in these programs, give a vivid and real experience of how the peer facilitators utilize their counseling skills in applied settings, how they feel about their work, and how their work affects their lives (see chapters 4-14).

We will not present so much a "cookbook format" of exercises as do some other texts that are geared for younger students. Rather, our approach will attempt to convey a sense of the modal discussions that evolve from the exercises we offer in peer counselor training. We have found, somewhat to our surprise, that the components of these discussions remain relatively consistent across the seven years that we have offered this course to a total of some five hundred college students.

Each week's class lasts for two hours; during this time we share journal entries, discuss assigned readings, view and review videotaped exercises, and occasionally watch a film on the subject of counseling. In addition, discussing students' own videotaped roleplays allows for a good introduction to the topic of how to give feedback supportively yet constructively. We encourage students not to omit positive feedback in reviewing each others' films so that they do not, perhaps erroneously, assume that people already know what they do well. We replay student-made films only with the permission of all participants involved.

The two hours go quickly; sometimes we could use more time. We encourage students to practice their skills during the week with an assigned partner and also to utilize their burgeoning self-observational skills in everyday life. The reports you read in chapters 1 and 2 suggest that most students do this with much enthusiasm, a good measure of success, and with benefit to their relationships and careers.

The Journal Assignment

On a weekly basis, students hand in journals in which they discuss how they observed or applied the peer counseling skills they learned that week, how and why it worked well or not, and their feelings about it. Since assigned readings are integrated with the classwork, these journals will often reflect references to published literature in the field of peer counseling as integrated with the students' personal experiences. The journal assignment, which is graded only as satisfactory or not in relation to the effort expended, gives students an opportunity to practice skills outside the classroom and invites them to write down interactions from their everyday lives which relate to the work of the class. Journaling is a respected vehicle for self-reflection and self-exploration; it is a personally therapeutic modality for students to appropriately separate their concerns from those of their counselees.

Weekly Agenda

We will now present a week-by-week semester-length agenda that works well with college populations. The blending of "old" and "new" peer counseling teaching techniques has led to positive course evaluations and enthusiastic participation by the class in the peer programs presented in subsequent chapters.

WEEK 1

To introduce ourselves to each other, we use a traditional icebreaker with a new twist. We go around the room and ask two people sitting next to each other to chat for five or ten minutes. We then ask each person in turn to introduce his/her partner and to reflect the content of the conversation between them. What we have added to this well-known icebreaker is the further instruction that the presenter try to *identify where the speaker showed the most affect or emotion and then to check this out with the partner.* This modified exercise teaches two things right away:

1. students need to begin to listen for feelings, an ability at the crux of peer counseling success

2. peer counselors need to learn to reliably check with their peer "clients" to be sure that they have heard them accurately

In professional psychotherapy, when a client makes a slip of the tongue, reports a fantasy or a dream, the counselor must not associate meaning or give an interpretation before the client has provided his/her own associations. In peer counseling, while one does not attempt to interpret such expressions at all, one still needs to check with the counselee for the correctness of any intervention that is offered, whether it is a clarification of what the counselee said, an identification of feelings, or the exploration of options in the process of decision-making.

Behavioral Attending Skills

Following our introductions, we continue with definitions of peer counseling and its history much as it is related in chapter 1. We also note the myths surrounding this work and, as in chapter 1, we discuss what peer counseling is and what it is not.

WEEK 1 (continued)

This is followed by a unit on behavioral attending skills—i.e., the importance of both the counselor's own use of facilitative body language and good listening posture and, at the same time, a sensitivity to and recognition of the client's body language and all that it can tell us.

When we talk about behavioral attending skills, we first practice not listening attentively with body language. The ideal of facing one's peer, having good eye contact, leaning generally toward one's client, having open posture and a relaxed attitude (termed by its acronym FELOR, Myrick & Erney, 1978) is turned into its horrific opposite, beginning with a demonstration from our teaching assistants. To the amusement of the class, we first demonstrate and then they practice in dyads, using the poorest imaginable attending skills. For example, an earnest student tries to talk about a problem that her roommate is drinking heavily and she is worried about how to approach this problem both because it is disrupting her own schedule and because she is worried about her troubled friend's welfare. In this initial round of practice of "non-attending skills," a teaching assistant demonstrates turning away from the client, picks at his/her shoes, looks at a watch, interrupts the client, talks about personal experiences with parties and drinking—all of the unprofessional, inattentive behavior that can be mustered so as to demonstrate "poor FELOR." While this may seem like unusual pedagogy, it effectively serves to highlight what many students, in fact, experience in their everyday lives. Students' journals of this first week describe a realization that they or others in their lives may have been "attending poorly" for some time; it is this first exercise, practicing wrong behavioral attending skills, that leads to such realizations (see Appendix B).

WEEK 1 (continued)

As one might hope, the practice of ineffectual attending behavior is followed by a demonstration of how to listen attentively to "the distressed roommate"—how to have good eye contact and patience and how to avoid self-disclosure of one's own experience so that the focus of attention is on the "client" and his/her particular concerns. The teaching assistants' demonstration of poor then good FELOR is followed by an opportunity for everyone to practice this exercise with a partner, usually the person seated near them. It is the experiential roleplay aspect of the course from which the students consistently tell us that they feel they learn the most. Readings, writings, films, and discussions, while all essential to the course, are not unique for teaching counseling. Few college courses offer the important component of practicing communication and counseling skills as they are relevant to the college students' everyday lives. In this spirit, we ask students during the first week of the course to observe good/bad FELOR and to try to practice it successfully. When we give this assignment and ask our students to report their observations and efforts in practicing improved attending skills, much enthusiasm and excitement is generated.

> *Student F*: I am sure that these peer counseling techniques have become a part of my everyday life. Thus, the skills will be helpful in everything I do. I am a better listener, more empathic, less judgmental, and therefore, I will be better able to correctly handle situations with friends, boyfriends, and my future career choices.

WEEK 1 (continued)

Ethics

Also in the first week of class we begin to discuss ethics, how confidentiality is a bottom line for all counseling work, how anyone who does not agree not to discuss the content of what people share in the class cannot be in the class. In the six years we have taught this class to more than five hundred students, we know of only one breach of confidentiality. Students sign a written oath of confidentiality on the first day of class; by all indications, they take this affirmation quite seriously.

We also address the limits of peer counseling, the need for constant communication with one's supervisor, and the importance of making referrals if the counselor is not clearly qualified to see the client or if for any reason the counselor simply cannot empathize with that client. We ask our counselors to always work for the benefit of the counselee, not their own gratification. With the exception of the rare client who is abusive, intoxicated, excessively disturbed, or violent, the peer counselor is asked to empathize long enough either to try to help that client personally or to make a suitable referral. It is not in their job descriptions to try to empathize with someone who is abusive to them—they need to know their limits in this way, too.

Personal Goals

We do not let the first week end without asking students to set personal goals. From a full-group discussion of what kind of person one would want to confide in (adapted from an exercise by Myrick & Erney, 1978), each student writes down which characteristics (such as empathy, non-judgmentalness, supportiveness to others, honesty, personal stability, etc.) he/she believes he/she already possesses to his/her satisfaction and which characteristics he/she would like to improve upon or further develop in the course of the semester. On the last day of class, we ask the students to retrieve their lists to see how well they achieved their stated goals.

WEEK 1 (continued)

Student A: The topic of peer counseling was relatively foreign to me prior to the start of this class. Besides finding out what it was all about, I didn't exactly expect that I would be able to use it in my future plans. I am glad that I was mistaken.

WEEK 2

Theories of Counseling

One of the early topics discussed in our course is the history of peer counseling as it relates to the work of Carl Rogers, including a film about his work (Rogers, 1965) and a discussion of the differences among his client-centered theory, cognitive/behavioral theories of counseling, and psychodynamic theories of counseling. We discuss how aspects of these theories may or may not be applied in professional versus paraprofessional settings; further, we illustrate for what types of problems and concerns each technique is best suited. We look for elements of these theories in the work of peer counseling and note the particularly strong underpinnings of client-centered theory and practice in most peer training curricula.

Roadblocks

During the second week of class we review what Carr and Saunders (1980) call "roadblocks to communication." Upon learning of this list, many students tell us that such "roadblocks" have, at times, been an unfortunate aspect of their family and peer relationships:

- Ordering and Commanding
- Warning and Threatening
- Moralizing and Preaching
- Persuading with Logic and Arguing rather than paying attention to feelings/affect
- Judging/Criticizing and Blaming/Praising/Agreeing
- Name Calling
- Ridiculing/Analyzing/Diagnosing/Reassuring/Sympathizing
- Probing/Questioning
- Diverting/Using Sarcasm/Withdrawal (146)

WEEK 2 (continued)

As with behavioral attending skills, we first practice these "roadblocks" in their most unconstructive form. Small groups of five or six students are given a controversial topic, perhaps something about current political elections. Four or more group members are assigned one of the above roadblocks and are asked to keep the nature of their assigned role private while at the same time acting it out in the small group discussion. At the end, each person must guess the role each participant played. This is a variation on an exercise suggested by Carr and Saunders (52) in that the topics we use are especially relevant for college-aged students. The exercise is useful in demonstrating how quickly a discussion deteriorates when people are using roadblocks, even though some participants are trying hard to keep the discussion on track. While students do not seem to enjoy this rather frustrating exercise as much as they do many of the others, which are more inherently gratifying, they are nonetheless reminded of the prevalence of such counterproductive communication in their everyday lives. From this work, students develop an increased sensitivity to unconstructive modes of communication and they become disinclined to use these in their interactions with others.

Teaching Empathy

Another model which we introduce in the second week of class relates to "empathy training." The question of the teachability of empathy has been one of the ongoing controversies in the field of counselor education. It is our conclusion from both naturalistic observations and research (Hatcher, et al., 1994) that for most college students, empathic listening can be taught and/or ameliorated.

WEEK 2 *(continued)*

To this end, we ask each student to listen to another student for five minutes and say nothing in response during that time period, only using the good behavioral attending skills the students have presumably begun to master from the previous week's exercises. We give them a suggested topic to work with, such as, "Something I would like to change about myself is...," but if they prefer, they may choose a subject of their own. As with most of our exercises, we ask a group of graduate and peer teaching assistants to first demonstrate the exercise. This is followed by the students trying it—some in dyads and some in triads—with one observer who provides important feedback to the roleplayers.

This is an interesting exercise because we are asking students to listen without talking for five or more minutes. In response, they tell us of their impulse to behave as they would in the dorm—to say, "Oh, yes, something like this happened to me as well"; they say how hard it is to listen, not to self-disclose, not to give advice, not to make judgments. The principles of client-centered work that characterize peer counselor training—such as listening to the other without interjecting one's own values, experiences, and judgments— come into clear focus with this early exercise.

After five minutes has passed, the student is asked to reflect back to the "counselee": "The most important thing I heard you say, was...." Prior to attempting the exercise we discuss how to identify what is likely to be *the most important thing* when a student may have been discussing a wide-ranging variety of issues during the allotted five minutes. Over the years, students have consistently enumerated these key variables to help in discerning what is, in fact, central for the speaker:

1. when the speaker shows the most affect

2. themes that may be repeated/recycled and therefore emphasized in the monologue

3. when the speaker may seem hesitant

WEEK 2 (continued)

This exercise often leads to an interesting discussion of the importance of the counselor's observing what is omitted by the counselee as well as what is overtly stated. In identifying the central feature of the client's communication, the peer counselor is asked to listen for both feelings and content and to reflect both of these back to the client, most especially the feelings.

Checking In with the Counselee

For each exercise in which a counselor verbalizes his/her observation about the counselee's communication, we ask that the counselor check out what he/she has summarized/clarified/observed with the counselee to ascertain whether it is correct or incorrect. We emphasize to our students that in most counseling situations, the truth is arrived at collaboratively by a series of trial and error, successive approximations. For that reason it is essential to verify that the peer counselor is "staying with" the client.

In this connection, we discuss the various ways one can tell whether the peer counselor is on the right track in his/her interventions with the counselee. We observe that if the peer counselor has correctly identified his/her "client's" main issue(s), then the client will "open up" rather than "shut down" the dialogue; additionally, the counselee may exhibit strong affect, laughter, or even tears when the peer counselor is "on target." Such criteria are also used by students of psychotherapy in their efforts to assess a correct interpretation. In our view, there is no reason that peer counselors-in-training should not similarly be made aware of these categories of response in order to correctly assess the aptness of their inventions as peer counselors.

WEEK 2 (continued)

"The Sounds of Silence"

This exercise, in which we ask students to summarize and clarify both content and feeling of "the most significant thing you heard the counselee say," seems to be one of the most valuable exercises in the course. Students discover how often they may unwittingly interrupt the "flow," even the meaning, of what another person is saying by not listening long or carefully enough. Sometimes students need to confront their discomfort with silence, which often occurs in the process of this exercise just as it does in actual counseling settings. It is useful to discuss the different meanings/feelings a silence can evoke: anger, peacefulness, patience, anxiety. This discussion is again similar to that in which graduate students engage in their courses on counseling. Yet, most standard peer counseling curricula for the high school or college student do not raise such issues. This may be the case because some peer trainers do not come from the mental health professions; others may assiduously avoid any topic which at all resembles what is taught to mental health professionals.

Principles of professional counseling and psychotherapy, while never actualized in peer counseling work, are nonetheless essential and infinitely useful for the education of mature college student paraprofessionals. Differences should occur at the level of technique and practice, where the professional clinician utilizes such techniques as Interpretation, Resistance Analysis, Identification of Transference and Countertransference, Assessing the Correctness of an Intervention, or Understanding the Sense of a Silence. An understanding of these phenomena is essential for the education of the college-level peer counselor. *While the college-aged peer counselors will not practice any psychotherapeutically derived techniques, they can benefit and enhance their counseling skills from knowing that these phenomena exist and what their meanings are.* For example, we know that such phenomenon as transference is not the exclusive province of psychotherapists, that "transferences" are experienced on a regular basis, in everyday life, across a variety of relationships: student to teacher, parent to child, partners to each other, and so on.

WEEK 3

Non-Judgmental Listening

In the third week—none too soon—we ask students to reflect on the difficulties and importance of listening to others in a non-judgmental manner. We do a number of exercises on values clarification so that people reflect on their ethnic, cultural, religious, and socioeconomic origins in order to discover with which groups they identify. We talk about Rogerian principles of non-judgmental listening and how hard that can be to achieve. We discuss why one should refer to another peer counselor a counselee toward whom one feels one cannot suspend one's inclinations to be judgmental. Counselees whose problems are best served by a professional must be referred to a counselor who can listen with equanimity and who has proper professional credentials.

An exercise we use to illustrate the pitfalls and value of non-judgmental listening is to ask pairs of students to find a subject on which they have polar-opposite views. On today's college campus, finding such a topic is often most challenging. This is another exercise in which content areas appropriate for college students will be significantly different from a high school version of this exercise. Rather than focusing roleplays on topics such as curfews or fashion, as many high school curricula suggest, the topics chosen here have often more to do with politics, worldviews, and physical/emotional separation from one's family of origin.

In this exercise, we ask our students to carefully listen to the other person's point of view without interruption and without imposing their own presumably different opinion on the interaction. They are asked to summarize the speaker's viewpoint as objectively, accurately, and empathically as they are able (Myrick & Erney, 1978). Accomplishing such objectivity with regard to a point of view with which they disagree is very difficult for many students.

WEEK 3 (continued)

Initially, our teaching assistants illustrate how this exercise can work; they model a roleplay in which a "client" tells the peer counselor that he/she was cheating on an exam, but that is not the "presenting problem" for which he or she is seeking help. Initially, the teaching assistants act judgmental and shift the client's agenda to their own judgment of the dishonest act; they might say: "How can you cheat on an exam?!" The class discusses this portion of the exercise and compares it with the followup version, in which the counselor plays the role in a non-judgmental way, listening to the focus and concerns the client presents, building trust in the relationship, and working with the client's agenda, not his/her own. The entire group then discusses the difference in judgmental versus non-judgmental listening and the respective effects of each on the counseling process.

Post-Practice "Debriefing"

For all the exercises utilized in our course, we spend time "debriefing/discussing" what it feels like to restrain one's judgmental inclinations, especially in those situations where strong feelings are generated. Students readily talk about how they are most accustomed to arguing opposing points of view, even in the college classroom. They tell us that they are not used to being asked to try to understand why someone else may feel quite differently than they do about a given issue. They furthermore tell us that to do this kind of exercise, while difficult, "stretches" their capacity to be empathic. Clearly such roleplays have direct application to understanding the diverse society in which we live.

WEEK 3 (continued)

How Empathy "Stretches" One's Experience

Often people ask psychotherapists if we need to have experienced all that our clients bring to the counseling hours so as to truly understand them. We usually reply by noting that if this were the case, we would be completely dysfunctional; i.e., we would have to be neurotic, character-disordered, and perhaps even more severely disturbed than that. We would have to have suffered endless losses, workblocks, and so on were we to have experienced everything our clients bring to discuss. While working within the realm of "problems in everyday living," the peer counselor cannot have experienced all that his/her clients present as concerns. We therefore tell our students that empathy—the ability to put oneself in the place of another in one's mind and in one's affects for just long enough to see what it is like to be that other person—is what makes it possible to help someone whose culture, feelings, and problems may not have been experienced by the peer counselors themselves. Teaching students to empathize with the "life spaces" and experiences of others who are different from themselves is at the very core of peer counseling, at the heart of prevention, and central to our potential to understand, respect, and treasure the fascinating differences among us.

WEEK 4

Content of College Student Roleplays

At this point in the semester we begin roleplays of the real issues and problems that those in the class are willing to share. Sometimes there will be a student observer in the roleplay, sometimes not. The value of having an observer is that it gives students a chance to practice giving feedback to others in the class. In effect, it gives them a "taste" of being on the other side of the supervisory process. Sometimes a third roleplayer will serve as a "co-counselor." Many peer programs use two peer co-counselors per "client" to ensure quality service delivery (see chapters 4 and 9).

If they want one, students are provided a topic in order to begin intensive practice of empathic listening skills; more often they are by now sufficiently comfortable with each other that they relish talking about the things which affect them in their everyday lives. They prefer to generate and indeed "work through" real issues in their lives, although they are never required to say whether or not the roleplay they construct is personal or fictitious. One of the interesting things that students tell us in regard to their roleplaying experiences is that if they really get involved in the role, it begins to feel personal and real to them, whether or not it began that way.

For those who want a suggested topic, we propose that the designated "counselee" think about a "problem you are having with another person." This prompt most often generates roleplays on roommate troubles, relationships with significant others, autonomy issues in relation to their families, experiences in confronting a professor about an "unfair" grade, and so on. From the thousands of roleplays we have both observed and filmed over the years, we have compiled an unique file of college-appropriate topics for practice in peer counseling (see Appendix A).

WEEK 4 (continued)

Sometimes students tell us that walking through these roleplays has the serendipitous effect of giving them clues to begin resolving similar issues in their everyday lives. For example, the student who wanted to tell her roommate to stop leaving old pieces of half-eaten pie and other food around their room transformed her approach from an initial communication of "You slob! Get that darn pie off my desk" to "I feel irritated when you leave old food around the room." The first statement is packed with "roadblocks to communication" and is therefore likely to raise the defensiveness of the recipient; in the latter intervention, the speaker assumes responsibility for the communication.

Confidentiality

In relation to all roleplays and classroom discussion, the essential nature of preserving confidentiality is reiterated throughout the semester. Students are most often sharing real issues from their personal lives and thus their anonymity outside the classroom must be respected. Whereas, in high school populations, reliable confidentiality is somewhat more difficult to achieve ("Don't tell anyone, but..." is sometimes followed by a public service announcement to the rest of the class or perhaps to a clique of friends), college students, while not necessarily used to preserving the confidentiality of others, nonetheless find it a feasible challenge to master.

WEEK 4 (continued)

Clarifying and Summarizing Statements

Also in the fourth week of the semester, students fine-tune the essential skill of learning how to phrase "clarifying and summarizing statements." College students excel in this exercise because they are readily able to grasp the notion that such statements must not only include a correct synopsis of the content of the counselee's communication but also include attention to and identification of "the client's" feelings. As most psychotherapists know either intuitively or directly, one does not get very far if one only addresses the content of a session, devoid of accompanying affects. We have seen student counselors attend to the details of a narrative storyline while a client is crying before their eyes; they are paying little or no attention to the tears because they are so concerned with "getting the facts right." The seasoned professional or paraprofessional counselor knows that, in most cases, one can be most helpful to the counselee when, in a counseling session, feelings are noted and empathized with *before* the content of a communication is addressed. This point is somewhat subtly reflected in Myrick and Erney's Empathy Model (1978), in which the peer counselor is instructed to say "You feel *(affect)* because *(content)*." An example of this model might be: "You feel *frustrated and angry* because *your professor refused to reconsider your grade*." This quite useful model is a challenge even for college students and must be very taxing indeed for those younger. I have seen even the most intellectually gifted college student say, "I am happy when you are happy," thus totally missing the point of the model.

WEEK 4 (continued)

With practice, students are generally able to sort out affect from content and pay primary attention to identification of the counselee's feelings. To practice this skill we use some briefer exercises originally suggested by Carl Rogers (1965) in which our teaching assistants repeatedly read the same sentences, each time varying the affect attached to it. For example, the teaching assistant might read the statement, "You slept through your exam," first in a judgmental tone and then in a quite empathic tone, which carries a vastly different meaning. For each sentence read, the class is asked to identify the feelings with which the content is related. This is most useful in training college peer counselors to begin to listen with their "third ears."

Carl Rogers' Work and Its Historical Relevance

Finally, during this fourth week, we show a training film of Carl Rogers working with a client (Rogers, 1965). We talk further about the impact of client-centered therapy on the peer counseling movement as we study Rogers' life and its impact on his theory. The fact that Rogers emerged from a very strict background in which he was not allowed to drink, date, or even go to the movies underscores the power of his so deeply valuing "non-judgmental listening" and "unconditional positive regard" as ways to be helpful to clients.

As we discuss the Rogers film, we reiterate the essential differences between client-centered psychotherapy and the more limited modality of peer counseling, while at the same time noting the extraordinary influence of Rogerian theory and practice on the entire peer helping movement.

WEEK 5

Open vs. Closed Questions

In the fifth week of our peer counseling course, communication skills are refined to include how one makes constructive interventions in working with a counselee. Here we teach two important skills which are cited in most peer counseling syllabi: the use of "I" rather than "You" statements (as in the pie-on-the-desk example) and how to phrase open-ended rather than closed questions. Most students don't have too much trouble mastering the former, though they may need to readjust their instinct to blame others when they feel angry. On the other hand, mastering the art of asking questions that are open—i.e., those questions that are not answerable with a simple yes or no, that expand the counselee's thinking about an issue—is harder for most students than it first sounds to them. Open-ended questions such as "How did you arrive at this decision?" or "What do you feel about that person?" usually elicit more information and are far less leading than such a closed question as, "Are you angry?"

While it is important to note that closed questions have a rightful place in the gathering of information (e.g., What is your major? How old are you?), the most valuable explorations in which clients have rare space to reflect will likely be prompted by a style in which the counselor poses non-leading questions.

Usually peer counselors are told to avoid "why" questions for two reasons. First, it is the province of professionals to delve into historically motivated issues from a counselee's past; second, to be asked "Why?" often puts people on the defensive. As some of our students say, "If I knew why, I wouldn't need to run this problem by an objective person." Defensive reactions to "why" questions begin early in life; for example, if you ask a child "why" he/she did something, he/she will likely either shrug his/her shoulders or cover his/her ears!

WEEK 5 (continued)

Surprisingly, learning to construct "open" questions—those beginning with "How...?" "In what way?" "What...?"—is one of the most difficult exercises for our students to master. Often, they automatically slip into asking closed questions, which because they contain a sense of their own beliefs and hypotheses are leading rather than exploratory in nature. When students find themselves unwittingly phrasing closed questions rather than open ones, we cycle back to discussing the issue of values: the assumptions we tend to make about what others believe and feel on the basis of our own reactions and our own beliefs. This occurrence exemplifies how our weekly topics are not discrete; they build upon each other and allow the opportunity for us to both recycle and blend important themes and techniques.

Practicing with Open-Ended Questions

Further practice with the particularly challenging skill of learning to ask open questions is accomplished by going around the room so that each person, in fairly rapid succession, must ask an open-ended question of the person on his/her left. If, as so often happens, a student unintentionally phrases a closed-ended question instead, he/she must now reverse the order in which the circle exercise proceeds, i.e., clockwise to counter-clockwise or vice versa. This fast-paced exercise allows for practice with a seemingly simply skill; however, it is one that does not come naturally for many students.

WEEK 5 (continued)

An original exercise that is also useful for practicing open and closed questions is one in which the instructor gives the class a quasi-personal scenario; for example, "My husband and I want to attend the peer conference together but he is also interested in attending another conference, which takes place in a different city, at the same time." First the class is invited to ask closed questions, which do not, as they soon see, yield much information. They ask such closed questions as "What date is the conference?" and "Can you afford to go to both?" Only when they are invited to switch to open-ended questions do they receive responses that address the complexity of the situation. They then ask such questions as "How do you feel about this scheduling conflict?" and "What are your options in this situation?" Clearly the open-ended questions yield more informative and enlightening responses. Students seem to enjoy this exercise not only because it is excellent practice in inquiry but also because it is a time when the professor shares something of her own life too.

"Dear Abby" College Style

An original exercise we use in the context of studying open and closed questions and "I" versus "You" statements is to ask each student to bring in an advice column from a current newspaper or magazine. Even though a written advice column is different from a "face to face" interaction with a counselee, students are intrigued to find how often such columnists use blaming-sounding "you" statements and rhetorically closed questions, statements that tell the reader more about the values of the columnist than the writing public. On the other hand, students sometimes find columns that manage, in the written word, to convey remarkable empathy and that offer thoughtful referrals. When they encounter an advice column that is non-empathic, they are asked to rewrite it; this challenges the student to put in writing, as well as speech, what he/she has learned about empathic communication.

WEEK 5 (continued)

Practicing "I" Rather Than "You" Statements

A popular exercise for the practice of "I" versus "You" statements—one that college students enjoy—is "The Coffee Table Exercise," suggested by Carr & Saunders (1980, p. 83). In this scenario, a student inadvertently puts his/her feet on the antique coffee table of a friend. In attempting to remedy the situation, participants first employ "you" statements: "You are ruining the antique coffee table that my aunt just left to me" and other similarly accusatory remarks. This is followed by the use of "I" statements in which the speaker takes responsibility for a request that the friend remove his/her feet from this valuable table; this time there is no negative judgment or assignment of blame: "I would prefer you take your feet off of the table because this is a valuable gift that my aunt left to me."

Upon completing these practice exercises, we discuss the value of each approach and how it felt to the participant. We discuss the variety of "I" statements and open questions that one can construct in one's own personal counseling style so as to advance the counseling process. Open-ended and non-leading interventions (such as suggesting to the counselee, "Give me an example..." or "How do you feel about that?") offer freedom to the counselee to explore a situation in the service of finding an eventual solution to a problem. This allows the class an opportunity to discuss how it takes much patience to be a peer counselor, that one cannot rush to a "decision-making process" before exploring and discussing the experience, goals, and feelings of a counselee.

WEEK 6

Giving and Receiving a Variety of "Feedback"

The "feedback" model is as widely applicable in everyday life as it is in counseling situations. It is designed for a counselor to give feedback to a client or the other way around; it is equally useful in grappling with a customer service representative when one has not received the book one has ordered by mail. The feedback model requires of the speaker an orientation to "I" statements, phrasing the feedback in the first person, and thus taking responsibility for the observations. As with good parenting techniques, positive or constructive feedback:

- is specific, not vague
- includes a statement about how you feel in relation to the other person's behavior
- includes a statement about how you then want to behave based on this interaction

In our college group, class members practiced a roleplay exercise in which one roommate was delinquent in doing dishes whereas the other did not relay phone messages. Each was to give "feedback" using the model described above (Myrick & Erney, 1878; Carr & Saunders, 1980). The first roommate in this roleplay might say: "When you do not do the dishes, I feel quite irritated; perhaps that is why I sometimes 'forget' to pass along your phone messages. Let's both try to consider the other's feelings."

Our classes tend to be quite enthusiastic about the feedback model as they find it useful in dealing with their families, co-workers, and friends. They notice that when they use it as prescribed, they do not bring up "everything" that annoyed them in the past in that particular relationship; rather, they are more able to clearly focus on the specific issue at hand.

WEEK 6 (continued)

Students note how many of them both give and receive positive feedback more rarely than "negative" (or what we prefer to call "constructive") feedback. The practice of giving each other (and themselves) positive feedback is an exercise that frequently begins with some degree of self-consciousness but, more often than not, ends with good feeling and greater attention to the importance of this kind of intervention. In this connection, we stress that as a peer counselor, one must never "flatter" a counselee—there is nothing healing in that. Rather, it is essential that the counselor be honest, much as a good parent who offers positive feedback in a trustworthy and thus credible manner.

Combining Skills

By the end of week six in the semester, students often feel they have been taught a set of discrete skills that are hard to put together in a natural way. We often use the analogy of learning to play an instrument; one needs first to know how to read music, then learn where the notes are on the instrument, and finally how to make sound. The last skills involve putting together these basics in a way that allows for fluidity, individual dynamic variations, and feeling.

The analogy to the paraprofessional counselor-in-training is similar. First our students must learn the basic skills of peer counseling and then they must blend these skills in a personal style of their counseling interventions such that it feels natural to them. They need to construct the language and tone so that their help reaches the peer both effectively and affectively.

WEEK 7

Decision Making

All skills are now combined for work on "the decision making model." Such models are variously offered in D'Andrea & Salovey (1983), Carr & Saunders (1980), and other standard texts on peer counseling; although arranged in various configurations, the basic elements of this model are similar. Counselees first need to *define their problem*. When someone first seeks out a counselor, peer counselor, or professional counselor, they often have waited a long time to "tell their story." They may spill a lot of information and feeling all at once. Peer counselors are taught to listen for what the counselee is most concerned with by paying careful attention to affect, to the frequency with which topics are introduced, and where feelings are expressed either in words and/or body language. Once the crux of the decision to be made is properly identified, *then possible solutions can be "brainstormed" in a collaborative fashion*. The peer counselor may ask the counselee, "What are the best/worst/most likely outcomes of the situation that concerns you?" or "Have you considered 'x' or 'y' possibility?"

It is helpful to begin a unit on decision making with a discussion of how people have made good and/or bad decisions for themselves. Students are then asked for what reason they consider that each decision was good or bad. Whereas younger students will often assess the wisdom of their decision making by its consequences—i.e., if they got caught doing something wrong then it was a bad decision—the morally maturing college student will more often identify a good decision by the *process* involved in reaching it. As one college student reflected, "I made a good decision in that I was true to myself and my beliefs even though things didn't turn out the way I had hoped they would."

WEEK 7 (continued)

College students' roleplays on decision making take account of the many "near adult" decisions with which they are faced. For example, roleplays address such issues as: With whose family should they and their fiancee spend the winter holidays? Should they take a year or two off before applying to graduate school? Should they accept the job of their dreams if that means that they will need to relocate far away from loved ones? Such topics are generated by the real life events of college students; these are problems with which they can identify. It is our sense that the more developmentally relevant the roleplays, the more engaged the students become and the more learning that takes place (see Appendix A).

Contracting, or Not?

In some texts on peer counseling (D'Andrea & Salovey, 1983), contracts are suggested as an aspect of the decision making model. College students often find such contracts awkward in terms of "the counseling alliance," and many tell us that they prefer to reserve this option only for serious situations, perhaps if a client were self-destructive and there needed to be an immediate contract in which the client promises to refrain from self-hurt in order to give the peer counselor needed time to make a proper referral. In such a case, contracting can be useful to preserve a "holding pattern" until supervisory backup can be accessed. Thus, we recommend the use of contracts for college students in selected crisis situations only. Most decision making can be successfully achieved in the context of the peer counseling "talking" relationship.

WEEK 7 (continued)

Exercises for Decision Making

A challenging exercise for decision making takes the form of a counseling "round robin." One person serves as the counselee and presents a decision to be made, e.g., Should I accept the job I have been offered in Alaska? Another student begins to function as the counselor, utilizing and integrating the various counseling skills learned up to this point. When yet another student in the class has something "counselor-like" he/she wants to offer, he/she taps the original counselor on the shoulder and takes his/her place. As many members of the class who wish to participate are encouraged to play the role of counselor. As with all these exercises, the group discusses and even debates the various counseling approaches they have viewed and roleplayed.

WEEK 8

Midterm Roleplay

This week is devoted to a late semester midterm, a videotaped roleplay in which one student is the counselor and the other a counselee. Students choose their own subject matter and are evaluated on their credibility and sincerity in the role of the counselee; those who play the role of the counselor are evaluated on their skills of listening non-judgmentally, empathically, with good behavioral attending, apt use of feedback and decision making models, and overall effectiveness as a counselor. Rating forms are completed on site by the teaching assistant who is filming the roleplays. After students film their roleplay, they are given an opportunity to watch it on "instant replay." Students' grades are based primarily on a written five-page critique, which they create independently and individually and in which they are asked to describe and evaluate the skills they did/did not use effectively in their roleplays. Therefore, students are not graded on stage fright or any other extraneous variable, for if they aptly and insightfully analyze what transpired, they can do well on the midterm (see also Appendix B, "Supervisor Exercise #1").

Most of the class find this an intriguing assignment; some even say it was "fun." The feedback provided to students on their work for the midterm roleplay and critique gives them a sense of their progress as a counselor and as someone who can evaluate the crucial elements of a successful counseling session.

WEEK 9

Values Clarification and Identity Exercises

While all along we emphasize multicultural awareness and issues of self-observation in our peer counseling course, we reserve an entire week to focus on issues of diversity; we do this once the peer counseling students have had sufficient experience with basic skills. A number of valuable exercises encourage both values clarification and the exploration of diversity; here are two we use.

1. Students choose among their many potential identities—student, family, religion, race, ethnicity, gender, worker—those three which they believe are most central to their sense of themselves. Individuals discuss their choices, going around the circle; this discussion tends to be quite emotionally intimate, as students offer the reasons for their choices. This sense of closeness in the group reflects the bonding that has taken place within the class over the course of the semester to this point. Students are often surprised to learn the ethnicity of their classmates; the assumption that ethnicity always "shows" is disproven many times over. Students learn that they are from a variety of cultures; that they have negotiated major family illness, divorce, losses, or, in some instances, that they have suffered traumatic illnesses such as cancer or infertility; that they have special talents in athletics, the arts, and academics—things that they didn't know about each other before. One senses that from experiencing this exercise, too, classmates develop an increased level of trust and come to regard each other with an augmented sense of respect.[2]

---

[2] This exercise is modeled after one used by IGRC (see chapter 14; Schoem, et al., 1993, pages 323-24).

WEEK 9 (continued)

2. "Take a Stand": This exercise, featured in the training of several of the peer programs presented in subsequent chapters (see chapters 7 and 14), involves posting signs in separate areas of the room that read: "Strongly Agree," " Agree," "Disagree," and "Strongly Disagree." Statements that assert specific values are read and students must physically place themselves in front of one sign or the other. In some versions of this exercise, one cannot hedge or find a "neutral" spot. Statements that college students often use in this exercise include: "I believe that students should not be allowed to drink on campus"; "Gay couples should be allowed to rent space in university family housing units"; "I would work with a client even if he/she were prejudiced against a religion or ethnicity with which I identify"; and so on. The divergence of opinion that this exercise stimulates yields a useful analogy to what it feels like to work with a "client" whose views or behavior may be different from those of the peer counselor. The "Take a Stand" exercise further highlights the difficulty involved in true non-judgmental listening while it serves to illustrate the different counseling attitudes within which peers can legitimately work. This description of the "Take a Stand" exercise is presented from the point of view of the participant; later chapters will describe this exercise from the perspective of peers who are trying to facilitate this exercise for others with equanimity (the Lesbian-Gay Male Programs Office, 1993).

WEEK 9 (continued)

The Importance of Self-Observational Skills

Parallel to the exploration of their value systems and identity affiliations, counselors are encouraged to reflect on their pasts, their personality styles, and their own areas of conflict so that they do not confuse their issues with those of their counselees. Student peer counselors-in-training often describe these exercises as exciting but also "tiring" and "taking up a lot of energy." This is true partly because skills for the practice of empathic and attentive listening are new for many of our students and partly because this new work is taxing for students as they are learning to listen closely to what another person is saying while simultaneously trying to observe themselves, their own feelings and motives. This combination of new tasks takes a great deal of psychic energy; what students may have initially described as "easy work"—to simply sit back and listen to another person—is increasingly appreciated by our students for the intense level of energy and attention that such peer counseling skills require. The conscientious counselor must always keep one eye on his/her own feelings while at the same time listen to the client. Combining self-observation with empathic listening ensures that the focus and outcome of the counseling are set by the client and not imposed by the counselor's "sympathy" or value system.

WEEK 9 (continued)

Inter-Generational Exercise

Another exercise that further generates self-observational skills for the peer counselor is one in which each of them is asked to write down three values that they hold most dear, then three that they believe their parents hold most closely, and finally the same for their grandparents' generation. This inter-generational exercise, often used in family therapy consultations, encourages the counselor to consider his/her values in a focused way. Once again, the discussion that ensues from this exercise yields valuable insights. For example, some students may be surprised by how similar or different their values are from those of their parents or grandparents; often they had not previously conceptualized family value systems in this way. In other cases, students discuss the struggles that have led to differentiation in their values from those of earlier generations. In general, it is interesting to note that, for the most part, the students observed more similarity than difference in value priorities across the three generations of their families (Lewis, 1993).

A Philosophy of Multicultural Counseling

While some students have suggested that we do this unit on diversity and values earlier in the semester, we have found that a certain level of trust, which develops over time, makes class members more apt to share deeply and honestly when we present these issues in the final third of the semester. That is not to say that we don't consistently emphasize the importance of multicultural counseling issues (Pederson, 1985). Our philosophy in this course is similar to the "universalistic," multicultural counseling model suggested by Fukayama (1990), in which good empathic listening allows the counselor to explore with another person's background and values different from their own in an atmosphere of mutual respect (see chapters 13 and 14 for more detailed explications of multicultural counseling issues).

WEEK 9 (continued)

Exercises to Identify "Countertransference Reactions"

Peer counselors are advised not to work with anyone whose behavior or beliefs are offensive to them, who threatens them physically or verbally, or whose problems are too serious for peer counseling interactions, i.e., whose problems go beyond those of "everyday living" and require the help of a professional counselor. Peer counselors must therefore learn to differentiate accurately when such a problem is presented by a counselee and when it is a personal reaction generated from within themselves.

To help with this differentiation, we conclude our unit on values by teaching college peer counselors another concept from the psychotherapy literature. This instruction is for the purpose of maximally developing and expanding the peer counselor's self-observation and objectivity. We explain to the students that as counselors they may sometimes react to a client on the basis of personal experience and values that are not necessarily in the best interest of the client. A peer counselor must attend to how events in his/her own life could impact on his/her own perception of the client's reported experiences. The value of such self-study is to make sure that the counselor "catches" such countertransferences and deals with them for the benefit of the client.

To illustrate this point, a roleplay was suggested by one of the students in the class based on an experience he had in dealing with a quite reticent counselee in another paraprofessional setting (Talmers, 1991). This "client" had a personality type that the peer counselor tends to avoid in his personal life. He tells us that he noticed that he had not offered this counselee the usual resources and opportunities that he routinely presented to his more talkative clients. In actualizing this scenario as a roleplay, students discussed the ways in which they feel inwardly "pulled" by different clients because of stereotypes, prejudices, their own real-life relationships, and strong, subjective feelings. Encouraging such self-observation is useful in preventing such countertransferences from going unnoticed by the peer counselor.

WEEK 10

Crisis Intervention and Related Issues

In this week the class reads about, practices roleplays on, and discusses the following important topics:
- crisis intervention
- how to make a referral
- the use of supervisory process

Teaching assistants demonstrate a roleplay crisis "embedded" in the client's presenting issues, i.e., a scenario not so obvious as someone walking in and saying he/she is suicidal. While students are taught to deal with an obviously suicidal client by learning to ask direct questions to assess lethality and to immediately seek professional supervisory consultation so as to keep the client safe, they learn that sometimes people ask for professional help via indirect messages to peer counselors.

For such situations, we teach counselors how to make appropriate referrals. In accordance with ethical counseling principles, students learn about laws which require reporting the following:
- child abuse
- intent to harm another, in which the "intended victim him/herself must be warned"
- potential self-destructive intent

WEEK 10 (continued)

Making Referrals

In addressing such critical issues and in teaching counselors constructive ways to make referrals to professionals and other appropriate community resources, we teach the peer counselors to identify and recognize his/her own limits in a paraprofessional role. Peer counselors are instructed to contact their supervisors immediately when any of the above situations occur so that proper referrals can be made.

For the more subtle situations in which a crisis is "embedded" in the client's material, we demonstrate a roleplay in which a student who comes in with an anorectic eating disorder does not come right out and say she is ill and weak but rather describes being vaguely "tired" and says that her roommates complain she is not eating much and that she is exercising six hours a day (see also chapter 7). Since an eating disorder may not be perceived as a potentially life-threatening situation, even though in some extreme instances it can be, and since many eating-disordered clients do not "own" that they have a problem at all, the student counselor is challenged to employ a judicious blend of open and closed questions, being careful not to confront the client before she is ready to acknowledge her problem. As we have constructed this demonstration roleplay, the counselor eventually ascertains that the eating disorder is severe enough to require an immediate referral to both a mental health professional and a medical physician. This scenario is usually quite educative for our students, who often did not think about a crisis as possibly embedded in other material presented by a client.

WEEK 10 (continued)

Another Roleplay to Study Crisis Intervention Techniques

A second demonstration roleplay is offered on how to make a referral so that the counselee will accept it. Sometimes, especially in a crisis situation, the counselor will walk the client to a professional service, make the necessary appointment, or otherwise make sure that the client has followed through on what is an essential referral. Students practice making referrals in a non-authoritarian, compassionate manner. The explanation of a referral to a client needs to be consistent with the stated and felt concerns. For example, if the counselee wants help with being "tired" but denies or avoids stating that she has what seems like an apparent anorectic eating disorder, then the referral to a physician must be made on the basis of the client's wish to deal with her exhaustion, thus avoiding any counterproductive argument as to whether or not the student has an eating disorder. Such a diagnosis is, in any case, one which a paraprofessional is unqualified to make.

Student H: I learned that when crisis intervention is necessary I can pick up on subtle cues. I learned that the person in trouble can make you feel a little how they feel and that this is important information.

The Supervisory Relationship

Since the peer counselor always participates in ongoing professional supervision, in a subsequent roleplay demonstration, the peer counselors share the content and feelings about the counseling session with their supervisor. The group discusses the role of the supervisor and the complex feelings that (peer) counselors may have toward the supervisor.

WEEK 10 (continued)

We have found that it is often helpful to begin such a discussion by talking about supervisors whom students had valued in work or other contexts. Usually, qualities that students liked in a supervisor in a job setting are the same qualities they want in a "clinical" supervisor. Many of these qualities are the very attributes that are desirable in a good peer counselor: a non-judgmental attitude, good behavioral attending skills, sensitive empathic listening skills, solid experience, emotional stability, reliable availability, a collaborative attitude, and the capacity to say when one doesn't know the answer—and then do research to find the answer.

Students discuss feelings they have toward those in authority and, as a consequence, the distortions that can take place in a supervisory relationship. Another concept from the psychotherapy literature that is useful for college students to understand is the notion of "parallel process" (Doehrman, 1976). "Parallel process" refers to how the supervisory relationship may affect the counseling relationship, but more often it refers to how the counseling interaction may be played out—in parallel, as it were—in the supervisory meeting.

A roleplay that demonstrates this occurrence is one in which we first depict a peer counselor with a provocative client who then goes into his/her supervisory meeting with the same attitude as his client had with him/her. Such a repetition of the counselee's provocative behavior is not a deliberate action on the part of the peer counselor; rather, it is an unconscious communication in which the counselor, who is likely unaware of how the session with his/her client has affected him/her, is instead showing the supervisor how it felt. An alert supervisor will detect this "parallel" and ask the peer counselor if anything similar was occurring in the counseling session.

WEEK 10 (continued)

Knowledge of "parallel process" is as useful a tool for the supervision of peer counselors as it is for supervisory work with mental health professionals. Parallel process is yet another concept that college students are intellectually and emotionally capable of comprehending and utilizing. As with the phenomena of transference and countertransference, the awareness of parallel process is well- utilized by maturing college students in service of their better peer counseling skills. None of this advanced teaching gives license to the college-level peer counselor to make interpretations of transference and countertransference or parallel process to the client; such interpretations are the province of professional psychotherapists. However, the *awareness* that these phenomena exist and that their existence affects the paraprofessional's work allows the college peer counselor to provide more useful and mature service to her or his clients.

WEEK 11

Applied Peer Counseling

This is the week we discuss the applications of peer counseling to a variety of populations. We address this topic in two ways. First, we discuss the students' term paper assignment, which is to design a peer counseling/peer education/academic peer advising program or some combination thereof for a population of special interest to them. Their proposed programs may be designed for a special cultural group (e.g., peer counseling with minority populations on campus; see chapters 13 and 14); for a focal age group (e.g., peer counseling with the elderly; see chapter 6); for a medical population (e.g., peer counseling in a physical rehabilitation unit); or for a sociocultural group in need (e.g., peer counseling with the homeless). Each of these examples and hundreds more have been produced by our classes over the past seven years. Students' program proposals tend to be varied, thoughtful, and specifically delineated enough that an actual peer program could be operated from them. The only hitch in actualizing a program from one of these papers is that our students have envisioned unlimited funding and generous "grant" awards. As we all know, in reality this is often not available, even though, as a time-honored prevention modality, peer helping is, in our view, quite deserving of such financial backing.

Reactions to the Guest Speaker Presentations

In this eleventh week of the term we discuss and review the presentations of the guest speakers, whose chapters follow. Their programs offer wonderful examples of peer work in all its many applications: a phone hotline (chapter 4); Resident Advisors in the dormitories (chapter 5); peer education on health issues related to healthy eating, alcohol and other drugs, contraceptive education, safer sex, and stress management (chapter 7); and many more.

WEEK 11 (continued)

Students in our class tend to feel strongly about their favorite presentations, and yet almost all the programs represented are at one time or another cited by numbers of students as "most valuable." The generosity of the guest presenters in taking their time to share with the class is an important component of the class, and thus we include their work and "the voice of their peers" in this volume. We hope that the format of this text will offer the reader many useful models for developing similar and/or new programs in subject areas related to their own interests. An equally important reason to include this applied peer work is to demonstrate how the teaching of basic peer counseling skills may be integrated in collaborative fashion with applied programs of a great variety.

Self-Care

We note that our guest speakers across peer programs emphasize the importance of self-care for their peer counselors. To be effective in this work, peer helpers need to attend to their own physical and emotional needs and stress reduction. While their job is to be "helpful" to others—and those who self-select for this work usually have strong impulses in this direction—peer counselors cannot allow themselves to be "on call" for twenty-four hours a day. They must learn how to postpone non-emergency requests to a time when they can honestly concentrate on peer helping: "I cannot meet with you right now, but I can see you at five p.m." is a tactful way to clearly promise help while protecting one's other commitments. Furthermore, peer helpers across programs must learn that (sadly) not everyone is equally "helpable" and that they cannot assume total responsibility for other people's lives. A peer counselor—or a professional counselor—can help a client only to the extent that the client is motivated to collaborate in the helping relationship.

WEEK 12

Summing Up the Basics/Effects of the Course

In this last week of the semester, we ask our peer counselors-in-training to do what every good counselor must do: reflect on their work and progress. We therefore request that our students retrieve the cards they filled out on the first day of class, on which they listed the qualities of a skilled peer counselor they thought they already possessed and those qualities they wanted to work on during the semester. By this point in the semester, many have repressed the whereabouts and/or contents of this list, but most students are interested in considering how much progress they have made as they reflect on this task from the first week of class.

> *Student E*: To learn how to be a good listener is not as easy as it sounds, and it is probably one of the most important skills a person could ever obtain. I have found through observation that there are many good talkers and too few good/effective/empathic listeners. Too often people search for a person to talk to without considering that at times other people need to be listened to without interruption equally as much. To be able to tune into others' needs and to help others can be done with peer counseling skills. Empathy, non-judgmental listening, the avoidance of roadblocks, negative and positive feedback, and the ability to seek outside help when necessary are invaluable skills for any type of personal situation. With my family, oftentimes communication is blocked due to the numerous roadblocks mentioned in class. It is important to be able to deal with parents at a deeper level than when we were kids. After all, we are now entering into an adult world and are gaining a deeper understanding of ourselves and the people around us. Why not take this development even further and use the

WEEK 12 (continued)

peer counseling tools to learn and better understand others in our lives?

Most students in our class conclude that they have been "turned on" to a level of psychological-mindedness that had not been available to them before. They feel more self-aware; more compassionate toward and more empathic with others; and more tolerant of a wider set of backgrounds, lifestyles, and values in others. While they tell us it is hardest for them to suspend their impulse to "jump in and give advice," they are more keenly aware of their tendency to do so. Students grow to feel respectful of allowing others to set their own goals at their own pace and for their own benefit. Even when our students forget to use skills of empathic communication, they are now conscious of such lapses.

> *Student C:* I have especially learned not to ever trivialize anyone's concerns for any reason. For example, I might envision a completely distressed freshperson coming into my room, utterly and totally distressed because a course he/she wanted was closed. Maybe also I just finished talking to a person who is dealing with a death in the family. The tendency would be to say to the person with the class problems, "Hey, would you stop your belly-aching! The class will be offered again. You're wasting my time and other people have much worse problems that you." Now I realize we all have problems that we must deal with, and for us those problems are very important. Others should never minimize them.

WEEK 12 (continued)

Most students say the course has impacted positively on their relationships with friends, though they tell us they sometimes have to be careful not to obviously wear their "peer counselor hats." In addition, they speak of improved family interactions, most especially when they keep in mind open-ended questions and the feedback model in their newfound repertoire. Students find their relationships in the classroom and in the workplace improved for their augmented open-mindedness and increased empathy. Some of our students write on their course evaluations that it was "the most important course I took at the university"; that "it should be required for everyone"; and that "whether or not I use it in my career, it will have given me skills and insights that I will use forever."

A Word of Caution: Selection Issues

If a course in peer counseling is to serve the very useful function of prevention of problems, it is best opened to all students. Our class is offered to freshpersons through seniors and is sometimes elected as a cognate class by graduate students. Occasionally school teachers, counselors, and others have elected or audited the class.

However, there are liabilities in opening up this class in such an unrestricted manner. For if taking the class leads to a subsequent practicum experience, then students in the class must be differentially evaluated since not everyone ends up a competent peer counselor. Sometimes it is hard both for the instructors and for students to have such personal work "graded." On the other hand, our system of evaluation is not appreciably different than the kinds of evaluations that helping professionals must undergo if they certified to work with others.

While most of our college students are talented as peer helpers and find the work of the peer counseling class to be enlightening, there are a few for whom it "hits a nerve." These few students may expect the instructor to be "all ears" for them whenever they choose; they may expect an automatic "A" because the class can be such an ego-supportive experience; they may on rare occasions even become angry because they are asked to consider issues that carry some amount of pain. Such reactions are rare; indeed, most students review the course enthusiastically; most are evaluated well by their instructors. Nonetheless, those who train peer counselors need to be aware that, in dealing with material so closely connected to personal life experience, complex "transferences" can occur toward the instructors in a way that would not so likely be elicited by a more "factual" college course in history or mathematics.

Format for the Chapters That Follow

In the following chapters, we will present a wide variety of successful peer helping programs designed specifically for the college student and elaborated upon by the voices of the peer helpers themselves. Many of the issues presented in this chapter will be addressed as applied issues in the text that follows. The interviews that we conducted on the 112 peers whose "voices" will be featured throughout were carried out by a single research team with a common semi-structured interview adapted as necessary for the content of particular peer programs (see Appendix C). All taped interviews were transcribed and coded according to a specified research protocol (see Appendix D). Interview material was inserted into the text of each contributor's chapter by our research team; thus, at the time authors wrote their chapter(s), they were unaware of the content contained in "the voice of (their) peers." After the research interviews were inserted in the text, contributors were shown their chapters for final approval.

Demographic findings in relation to the peers who were interviewed for this project and commonalities across programs will be reported and discussed in the final chapter of this volume (see chapter 15 and Appendix E). We hope that you will enjoy reading about and perhaps even replicating some of the programs presented and that you will find as engaging as we have the voices of the peer helpers on campus.

REFERENCES

Carr, R., & Saunders, G. (1980). *Peer counselling starter kit.* University of Victoria: Peer Counselling Project.

Erikson, E. (1968). *Identity, youth, and crisis.* New York: Norton.

Damon, W., & Hart, D. (1982). The development of self understanding from infancy through adolescence. *Child Development, 53,* 841-864.

D'Andrea, V., & Salovey, P. (1983). *Peer counseling skills and perspectives.* Palo Alto: Science and Behavior Books.

Doehrman, M. (1976). Parallel processes in supervision and psychotherapy. *Bulletin of the Menninger Clinic, 40* (1), 9-40.

Fukayama, M. (1990). Taking a universal approach to multicultural counseling. *Counselor Education and Supervision, 30,* 6-13.

Galea, J. (1991). *The basics of peer counseling* [Videotape.] Ann Arbor: University of Michigan Department of Psychology.

Greenson, R. (1960). The vicissitudes of empathy. *International Journal of Psychoanalysis, 41*, 417-24.

Hatcher, S. (1989). Aspects of turmoil and self-containment in the adolescent psychotherapy patient. In E. M. Stern (Ed.), *Psychotherapy and the self-contained Patient* (73-83). New York: Haworth Press, Inc.

Hatcher, S. (1994). Personal rites of passage: stories of college youth. In A. Lieblich & R. Josselson (Eds.), *The narrative study of lives, Vol. 2*, 169-194.

Hatcher S., & Litzenberger, B. (1994). Reactions to peer teaching assistants in a college level course on peer counseling. The Peer Facilitator Quarterly, *11* (3), 20-23.

Hatcher, S., Nadeau, M., Walsh, L., Reynolds, M., Galea, J., & Marz, K. (1994). The teaching of empathy for high school and college students: Testing Rogerian methods with the Interpersonal Reactivity Index. *Adolescence, 29* (116), 961-74..

Hoffman, M. (1980). Moral development in adolescence. In J. Adelson (Ed.), *Handbook of adolescent psychology* (295-343). New York: Wiley & Sons.

Ivey, A. E., & Authier, J. (1978). *Microcounseling*. Springfield, IL: Charles C. Thomas.

The Lesbian-Gay Males Programs Office. (1993). Classroom and workshop exercises: "Take a Stand" exercise. In D. Schoem, et al. (Eds.), *Multicultural teaching in the university* (323-4).

Lewis, E. (1993). Classroom and workshop exercises: "Ethnograph Charting" exercise. In D. Schoem, et al. (Eds.), *Multicultural teaching in the university* (327-8).

Litzenberger, B. (1993). Personal communication to the author.

Myers, P., & Zúñiga, X. (1993). Classroom and workshop exercises: "Concentric Circles" exercise. In D. Schoem, et al. (Eds.), *Multicultural teaching in the university* (32?-?).

Myrick, R., & Erney, T. (1978). *Caring and sharing: Becoming a peer facilitator*. Minneapolis: Educational Media Corp.

Pederson, P. (1985). *Handbook of cross cultural counseling and therapy*. London: Greenwood Press.

Rogers, C. R. (1965). Client-centered therapy [Film No. 1]. In E. Shostrom (Ed.), *Three approaches to psychotherapy* [Three 16-mm. color motion pictures]. Orange, CA: Psychological Films, Inc.

Schoem, D., Frankel, L., Zúñiga, X., & Lewis, E. (Eds.). (1993). *Multicultural teaching in the university*. Westport, CT: Praeger.

Sheir-Younis, L. F., & Weingarten, H. (1992). Social identity groups exercise. Ann Arbor, MI: FAIRteach Workshop.

Simon, S., Howe, L., & Kirschebaum, H. (1972). *Values clarification: A handbook of practical strategies for teachers and students.* New York: Hart Publishing.

Talmers, P. (1991). Countertransference in peer advising. Unpublished manuscript, University of Michigan.

Thorne, B. (1992). Carl Rogers. Thousand Oaks, California: Sage.

Truax, C. B., & Carkhutf, R. R. (1967). *Toward effective counseling and psychotherapy.* Chicago: Aldine.

Zúñiga, X., & Nagda, B. (1993). Classroom and workshop exercises: "Identity Group" exercise. In D. Schoem, et al. (Eds.), *Multicultural teaching in the university* (323).

Peer Counseling Practica

Chapter 4

A Peer Counseling Phone Line

Doreen Murasky, ACSW, and Todd Sevig, PhD[1]

Introduction

In the past twenty years, programs have evolved across student affairs offices in campus communities that focus on the use of specially selected, trained peers to serve as advisors and counselors to other students; these programs are called paraprofessional or peer programs. Such programs have been developed to provide services in areas in which professionals are short-staffed and/or to augment and supplement services that professional staff provide. Indeed, the use of paraprofessionals in a number of counseling and guidance centers on campus is a trend that has gained momentum in recent years (Carns, Carns, & Wright, 1993). As D'Andrea and Salovey (1983) note, seventy-eight percent of colleges and universities utilize peer counselors in some capacity.

Peer counseling programs have a distinguished history in university counseling centers. While peer counseling takes many forms and functions at the college level, the crucial and most basic tenet is that peers enlist people similar to themselves in order to learn how to help themselves. There is much indication that the college-based peer movement is

---

[1] Having contributed equally to this article, the authors' names are listed alphabetically. We would like to acknowledge the efforts of previous coordinators of the 76-GUIDE program: Alice Brunner, PhD, Evie Gautier, PhD, Laurie Loevinger, MSW, Tom Morson, MSW, and David Patch, MSW.

growing both within and outside of counseling centers, in such specific areas as career concerns, eating disorders, AIDS prevention, multicultural issues, and relationship enhancement (see chapters 7 and 14). As strict outcome research is hard to conduct (Varenhorst, 1984), it appears that the benefits of having a peer counseling program are numerous to the center, the campus community, and to the peer counselors themselves.

> *Peer K*: Although there are other lines, they deal with specific things where 76-GUIDE handles everything. And there's also the stress and time management part of it that deals with students' inability to handle their stress and manage their time. And we also help Counseling Services in a way because we get the runoff of the clients they get. They get overloaded a lot, so we help the people out at least until they can see a professional counselor. But the focus at 76-GUIDE is dealing with your peers.
>
> My role is to help my peers to the best of my ability. But at the same time, I don't know if this sounds selfish or anything, we just learn more about other people's experiences and we learn more about things we may not have known about ourselves. We learn things that we can apply to the rest of our lives. But essentially for me, it's just helping. If someone calls with a problem and I might not have the answer, I can still be there to listen. There are a lot of things that I'm going through that I know a lot of people might be going through. And I think that I bring a lot of different experiences to this program.
>
> *Peer A*: It's just a place for people to call when they don't feel like they can talk to their friends about a problem or they don't really have a big support network. And I think it's really valuable to have something anonymous. You know, a lot of people are wary of going in and seeing a therapist. There's a stigma attached.

> But, it's easier to pick up the phone and talk to someone you're never going to see and to try and work through immediate problems. It's not long-term counseling; it's short-term, very short-term.

This chapter describes 76-GUIDE, a phone counseling service line that has been in existence for more than twenty years as the main peer counseling crisis service for the university community. Over the years, other 76-GUIDE peer programs have been developed, including an educational workshop series, a suicide workshop for advisors in the residence halls, and a time and stress management program (separate from that described in chapter 7). While the program has changed and evolved over the past twenty years, the basic mission and philosophy have remained intact: that of providing a humane response to all those who are in need of services. In this spirit, 76-GUIDE has provided peer counseling programming for thousands of students over the years.

> *Peer I*: We've taken a lot of different kinds of calls. It can range from student concerns—roommate problems, relationship problems, grieving, things like that—to academic concerns, to any counseling concerns that are very serious like suicide. I think a really valuable part of our service is handling emergency situations. Because in the later hours of the night there aren't a lot of resources out there for people that all of a sudden they're in an emergency situation. Basically we are able to direct that person to the best course of action, whether that be taking them to the psychiatric emergency room or another appropriate resource. The other smaller part of our services is the stress management face-to-face consultation for students where they come into counseling services and we would see them about any stress management or time management or academic-type concerns. And we help them with strategies to help them to try to relieve

their stress or manage their time better. We use different tools and paradigms to help them focus on whatever they want. We see what will work for *them*.

76-GUIDE operates under Counseling Services, which is housed in the Division of Student Affairs. Counseling Services is a comprehensive university counseling center that provides clinical services, outreach and consultation, and training for psychology and social work graduate students. 76-GUIDE is coordinated by one professional staff person; however, other professional staff and interns become involved in the program by helping with training, serving as professional back-up to the phone line peer counselors, and providing consultation and supervision.

We will proceed by outlining the following:

1. the mission of the program

2. the history of the program

3. the services provided

4. the peer counselor selection process

5. the training and supervision processes

We will also discuss the supervision/training processes and address the peer counselors' own development through their involvement in the program.

Mission of 76-GUIDE

The mission of 76-GUIDE is to serve the emotional needs of the university community through quality peer counseling, consultation, referral, and educational programming and to provide responses to all who request our services. The peer programming philosophy at Counseling Services views peer counselors as service recipients as well as service providers. The goal of our peer programming efforts is to provide quality training to selected students, in turn enabling them to be effective service providers to the University community. The original 76-GUIDE philosophy statement is a one-page document that dates back to early in 76-GUIDE's history. The philosophy places the peer counselor in the role of a mentor and supporter whose main task is to listen, empathize, model effective communication skills, provide relevant information, and offer referrals when appropriate. The philosophy is "client centered"; it moves away from pathologizing "clients" and focuses on struggles shared by all humans. The tenor of this philosophy has remained central to the structure of 76-GUIDE throughout its history.

> *Peer O*: It was developed to provide students on campus with a place to call and talk. It's not meant to offer any kind of diagnosis and it's not meant to offer any kind of long-term care. It's more like when you're really stressed out or you're really depressed and you don't have anywhere else to turn, you can call. And it is a place to talk about your problems without seeing the person, without knowing who the counselor is, in a very non-judgmental kind of atmosphere.

> *Peer A*: I'm part of a team of people who try to reach out to students or their community members who are going through small or large crises and my role is to be there for them when they call, to try to help them to get in touch with what they're feeling and what they're going through, and to a lesser extent to help them work through their problems. But that's secondary to just "being there for them," which I think is our main goal.

> *Peer J*: I had gotten a call from this guy who said that he had just cut himself and he was bleeding and the knife was in his hand. And at that time my heart was racing; I had been woken up—you know, you're there overnight for overnight shifts. And at first, my first reaction was to say, "Oh my God!" But at that point it's the stress of the moment. I don't know how I got through that call, but I just followed everything that we were trained for. I pulled

out my paper and did it almost pragmatically, "Put the knife away. Can you put it away? At least that way I can talk to you." It was a really stressful call, but it was very rewarding because I got him to put away the knife and he called the next day so I knew he was alive. At least I had gotten him through that night. That's our purpose; you've got to get these callers through that time temporarily. You can't fix their lives for them. I mean, we could if we were gods and goddesses, but I got him through the night and that was my purpose.

Peer E: A lot of these people are calling because they're having a new feeling and they don't want to think they're the only ones going through it. We say we've been there before. We don't say that if we haven't been there before. We can try to understand; we can relate to the feelings at least.

Peer B: It's taught me a lot about skills that I might not have realized that I have in terms of forming a connection, I mean, forming a bond with the person on the other end of the phone and a basic understanding, a basic trust between two individuals, so that the person I'm speaking with on the phone shares with me a problem that they might not have wanted to disclose. Just an empathic connection to really get a genuine feeling for what the other person feels.

Peer N: Some situations I've realized might not be a situation that's a crisis to me, but to other people it is. There are different levels of needs and goals for various people and different ideas of what achievement means.

Peer L: I've learned that other people go through some of the same things that I go through and some people struggle with much different things than I've ever struggled with. Some

A Peer Counseling Phone Line

people struggle just getting through a day whereas I tend to focus my struggles on more futuristic things. It's definitely put me in touch with family problems that I've experienced and relationship struggles too.

Peer J: It's taught me that there are a lot of people out there who are very fortunate to have a good support group, but there are also many people out there who don't have a sufficient support group. And that sometimes people are the way they are because of circumstances.

Peer C: They're calling and looking to elicit some help, but for me the key thing on my line when I'm working with a client is that they have the answers. I'm there to help them come up with those answers that they have and to find those skills for themselves because they know what works best for them. It's just a matter of finding their strengths and helping them to see their strengths. For the most part, it is just a relationship in which I'm helping them to find what's already there inside themselves. I don't have any magic cures. I try to make that really clear to them because occasionally callers look for that.

History

The evolution of the 76-GUIDE program began in 1967 when the Student Affairs Counseling Office began operating the "Referral and Information Services Program." This service was staffed by students and operated weekdays, 8 a.m. to 5 p.m. It was well received by the campus as it was responsive to students' informational needs as well as to students in need of psychological help. Soon it was recognized that student life keeps a schedule that does not easily parallel the hours of university administrative offices, and alternatives for better access were considered. In 1970, the service was expanded to provide twenty-four-hour operation and the name was changed to "Focus." After a short period of time, the name was changed one final time to "76-GUIDE." Over the years, this name has remained because it is somewhat descriptive of the services provided and it spells out the telephone number of the service. Indeed, 76-GUIDE has become a well-known name and service across campus.

During the late sixties, other universities were also establishing twenty-four-hour telephone operations aimed at dealing with students in crisis or in emergency situations. In the formation of 76-GUIDE, great effort was placed on publicizing the service as one that is responsive to a broad range of needs and services: counseling, referral, and information. 76-GUIDE's first slogan was: "Any question, any problem, any time." The publicity and highly visible location were successful in promoting 76-GUIDE and in producing some five hundred calls a day. The majority of calls were inquiries about campus events, and the high volume of requests for information left 76-GUIDE workers feeling overextended, negatively impacting the ability of the workers to provide peer counseling to students calling for personal psychological assistance.

In 1972, a decision was made to refer informational questions to the appropriate campus units. During the rest of the 1970s, the 76-GUIDE program had two peer counselors offering service to students twenty-four hours a day, every day except Christmas and New Year's day. During this period, 76-GUIDE offered both telephone and drop-in service.

In the 1980s, a decade marked by leaner budgets across the university, "Smaller but better" was the slogan. Like many other departments, Counseling Services faced budget reductions and difficult decisions about how to spend limited resources. During this period, services provided by 76-GUIDE were scaled back and operated when Counseling Services was closed: 5 p.m. to 9 a.m. Monday through Friday and twenty-four hours on the weekend. In addition, the 76-GUIDE drop-in service was closed and the 76-GUIDE telephone operation was moved to a confidential location.

In 1984, university students staged a demonstration and demanded services focused on the problem of sexual assault. A year later, the Sexual Assault Prevention and Awareness

Center (SAPAC) was developed (see chapter 8). Part of SAPAC's mission was to operate a twenty-four-hour sexual assault telephone line. Thus, in 1986, SAPAC opened a telephone counseling line specifically for survivors of sexual assault and their friends and family. 76-GUIDE collaborated in the operation of this phone line, answering calls during specified periods of the evening and night.

The future will no doubt bring more changes to the 76-GUIDE program. The 1990s began with a national economy in recession, which may mean further budget reductions in higher education.

Services Provided

While services provided by 76-GUIDE have developed and changed throughout the years, the service that has remained consistent over the years is the peer counseling telephone line. Although the counseling line receives the majority of its calls from students and others affiliated with the university, individuals from neighboring communities also utilize the service. People may call 76-GUIDE to request a wide range of assistance ranging from suicide emergencies to exam anxiety to advice on helping a friend confront a suspected eating disorder. 76-GUIDE also provides an after-hours link between professional counselors and the campus community since there is always a professional counselor "on call."

> *Peer O*: Having a student call with a problem that you can honestly help them with is gratifying. Generally the callers want to vent their feelings and just say, "Oh, oh, I'm so frustrated," and then talk about it for a while. But then to actually get to exploring the caller's options and to get to the point where they say, "Yeah, that's a good idea. I think I'll try that," is great. Sometimes, though, they still realize that they've still got a problem, but it's like something to tide them over that we can do for them.

Because the phone line is anonymous and confidential, obtaining detailed evaluative data regarding effectiveness or consumer satisfaction is difficult, if not impossible. In general, the 76-GUIDE coordinator receives evaluative data in five distinct ways:

1. a caller calls 76-GUIDE back to report the outcome of the issue(s) discussed and to offer feedback

2. callers in counseling with a Counseling Services staff member report their experience with 76-GUIDE to their counselor

3. a student reports his/her experience in calling 76-GUIDE to faculty or staff and that person reports back to 76-GUIDE

4. the caller phones the 76-GUIDE coordinator directly with feedback

5. in rare and extreme circumstances, an actively suicidal caller is connected to life-saving services through 76-GUIDE and feedback is received from the police, security, Housing Department, and/or the hospital.

Overall, feedback received through these means has been positive to extremely positive. Whenever criticism or constructive feedback is reported, every attempt is made to correct the problem.

In addition, peer counselors receive feedback on each call through an extensive write-up system. In brief, each call is recorded on a "write-up" form and placed in a log book. All peer counselors and the coordinator are expected to read each write-up and offer feedback. This system serves to provide workers with ongoing feedback, to gain insights on different approaches to peer counseling, to keep the coordinator informed about the day-to-day functioning of the line, and to provide a sense of continuity to callers who call again. This process reinforces the "team aspect" of 76-GUIDE.

> *Peer H*: A lot of times, you don't know how you're affecting this person, if you're helping or not. I mean, sometimes you can kind of tell. Other

times that person may hang up and you'll never hear from them again and you don't know what's going to happen. It's neat sometimes when you talk to someone and they'll come to a decision about something they want to do; sometimes they call back and say, "Oh, I did this and it worked out really well. Thanks for your help." And that's always nice to hear.

Peer H: We got feedback in a number of ways. First of all, you get feedback in a sense from the caller and how they react to how you're helping them. Secondly, we get feedback from each other on the team. Our team was very small; there are fifteen of us on the team. And we would do a write-up after each call. And we are required to read every write-up and write comments on the write-up as to how the particular worker handled the call: "This was a really great technique that you used here," "I think that's good," or "I would have tried something a little different here." So that's how we got some feedback. We also did self-evaluations, which we talked over with our supervisor. We also got feedback directly from the supervisor because he reads all the evaluations and has individual meetings with us. And we also, in addition to clinicing in the large staff team, would break up into small groups of four with a professional staff person from Counseling Services and "clinic" in a small room. So we get feedback there also, lots of feedback.

Peer F: I mean, you can get some feedback from callers and how they respond. And, yeah, slamming down the phone is definitely feedback and sometimes people say, "You're very helpful" or "Thank you very much." And other times you can't really get a sense of it. In terms of staff, we do have a written log of all the calls we have, so at the end of the write-up you can say, "I really don't know what else I would have done with this" or "I felt really great about this call; it went very well." Everybody on the team reads that log and so you'll very often get responses on that. And sometimes, especially with really difficult calls, we'll talk about it in our staff meetings the following week. The person who took the call is generally given the opportunity to tell what the call was about and what they did. If there's been any kind of follow-up situation, the supervisor might mention that, and then the team could process it. Generally it's a tremendously supportive thing. People say, "You did a great job," "That was a great call," and all sorts of stuff. And people will bring up, "I've found that this is really effective in situations like this" or "I know this person doesn't respond well to this, it was a good try." So you get stuff like that. And sometimes, if somebody just reads that you had a really tough call in the log, you might just get a note or something, or if you run into them on the street. So definitely, there is a good amount of feedback.

Peer B: Most of the time, most of the feedback you get from another team member is just really positive, so it feels nice to hear. I mean, it's good when you feel bad about a call to read someone's comment saying that you did the best you could; you know, remember to take care of yourself. People are really supportive when they give feedback.

Peer A: I guess I'm a person that's pretty open to feedback, just because I want to be doing a good job. So I like it when people on the write-up forms don't just write, "Good call," they write what they liked about the call. And also I don't mind when people say, "This is what I would have done..." because a lot of the time I don't think of things. Even when the call did go well, maybe it would have gone better or differently if I had tried out these other things, just to give me a sense that what I'm doing really is helping people, that I'm not just sitting there going, "Uh-huh, uh-huh, uh-huh. How do you feel about that? Oh. You sound upset." I mean, I'm not some robotic comforter, you know.

Peer N: I think it's very helpful. Nobody gives feedback in a negative way. Even if there's something we could have done differently, it's never said, "You did this wrong thing." It's more like we work together and we have a concern for each other, so therefore it's not our objective to make others feel bad, it's just to improve our services. I'd rather get the feedback and make a good call than do something wrong.

76-GUIDE has intermittently offered workshops to the campus community. In 1986, a major effort to launch a workshop series was initiated. The topics offered were: assertiveness training, peer relationships, suicide intervention, test anxiety, and family-of-origin relationships. Overall, the response by participants to the workshops was quite positive. However, since many of the workshops were poorly attended, it was not viewed as a good use of limited resources.

In the winter of 1990, 76-GUIDE renewed its program of face-to-face counseling, focusing on stress and time management consultations to students. The evaluations from students who utilized this service were quite positive. Students rated the service on five-point scales, tapping helpfulness, usefulness of the strategies suggested, empathy of the counselor, and knowledge of the counselor. No mean of any of these areas in any year was below 3.5. Most means ranged above four. Additionally, comments were often forthcoming regarding students' appreciation of the peer-aged counselor in contrast with older professionals.

Peer E: The time you do "time and stress management" is really rewarding because you can see the person's face. The phone is good too because you can hear them say, "Oh, yeah. Thanks a lot." People thank you and everything. But when you see a person's face and they're happy about something, that is a totally great feeling. We hand out a lot of worksheets and during time and stress management and try to help people understand their problem better. This part of the program is actually more solution based. It's a really rewarding experience because they walk out of there saying, "Thanks a lot, I'm going to use this." And you know you haven't solved their procrastination problem for life or anything but at least they realize there are ways around it. The callers are generally people who aren't looking so much for solutions but looking for someone to vent with, someone to empathize with them, someone to make them feel not-so-alienated, because this is a big university and it's tough to talk to friends about things because you might feel like they're not really listening to you. The people who come in for face-to-face time management counseling have more specific problems that they have to work on.

Selection Process of Peer Counselors

The selection of 76-GUIDE workers is an important and time-consuming task for the 76-GUIDE team. It is one of the most vital administrative tasks because the quality of the program is based on the skills and knowledge of peer counselors who staff the telephones. 76-GUIDE selection is a multi-faceted process which occurs once a year. It is a three-stage process consisting of the following:

1. a written application

2. a group interview

3. an individual interview complete with roleplays

The selection process is designed to be consistent with the aforestated mission of 76-GUIDE. All current 76-GUIDE workers are part of the selection process and provide input into the selection decisions. In this way, current peer counselors learn how to screen applicants, about fairness in employment decisions, and how to implement and achieve affirmative action. The process is also designed to challenge applicants to reflect upon their own problem-solving skills, motivations, and personal growth. Feedback is provided to each applicant regarding his/her participation in the process. In so doing, it is hoped that each applicant gains something simply from going through the process, whether or not they are selected. Each stage of the selection process emphasizes different peer counseling criteria. First, to apply for a peer counseling position, a student must pick up an information sheet and a four-page written application. The information sheet describes what qualities are desired in a peer counselor, the time commitment required, the training, and an overview of the selection process. The application asks many personal, open-ended questions that require time, reflection, and openness on the part of the applicant.

Each year, more than one hundred applications are distributed, and between sixty and one hundred students actually apply to be a peer counselor. Some students apparently decide not to apply after reading the information sheet and reviewing the application. This self-screening aspect of the process is important in that there are only five to ten open positions each year. Once the application is turned in, it is read by the 76-GUIDE coordinator and at least half of the current team. The written application helps assess an applicant's awareness of self and process of dealing with personal problems, his/her ability to express him/herself in writing, and his/her expectations as a helper and member of a team. Students screened out at this stage generally seem to lack either the emotional maturity needed to cope with the demands of the job or the skills needed to express themselves.

The second stage of the selection process involves a group interview. During the interview, six applicants are asked to respond to a series of four questions. Two current peer counselors facilitate the interview and the process is observed by an additional three to four peer counselors and the 76-GUIDE coordinator. The first two questions are designed to put the candidate at ease and to allow the selection team to get to know each of them better. The third question is a group consensus exercise designed to give the selection committee clues as to how each candidate operates in a group given a time-limited task. The exercise is issue-oriented, which also allows the selection committee to experience each candidate's comfort level and knowledge about various current issues. The last question gives each candidate the opportunity to reflect on his/her personal participation in the group interview and to offer feedback to the facilitators about the selection process. This provides the selection committee with additional information about each candidate's level of self-awareness. It also provides valuable information about the selection process from the candidates' perspective.

After each group interview, the selection committee discusses the interview and makes tentative decisions about which candidates are to be asked back for the final stage of the selection process. At the conclusion of all group interviews, a consensus decision is made regarding which candidates are asked to continue in the selection process.

> *Peer K*: One thing that we look for in the interviewees is people who show a certain amount of common courtesy. When you're speaking to someone else, I mean you should at least respect what they have to say and the way in which they're saying it. There are so many ways, like not cutting people off. That's kind of one thing that I think this program looks for, is to show common courtesy and respecting others' ideas and to show that you're open. You have to be open to work on this phone-line to have an "open line."

The final stage of the selection process is an individual interview, which consists primarily of two roleplays, a few standard questions, and an individual meeting with the 76-GUIDE coordinator, who makes the final decisions. After each roleplay, the coordinator, peer counselor, and candidate process the roleplay. The candidate is then offered feedback on how to improve in the role as counselor. Allowing each candidate two roleplays provides information both about the candidate's current ability and style as a helper and his/her ability to incorporate and apply feedback.

Finally, the coordinator collects the feedback on the candidates from current peer counselors and schedules a staff meeting for final input on hiring decisions. After this meeting, the coordinator uses the team recommendations, balances factors such as building a diverse team, takes into account how many people are returning, and makes the final decisions. Full positions on the team as well as alternate positions are offered at this time. Students who have been offered a position are invited to attend a staff meeting to receive further information regarding the program. The 76-GUIDE coordinator also is in contact with new workers throughout the summer.

Once the new worker starts in the fall, he/she is on probation for the first three months. This period allows time "on the job" for candidates and the coordinator to evaluate if a good match has been achieved through the selection process.

Training and Supervision

The initial and on-going training of the peer counselors and the supervision process are crucial to the success of the program both in terms of service delivered to the clients and for the peer counselors' own education. The theoretical approach to the training is one that is grounded in college student developmental theory, helping skills training (Ivey, 1983; Egan, 1982), experiential learning, and various approaches to peer counseling (D'Andrea & Salovey, 1983).

Two full days of training and orientation are held at the counseling center. First on the schedule are team building, introducing peer counselors to the confidential suite where the phone lines are located, helping skill development, and practicing going through the 76-GUIDE manual[2] and crisis/suicide intervention. There is also a weekend retreat at a local state park. The "atmosphere" of the retreat is conducive to a relaxed setting for more in-depth team building and to begin training on a variety of "difficult" topics, such as suicidal callers, sex callers, repeat callers, and chronic callers. The sequencing of training topics and formats aims to incorporate developmental aspects of learning. For instance, in presenting the topic of crisis intervention, we present conceptual material, encourage students to become aware of how they have experienced crises in their own lives, and then invite them to engage in related roleplays.

Additionally, we try to capitalize on returning workers' knowledge and experience by having them present/facilitate some of the training. The benefit of this is twofold: 1) this is, at times, the most effective way to present material to new workers because the returning workers will communicate material in a way that can be easily heard, and 2) this presents returning workers with a new challenge in which they can increase their own skills.

> *Peer H*: We did a variety of things in our training program. We started out by going over basic helping skills, such as empathy and listening skills and identifying feelings, talking about different kinds of issues that people might have to deal with, real basic things. From there—those were the first two days of our training—we went on a weekend retreat where we spent a lot of time practicing those skills with other workers, as well as really looking at how we felt about a lot of different issues. Much of it was very introspective that weekend. We spent time talking about a lot of different issues that are really tough and how we might deal with

---

[2] The 76-GUIDE program has developed a manual that peer counselors use as a resource during training, for reference on specific topic areas, while on the phone line, and for their own growth and development. The manual contains sections on mission and philosophy, policies and procedures, general counseling, phone counseling, and a quick reference page of information for several specific topics.

them: multicultural issues, issues of sexism and sexual assault, AIDS—just different kinds of issues and how we react to them and how our reactions might affect how we help people. And so we did a lot of introspection which was very helpful when you're confronted with a lot of these issues on the phone. The initial training was those first two days and the weekend retreat and then we had on-going training throughout the entire year at our weekly staff meeting, which is a two-hour meeting. We'd spend some time doing business but also some time training on a variety of issues. We had Lesbians and Gay Males Programs Office come and talk to us; we covered multicultural issues; we talked about issues of transference and countertransference and how that came through on the telephone; we talked about grief and loss; we talked about self-esteem; we talked about burnout and how we were affected by our work. We did a lot of self-evaluation, looking at how the program was affecting us and how we were helping people, and how our skills were improving and where our strengths were and where our growth areas were. We did a lot of stuff. And it didn't really end; I mean, training was basically constant.

Peer I: The new workers are getting more of an indoctrination into counseling—what is counseling? what is a helping profession?—and also basic counseling skills—how to listen, how to be empathic, and those kind of things. And also the returning workers help in that they do some of the training along with the 76-GUIDE supervisor. And a lot of roleplaying! I think that's especially helpful for new workers so they get their feet wet, so to speak, and also for returning workers to get back into the swing of things. And it's valuable in the sense that new

> workers are seeing how old workers handle different situations, so that they learn from the experience that the returning workers have. So, it's a lot of different things. And also, it's not only counseling skills and learning about the profession, but it's also personal development: How do I fit as a helper? How do I take care of myself? How do I set my own limits? Those kind of things. So that's another part of the job. And also a lot of teamworking-type things are built into the training because we do operate in a team environment—so it's really important to build those relationships. And that's the initial training, and from there I think the training is on-going.

With the conclusion of the retreat, the initial training period is over; evaluations of the initial training period are collected to assist the coordinator in determining additional training needs. On-going training is then conducted in the format of staff meetings. These meetings are a combination of administrative matters, announcements, and pertinent training topics; these include eating disorders, working with lesbian/gay/bisexual callers, sexual assault issues, counselor self-care, and so on.

> *Peer E*: Like, it's really loose how we do it but there are basic guidelines on how to handle a call. First you have to identify the problem and then go through steps to get out the caller's emotions. That's pretty much the main thing in any psychology discipline, working with feelings and then actually helping the client solve the problem. You might not even get that far in the call because so many problems are unsolvable. If we see a specific thing they can do to help themselves we try to point out these things and make them aware that there are things that they can do to help themselves. We're trying to help and we're trying to validate. Validation is a form of help and we're trying to validate or help the people help

themselves by pointing out certain things or by asking certain questions that get at the heart of their feeling in order to help them understand themselves better. We're not professional counselors. The whole thing is peer stuff; "peer" is like the key word. So we're trying to help them on a totally equal level, you know?

Peer J: We go through the four-stage model: discussing the problem, establishing a rapport with the caller, giving suggestions, and the final one is like summarizing the call to them. And so throughout the call we'll ask, "What's the problem?" And then, you don't give advice, but you give a lot of suggestions because in the end our most important goal is that this caller has to make a decision—him or herself. We can't make the decision for them. So you can help them with suggestions, but in the end it has to be their decision.

Peer F: I think that to an extent you can only give so much training. You can give people an idea about the skills or about the kinds of issues, but I think it takes getting on the line and talking to people and kind of figuring out what's your style, what you seem to feel comfortable with, what things you have a harder time with—and from there, once you really see what you've got in the working situation, you go back and say, "OK, I want to work on this and I'm really happy with how this is going." There has to be an on-going training.

Peer A: A lot of what you learn on this job, you learn on the phone actually doing it.

Team building is a process that is worked on throughout the year, since the counselors offer support not only to callers but also to other team members.

Peer O: You go and you work and you answer the phones. So you're a peer counselor trying to work with clients. But there's also offering your support as a team member and helping the other peer counselors figure out what other things they could have done with that call.

Peer N: My role is to work with people on the line and work with other people in the group to make the program successful. I have responsibilities within the group and yet I have a responsibility to the people to share the skills that I have learned through the program.

The supervisor meets individually with each peer counselor to solidify the student's own goals and what he/she needs for support and for challenge; the supervisor gets to know each peer counselor. It is important to have this one-on-one supervisory contact and to establish a good working rapport between the coordinator and the peer counselor. The coordinator maintains office hours throughout the year so peer counselors can stop by and receive additional supervision as needed.

Peer L: It's a really positive experience because it's not the supervisors telling you what you've done well, necessarily, and what you need to improve on; it's his being a sounding board for what you see you've done.

Peer A: He is the supervisor, but he's very much a part of the team. He really values what we have to say and he encourages us to bring up ideas. And when people bring up things in the staff meetings we have each week, or if you go and see him on an individual basis, you can tell that he really takes what you're saying into account and a lot of times tries to implement your ideas.

Peer K: Our supervisor also elicits our help, our concerns about how we should go about the work, especially since we're involved. He gets lots of input from us and we get a lot from him. But he just makes sure that we stay within our guidelines, I should say rules. He also prompts us to discuss our norms and values with this job, such as professionalism, common courtesy, things like that.

We also have "clinicing" teams; these are small groups of peer counselors who meet with one professional staff person. The purpose of these teams is to provide a safe, small group atmosphere in which to discuss calls, issues, and personal development issues in detail. A secondary benefit of such "clinics" is that peer counselors get exposed to other professional staff besides the supervisor.

Peer E: At the beginning of the term, before classes, we had a weekend retreat, four days of training. Actually, we're trained throughout the year. We have two hours per week of meetings and that's training because we talk about calls we get, we talk about how we could approach what we did differently, and we get different counselors from Counseling Services to come and talk about different sorts of things. Also once a week for one hour, we have clinicing teams where we're all split up into groups of three and then we go and talk to a counselor for one hour. A lot of times we talk about the calls, specific calls, what we could have done, how we thought we handled it, and different approaches. We also talk about our personal lives and issues, about how a call could have affected us, how we could relate to the call, or even just things that have nothing to do with the calls, just things that have to do with ourselves. Like a counseling session for ourselves. It kind of brings about self-awareness.

Peer F: Working in an agency with social workers and psychologists with all these great listening skills, when they're teaching you how to be good listeners and how to give feedback and how to phrase things, in some ways it's just part of who they are now because it's what they

> do professionally. And so just watching them, I
> find that now I do it myself too. You know,
> kind of just watching them kind of helps you
> learn the skills that they're trying to train you
> in anyway.

With the combination of the total team, the small groups, and the individual time with the supervisor, training and supervision are comprehensive and allow for flexibility (i.e., some people learn and are supported best in a big group; others learn best in individual situations, etc.) Also, this approach allows for people to grow and develop in ways that may be challenging for them (i.e., a person uncomfortable in groups or in working as a team is challenged to work on this issue throughout the year).

> *Peer C:* I think there's very few counseling lines in
> which you get the kind of ongoing training
> throughout the year that we got. Most
> counseling lines I know use volunteers and
> they may get three days of training every year.
> Our training was incredible, along with the fact
> that the supervisor did see us as being very
> mature, capable, professional people, that he
> helped us draw a lot out of it; the teamwork
> was critical. I think without that, it wouldn't
> have been the experience it was, either for me
> as a counselor or for the callers who called,
> because I don't think I would have been as
> effective.

Special Challenges in Peer Phone Line Work

Suicide intervention is one extremely challenging component of phone counseling work.[3]

---

[3] If a caller mentions that he/she may be feeling suicidal or is thinking about suicide, even though it may be vague, 76-GUIDE workers are trained to do a standard lethality assessment. This includes asking about intent, method, availability/access to certain means, specific plans, drugs/alcohol, previous attempts, and the caller's present social situation. If a caller discloses that

> *Peer F*: I can definitely tell you what my most challenging or frustrating experience was on the phone line. It was this past December, and a woman who called late one evening was suicidal. It was around 10:30 p.m. She had been a "regular caller" and we knew her well, as she had been suicidal on and off. I contracted with her not to hurt herself, but she called back about half an hour later having taken a huge number of pills. This is one situation in which we must break confidentiality and so I was doing my best to get a call trace going. I was also doing my best to keep her awake and to try and keep her on the phone; it was literally a huge juggling act. I was very fortunate to have another staff member who just happened to be working down the hall.

Peer counselors often report frustrations of dealing with chronic and abusive callers, sex callers, the mentally ill, and other non-peers.[4]

> *Peer J*: We have some callers who call almost everyday; they are mentally ill and they've been calling for five, six, seven years. Those are what we call "regular callers." And those callers sometimes know exactly what you will say. Some callers just call up and say, "I did this today"; they just need another human voice to talk to. Everybody has a different

---

he/she has done or could do something that could be self-harming or even lethal, the peer counselor calls the professional back-up counselor. If confidentiality needs to be broken, we have a "call tracing procedure" by which we can identify the location of the originating call and thus provide life-saving assistance.

[4] In training, time is devoted to addressing strategies that prevent callers from "abusing" counselors. This involves having peer counselors understand their own reactions to a particular caller, addressing the presence of a mental illness, setting limits with callers, and ending clearly inappropriate calls in a functional and responsible manner.

reason for calling, but you have one purpose with them: to help. There's all these people with all these different problems, all these different backgrounds. You're one type of person and you have to listen to them and try to adapt your one way of dealing with people; you kind of mold it to them.

Peer P: The most frustrating thing I suppose would be regular callers, who after a while get to know your voice and after a while start telling you about yourself. Like, "You're not a good counselor. Why do you do this?" And they know more about the subject of schizophrenia and every disease they've ever had than you do and they like to tell you that. That's frustrating because regular callers usually aren't university students—they're not really peers. They're people way older than yourself and it's good experience to deal with other people, but at the same time it's disappointing because you come into the job thinking that you're going to deal with people your age. The regular callers call with the same problem and it never gets anywhere. It's never really a crisis.

Peer J: We had this one caller who called a lot and he'll test you. He'll test you over the phone, like, "You're a lousy counselor, you're not helping me." Because he had a psychology degree himself so he knows exactly what you're doing. And it's frustrating. Whenever he'd call, I just didn't want to talk to him. But then you figure out ways to deal with it, you talk to your supervisors, you talk to your counselors. You always have professional advice.

Peer H: Probably the most challenging for me was a caller we had who talked a lot about his sexual orientation and he was really struggling with that and he got very pushy with us about how we felt and how we felt about our own sexual orientation. And sometimes it was kind of borderline as to whether this was a sex call or not. You know, "Is this guy really struggling with these issues or is he trying to be manipulative with us?" And it always seemed kind of that way because none of the men on staff had ever talked to this guy even though he called back regularly. So that was really tough. And I think it was interesting because we never really did come to a conclusion, but nobody ever terminated the call in case this guy really needed somebody to talk to. But that was really tough, to try and figure that out. And sometimes it could be really frustrating and he could almost get really violent with some of things that came up in the call. He really tried to push your limits. Sometimes we had to set limits with him which was tough too. To say, "You know, look. I'm here to help you but I'm not here to take any kind of abuse from you. And that's not going to be helpful to you at all." And that's been really tough to do.

Peer D: The most frustrating would probably be a psychotic caller who called up. I didn't really realize that the person was psychotic until ten minutes into the call and it was just very hard to follow their train of thought. And it was really frustrating because at the point I realized what was going on, the call was not where I wanted it to be; I needed to make a referral for professional help.

Peer B: One of the most frustrating things about working at 76-GUIDE is the fact that we don't get enough students that call. I'd say twenty percent of our calls are from people in the community that have been calling 76-GUIDE for like ten years; they're regular, chronic callers. And that's frustrating because the population we're out to serve is students and staff. One of the reasons why it is a peer line is because we are peers with our fellow college students. We should be better able to empathize maybe with fellow college students. Basically, we can empathize and sort of get them through the day, but it's not what we're there for as a 76-GUIDE line.

Peer M: Well, I think it's interesting that many people we talk to are older than us, older than me. I mean, pretty much everybody who works on the line is younger than twenty-one, there's like one twenty-three year old, twenty-two or something. But a lot of the callers are either grad students or adults in the community with emotional/mental problems. And so it's very hard, a lot of issues that come up have to do with jobs or grad school and long-term, various type relationships. A good portion of the calls are like that and I don't think we've been through those things ourselves. So we can be sympathetic to a degree. We can say, "You sound like you're feeling such and such" and "It's okay to feel that way," but it's hard to relate to sometimes. Whereas with undergrads, their relationships, their being in school, it's much more close to home.

Peer counselors also report being challenged by recognizing callers from other interactions.

Peer F: Another component of 76-GUIDE is working face-to-face stress and time management consultations. And it did happen once that I saw a client in that setting that I had also spoken to over the phone, but I don't think that she made the connection. I certainly did. It was funny. I mean, she was kind of a difficult person to help because she was just so overwhelmed and really I felt for her; she was difficult in any situation. In some ways, it might have made it easier for me because I was seeing her where I knew a lot of the background. I knew how she responded to different questions and different suggestions, and at first it was a little weird. I thought, "Wup, guess who this is!" It's strange because we usually don't meet our callers face to face. There are other people I've talked to dozens and dozens and dozens of times. I wouldn't know them if I ran into them on the street. And so here's somebody sitting right here in front of me. It's information that we don't usually have about our callers, so it was strange.

There was a faculty member that we had a number of conversations with at 76-GUIDE and he called the office of orientation at some point in the summer and I recognized his voice. I had talked to him a number of times, a very distinctive voice. And he was calling about something related to orientation; he had a question or something and I could have very easily found out his name. I could have just said, "Can I ask who's calling?" before connecting him to someone else and I said to myself, "You know you can't do that." There is a certain amount of curiosity, "Who is this person?" And I thought "That's not the kind of information that I should have." And I just kind of let it go. Things like that are kind of interesting because you do encounter them again in other ways. We really adhere to professional values.

Calls during which peer counselors are unable to extract needed information or to make a connection with the caller are challenging as well.

Peer N: My most frustrating call I would say is a third-party call. There's a person in need and that person doesn't call, but another person who's a friend, or it was an RA in this situation, called. And it was a suicide call. And the person in need didn't seem to want the help, but yet the RA was calling me and wanting help from me. And it was really frustrating because the person in need wouldn't talk to me. She was there in the room also and it was uncomfortable talking about her with the RA in front of her. I wanted to help the person but she didn't seem to want to be helped. In a way it was kind of a manipulative thing—she wanted the attention, she wanted things, but yet she wasn't giving me anything to work with.

Peer G: One time a man called and he wouldn't talk. When he did talk he was very abrasive and very rough. So it was really frustrating when I hung up the phone. I felt like I almost, not created a problem because I knew he had his own problems, but I just felt really bad because I knew I couldn't help him. And it's frustrating because from a phone you can only do so much. So it's really hard sometimes. You just want to reach out and help the person, but you can't always do that. You have to accept that.

Peer E: A general situation is when you don't "click" with a caller and you can kind of tell. And that happens a lot when someone calls with a problem and they want a solution. They're looking for us to tell them the answers and we really don't know the answers because they know what's best for themselves. Generally you can't tell anyone a solution. One time, this person called up about some racist incident that happened to her. I was there to empathize with her and I said, "Yeah, you know, I know how that feels and that was really terrible" and I talked to her about it and all this. But I think that she wanted a little bit more than what I could offer, like kind of a solution. I tried to let her vent about the whole situation, but she wanted something to do, something specific. The call went really badly.

You can't really help clients more than they want to help themselves.

Peers are also challenged by trying to form a connection with a peer while not offering too much self-disclosure or feeling personally responsible for the caller's problems.

Peer L: My experience with counseling peers had probably been the least frustrating because the reason we have a peer line is that we assume that peers can often relate to peer problems and that's really true. I think part of the frustrating part is we're taught not to self-disclose too much, not to say, "Oh yeah, I've had that problem." But, you know, a lot of times that really comes up and you just want to tell the person, "I feel the same way." But, it doesn't help them to know your problems. The focus here is one them!

Peer K: During a stress and time management consultation, one person came in and she checked off a lot of issues to work on. For example, procrastination and stress-reduction techniques, she wanted to know how to deal with those. But she had a lot more problems. They were a lot more deeply rooted, really extensive. And so she pretty much cried a lot of the time. And I didn't really know what to do because as a counselor I had to keep my distance. But as a person, I wanted to hug her or comfort her in some way. I guess that is what empathy does verbally.

Peer A: Now I've realized that people are going to do what they want to do and you're not helping them by telling them what to do. All you can do is help them realize what's going on in their life and realize how they're feeling and help them think of some options. It takes a lot of pressure off, that you don't feel so personally responsible for what that person is doing. Each individual is responsible for what they're doing. People that know I'm a peer counselor expect me to know everything. But, you know, that's unrealistic.

Some phone counselors report feeling as if they must perform in a counseling capacity even when they are off duty.

Peer M: When friends want to come and just talk about little things, in the past I wouldn't have noticed. I mean, I would have done it, no problem. But when I get home from work, I don't really want to talk to anyone for hours and hours about anything. It's sort of like a certain time I need for myself. It gets old really fast when people want to take up my time outside of work, and I try not to be selfish about it but I really have to separate myself from listening to problems at work and doing it at home.

Peer F: Ask my roommates. Part of what I've learned about myself is that I know that when I come home from being in a helping position, I can have no more demands put on me. I had a very non-demanding roommate when I started 76-GUIDE and I'd come home from work and she would say, "Oh, you know, I lost my bookmark" or something and I would say, "I don't want to hear it!" I just could not hear one more thing. It was like, I get paid to deal with this, I can't deal with this now. So, I think that that was something that was hard at first, but I've learned how to deal with it better. I think, at first it was probably a little bit damaging to relationships but that was part of my adjustment to the work.

Other challenges involve trying to balance one's own student life with the level of time and energy involved with peer counseling.

Peer M: I had a hard time fitting it in emotionally with other things because it's such an emotional job. It's hard to just leave. It's hard to just leave work and forget about it as if you were working at an ice cream place. So I found that it does cut in a little bit to my other commitments, like school or my friends. But basically, it fits well because I just like to work with people and it's nice to be at school and really have a good idea of what's going on with people on campus as opposed to just sitting in the library and not really paying attention to it.

Peer P: This term I don't have a problem but last term I was new and I was really under a lot of stress when I went to work because some of the calls are quite difficult and I would have to study for all of these chemistry and physics tests and have to go to work for eight hours because we have shifts like that. And it would be crazy. It really stressed me out and I was like, "I can't do this!" So, I'd take off work for a little while and then get back to it when my schedule was a little bit better. So when I'm not really pressured or stressed from schoolwork, I am better on the phone.

Peer O: It was nice in that it is a helping role and it's a helping job. And it's definitely nice to have that, to have that kind of outlet so you can say, "Yeah. Okay, I'm actually doing something productive." It's a really good feeling. In terms of being a student, when you have an overnight and you don't get much sleep and you have classes the next day, it can be a bit of a strain.

Peer H: It takes quite a bit of time. The evening shifts are three hours apiece and then the overnight shifts are ten hours. And then we'd also have two-hour-a-week staff meetings, so it's quite a bit of time we spent there. You have to be very committed to this job to make it work because it's a lot of time. But I was willing to work around it because it was such an important part of my life. The team was so supportive that if I needed to take time off for an exam or something like that, somebody else would take my shift. It always worked out very well. We were really "there" for each other and always willing to help the other team person out.

Peer L: It takes a lot, especially if you are sick. That's really hard to put out one hundred percent when you're feeling at twenty percent.

Peer C: When I had a particularly difficult call in one night, it can really wipe a person out. It would be six o'clock in the morning, I hadn't slept yet. I'd get off that shift at ten or eleven that morning, and have no sleep. It does affect things, especially in the sense that I tried to find ways to get the support that I really needed, but it's hard not being able to talk about what had happened that night with other friends outside the team. The teamwork became definitive for me, because I could draw on the support of the people who I could talk to about the calls.

A major responsibility of the 76-GUIDE coordinator is to structure the program with adequate support. Support is provided in a variety of ways. Initial and on-going training provide peer counselors with theories, knowledge, and skill-building exercises that are necessary in order to effectively respond to incoming calls. In addition, the development of respectful, caring, supportive, and cooperative working relationships among peer counselors is a vital aspect of the program. From the time a student picks up an application to become a peer counselor, the notion of "teamwork" at 76-GUIDE is introduced. The spirit of teamwork is modeled and emphasized throughout selection, during training, and throughout the whole year.

Peer Q: Sometimes when I was done counseling I kind of felt this big let-down. You can't really share it with a lot of people, and people that you share it with usually get really tired of hearing you talk about it, and sometimes you need more processing than they can give you. Sometimes you're just kind of left with the "baggage." Those times I rely on my friends. I don't tell them specifics, but just kind of what's happening, and then they give me support, like, "Oh, I'm sorry," and I feel a lot better.

Peer C: There was never any doubt in my mind that if I was having a hard time on a call at, say, two o'clock in the morning, it doesn't really matter, I can pick up the phone and call one of my team members. When you're sitting in this room alone, and if it's late at night in this building, and you have someone who's in major crisis on the other end of the line, you really need that sense of assurance that you're not alone.

Peer O: I think that I personally don't utilize the team as a resource as much as I could. I just kind of isolate myself from work. Like, there's work and then there's my life. And so they don't mix that much. I think that's kind of a disadvantage. The team has really cool people and it would be fun to go to parties and stuff with them or go out and have coffee.

Peer F: You've got twelve people who you know are good listeners and who you know are well trained and whose work you've seen a lot, and they're there for you. On both teams I was on, people said, "Whatever it is, if you have a tough call, if it's three in the morning, you're welcome to call me." And I've done it a number of times. I've just gotten a tremendous amount of support. I have developed some social relationships with people there. They haven't become my best friends, but they're people I certainly do enjoy going out with socially and it's nice to know people in both contexts. But, in general, I just really enjoy the people I've worked with and been so impressed with their honesty and openness and hard work. I feel really honored to be a part of the team.

Peer O: The people that I work with are just amazing! They're all so nice and supportive. And especially during training. I had never been in a more supportive, kinder environment than with these people. We don't really hang out together outside of the group and there's a lot of opposing personalities in the group. But when you're working and when we're at the meetings, it's just a very supportive environment. It's really encouraging to know that that can happen because in many other work environments, there's so much politics in an atmosphere like: "Oh well, I'm going to get a promotion."

Peer A: I can't emphasize enough the value of the team. It's something that's really important to the job when you go into a work situation. It really helps to know the people you're working with and to be able to rely on them. I guess also that being a peer helper is just that we're on the same level as the people who are calling and I don't feel better than any of them or worse than them. I really feel I can identify a lot with what they're going through.

Peer M: Everybody needs an outlet to discuss whatever stress they have in their life. People "on the line" with a suicidal client need a release at times for themselves. Everybody has feelings that build up over time, including us, and occasionally we need to step back and talk about it. In the past I thought that others were just kind of oblivious and stressing out when big problems occurred. Now I've learned about myself and everybody else I work with and everybody has times when they need to vent.

Peer G: It was a different kind of working atmosphere because we really support each other and work as a team. You can't do this with one person, you need everyone, and they all help you and they're all there for you when you need them. If I had a bad call or I needed help, I could call them, in the middle of the night or whenever I needed help. Or if I had a problem with my own life, I could call them anytime and talk to them. We all volunteered to take each others' shifts. In a lot of work settings you don't know people, so people don't really go out of their way to help you. But this is different and they definitely do.

Peer E: People on the 76-GUIDE team think I'm a little blunt. Some people are really empathic and I can learn from that because I feel like I need to be more empathic. Some people are really patient. And for me, that's a quality that I really need to work on. Everyone has a different style and everyone has different strengths in their counseling techniques, so it's totally helpful to have a big team to learn from each other.

Peer M: I have always had doubts about whether what I'm saying to the people on the phone is right, if I'm doing the right thing. You know, it's nice to talk to other people and let them remind me that there's only so much we can do.

Peer B: Being part of a team at 76-GUIDE and feeling that team environment is a very different work experience than I've ever had before because it's such a supportive atmosphere. It's not a hierarchical structure— we decide as a team what our policies are going to be, we decide how we're going to handle different callers as a team. Just being part of that supportive atmosphere as been really rewarding.

Peer K: I hope I can find this sense of teamwork at another job, somewhere else in my life, although I seriously doubt it. The other workers are really important to me. And this is the only job I've ever had like this. Some other jobs are just work and you leave. But here, you don't exactly leave. It's something that you take with you for the rest of your life.

Growth and Development of Peer Counselors

A literature exists on the benefits to peer counselors of their work in this capacity. Yamauchi (1986) noted positive effects on self-worth and interpersonal skill development for peer counselors. These findings are corroborated in other studies (i.e., Frisz, 1984; Winston & Buckner, 1984). Similar outcomes have been found over the years for peer counselors in the 76-GUIDE program.

Peer P: One thing is that I was really, really scared and nervous to do this job. And I learned that with a little bit more self-confidence you can basically do a lot of things that you couldn't do before. I had a lot of problems dealing with relationships and school and career decisions, just like most people our age, you know? And I thought, "How am I going to help someone on the phone line if they're breaking up with their boyfriend and I could not handle mine just three months ago?" But you realize that you can help other people.

Peer D: One big thing I ask myself is, "What do you think you owe to your peers?" Not "What do you think you owe to your country?" Not "What do you think you owe to people who aren't as fortunate as you?" I mean, "What do you owe your peers?" I think that's a big question. I'm not really sure, but I think I owe something to them.

Peer N: I think it gave me a good break from school and my problems and things that were going on in my life. It gave me time to step away from that and focus on something else. And I think it was really good for me. Because sometimes I just get too caught up in what's going on in my life and get stressed out about that. I think this was a good break from my reality into somebody else's.

Peer counselors report feeling rewarded from having the opportunity to help others.

Peer L: I think that anyone, pretty much anyone, can do peer counseling because, if our team is representative, they have various majors and interests at this university. Anyone who can handle the problems can do the work. You don't have to be a psych major to understand what people are struggling with. You just have to have some sort of connection, and making that connection is the most rewarding part.

Peer C: It is very rewarding when the caller sort of has that light bulb go off in their head. You can sort of "hear" it over the phone and you know you have done something, that you have helped them and they were able to say, "Yeah! I see this now." I also call it reaching that "eureka point."

Peer M: The most rewarding for me was a suicide call, just because the caller became more positive as the call went on. It was just good to see that I learned all my peer counseling skills and they worked. I didn't think that I would remember things, so I was happily surprised to see myself making a contract with her not to kill herself and doing a lethality assessment and just getting her to stop crying and talk about it.

Peer G: I think probably my most rewarding peer counseling experience was when I was on the phone with a man for two hours and he was having problems about a relationship and we brainstormed for a long time. Although he seemed really frazzled, we actually worked up to a solution together. He was so thankful and I could tell his voice sounded happier. I felt like I really put a lot into it and got a lot out. And we worked together, he and I. So, it was a clear-cut example of how the program works for a peer counselor and for the client.

Peer N: Peer counseling not only helps the person that calls, but it also helped me. And it's really positive when someone says, "Thank you, you know, you helped me get through the night." It's a really good feeling and it's important to me. Because sometimes when you're doing research and you're in class, you don't realize what impact you're having, but this is a very direct impact that you've had on someone.

Other students mention a new emphasis on the value of feelings and being able to recognize counseling techniques in other settings.

Peer O: If a feeling exists, it is valid. All emotions are valid, however you experience something. This work has definitely encouraged me to place more weight on my feelings and emotions than I had been.

Peer A: Everybody carries around their own issues and when you look at a person, you can't tell right off what's "going on with them." There are reasons behind their actions and there's more depth to people than what you see at a party on Friday night. First impressions aren't always true.

Peer O: After the intensive training period, I went into the real world and all I ended up doing was speaking in counselor-speak, like, "It sounds like you're feeling frustrated," just all of the stuff that we'd been trained to do, like reflecting the emotions of the other person. Because the experience is over a phone line and it's very isolated. I think I "practiced" some in other situations.

Peer M: Sometimes when you talk to other people you see yourself using empathy. I never even knew what that word meant before this school year. And it's funny to see how people can be empathic in TV shows and newspaper articles—it just comes up a lot. And I'm just much more aware of how to be empathic. I used to do those things once in a while just by luck.

Many peer counselors feel benefited by the opportunity to learn to set limits and to avoid overextending themselves.

Peer N: I'd say I've learned my limits, what I can and cannot handle. When I know I'm pushing myself too hard or certain situations arise that I feel uncomfortable in. It can really "hit home." I know more what bothers me because of the experiences I've had with other people.

Peer K: I learned that I have my limits in a major way. I took a lot of classes last year and a lot of hours at 76-GUIDE. And I was sick a lot—I never really get sick—and I wasn't really sick last year but I wasn't feeling too healthy. I was feeling really ragged and tired. And so I learned to give myself some time to just relax and just process things that were going on around me without jumping into more things. I learned not to overextend myself.

Others report an enhanced level of self-awareness.

Peer H: Peer helping has helped me to see that I'm a lot stronger than I thought I was and it's really put my life in perspective. I feel thankful for all the things that I have and the things that I've been able to accomplish because I've talked to a lot of people who didn't feel that. And so it's been really helpful to put my life in perspective because this past year has been kind of a tough year for me because it's my senior year and I'm graduating. I've learned that I'm capable of helping people. I've learned that I can be confrontational and not be offensive. That was always a big thing for me. That was one of my major problem areas was learning how to be confrontational with people because I was the peacemaker and didn't want to disrupt things. Sometimes you just have to be confrontational with people and I've learned when it's appropriate and how to do it. I've learned that I sometimes need to put my needs first in order that I don't get walked on. That sometimes happens to a lot of workers. And that was one thing we talked about a lot, your needs have to be important, too. You can't just ignore how you're feeling.

Peer E: It's totally made me more self-aware. What I feel the whole job is about is sorting out people's feelings and in the process you have to get a grip on what you are feeling yourself. So it's totally an introspective process. It's like you're helping others but you're helping others by relating to them with empathy and that gives you a better understanding of yourself.

Peer E: I found that stuff you don't like in other people is really stuff that you don't like that you see in yourself. You want to pretend that you don't have it, you know? So when I see stuff that I don't like in other people, before I judge them I think, "Okay, I see that in myself. Why don't I try to work on that in my own self and try to change that part of myself?" I can try to make myself a better person by emulating the good qualities of those I work with. I think we're all more alike than we realize, like shadows of others in ourselves. To know that you're not the only one who's ever felt totally confused, scared, upset, grieving or whatever, makes a world of difference.

Peer A: It definitely has helped my self-awareness in how I deal with situations and how I deal with problems. First you start listening to somebody on the phone and you get so frustrated with them; why don't they just change what they're doing! And then you start applying what they're talking about on the phone to your own life and you see that things aren't that easy. The work helped me become more active in my own life.

Peer D: The job makes you think a lot about yourself. It makes you think of your own personal culture and how that sometimes gets in the way of counseling someone. You know, being a man, being a woman, being white, being black, coming from a small town, coming from a city, you learn a lot about your own personal beliefs and your biases. The peer counseling stuff is very practical; it's like a model for the way you deal with your peers. So it's not something that you necessarily turn on when you go to the job and turn off when you're not on the job.

Peer counselors can also gain greater empathy for the extent of their peers' personal struggles and dilemmas and an appreciation for the importance of support networks.

Peer M: You realize that a lot of the people you talk to on the line have really big problems or big issues in their lives and it minimizes my day-to-day concerns which I get stressed out about. I can sit back and say, "Well, this is really not a big deal." You know, if I have a big test next week, it's not a big deal compared to somebody on the line who's pregnant and her parents have disowned her. My test is important, but I don't have to feel like it's life or death anymore. I've become much more self-aware and very sympathetic to other peoples' problems. For example, there are lot of people that call about their relationships. If you hear about people, how they run their relationships with other people, what they do well, what they don't do well, it gives you hints, things I try to implement in my own life. I think about the right way to treat people and different ways of thinking and living.

Peer G: It's taught me a lot about other people who are very much different from me. It's taught me that people who have a mental illness have a lot of good qualities to offer, if you just give them a chance to talk and get their story. It's very interesting; you can learn a lot about what they're going through. Fellow students who see things differently than me and have different backgrounds than me just handle things differently. I kind of feel like I understand that a little more than being caught up with my own friends who all have similar backgrounds.

Peer F: I've really learned that everybody knows their own situation better than anybody else can. I think that one can easily get caught up in the idea that "I'm a trained counselor, I know what to do, I know your situation." But nobody knows anybody's situation like the people themselves. And I've certainly learned that from working with chronically mentally ill people, with survivors of sexual assault, and others. I can get all the training in the world but these people know what it's like to live their lives on a daily basis, to be faced with these concerns, to always have that as a part of their life. And so in some ways, it's been real humbling. I might know how to respond and how to be empathic and how to be helpful, but I certainly can't speak for others' situations as relevantly and honestly as they can.

Peer F: I think to an extent this work has helped me with learning to ask for help. So many people honestly believe that asking for help is a strength, not a weakness. This new attitude has certainly increased my support network. I've had a lot of people around me who are just great listeners and great problem solvers and I've probably grown a little more comfortable being willing to ask for help.

Peer H: A lot of people who call our line have support networks which have completely disintegrated and they really count on 76-GUIDE to help them through some tough situations. I realize now that it's really important to have a support network—that people really need that, no matter what they may say.

Peer O: I found out that there are a lot of people in this world who just don't have anyone to talk to. And, because of that, I've really come to appreciate my friends and family. And now I like to tell them all the time how great they are and how glad I am that they're around.

Changes in problem solving strategies and attitudes also occur.

Peer B: I think every experience you have with another person teaches you something, even if that experience is bad—just because peoples' experiences are so diverse and there's no way that you can ever learn about everybody's experience. This work has taught me a lot about different kinds of people and problems;

about different ways that people think about things and different ways people cope.

Peer N: I find myself thinking of pros and cons with situations that arise with myself concerning school, even time and stress management. We've been working on that too and I've found that to be really helpful with learning how to schedule my time.

Peer B: I guess that the skills you learn in peer counseling are to look at all your options, to weigh your different options, and then to develop the best outcome, the worst outcome, and the realistic outcomes for each of the options.

Peer H: It's really interesting because I think that a lot of times I was too quick to "problem-solve." And now I'm more willing to sit back and really explore how I'm feeling about a situation before I get all anxious about trying to fix it. I feel that I've taken a much more introspective route to solving problems because I don't jump to conclusions. And I think that in the long run that's helped my problem-solving skills because the decisions that I come to are more thought-out.

Peer E: It's helped me understand my own problems better. In terms of solving them and accepting that certain problems aren't solvable. Like insecurities you have about yourself or things that you don't like about yourself. Sometimes you can't really change stuff like that. You kind of can but if they're insecurities about yourself, it helps you become more accepting of yourself.

Peer counseling experiences can also have an impact on listening skills and personal relationships.

Peer Q: I feel really more comfortable in situations where I'm working with people and interacting

A Peer Counseling Phone Line

with them. My listening skills have improved the most. I think those are really important. Just basic counseling skills and keeping conversations going; like when I'm talking to friends, asking, "How do you feel about that?" I just find myself in a kind of counselor mode, but also a friend mode.

Peer C: This work has also helped me in terms of friends who approach me in situations where they're having a difficult time. I find how I relate with my friends and how I relate with clients on the phone to be very different, but some skills have carried over.

Peer B: I think I find it easier now just to talk with people that I might not know well, to carry on conversations with a stranger, meeting someone for the first time. I think I'm a lot more confident now, as a person, from my experience on the phone line—confident in my skills, my peer counseling skills, and more confident in general about dealing with certain situations. On the phone line, you're there by yourself and you have to handle whatever emergency situation comes up. So when you get a call, like a suicide call or something, and then it goes well, you feel a lot better about yourself and a lot better about what you can do.

Peer F: I've become more articulate and can respond to a lot of things and like to think that I'm a better person for it. I can respond to people in a more sensitive and rational way. I think that some people who I've just always had conflicts with I've learned to treat like a difficult caller. I empathize and say, "I can see completely where you're coming from," even if I don't, and then say, "But another side of the story might be this." And I just would have never thought of doing that with some of these people who I crash heads with—just to treat

> them like a caller. If this person were calling you on the phone you'd have no problem handling them, but because you know them in a personal situation, you're having a hard time. And so, I think, "Okay, I'll treat them like a caller." Just offering people basic respect and empathy and not arguing so quickly helps in terms of just dealing with people I have a hard time with personally.

Many peer counselors report that their plans to pursue careers in helping professions were solidified by this experience or recognize ways in which their skills can be applied in fields outside of psychology.

> *Peer F*: I have a greater awareness of the world around me. I don't consider myself particularly sheltered, but I certainly know that I have only experienced a very thin slice of life; I hadn't had a lot of contact with a whole wide range of people. Now I think I have a greater awareness of the world around me. I think it helped me decide career-wise what I want to go in to. That was part of my motivation: to find something I could stand doing the rest of my life. I think I learned some things that I really do enjoy doing and so as I go into social work school next month, I can keep an eye on those things and know better where I want to go.

> *Peer C*: It also opened me up to a lot of just sort of hands-on experience in a lot of things I got in textbooks being a psychology major. I think one thing that it did, that not every peer counseling program does, was to help me develop a sense of professionalism. It's the first job that I've actually been able to say, "Yeah, I'm good at what I do."

> *Peer B*: I basically knew I wanted to be a clinical psychologist before, but volunteering for this phone line has really made that concrete. It's really let me know that I can work with people

on an individual level, that I can make the
connection with people on the phone line. I
have the ability to empathize. Knowing that I
have the skills has really helped me to declare:
"Yes, this is indeed what I want to do."

Peer O: I think that it definitely showed me the
extent to which I want to help people. I do
want to help people and especially I want to
help my peers. When you get calls coming in
from people where it's really hard to relate, I
realize that there is a limit to what I could do.

Peer Q: When I started out I wanted to go into
social work, and so I thought I would try out at
76-GUIDE and see how it worked for me. I
realized at the time that it takes a very strong
individual to do this work. I did change my
career plans, because I was a psychology major,
and I changed away from that. I have a lot of
respect for people who can do that, but I
noticed that wasn't for me.

Peer K: I'm going into law so I don't know how
much it's affected my career plans but I guess
the way I would deal with my clients might be
affected. I might be a little more
sympathetic/empathic towards situations in
dealing with them. I know it sounds really
manipulative, but this program's kind of
shown me ways to elicit little things from
people that I want. So that might help my
career. I want to be a defense lawyer so maybe
I can ask a question in a certain way that might
get them to respond with the answer that I
want.

Peer O: I'm kind of thinking of medicine, in which
case I was thinking peer counseling is really
helpful because when you're a physician, to be
able to listen to people and hear that what
they're saying is important because often
ailments aren't necessarily physical.

Peer P: Going into medicine, I'm going to have to have a lot of communication and patient contact in dealing with people's personal lives as well as their medical problems. So in that sense I think I've gained a lot. But at the same time, it's kind of helped me realize that I don't want to be an academic psychologist. I want to be a counseling psychologist or a clinical psychologist.

Finally, many peer counselors believe that the opportunity to provide help for others ultimately benefits themselves as well.

Peer H: 76-GUIDE is a helping line to help the clients that we serve but it also helps us grow and to learn about ourselves, who we are. I grew a lot this past year.

Peer J: In high school I always found myself to be a listener—I used to listen to people a lot and solve their problems. But I wanted to do it on a broader basis. The thing that I got most out of it is just knowing my personal limits. You can't do everything for everyone even though you'd like to. It helped me realize that when you think for yourself, it's not doing something selfish. And it helped me in dealing everyday with people. Little skills that you use over the phone, I use with parents, family, friends, anyone. I think it made me more sensitive to issues like domestic violence, rape, sexual abuse.

Peer I: Something I think is really an important aspect of the program is personal development and service to the community: serving the university community, growing and learning from it, becoming a better person.

Peer H: I just want to say that it's one of the most positive experiences that I've ever had here at the university and in my life as a whole. It gave me the opportunity to help others, which is something I've always wanted to do, as well as learn about myself and really grow. The friends I have made through working at 76-GUIDE will always be my friends and these memories will always be really special.

REFERENCES

Carns, A. W., Carns, M. R., & Wright, J. (1993). Students as paraprofessionals in four year colleges and universities: Current practice compared to prior practice. *Journal of College Student Development, 34,* 358-63.

D'Andrea, V. J., & Salovey, P. (1983). *Peer counseling: Skills and perspectives.* Palo Alto: Science and Behavior Books.

Egan, G. (1982). *The skilled helper* (2nd ed.). Monterey, California: Brooks/Cole Publishing Company.

Frisz, R. H. (1984). The perceived influence of a peer advisement program on a group of its former peer advisors. *The Personnel and Guidance Journal, 62,* 616-9.

Ivey, A. E. (1983). *Intentional interviewing and counseling.* Monterey, CA: Brooks/Cole Publishing Company.

Salovey, P., & D'Andrea, V. J. (1983). A survey of campus peer counseling activities. *The Journal of American College Health, 32,* 262-5.

Varenhorst, B. (1984). Peer counseling: Past promises, current status, and future directions. In *Handbook of counseling psychology* (716-51). New York: Wiley & Sons.

Winston, R., & Buckner, J. (1984). The effects of peer helper training and timing of training on reported stress of resident assistants. *Journal of College Student Personnel, 25,* 430-6.

Yamauchi, G. (1986). Students helping students: The emergence of paraprofessionals in campus activities. *Campus Activities Programming, 19,* 39-43.

Chapter 5

Resident Staff As Peer Mentors

Robin Sarris MPH, MBA[1]

Residence Education: The "Other Curriculum"

Life in a residence hall can be integral to the college experience. Young adults away from home and experiencing a new community begin to formulate and test their own values and ideas. The University of Michigan Residence Education Department seeks to nourish students' personal development and, at the same time, to promote a sensitive, tolerant, and humane community in the residence halls.

The University of Michigan houses nearly ten thousand students in twelve residential complexes. More than ninety-eight percent of all first-year students live in the residence halls. The Residence Education Program described in this chapter is funded by student housing fees. The Housing Division Resident Staff program is part of the Residence Education Department, one of the three major components of the Housing Division. The primary task of this unit is to meld together the process of learning within the classroom with the learning that takes place outside the classroom.

---

[1] The author wishes to acknowledge Dr. John Heidke, Associate Director of Housing, UM, for the concept of the "other curriculum"; Alan Levy, Director of Housing Information and Public Affairs, UM, for the extensive work on the development of the staff selection process, criteria and program philosophy, as well as the University of Michigan Housing Division Credo; Ed Salowitz, Director of Research and Development, UM Housing, for historical information on the UM Housing Division.

This mission is carried out within each residence hall by *trained* students under the supervision of a Coordinator of Residence Education (CORE). These supervisors are responsible for overseeing the resident staff and the educational/developmental mission of the Housing Division. All COREs are trained at the Master's level in counseling, student personnel administration, social work, or other related fields, and come from a range of cultural backgrounds.

Reporting to the COREs are resident staff who are graduate and undergraduate students residing on the floors. These staff are appointed for between twenty and thirty hours per week, yet they interact with residents on a twenty-four-hour basis. The experiences of these resident staff persons are illustrated in later sections of this chapter. Also active within the building are student employees who work as library assistants, computer consultants, and desk receptionists. As peer leaders, all resident staff are presented with a unique challenge—that of living where they work. This challenge, along with their other experiences, is further explored throughout this chapter.

History of our Program: A Shift from *In Loco Parentis*

A version of the present-day resident staff program existed as early as the 1950s. During that time, a number of societal and attitudinal changes on campuses began to alter the nature of university housing programs throughout the country as universities reconsidered the mandatory live-in policies for women students, residence hall closing hours for women, and the restricted visitation privileges for members of the opposite sex. The dress standards at meals were also relaxed at many schools. The 1960s brought even greater changes in behavioral standards. This was the beginning of the swing away from an *in loco parentis* philosophy for university housing.

For example, at the University of Michigan in 1962, a report from the Special Study Committee for the Office of Student Affairs reinterpreted the university's purpose in relation to student life outside the classroom and provided a proposed plan of more effectively administering student affairs. These goals included extra-classroom experiences and a clear rejection of *in loco parentis*, which was now viewed as "excessive paternalism." Following this shift in philosophy, live-in "house-mothers" were phased out and peer Resident Advisors began to play a greater role in the advising, counseling, referral, and discipline issues in the residence hall community.

> *Peer F:* I think a lot of it is discipline and just maintaining some norms and standards in the hall. People don't realize that if they turn their stereo up, stuff will shake off people's walls. A lot of it is just purely because people are experiencing freedom for the first time; they go a little crazy. I think that's the easy part. The hard part is dealing with people who are depressed or just not doing well, and they don't understand why. It's an adjustment. Unfortunately, a lot of people tend to cling to their RA, because their RA is next to them, asking them how they're doing. People think their RA is their best friend, and they think it goes both ways, I am their best friend and they are my best friend, but I have to be friends with everybody else. You have to maintain a professional distance.

The resident staff system within the Housing Division has for some time consisted of Resident Advisors (RAs) reporting to Resident Directors (RDs) within a house configuration. Each RA is responsible for a group of between forty and sixty residents on a floor. Their role is to assist students through counseling and referral, to provide programming, to foster a sense of community, and to maintain conditions conducive to academic and personal development.

The RA position is a twenty-hour-per-week appointment and is remunerated with room and board. RA positions are held primarily by undergraduate students. Resident Directors are responsible for a portion of a building (a "house") containing 80 to 350 residents; they supervise resident staff (RAs) appropriate to the size and structure of the building. The Resident Director reports to the CORE of the building.

RD positions are thirty-hour-per-week appointments and are remunerated with room and board along with a stipend. RD positions are held by a mix of undergraduate and graduate students.

Resident staff are expected to view the residence hall as their primary place of residence and to spend sufficient time in the building to be seen as a leader in the hall community. Over the past several years, participation by minority students in these positions has been exceptional, with approximately thirty-five percent of the positions being held by such students.

> *Peer C*: A lot of my strength as an RA comes completely from how the residents perceive me, not how they perceive the title. Because "RA" means so many different things to so many different people, it's up to me to give them a definition for it. And if it's a guy down the hall who's pretty nice, who I can respect, then that's somebody who's going to listen more. So, because I'm on good terms with them, and they know they can come to me and that I welcome their opinions no matter what they are, I feel like when I approach them they aren't going to take it as me being hypersensitive or just promoting some personal agenda.

Recent Trend Toward Specialization

Over the last ten years, a trend in resident staff positions has been the creation of a greater number of specialty positions that focus on particular services offered to residents in the halls. These now include the following:

- the Head Librarian, who is responsible for the operation of the residence hall library
- the Minority Peer Advisor, who is responsible for advising, counseling, and programming related to the retention of minority students

- Minority Peer Advisor Assistants, who are responsible for assisting minority students throughout the building
- Academic Peer Advisors, who are responsible for linking residents, staff, and building organizations to appropriate academic support resources within and outside the residence hall
- the Resident Computer Systems Consultant, who is responsible for the operation of the residence hall computing sites and teaching introductory computer concepts and applications in the residence hall.

These exist in addition to the traditional RA and RD positions. There are currently a total of 325 resident staff across the entire system.

Program Philosophy

While intellectual development is a major concern for students in college, personal, ethical, social, and political growth are considered important as well. A unique feature of living in a residence hall is the need for every community member to share responsibility for the entire community. Community standards insure that basic responsibility for the enforcement of rules and regulations rests with each member.[2]

The goals of our Residence Education program fall under three crucial areas that form the foundation of work with residents. It is expected that our resident staff understand and feel comfortable with these goals and that they are prepared to build and develop them in their halls:

---

[2] The University of Michigan Housing Division is committed to the creation of a diverse community and, as is outlined in our *Living at Michigan Credo*, a sensitive, tolerant, and humane community in our residence halls in which individuals are not harassed, excluded or made to feel uncomfortable because of sex, color, religion, sexual orientation, disability, lifestyle or political belief."

Resident Staff As Peer Mentors

1. Human Rights
2. Personal and Community Development
3. Academic Advising

Successful resident staff members are self-motivated and base judgments upon respect for evidence, ideas, and concern for ethical values, both public and private. They are individuals who are interested in growth in others and themselves. Staff are expected to be active community members and to understand that a university education is not limited to the classroom but rather is a lifelong process, one in which academic and personal learning and growth go hand in hand. Resident staff spend a great deal of time working with students. As peers, they serve as positive community builders, active listeners, creative leaders, peer counselors, peer academic advisors, referral agents, problem solvers, conflict resolvers, educational programmers, and change agents.

> *Peer C*: Part of my competency was trying to remember where my residents were at and how I had "been there" a year or two before. And that's one of things I remind them of. When I talked about the alcohol policy, one of the first things I said was, "I used to drink as a resident. I did it a lot. Well, not too much, but you know...." I wanted to get across to them that I was being honest and that I'm not so far out in left field that I don't understand where they're at. And I think that's one thing that I really came to appreciate about myself, that I try not to forget where I've been and where I am.

> *Peer D*: You can do a minimum or a maximum. You can put a lot of time into it and I think that's when it gets to be the most rewarding position. But the residents have to come to you. I can sense problems, but I can't force anyone to come to talk to me. They know I'm there and I'm available. I make myself available in person and with weekly newsletters. But I can't do more than that. I can't probe into their lives.

Staffing

Each resident advisor (RA) is directly responsible for a certain area within a residence hall. RAs are the staff persons with whom the residents have most frequent contact. They live in the area for which they are responsible and are expected to get to know all of their residents and to serve as informational resources and peer counselors. Many resident staff members feel that establishing positive peer relationships with their residents, without becoming overly involved at a personal level, contributes to their abilities to meet these goals.

> Peer B: I have a really good rapport with my residents, which I actually worked very hard to achieve. I think it wouldn't have been as effective if I went out of my way to become friends with those people. But it worked out great! They call me "RP," for Resident Pal.

> Peer G: I try to see myself not like an authority but more as a resource and a friend. Not necessarily like a "big" friend, but someone you can come to and I'll listen and we can talk. I see myself as a big resource.

> Peer D: I gave my residents the chance to take advantage of me by becoming too much their friend and not enough their role model or their supervisor. And I just brought myself down to their level and I didn't draw any fine lines. So, therefore, they got away with a lot of things. And so in my evaluations, as far as my building director and my resident director thought: "You need to be more patient. You need to be less emotional when you're involved." I was getting involved to the point where they were my friends and I didn't want to see bad things happen to them. So, I needed to pull away, which is what I've done this year. Not so much that I'm not anyone's friend, but there is a

Resident Staff As Peer Mentors

> difference between me and them. There's got to be if you're going to do the job.

Peer F: I think it's really rewarding when a resident comes and leaves messages on your door, and it's nice when they bring you things for Christmas and holidays, things like that. I think one of the best things that happens is when they tell you something very confidential, very personal; it just reinforces the fact that they trust you.

RAs are responsible for providing educational and cultural programming for all residents as well as enforcing provisions of the lease, building policies, and the Statement of Student Rights and Responsibilities.

Peer D: It's a community living environment, and as Resident Advisors we are there to uphold those standards. I'm there to resolve any problems, form compromises between residents. If they have to live day-in and day-out with some other people they don't get along with or they don't like the music being turned up or they want to be in bed at a specific time, you kind of try to encourage some tolerance and compromise, implement programs for educational and social needs, provide resources for people who have special needs, make referrals to counselors, help them chose their classes, just be there for them to have someone to talk to.

The Resident Director (RD) works with the RAs in a training and supervisory role. Due to their administrative responsibilities, RDs may not have as much contact with the residents, but residents may use them as a resource or arbitrator.

Peer A: I prefer being an RD. But it's harder, more stressful, and we have a lot of responsibility. You're accountable for almost all of your actions and you can't go unrecognized anywhere in the building. So, it's definitely a harder position, but I like it better. Something can come up at any moment. Sometimes I sit there with the lights off and I won't open the door. If I'm not feeling well, it's really difficult.

RDs frequently become involved in disciplinary situations of a serious nature. Each residence hall also has at least one Minority Peer Advisor and, in most cases, a Minority Peer Advisor Assistant (MPAA) as well.

Recruitment

Recruitment for resident staff positions begins in the fall semester each year. We initiate our media campaign to attract candidates in November with posters, bus signs, campus newspaper advertisements, residence hall dining room table tents, and flyers across campus. Anecdotal data collected from applicants suggests that the most effective recruitment mechanism is word of mouth between current resident staff members and residents in the halls who they think would make good future staff members.

In addition, we place a strong emphasis on minority student recruitment. This effort includes letters of invitation to minority residents recommended by our current staff, networking with related campus offices, and Minority Candidate Information Sessions. These sessions are open to all minority students interested in learning more about resident staff positions. Each session includes a panel of minority students currently on resident staff talking about their experience and is hosted by minority professional staff members from the Housing Division.

An additional source of applicants comes from our out-of-town pool of candidates. Resident staff programs are institutionalized on college campuses across the country. Many students entering as transfer or graduate students are interested in being considered for positions and may do so by mail.

Selection

Mandatory Information Sessions: In January each year, the first step in the process is a mandatory information session. Each candidate is required to attend only one mandatory information session. This is the only forum through which to receive a staff selection booklet with instructions and the staff application.[3]

This session covers the details of the complex application process, the expectations of resident staff in general, and the minimal requirements to be eligible for hire. These include a satisfactory cumulative grade point average, at least forty-eight credit hours toward a degree program, junior status, and at least four terms of enrollment on a college campus. We believe that these minimum standards assure that each applicant has a proven history of academic achievement in a college environment, suggesting the ability to take on an additional responsibility during the academic year. We are very strict about these minimum requirements and will not accept applications from those who do not meet these standards. Current staff members who drop below a 2.5 GPA are placed on probation for one semester to allow them to improve their grades. If they do not succeed in doing so, they are removed from their position.

Written Application: The application process requires applicants for all resident staff positions to fill out a standard hiring application, which is submitted to a central location. Candidates can apply for more than one type of staff position and may request their preference for up to five buildings. In any one year, we have approximately five hundred to seven hundred applicants for the 150-200 resident staff positions that are available from among our 325 positions.

Mandatory Classroom Session: A mandatory classroom session includes two observed and rated exercises as well as a "homework assignment" completed in advance of the session. The homework assignment consists of a visit to two

---

[3] Exceptions to this rule are only granted in extreme circumstances (except for out-of-town candidates, who follow a process with different deadlines) through an appeal process to the Assistant Director of Housing.

different residence halls on campus during hours when current resident staff are available to meet and discuss their positions with the candidates. The goal of this assignment is to increase the candidates' awareness of the differences in residence halls on campus and to learn about the particular services that are offered in the buildings in which they are most interested.

The exercises in the classroom session are observed, and candidates are individually rated by current resident staff. Candidates are rated based on the selection criteria outlined in the application materials:

- Ability to conceptualize and communicate
- Ability to engage in educational and program planning
- Capacity for group participation
- Identification with staff role
- Potential for leadership
- Self-confidence and maturity
- Tolerance of others/empathy

The classroom sessions generally include a group process exercise lasting about forty minutes and a set of roleplays in triads lasting about forty-five minutes. Group process sessions focus on programmatic, educational responsibilities of the position and test the applicants' ability to work in groups. The roleplays stress peer counseling and listening skills. At the completion of this session, all candidates are scored by resident staff observers and the quantitative data is entered into a database. The data is then compiled and candidates are ranked by quantitative score. Approximately twenty-five to thirty percent of the candidates with the lowest scores are cut from the process at this point, depending on the size of the pool and the number of open positions in any one year. Those cut from the process at this point are not eligible to apply for a resident staff position at any time during the following year.

Group/Individual Interviews: Those candidates who have successfully completed the centralized class session move to the next stage of the selection process. This consists of group and/or individual interviews with the Coordinator of Residence Education, Resident Directors, and Minority Peer Advisors. Candidates may interview in more than one building depending on the number of openings and the number of interested candidates for that particular building.

Position Offers: Position offers are extended during the first week of March, and candidates must return an offer of acceptance promptly. Staff are given letters of appointment before leaving campus in the spring. Finally, a small number of positions are filled after the semester ends, due to changes in returning staff members' plans for the coming year.

Training

Resident Staff training takes place throughout the year and is based on specific criteria, which include:

- Relationship with Students: promoting a residence hall community that is supportive of human rights and academic and personal development; displaying sensitivity to the needs of minority, disabled, and international students; educating residents with regard to rights and responsibilities within a community living situation; instilling group norms and spirit; being perceived as approachable and available, knowledgeable about housing and university resources; acting as a good referral source; enforcing housing and university policies in a manner that earns respect.
- Programming Skills: establishing clear goals and objectives; conducting needs assessment of resident populations; planning, implementing, and evaluating social, recreational, educational, and cultural programs; participating in programming on community building, diversity, academic support, and health; understanding the impact of technology in residence hall environments and applying technology as a resident staff member; carrying out programming that challenges residents to learn about new ideas or think in new ways.

- Counseling/Advising Skills: displaying sensitivity to the needs and feelings of others; creating an atmosphere in which students feel comfortable to discuss personal, social, and academic concerns; demonstrating constructive and creative problem solving; establishing a positive climate of openness and trust; managing interpersonal conflicts; utilizing crisis management skills effectively; being perceived as a good listener; effectively advising resident government councils and officers.
- Resident Staff/Building Staff Relationships: working cooperatively with other staff; supporting programs and efforts of others; developing effective relationships with non-Residence Education building staff, including Facilities, Dining Services, and Security; being supportive of group goals and decisions; handling on-duty shifts as expected; ability to lead and inspire others; disagreeing in a constructive manner; being perceived as available and willing to assist in emergencies or when requested; attending and participating effectively in staff meetings.
- Organizational/Administrative Skills: managing time commitments effectively; regularly attending meetings; meeting administrative deadlines; demonstrating ability to plan, organize, and participate in several different tasks concurrently; able to follow through and complete tasks.

Resident Staff training begins during an intensive one- or two-week period (depending on position) in August before school begins. It consists of a combination of sessions for the entire staff, for each building staff, and for groups by position. A general framework and schedule is provided to each professional supervisor, who then plans specific sessions to address topic areas. Often members of other Student Affairs offices or specialists in various topics provide supplementary training.

Topics covered in this training include the following:
- counseling and helping skills
- alcohol and other drug issues and policy
- conflict management and mediation
- preparation for emergencies
- crisis management
- sexual assault
- group facilitation
- diversity and multicultural issues
- roles of resident staff
- programming planning
- team building
- student account management for working with student government
- computer and electronic-mail training
- becoming acquainted with non-Residence Education building team members and Housing/Student Affairs organizational structure

In addition to training on these topics, each staff member receives an extensive resident staff manual when arriving on campus and "all-staff" training on the following topics:

- Discipline Policies: Covered with the entire Resident Director group during the first week of training. RDs are then expected to facilitate this training under the supervision of the CORE for the other staff during the second week of training.
- Behind Closed Doors: An interactive series of roleplays done with all staff. Working in small groups, staff are placed in a situation and asked to roleplay the part of a resident staff person. The scenarios include roommate conflict, a hall party where alcohol is present, a depressed resident, and a sexual assault situation. Returning staff serve as actors and small group

facilitators. This is regularly the most highly evaluated session during our training.
- Resource Fair: An exhibit-hall-style session that includes representatives from various campus offices and services. Resident staff browse through displays, talk with staff, and collect information for programming and referral.
- Social Events: Several social events are scheduled throughout the week for the entire staff, including picnics, movie theater passes, karaoke, and recreational activities.

Ongoing Training

During the academic year, staff in every building attend two-hour staff meetings every Monday evening. These meetings are used for discussion of current issues or problems, planning and information sharing, and in-service training. Topics covered during this time vary between buildings, depending on the most prevalent issues in the hall. They may include cross-cultural communication, mental health and stress management, suicide prevention, security, leadership issues, computer training, eating disorders, domestic violence, academic issues, counseling skills, sexually transmitted diseases, alcohol issues, and so on.

During the fall semester, one evening meeting time each month is devoted to a centrally designed, conference-style set of workshops from which staff elect to attend one session. They are assigned to sessions such that each staff group is represented at each session. In September, the sessions focus on health themes and include such issues as alcohol and other drugs, eating disorders, sexual health and HIV, mental health issues, stress management, University Health Service resources, and the relationship between alcohol and sexual assault (see chapters 7 and 8). In October, all staff attend sessions on lesbian/gay awareness issues. In November, another conference-style group of sessions focuses on issues related to oppression, racism, interracial relationships, intergroup dialogue, being white in a multicultural world, homophobia, sexism, sexual harassment, and issues related to students with disabilities (see chapter 14).[4]

Training for resident staff is designed to be extensive and on-going. Not only does the training provide background that they need to be more effective in their roles as resident staff, but they also gain skills and experience that will be valuable to them regardless of the careers they may choose. Personal growth is one of the frequently mentioned incentives that draws students to our staff.

An additional benefit often mentioned by resident staff is the opportunity to participate in the resident staff computer loan program. Through this initiative, every resident staff member receives a computer and network connection in his/her room. This program is designed to provide peer modeling for the advancement of a technological culture in the residence hall. Resident Advisors are seen as resources for computer information by residents on their floors. Through the provision of workshops, resident staff assistance, and role modeling, students are offered the opportunity to learn computer skills in the smaller, friendly environment of their residence hall.

Program Evaluation

Our resident staff program is evaluated at many levels throughout the year. During the selection process, both successful and unsuccessful candidates are given the opportunity to evaluate their experience. During training, every session is evaluated by participants. For both selection and training, feedback is reviewed and incorporated into revisions of the process for the following year.

As staff members, individuals receive on-going evaluation and feedback. The primary purpose of this evaluation is to provide the staff member with empirical and subjective assessments of his/her development over time in his/her

---

[4] These conference-style sessions allow us to touch on a broader number of topics than would be possible if all staff attended all sessions. The philosophy is that if each staff is represented at each session, those attending will then become a resource for referrals.

position. This data is also used to evaluate whether an individual should be rehired in the future. The five core criteria listed in the training section above are also used for evaluation purposes. Staff are evaluated by their supervisors and by the residents on their floor. This information is included in the supervisor's assessment. Many RAs find that this feedback is very useful in improving their performance in their roles.

> *Peer D*: The feedback I got the past years as an RA was like, "You didn't do this correctly; you should have done this," which makes you feel like, "Wow, I know I could have done a better job. I have potential there. Why didn't I use it?" This year the feedback made me feel much better because I haven't received one word of criticism, not one this year! You learn. This job is an experience, on-the-job learning. You just can't get training for it; you just can't. You can learn and have things in your mind you can say, but it's got to be what you pick up on the job.

> *Peer E*: Usually the feedback has been pretty positive, so it's felt pretty good. I felt that the work's being appreciated. I've never been the best person to take criticism. It's something that I work on, but those few little things kind of bother you. Sometimes you don't feel that it's justified, but for the most part you see where they're coming from. "Yeah, that is an issue that needs to be addressed." For the most part it's been pretty positive overall.

Resident Staff Experience

Unlike some of the other single-function programs presented in this book, resident staff experience is a combination of peer counseling, peer education, peer advising,[5] and peer

---

[5] Some interviews with LSA academic peer advisors (e.g., Peer E to follow) are included in this chapter with the cooperation of the

tutoring, and yet it is also unique and different from other such experiences on a campus.

> *Peer E*: The purpose of the residence hall experience is just to try to get first-year students used to the idea of community living—no longer just at mom and dad's house but as part of a community. Once you leave a university, you're going to be living on your own and part of it's just to supposedly get them to respect other people and other ideas and stuff like that. Another part of the program is education. We try to provide programs throughout the year that might be useful to students, that deal with professions, their career, diversity, things of that nature. So, I think that probably provides them with a good environment for living and learning.

> *Peer E*: My role is kind of two parts. The big part would be peer advising. RAs usually have to be at least a junior in status and the reason why is because they feel that after having two years at the university, you've acquired some skills that might be useful for first-year students to know. Hopefully you'll have resources to help people out—where they've gotta be, who they should talk to if they have problems, how to help people through the problem solving process in getting what they want for themselves. The other part is policy enforcement, making sure that the halls stay in pretty good shape, that people are respecting each other, that roommate conflicts are being mediated...

Being a resident staff member is a complex role that includes several unique dilemmas not present in other peer roles.

Coordinator of Academic Programs/Residence Operations, Virginia Reese, AMLS.

Peer C: I guess I know one thing that I've learned that probably couldn't happen in another situation is that I saw how people react to authority and how inseparable a person is from the position they hold. I don't think you can take off the resident advisor hat and put on the "Hi, my name is Joe, I'm just an average guy" hat.

Peer D: I just get so wrapped up emotionally and passionately in things. I just don't stop and think about the consequences. And this position has helped me to stop and say, "Look, you can't say the first thing that pops into your mind. You have to stop and think of what you're saying and how you're wording it and how it's going to come out—not to offend anyone, making sure it's coming out in a positive way, positive tone. It's definitely going to help me in the future. I know where I can go for help; I know how to do it. It's amazing that you take care of forty to fifty people and you have to watch that they can get along and that you get along with them. And then, hopefully they're not having personal problems they can't deal with, that are detrimental. I mean, it's all wrapped up in the midst of your own work, your own social life, your own programming. You have to give to them. The amount of paperwork is unbearable and this all builds your time management skills. It's really amazing.

Peer E: The big thing is, you're not frightened to get into conflicts with people anymore. You have some sense of being comfortable dealing with people who have trouble with you, people that have trouble with other people, and interacting with that. So that fear isn't there anymore. It used to be hard for me to confront conflict with other people, whether it be best friends, girlfriends, parents. Now I think I just go into it saying, "Well this is something that needs to be taken care of and I know that I've handled a situation like this before." I'm comfortable and confident handling the situation.

Resident staff are peers and yet, unlike positions that include only counseling or education, they are expected to be "agents" of authority. At the same time that resident staff are primarily educators, they are responsible for assuring that community standards are maintained.

Peer C: The most frustrating would be the almost daily enforcement of quiet hours last year. Just the frustration of knowing that I had to face that every night. Some nights I was the only one on the hall that wanted to get to sleep. And it was a question of "Do I stay up or do I become a jerk?" It was like, if I asked them to be quiet, they'd be quiet for two minutes and then forget. And since most of them were going to leave anyway at the end of the year, they didn't care. So I felt powerless. I could have written them up, I could have threatened to kick them out of the building—that was just a sense of powerlessness because being an RA doesn't mean a whole lot sometimes.

Peer F: The noise level is very frustrating. It's just that people don't think, and people aren't considerate enough to realize that people right next to them might be studying or sleeping. My neighbor turned his stereo up so loud that stuff has actually fallen off my walls, everything was shaking so bad. But that situation wasn't a problem, I just said, "Here, I want to show you something," and he came over and looked at the stuff falling off my walls and was so shocked and so apologetic. We haven't had a problem since.

Peer E: I think that the biggest thing it's probably taught me is that people, in a way, just want to be told what to do in some situations. It's not blatant, but people want to be given a set of rules to follow, as long as they're fair.

Resident staff are expected to respond to problems and crises that may be difficult even for a professional to handle, yet they are students who may themselves be experiencing the ordinary problems of college life. They are expected to take action and at the same time be aware of individual and positional limits, making use of resources as needed.

Peer A: Being an RA makes you react faster, kind of in a crisis mode. And it makes you always look for an answer. You become more analytically creative in your problem solving.

Peer C: There was a resident who came to me after being sexually harassed by her boyfriend; I knew her and her boyfriend. She was very upset about the whole incident. Just before, as part of the training, I was assigned to a sexual assault roleplay. My facilitator drew out a lot of things that I should be aware of and that I could have looked at, all of which were very helpful. The woman's boyfriend was making advances toward her as he walked her to her door and said goodnight. He was drunk and she pushed him away. And she was very upset that he wouldn't care about her any more or that he wouldn't have anything to do with her—that she did the wrong thing, that she shouldn't have been so aggressive, that she shouldn't have resisted him, this and that. Had I not gone through that roleplay I never would have known what to do. Staff training really helped me out with my friend in that situation. I probably would have been a total klutz about the whole situation had I not gone through training.

Peer F: You get a Mother Teresa complex. You want to take care of everybody. Once you see one person get really depressed and hit bottom, you look for it in all your friends, and if you see one of your friends slipping, you start to go into the RA mode. You start asking questions like, "How can I help you? What's going on?" The other thing is, I think as an RA you learn about a lot of resources, you know where to refer people. I'm not a trained counselor, I'm not an alcoholic, and I don't know a whole lot about it; so part of what I do is refer people.

While their training and experiences are useful in their roles as RAs, staff members also find that the experience is helpful in developing their career-oriented skills.

Peer D: Up until September of this year, my senior year, I was going to go to law school. I had everything set up and then I had just a sudden feeling that this was not the right way for me, not the correct course for my life. What I want to do is manage a staff, administer something like a hospital or community center. I like to oversee people. I enjoy being there for them and giving what I have, but I also like to have people look up to me and say, "This is what I need from you." That's what this job is.

Peer B: Actually, I've always wanted to work with people. I don't know exactly what I want to do but I do know I've either wanted to teach children or teach the hearing-impaired. This RA experience couldn't be better for that. I'm working with groups of people and I'm advising them and I'm teaching them and I'm living with them and getting along with them. It's definitely the best experience I could get for my future career goals.

Resident staff also find that their training has an impact on personal relationships.

Peer E: When I talk to people, I'm a lot more patient. If somebody's doing something wrong, I don't go overboard and I don't yell at people anymore. I've acquired techniques to resolve conflicts in my personal life. If I had a problem with my girlfriend, I'm more apt to talk—sit down and talk it through with her. Earlier I might have either held it in and waited for it to build up or just exploded.

Peer B: I work with people a lot better. I used to be very shy and introverted, but because I've had to take charge of a hall and meet new people I interact a lot better now. And I have a much better time doing it. I'm learning how to deal with people on a counseling level, as well as a personal level. I used to be a very impatient person. But, obviously, I can't be impatient with people who come into my room crying. And I've learned how to budget my time. And I've learned how to help people better. I really take a step back and try to see a situation from every angle and try to have a very objective view about it.

Resident staff also report being supported by each other and their supervisors.

Peer C: Because there are so many diverse opinions on staff as to how to handle a situation, I've had a few conflicts with staff members about policies. Generally, I'd say we're all really good friends. There's a real feeling that we need each other because, in a way, we are unique as staff members. We're the only ones who understand each other. As good friends as I may be with my residents, if some of my residents have me feeling down, I can tell them about it. And there are also things that I shouldn't bother residents with. If I've got a problem, there are some things that it's best maybe not to expose. If there's something they feel they need to talk to me about, I want them to feel like they can, no matter what's going on with me. But, with the other resident staff, I feel very comfortable being open with them, being honest and very straightforward—it's not like we're one big happy family, but there's a sense of family there I think.

Peer G: Sometimes I try and go it alone and be real overly responsible and try to handle everything myself. I've learned a lot about delegating responsibility, asking for help and looking for support.

Peer F: We're the ones that the residents come to weeping or sobbing when anything goes wrong. I mean, if their light burns out, it's my fault. You know, things like that. So we're definitely the front line. The first year I was a wreck; I was so concerned if the students were going to like me, and how I was going to balance the discipline and the friendship. So, it really helps to have a lot of support from your Resident Director and from other RAs.

Peer E: There is camaraderie in this type of support system. You're not the only one going through the experience. That helps a little bit and gives you a sense of security knowing that you're not alone. Often you'll be able to bring up problems with other Resident Advisors and they'll be able to help provide solutions or, at the very least, they are able to empathize with the situation that you're in.

Finally, the resident staff person's home and workplace are one and the same. In spite of the twenty- to thirty-hour-a-week job description, it is difficult to ever be entirely "off duty."

Peer D: This is so different from any other peer counseling position in that you live with the residents. You see them every single day, in every environment. You see people come in and out of their rooms; you know what they're doing in the bathroom. So, it's not like you see somebody for thirty minutes or an hour and then they leave and you never see them again or you see them once or twice a week. It has its pros and cons, but it's a very different experience. It's in a class by itself.

Peer D: I would say it's difficult to maintain friendships when you have so much work to do and not enough time. I've really found this year that I know who my friends are. I've lost touch with a lot of people except for people that are really significant to me. The job takes up a lot of your time and you've got to set your priorities. It's hard to date, have a steady boyfriend, especially one who's very jealous of your time. You never leave. And everyone sees you. Everyone knew my life.

Peer C: There's a financial problem because I don't have another job, so I don't get to have a steady paycheck. And even though the RA job is saving my family money, it's not necessarily saving me money and that's kind of complicated. I wanted to be in a few shows that are difficult to get into because of my staff time constraints. I'm going to try for it again in January, but I don't know how much time I'll have. Plus, I might want to take the LSATs too. I dropped a class this term because I had a lot of stress and part of it was the job. Not all of it, but a big part of it. The thing is, if you procrastinate as an RA, you're not procrastinating for yourself, but for your residents also. If there's something that needs to be done, you have to do it for them as much as for yourself.

Peer B: Occasionally, if there's a program or something that's planned for a certain night, I can't do homework. Like tonight, for example, I have a program from 8:00 to 10:00 and then a cluster meeting and then "hall munchies." So I have no time whatsoever to do homework tonight. But, I take it as it comes. That's part of being on staff. I just work harder on weekends.

Peer F: I'm heavily, heavily involved in community service, and it's something that's very important to me, and it's something I will not give up. You know if something's important enough you can find the energy. Unfortunately, it catches up with you and then you get really tired and sleep all weekend, but hey—that's okay!

Peer F: You learn your limits. You learn how far you can be pushed. It's crazy, everything always happens right at once. It's usually around exam time. When you're stressed out, they're stressed out, and as soon as they start having problems they forget that you're a student, they forget that you have problems of your own. They forget that you have other people down the hall to care for too and all of a sudden they think that you are there specifically for them, twenty-four hours a day. I pull eighteen credit hours; I did all through last year, and I am this year. You learn how to manage your time a lot, but that's not learning about yourself, that's learning how to do something. You learn about yourself that you can't help everybody, and there are some roles that you might want to take on that you can't, because you're not professionally trained.

Peer D: If you don't work well with people, you are not going to do well on this job. You get no sleep, you have to be there all the time, every hour of the night when you're on duty because people come to you all the time and just want to talk. And if you shut them out, they could do something really wrong and then you'd feel guilty. It's just a very difficult job, but it can be enjoyable.

The resident staff position has been identified in the college personnel literature as one of the most demanding assignments on a campus. In spite of these complexities cited by the RAs, they handle their responsibilities exceptionally well and generally speak favorably of their experiences. Studies show that RAs list personal growth and development, friends made as a result of being an RA, and experience gained by developing a sense of responsibility as important benefits of being in this position.

> *Peer E*: I think that being an RA just shows you that if you make every experience you have with a person a positive experience, you can make people's lives better just interacting with them a little bit. You are the role model, people are looking up to you, and you have a chance to affect people's lives for the better.

> *Peer E*: A lot of people coming from the university are going to go on to professional-type jobs. These professional jobs are going to require a great deal of personal interaction, problem-solving, and conflict resolution skills. I recommend the RA experience because it will play a huge part in your success in whatever you do professionally. Nowhere else can you find that intensity of experience than as an RA! The only limits are those that you impose on yourself.

> *Peer B*: I just think that being an RA was the most rewarding experience I could have had at the university. Even better than getting an A!

Chapter 6

A Peer Counseling Program for Older Persons

Ruth Campbell, MSW

Editor's Note: The inclusion of a geriatric peer counseling program in a volume on counseling for college students may seems anomalous. We choose to bring together our college class on peer counseling with elderly peer counselors both to compare the work at different points in the life cycle and to illustrate the applicability of peer counseling for prevention throughout the life cycle.

Background

The peer counseling program at our geriatric clinic began when it opened in 1978 as an outpatient clinic of our University Hospital. We offered comprehensive health assessment and diagnosis along with on-going healthcare for people over the age of sixty. At the time there were few models for geriatric care in the United States, prompting staff to turn to older people in the community for assistance in developing programs. The plan that evolved was distinctive in several respects:

- From the start, the medical director of the clinic viewed community involvement as a basic component of the program.[1]

---

[1] A Turner Advisory Council was established with representatives from community agencies, hospital and university groups, and consumers to guide the development of the clinic.

- Multidisciplinary care was the mode of practice. A physician-nurse-social worker team was seen as necessary to meet the complex medical and psychosocial needs of the elderly and their families.
- The clinic felt a responsibility to share useful knowledge with the elderly consumer and to make its services available to the community so that, from the start, programs were open to all interested older persons. No referral was needed to obtain medical care at the clinic; family members or older adults could simply call the clinic for an appointment.

Getting Started

Shortly after the clinic opened, a social worker and a psychiatric nursing student invited older people from the local community to an exploratory meeting to discuss community needs with their peers. Volunteers were recruited from the local Council on Aging, the university's Institute of Gerontology, church groups, and new clinic patients. We were looking for people to collaborate on creating services for the elderly. We did not have a preconceived idea of what we wanted to offer.

Out of the first few brainstorming sessions, a sense of excitement emerged. Although the idea of peer counselors was based on a growing literature on peer support networks for the elderly (Waters, Fink, & White, 1976; Bolton & Dignum-Scott, 1979; Becker & Zarit, 1978), the group initially approached the issue of peer support from a different angle.

The reluctance many older people feel toward participating in mental health programs, despite the need for such services, is well known (Blazer, 1990; Butler, Lewis, & Sunderland, 1991). Therefore, instead of initiating a traditional individual or group counseling program, a peer counseling program was organized. These began with health-focused workshops that were designed to attract a broad audience of older adults. The peer counselors were designated to provide a link between the health-oriented informational groups and more individualized support services.

> *Peer I:* I think probably the biggest thing as far as the actual work with the client is deciding where to start and which direction to take until the experience with her indicates that we should go in a different direction and figuring out what would be most helpful. The actual experience of getting to know the client and trying to pick up what would be most helpful is challenging.

In effect, the peer counselors acted as the eyes and ears of the program. Initially the peer counselors facilitated small discussion groups within the large workshops of about sixty to eighty people. Workshop topics covered a range of issues such as coping with arthritis, heart problems, and consumer issues, developmental/physical changes of aging, depression, sexuality, and so on. Following the presentation of the speaker, the audience divided into small discussion groups, which were facilitated by peer counselors. Peer counselors and staff followed up with those workshop participants who expressed the need for individual attention; thus individuals who might not normally use support services were identified.

Funding from the Administration on Aging made it possible to implement this project in four different sites: a medical center, a senior nutrition center, a nursing home, and a community hospital in a rural area. During a two-year period, forty-eight peer counselors served 2,500 "clients" in some 5,000 participant contacts (Campbell & Chenoweth, 1981).

Professional supervisory staff consisted of one part-time social worker, one full-time psychiatric nurse, one part-time program assistant, a psychiatrist, a geriatric nurse, and seventeen graduate students. At the end of a two-year period, program staff gradually transferred responsibilities for the nursing home site, nutrition program site, and community hospital site to other sponsoring agencies. The program at the medical center continued to expand in ways consistent with the skills and interests of the peer counselors and the needs presented by their contemporaries. The remainder of this chapter will discuss the development of this program.

Program Staff

Currently, at our geriatric clinic, there are about twenty-five peer counselors, one social worker, and one social work graduate student. The peer counselors meet together monthly for in-service training and discussion of their activities. The social work student meets with the peer counselors who are doing individual counseling at another monthly meeting to discuss client issues.

A current grant funds a quarter-time social worker and an assistant to recruit and train African-American and low-income peer counselors. This program works closely with black churches and recruits African-American professionals to assist with the training. The goal is to serve a diverse population of elderly clients.

Recruitment and Training

Recruitment of peer counselors has been accomplished in a variety of ways:

- Fliers announcing training programs are sent to about 250 community organizations, including groups that serve the elderly, such as churches and civic groups.
- Press releases are sent to local newspapers, radio stations, and newsletters.
- Volunteer offices and university hospital staff make recommendations.
- Current peer counselors bring their friends into the group and they, in turn, may become interested in joining the peer counseling program.

Potential peer counselors are interviewed by staff to discuss program opportunities. The following are important considerations for acceptance:

- a stable emotional state
- the ability and willingness to commit at least ten hours a month to the work
- a motivation to be a peer counselor
- the ability to listen

> *Peer F:* One of the best things I got from the counseling I thought was listening to people and not telling them your story, but listening to their story. It's a wonderful thing to learn to listen to people.

Nevertheless, there is no attempt to do extensive screening of potential volunteers. The flexibility of roles that a volunteer can play allows us to involve people with different skills and talents. For example, one volunteer can be a "communications" specialist. He/she takes pictures of workshops, group activities, and special events and makes copies of audiotapes of workshops to distribute to people who couldn't attend or to those who want to review the material presented.

Another volunteer compiles our resource guide of services in the county, a one-hundred-page guide that is updated every two years. She also answers the telephone in the clinic's social work department one afternoon a week. Bonafide peer counselors have one client they visit weekly; they may continue this relationship over many years. Although the term "peer counselor" is accepted and preferred by the volunteers, the roles they play vary with their ability and interest.

> *Peer A:* In my case that little woman that I visit had a couple of daughters, married, you know. One of the daughters had charge of her affairs, paid the bills, and brought her groceries. She requested a visitor for her mother, and she happened to get me. Some of the peer counselors are called facilitators, and they plan workshops. I don't feel that I'm up to that.

Training has varied, depending on client needs. When more people are needed to do individual counseling, training emphasizes peer counseling skills rather than group facilitation training. The following are overall training goals:

- to develop a sense of awareness in each peer counselor of his/her own special skills and interests
- to acquaint the peer counselors with each other, thereby establishing a group identity as peer counselors
- to cover topics of importance to the elderly; these include bereavement, depression, management of chronic health problems, and availability of community resources

Although some basic counseling skills and group techniques are taught by utilizing roleplays, an effort is made to encourage the peer counselors to discover and develop their own talents and resources. There is more flexibility in this regard in our program than in some others covered in this volume.

Peer A: Well, we had this three-week course. I have since taken another one. I think that was four weeks total. They invited a lot of new people to join, and I took it again. When you get through the training you learn a lot. It tells you to keep things confidential, and don't go blabbing things around, and to accept people the way they are, and just go on from there.

Peer I: Information was given about what should be done if you would run into a problem that a client was having, because even though the word "counselor" is in here, it is my understanding that you're not really a counselor, but more of a friend. And, if you see something that needs some kind of professional intervention, we would refer this to the people at the medical clinic.

The basic model for training was eighteen hours in six weekly sessions of three hours each. Crucial to the success of the program has been a bi-weekly or monthly meeting offering in-service training and/or exchange of information by the peer counselors about their activities. This has helped create a cohesive group, many of whom have become close friends outside the peer counseling meetings.

> *Peer A*: I do think it's a wonderful thing to have that clinic, because not only did I join a support group, which now meets every other Wednesday morning but also a readers group that meets once a month at somebody's home. I joined that too because I love to read, and we read books and report on them to each other. Then I joined the peer counselors and got to do visiting, and besides that the monthly meetings. I volunteer at different events they're having, so it keeps one involved and among people. I think that's very important. It would be so easy just to stay home all the time and then get scared to go out.

> *Peer H*: The peer counselors are all more or less alike. And, we all had a very good time, because Ruth, the program director, is just wonderful; she just inspires people.

> *Peer D*: Several of us peer counselors have been together for fifteen years. We've become good friends, and we pass anecdotes along, what we're doing about particular things, and what we get into.

> *Peer A*: Knowing any of the peer counselors is enriching; they are all wonderful people, very friendly. I am not a university graduate, and I think many of them are, but that doesn't seem to matter.

Program Workshops

The first activity developed by the peer counselors were workshops on vision loss. It became clear from the turnout of almost one hundred people that this was an enormous problem for older adults. Unsuccessful cataract operations, the problems of macular degeneration, and glaucoma often result in significant vision loss with aging.

Spurred on by two legally blind peer counselors, a low-vision support group was started and has continued to meet monthly, consistently attracting new members since 1978. Peer counselors and staff also work closely with staff of The Detroit Society for the Blind and the Michigan Commission for the Blind to help them more effectively service newly blind older adults. Besides the support group, telephone counseling by the peer counselors and some support group meetings became an important part of the program, giving participants a chance to talk about their feelings with those who had similar experiences.

Another example of a significant workshop were those run by the peer counselors on housing. When the peer counselors themselves met in small groups, several were surprised to hear how often housing problems came up with their clients. People were lonely in their houses after spouses died and they had problems maintaining their homes and in paying high property taxes on a limited income.

> *Peer E*: Sometimes there's business. Sometimes it's a question. One meeting we talked about housing because three of us had recently moved into retirement homes. We talked about how it felt to move into a new home.

Support Groups

A key feature of this facet of the peer counseling program has been the growth of support groups.[2] In 1992, the clinic held seventeen different support groups with a total of 294 sessions. Support groups average about twelve to twenty-five members each; some of the more popular groups were Low Vision Support and GLOW (Gay and Lesbian, Older

---

[2] Support groups of a wide variety exist in our society; some are leaderless and/or run by untrained/unsupervised group members. Only a responsibly trained and supervised support group format such as this one can be legitimately considered "peer counseling."

and Wiser). All support groups are facilitated variously by staff social workers, social work students, peer counselors, and other volunteers.

Groups started specifically by the peer counselors include a memory improvement course, a newcomers group for people who have recently moved to the area, a men's support group, and lunch and dinner groups in which people dine together on a monthly basis. A peer counselor facilitates the Divorce Over 60 group for people contemplating or going through divorce in later life. Another peer volunteer facilitated a weekly writing group for five years until his recent death. Peer counselors also participate in a bi-weekly support group led by a clinical social worker for people with chronic depression or coping with changes and losses occurring in their lives.

Individual Peer Counseling

About half of the peer counselors have clients whom they visit, usually in the client's home, on a weekly or bi-weekly basis. Client referrals usually come from social work or medical staff at the clinic. Peer counselor clients may also be seeing a social worker or psychiatrist for counseling. They are often people who are homebound because of physical or psychological problems and need more support than they are currently receiving. A peer counselor fills an important role, bridging the gap between professionals and friends. They may take their clients out to lunch or to a doctor visit; they listen and provide encouragement and support to their clients.

> *Peer H*: We did some one-on-one visiting to our clients. I liked that; I thought that was quite interesting. Often old people who can't get out very much are bored and need companionship.
>
> *Peer G*: My role is just to provide visits to people and provide social activity and encouragement for these people. This one guy acted very depressed, very often. I tried to cheer him up,

and every time I left he seemed to be in a much better mood than when I got there.

Peer C: One of my clients died; her daughter called me a couple times afterward to tell me how beneficial she thought the visits had been. Her mother was, I think, ninety-one or ninety-two. I don't know whether it was Alzheimer's or what, but she was kind of out of it, and many times she would forget who I was from one visit to the next. But the daughter, who was a woman almost my age, said that her mother would look forward to my visits.

Peer E: The other thing that happened was that I came into a woman's life at exactly the moment that there was so much publicity about her great grandchild having been murdered. And, her daughter who lived in the same building with her went to the funeral, had a stroke, and could not come back home. So the client needed someone to talk with. Having had an experience in my own family where my brother was murdered, this I could understand; I think this was a help as far as she was concerned. She was able to speak very freely. Sometimes something like this happens when a person needs outside help. They don't feel like discussing it with any relatives or their neighbors. She avoided everyone; she didn't want anyone to know how she felt. She was not willing to discuss her problems with anyone else. She needed an outsider. This is what we try to do for people.

Peer E: Well, part of it is social, meeting other people who are doing the same thing. This is very important. And, reaching out to people who are lonely and need a contact, need someone to talk with, because sometimes physicians are not very good at giving any help at all personally, except in the physical.

Peer C: I feel very strongly to put forth to the public that there needs to be more stress on the fact that just because we're seniors, old folks, doesn't mean that we don't still have problems to solve. Many people deny their problems, so I think there should be more stress on the fact that seniors can benefit greatly from counseling.

Peer I: I see this as one more opportunity for service to the community. I assume the purpose is to help people with their quality of life and to be the person that would intervene, even though not directly, in case of a problem.

Following are three additional examples of individual counseling done by peer counselors.

Mrs. J's daughter called the clinic social worker. She was very concerned about her seventy-two-year-old mother, who was depressed and never left the house. Her mother was also a chain smoker, which had a devastating impact upon Mr. J, who had pulmonary problems. An artist many years before, Mrs. J had for the last ten years allowed her life to shrink so that she no longer had friends and depended entirely upon her husband. In addition, she refused to see a doctor. After coming in to talk to the social worker at more length, Mrs. J's daughter was able to persuade her mother to see a doctor. Eventually, she also saw a psychiatrist and began to take antidepressant medication. She still did not leave her house and continued to chain smoke. A social work student was assigned to visit her at home, but Mrs. J could not relate to the student and said it made her "nervous" to have her there. She did not know what to say to her. A peer counselor, a woman in her early seventies, was assigned to Mrs. J. Mrs. J felt comfortable with her and could talk to her. The peer counselor visited weekly, during which time she encouraged Mrs. J to stop smoking. Mrs. J then accepted the nicotine patch prescribed by her doctor. She began taking short trips in the car with the peer counselor, visiting areas on the outskirts of town, where she used to live. Now, the peer counselor is encouraging her to start painting again with the possibility that she can have an exhibit at Turner Clinic.

Peer B: I think Mrs. J thought of it as one senior talking to another senior rather than a social worker talking to a senior, and it seems to have worked out well.

Mr. K was an eighty-year-old man who suffered a stroke with resulting aphasia. It was difficult to understand him and this made him angry. He was a retired fireman who had had a troubled relationship with his three children. Although they tried to help him, he was hostile toward them. As a result, he was quite often alone, sometimes feeling suicidal. When he was discharged from the hospital after a suicide attempt, he was referred to a doctor and a social worker. A male peer counselor, recently retired, was assigned to him and visited him weekly for about five years. Through writing and other techniques, the peer counselor developed a facility for communicating with Mr. K, and Mr. K routinely called him when he was having problems with his family or when he had concerns about his health. The peer counselor had numerous contacts with Mr. K's son and tried to improve the relationship between the two of them, even to the point of inviting Mr. K and his family to the peer counselor's house for a picnic. During this post-stroke period, Mr. K became angry at others but maintained his relationship with the peer counselor. About a year before his death, he became angry with the doctor at the clinic, blaming him for his medical condition and refusing to see the peer counselor because he was part of the clinic. This was difficult for the peer counselor, who made numerous attempts to renew the relationship. Mr. K's son kept in touch with the peer counselor and thanked him for his assistance over the years. The peer counselor has had several other clients and is especially interested in another stroke patient. While other client contacts have gone more smoothly, the peer counselor believes that he learned a lot from his first client and remembers him fondly.

Mrs. L is an eighty-eight-year-old woman who was a long-time member of the clinic's writing group. She wrote many stories about the farm community in which she was raised. She lives with her husband, who is wheelchair-bound after several strokes, and her daughter, who moved from

A Peer Counseling Program for Older Persons

Indiana to take care of them. Mrs. L has made quilts all her life and still sits with her sewing on her lap, occasionally making stitches. She was matched with a peer counselor in her late seventies, who had moved to Ann Arbor about ten years ago to care for her sister, who had Alzheimer's Disease. The peer counselor loves to sew and visits once a week with her sewing basket and chats with Mrs. L. Mrs. L repeats her stories over and over, but the peer counselor enjoys the companionship of sitting side by side "sewing," even though Mrs. L hardly picks up the needle anymore. The peer counselor is also aware that she is relieving Mrs. L's daughter and giving her some time to relax.

> *Peer A*: Little things happen, like with this lady that I visit to sew with. One day I happened to have some nice cookies around here, and I thought I'd bring her a half-dozen, and I put them in one of those baggies with the zip-top, and I took them to her. I think they were sugar cookies. And when I gave them to her, she sort of snuck one right away, then took them into her bedroom. I thought maybe I shouldn't have given them to her, I don't know.

Depending on individual interests and skills, the peer counselors have been encouraged to develop individualized projects. One peer counselor, Bea Wooley, became interested in what happened to "normal" memory as people grow older. Together with other peer counselors, she developed a memory course and went on to teach this material at senior centers and church groups. She also published two books on memory, which were printed and distributed by the clinic.

Another peer counselor, Kathryn Flynn, produced three resource guides. One is a comprehensive guide to services for the elderly in the county, which has become an essential resource for professionals as well as the general public. She also wrote a resource guide for people with low vision in collaboration with the Low Vision Support Group. This guide has been updated and expanded to include a chapter on low vision aids for children. Her third effort came out of a workshop on housing. Many people spoke about how difficult it was to get rid of possessions that had accumulated over the years. Kathyrn researched and wrote a popular guide to recycling, giving away, and selling furniture, empty plastic containers, art, and all the other accumulated "treasures."

Peer counselors also are responsible for planning together with staff two annual events—a picnic in July, which draws more than six hundred seniors from the community and nursing homes, and a health fair in the fall, which features medical screening and flu immunizations. Peer counselors work at the various stations in the health fair, guiding traffic, registering people, and generally keeping things running smoothly.³

> *Peer C*: At the picnic they urge that seniors come in from all walks of life. They usually have several busloads of people from nursing homes. That's both pitiful and kind of uplifting. Pitiful because a lot of these people are terribly debilitated, and uplifting because they're like little kids getting to do something.

Outgrowths of the Peer Counseling Program

The vitality of the peer counselor group has produced several projects. The Housing Bureau for Seniors is one example; the energy and commitment of two peer counselors created this unique program, which helps seniors find housing.

It was also at a peer counselor meeting that several people said that they would like to have a program similar to the successful Elderhostel program, in which organized, week-long courses are offered at colleges all over the world for people fifty-five and over. The peer counselors thought it would be interesting to have a home-based, year-round program focusing on academic topics rather than the health-related ones.

---

³ The older peer counselors so much enjoyed lecturing to the college peer counseling class that they invited our students to help at their picnic. Inspired by their presentation, numbers of college students volunteered to help at the seniors' picnic. Cross-generational friendships were thus formed in the process.

A committee was selected to study this, and out of their discussions the Learning in Retirement program was created. The first lecture series was on China and Japan. The peer counselors thought we should charge a modest $20 fee for the six-week series. Social work staff were somewhat concerned about charging because our previous activities were all offered free. When 150 people signed up for the program, it was clear we had no worry in that regard.

Evaluations

We conducted two sets of evaluations: one among workshop participants and one among the peer counselors.

Workshop Evaluations: Participants filled out evaluations at each workshop to monitor the effectiveness of the program. About one half of the participants were later followed up for interview by telephone. Most found the information presented at the workshops helpful, especially those programs that suggested concrete techniques and information. Significantly, three quarters of all participants reported sharing information from the workshops with others—with a friend, with adult children, or with a spouse.

Besides giving us information about the value of each program, evaluations also provide suggestions for future programs that can be facilitated by the peer counselors. Evaluations have also been important in development of support groups. When many participants write that they would like to have more information on a certain topic, it serves as an impetus to start a new support group.

Observations of Peer Counselors: To assess the impact of the program on peer counselors themselves, three types of evaluations were done:

1. Self-evaluation forms were filled out by the peer counselors at six-month intervals.

2. Structured group discussions were facilitated by each of the four peer counselor groups to evaluate their services.

3. Staff observed the work of the peer counselors.

Peer counselors reported better understanding of their own problems, greater empathy for those with chronic illness, and a sense of achieving something worthwhile. A feeling of accomplishment was the repeated response to the question, "What did you enjoy about this program?"

> Peer I: As a peer counselor I'm dealing with someone approximately my own age, so it's a reminder that some people have a really difficult life. Well, let me just say that I'm grateful.

> Peer G: Maybe being a peer counselor teaches you that there is a group of people who are much less fortunate than we are. Most of these people we see are really terribly handicapped and you appreciate your health a lot more when you see somebody with a handicap.

> Peer B: It was just a very rewarding experience at a time when I probably would have been at a loss as to what I was going to do because I had just retired from teaching.

> Peer D: Years ago I was waiting on older people, selling shoes, and sometimes I would get upset at the questions they would ask and the complaints that they had. I would think, well, they're just cantankerous old people, you know. Then after I had been a peer counselor and retired, I realized that I was probably the same way; I had certain likes or dislikes. It's been a good learning experience, and I wouldn't give it up.

> Peer C: I think, well, it's my opinion that practically everybody that gets into this kind of work has got problems of their own, and that's how they get in. And yes, I think it has affected my own problem-solving ability. I look at whatever problems I have more honestly.

> Peer G: I think the most rewarding experience I can remember was when I got to my client's place,

he was furious and didn't want to talk, and I told him, "I'm really here to cheer you up, and I feel like a failure if I can't cheer you up." And then he turned into a good personality, and I had a good time with him for an hour. When I left he was smiling, and it made me feel good. You feel inadequate if you don't succeed in what you're supposed to do. And if you suddenly succeed, it makes you feel good. I'm not a very ambitious person, but it makes me feel good if I do something right.

Staff observed that peer counselors became more assertive in their counseling roles, gradually assuming more responsibility and taking the initiative rather than delegating responsibility. Counseling and group facilitation skills markedly improved. Peer counselors also wrote self-evaluations, and the overwhelming feeling was that they had benefited themselves from the program more or as much as they had benefited others. The pleasure of being part of the peer counselor group itself and the friendships that had developed were seen as significant outcomes of this program.

Peer B: I think probably most of the older peer counselors would tell you that their friendship that has developed among the older peer counselors is probably one of the most important things that they can get out of it. Because, we still go to lunch together. It has nothing to do with peer counseling; we just go as friends.

Peer F: Yes, one of the nicest parts about it is that when we came here, we had just moved here from Flint, and I wasn't acquainted with anybody. I was very fortunate. It's been about fifteen years that we've been together, and we've become real friends.

Evaluations have never been attempted with peer counseling clients, mostly out of reluctance to label people as "clients." However, evaluations of this group would be quite useful in examining the dynamics of the peer counselor/counselee relationship.

Conclusions

The success of this program for more than sixteen years has demonstrated the effectiveness of utilizing the skills and experience of older people to provide services to their peers. It seems miraculous that the program survived long after initial grant funding ended, since no additional funding specifically for the peer counseling program has been allocated. Social work staff and students have incorporated peer counselor activities into their schedules.

An issue we are currently struggling with is the aging of long-time volunteers. As new, younger peer counselors are trained, the question has arisen about the retention of those who no longer want to be as active as before but who still want to keep their identity as peer counselors. The unique spirit of those who helped develop this program has to be recognized as new peer counselors are recruited. We are still struggling with this issue and hope to come up with innovative solutions. The peer counseling program has historically taken change as a challenge and has continued to thrive. Given this history, the future should be interesting to watch.

> *Peer D*: Well, the purpose of the program, I think, is sort of to bring home to people my age the fact that there are lots of things in life left to be done. There's a lot of learning and there's a lot going on. And, if you're going to be alert, you have to keep busy, as well as active physically, if you can. And it's been a learning process all the way through, both for the peer counselors and for the people who come to see us.

REFERENCES

Becker, F., & Zarit, S. (1978). Training older adults as peer counselors. *Educational Gerontology, 3*, 241-250.

Blazer, D. (1990). *Emotional problems in later life: Intervention strategies for professional caregivers.* New York: Springer Publishing Company.

Bolton, C., & Dignum-Scott, J. (1979). Peer group advocacy counseling for the elderly. *Journal of Gerontological Social Work, 1*(4), 321-331.

Butler, R. N., Lewis, M., & Sunderland, T. (1991). *Aging and mental health.* New York: Merrill Publishing.

Campbell, R., & Chenoweth, B. (1981). Health education as a basis for social support. *Gerontologist, 21*(6), 619-627.

Waters, E., Fink, S., & White, B. (1976). Peer group counselling for older people. *Educational Gerontology, 1,* 147-50.

Peer Education Practica

Chapter 7

Peer Education at University Health Services

Janet Zielasko, MPH, CHES, Polly Paulson, MPH, CHES, Robin Nwankwo, MS, MPH, RD, Gen Stewart, MPH, and Kristin Hoppe, MPH, CHES

College-aged students, particularly those eighteen to twenty-five years old, are often "on their own" for the first time and are thus confronted with numerous experiences, some threatening, others enhancing to their health. Students' knowledge and understanding of health risk behaviors varies dramatically depending on their past educational experiences, family situations, and peer influences. At the same time, they have a great potential for good health. Therein lies the challenge for college health providers: how to effectively build awareness of health issues in this age group.

Since the 1960s, the use of peer health educators has been increasing both in terms of the numbers and types of services they provide. Although peer education is not a new concept, it takes on additional importance in college healthcare, where budget reductions and staff limitations are common. Peer educators provide a cost-effective solution to some of these problems by providing services to a university community at a low cost. Many additional attributes to this alternative form of service delivery make it appealing to the youth themselves.

In reviewing typical advantages of model peer education services, Baldwin and Wilson (1974) highlight the following:

- their informational style in presenting material
- a less rigid organizational structure
- their practical orientation to information
- the ability to insure confidentiality of participants, in part due to decreased data collection and record keeping
- a balanced educator/participant relationship, which can lead to more open discussions about important health concerns
- an increase in perceived and actual acceptance of student behaviors and lifestyles
- free services

Many of the facilitators themselves believe that the peer aspect is a crucial dimension of the education process.

> *Peer B*: It's hard to know in terms of actual, well-designed evaluation the impact of these programs, but it does seem to be well-received when people who can relate to others' experiences share and facilitate those experiences to other peers and talk about things that everyone is dealing with, not coming down from the official university standpoint. Our programs do seem to be well-received, and hopefully that translates into making an impact.

> *Peer D*: It's reinforcing for me not to be judgmental, to be able to go to a fraternity and say, "Hey look, I'm not going to be here just being like Nancy Reagan, 'Just Say No'—because I go to the bar, too. And I'd be a liar if I said I didn't." So, I think in that way I can relate to other students a little bit better than adults would and I think I can get my point across because I'm more believable.

> *Peer A*: I think the best thing about it is that it is peers who are talking to students instead of having some health professional come out and say, "Okay, you students shouldn't do that."

> Then I think people would automatically tune themselves out. But since it's people our own age, sometimes you might even say something like, "You know, I've gotten through this too." That just helps people to be more comfortable. So, I guess that's almost the biggest thing that I like about it: it is a peer thing.

Peer education programs not only benefit the participants but also benefit the peer educators involved in programs. The educators are provided an opportunity to acquire leadership skills, public speaking experience, group facilitation training, interpersonal communication skills, and in-depth training in specific content of health issues; furthermore, they are offered an arena for career testing and development.

Most university health service peer education programming began in the mid 1970s. The first such program was developed in conjunction with the needs of the gynecology clinic and focused specifically on contraceptive information. In light of the success of that program, peer education has been applied to other health-related topics that concern the college student. Peer education programs are now offered on not only "Contraceptive Education" but also "Alcohol and Other Drugs," "Safer Sex," "Stress and Time Management," and "Body Image: Healthy & Disordered Eating." Each of these programs is available on request in residence halls, sororities, fraternities, and for other university groups and classes. Peer education programs are interactive and informative, are co-facilitated by peer educators, and provide a relaxed atmosphere where students can openly discuss health issues.

Structure of Health Education Programs

Any effective and efficient peer education program requires a clear delineation of duties and responsibilities among those staff and peer educators involved. Typically the responsibilities of the health education staff include balancing the time they spend with peer facilitators, other students, various university departmental staffs, and administration personnel. On-going coordination and communication among the staff, the peer coordinators, and peer educators is the key to success.

The main function of the professional health education staff is to develop, design, and evaluate the programming for each group and provide initial and on-going training of the peer educators. In addition to professional supervisors, each peer program has one or two peer coordinators, who are selected by the professional staff to assist them with training and day-to-day running of the program as well as scheduling and implementation of the programming. Peer coordinators are students who were peer educators for at least one year and who are interested in assuming additional responsibilities within their program. Peer coordinators receive two academic credits per semester through the School of Public Health and serve in this capacity for at least one year.

Peer educators are trained to facilitate their respective programs in various settings on campus; they receive one academic credit per semester for their involvement in the program. Grading is based on attendance at the fall and winter training, regular attendance and active participation in monthly in-service discussions, facilitation of one to two programs per month, and weekly check-ins on the peer computer conference for updates and messages.

Recruitment of Peer Educators

Several methods have been used to recruit potential peer educators:
- Fliers have been posted in various locations on campus.
- Announcements have been made in classes.
- Ads have been placed in the student newspaper.
- Information recruitment sessions have been held at strategic locations on campus.
- Peer educators have made personal contacts with friends, acquaintances, and other students.

Peer educators are actively recruited each spring from the undergraduate and graduate schools, including Public Health, Medicine, Nursing, Education, and Liberal Arts. Diversity of age, gender, ethnicity, and sexual orientation are important considerations in recruitment of the peer educators so that the group selected will be representative of the whole student population. Many peer educators recognize the impact that cultural and gender differences can have during their educational presentations.

> *Peer F*: One thing I did notice is that, whatever background you come from, alcohol may have different effects on people. That's one thing you really discover in this program. Coming from an African-American perspective, I explain to them how our parties are usually in the Student Union, so there's no alcohol there. The central focus isn't on alcohol. We go to a party just to dance and things like that. And they sit there and say, "Wow, you go to a party—you just dance?" And we get this response just from telling our different experiences. It's just very interesting.

> *Peer B*: It depends on who's available for the program that night. Unfortunately we have a lot more women than men peer educators and so it's hard for us to always arrange for co-ed teams. I think there are a lot of important issues that peers can relate to other peers. The last program we did was in a fraternity and both of the educators were women. Although it did go really well. Gender is not everything; it doesn't override common experiences, but I think that's unfortunate in general that there just aren't as many men advising in peer education, at least in the programs I've been in.[1]

A student interested in becoming a peer educator is interviewed to ascertain that she/he has the skills, experience, and attitude necessary to facilitate discussion and to present

---

[1] It is a national trend that more women than men volunteer as helping professionals and paraprofessionals, whether one considers clinical psychology or peer education.

the requisite health education information in an unbiased fashion. Students can serve more than one year as a peer educator, and those students who do return for a second or third year are often excellent mentors for new peer educators. Some of these students step into the aforementioned "peer coordinator" role.

Training and Supervision

In-depth training of peer educators in fall and winter semesters is planned and conducted by the health education staff and the peer coordinators. The purpose of the training is to facilitate knowledge of those skills and attitudes important for the peer education programs. The training is also intended to familiarize students with and stimulate interest in and enthusiasm about the health education material. All five health content areas include training in skill building exercises in group facilitation, issues of diversity, and knowledge of health education principles. For each of the peer programs, peer educators receive a "manual" that contains background information and the step-by-step program agendas. Monthly in-services are held to discuss problems or situations encountered during presentations and to schedule upcoming programs. This time is also used to introduce additional information on requested subjects, often with a guest speaker.

> *Peer B*: At the beginning of this year we had a training that was twenty hours long; when we came back this semester, we had additional training at the start of the winter term. We learned about alcohol and other drugs, watched some videos, talked, addressed peer issues, and discussed college life. We had a speaker on diversity issues so we can try to be sensitive to different populations and their different needs. Part of our training this term is for information on "other drugs." We tend to focus more on the alcohol than other drugs. We also had a session on gay and lesbian populations. We did have some sessions on

group facilitation and how to handle different scenarios. We also had practice sessions. We would give our program, and others would critique us; then they gave theirs, and we critiqued them and said what seemed to work or what they could do better. So that was really helpful.

After each peer educator has facilitated one to two programs, the health education staff or peer coordinators observe and evaluate each educator facilitating a program. The purpose of the observation and evaluation is twofold: 1) to provide an opportunity to observe the "flow" of the program with an actual audience and 2) to provide feedback to the peer educator regarding her/his facilitation skills. Through this evaluation, the staff or peer coordinator can provide positive, encouraging feedback to the peer educator, gently correct any misinformation she/he might be giving, and offer suggestions for improvement.

It is important for peer educators to receive training and supervision in order to facilitate mastery of information as well as methods of education that are most likely to impact a learner's behavior. Health Service trains and supervises peer educators in programs addressing several different health issues.

Alcohol and Other Drugs Peer Education Program (ADPEP)[2]

The Alcohol and Other Drugs Peer Education Program (ADPEP) is a peer-facilitated interactive workshop that addresses issues related to substance use and abuse among college students. ADPEP was created in 1986 in response to student concerns about substance abuse and their desire to create a forum where alcohol and other drug use and abuse could be discussed in a non-prohibitionist, non-judgmental manner.

---

[2] The current coordinator of ADPEP is Marsha Benz, MA, MPH.

Peer K: We did a lot in the Greek system, so we would go to the fraternity or sorority and do a workshop for them. We worked with the Sexual Assault Prevention and Awareness Center on developing an alcohol and sexual assault program. We had big programs in the Union Ballroom and then we would have smaller ones in classrooms. We did a couple for the peer counseling class and a few sociology and women's studies classes.

Peer A: The basic purpose is to just alert students on responsible decision making in regard to alcohol and other drugs. I guess the basic plan is not to tell them whether or not they should or shouldn't take drugs, but if they're going to do it to make responsible decisions. So we alert them to the dangers and different things that can happen and how to tell if you have a problem in the first place and where to go for help.

Peer D: We call it ADPEP for short; it's Alcohol and other Drug Peer Education Program. And it's supposed to promote awareness of issues surrounding alcohol and other drug use on campus. And it's not like a "Just Say No" program; it's supposed to get people thinking about the choices they make. We do activities that highlight some of these things and make them think. We don't ever preach any kind of "Drink responsibly or don't drink." We don't say anything about which choices they make, just what they need to think about.

Peer C: I'm a peer educator at Alcohol and Other Drugs. I like people to consider the role of alcohol and other substances in their lives. I want to educate, spread awareness through education, get people to know if they choose to drink alcohol what this alcohol can do, what other drugs do, make them more aware of the consequences to them and others.

Given the high level of knowledge about alcohol and other drugs among students, there is relatively little specific descriptive content in this program. Rather, the bulk of the presentation focuses on problem solving and development of coping skills. Objectives of the program include:

- to encourage thinking and discussion about the role that alcohol and other substances play in students' social lives
- to enable students to accurately determine when the use of alcohol (or another substance) becomes problematic
- to give students the information they need to intervene in the case of a medical emergency involving alcohol or other drugs
- to enable students to approach someone in a caring and supportive manner who may be having a problem with alcohol or another drug so as to encourage that person to examine her/his behavior
- to provide information about where students can obtain further information or assistance on campus

Many peer educators see these objectives as being tied to their roles within the program.

> *Peer C*: One of my roles is as a facilitator. We work in pairs. We work as co-facilitators and make presentations to groups of between twenty and forty. We want a program that teaches basic facts about alcohol and other drugs, makes people think about a scenario concerning alcohol. And then we do a roleplay that teaches people how to deal with alcohol emergencies. Not being an expert on the topic, in addition to fielding any questions we can refer people. We know what resources are out there.

[handwritten: This is important]

Peer B: Some parts of the program end up running themselves once you get them going. We introduce the program, set the ground rules by saying, "We're here just to talk about the issues. We're not here with all the answers or to tell you that what you're doing is wrong," that kind of thing. We sort of set the tone for the program. Then we just try to facilitate discussion between people that will hopefully make them aware of things. We also try and answer all their questions and provide them with factual information. But one of the things we always say is, "We're not experts on alcohol and other drugs." And sometimes it's hard because they ask all these questions that we don't know the answer to, and then you kind of feel like you're losing your credibility. So we make a referral to an expert. During the other parts of the program we try to draw out people, get different opinions heard.

The format of the program is almost entirely interactive. It takes approximately one-and-a-half hours and usually involves ten to fifteen participants. In addition to these fairly small programs in residence halls, ADPEP is also often invited to present to members of fraternities or sororities. These programs are much larger, fifty to seventy-five people, and usually involve teams of four peers, who facilitate parts of the program in one large group and then break into smaller groups for the more interactive portions of the program.

Our program begins with an overview of goals and groundrules. This is intended to create appropriate expectations and an environment in which participants feel safe sharing experiences and opinions. Then there is an ice-breaker, which involves eliciting information in a round (for small groups) or random voluntary participation (for a larger group). Some of the ice-breaker questions require personal disclosure of the participants' decisions about alcohol/other substance use, while other ice-breaker questions elicit participants' opinions about why some people drink to excess or what they expect to get out of the program.

The component of the program that most specifically addresses alcohol and other drug information is a game called "Just Say Know." The game board is a grid that has classes of drugs (depressants, stimulants, narcotics, hallucinogens, and marijuana) along the top and some characteristics (examples, psychological effects, and dangers) of these drugs along the side. Participants are asked to work as a team to place cards with information that correctly corresponds to each category on the grid. The facilitators then review the categories and answer any questions.

Another major component of the program involves values clarification. An exercise called "Take a Stand" is used to explore participants' opinions and values regarding alcohol and other drug use. In this exercise, controversial statements such as "Marijuana should be legalized" and "The drinking age should be lowered to eighteen" are read and participants are asked to move along a continuum marked "Strongly Disagree," "Disagree," "Agree," and "Strongly Agree." After participants have chosen a place on the continuum, opinions from people in each area are solicited and discussed by the entire group. After several minutes of discussion, the facilitators summarize the main points and move on to another controversial statement, and so on (see chapter 14).

> *Peer B*: We have the "Take a Stand" session to get people just thinking about how other people view issues around alcohol and other drugs, to get them aware of other people's opinions, maybe ones they hadn't thought about before. We talk about how to recognize alcohol emergencies, how to "caringly confront" someone if you think they might have a drinking problem, when they show characteristics of problem drinking. We try to convey some factual information and information that will help them recognize problems. Then they might want to say something to a friend. We cover some factual information through this game we have called "Just Say Know." The rest of the program is more attitudinal or asks, "How are you

> handling it?" "Just Say Know" is where we try to clarify facts: this is what this kind of drug does and it's very dangerous in combination with this kind or that. We always say that the name of the game is "Just Say Know" and the "know" is spelled k-n-o-w. This is not about morality. We're not going to tell you what to do, we're not going to tell you what the laws are. It's very much not saying you shouldn't be drinking. It's saying, "Let's think about what you're doing" and making sure it's what you actually want to be doing and so on.

In order to connect knowledge and values with the development of problem-solving skills, participants are asked to engage in a fairly lengthy exercise that is part discussion and part roleplay. The group is split into three subgroups and each subgroup is assigned to a role. The typical scenario involves one person who quite clearly has the substance abuse problem, a friend who is concerned about the person who has the problem, and a peer who is in a position of responsibility (perhaps a resident staff person, fraternity president, etc.). The procedure involves describing each of the three characters and their situations vis-à-vis an alcohol emergency.

Each of the subgroups is then asked to consider the situation from her/his perspective and to answer the following questions:
- What is happening in this situation?
- How do you feel about the incident?
- What do you need to have happen with regard to the situation?

Information about characteristics of substance abuse, how to handle such an emergency, and how to approach someone with this problem are reviewed with all three groups. The three groups then discuss these questions among themselves and share their reactions with the other two groups.

Volunteers are variously asked to do a roleplay of a discussion among the person who has had the emergency (the "client"), the person's concerned friend, and the peer in a position of responsibility. Other program participants are asked to watch and provide feedback to people in the roleplay. The roleplay is repeated using different players and incorporating feedback from the group. A general discussion following the roleplay helps to summarize the information and provides closure to the exercise.

To end the program, the facilitators provide written material about a number of issues related to substance abuse and make themselves available for individual questions for fifteen or twenty minutes after the program.

> *Peer D*: It was the very first program I did and it was at a fraternity and I was scared to death. Actually all of them were very interested during the whole thing but three or four of them came up afterward and said, "Thanks for coming by. You guys did a really great job." And I was like, "Wow! They listened!" And then they came up and asked all kinds of questions and they were really concerned about some of their friends. And it felt really neat that I could be a resource for them.

The ADPEP program is particularly popular during our Alcohol Awareness Week, which takes place in the middle of November. In addition, the program is often requested by student leaders in response to alcohol/other drug-related incidents. As might be expected, requests for the program drop off considerably at the end of the semester, when students are busy preparing for final exams.

ADPEP is evaluated on several levels. At the end of each semester, peer educators are asked to evaluate and suggest modifications for each of the program components. In addition to evaluation of the program itself, peer educators are asked to provide feedback on training, monthly in-services, the training manual, the computer conference, staff supervision, and the work of the student coordinators.

> *Peer C*: And in addition to running the program, we also work to help the program to change and give suggestions as to how it's run so it can be more effective, reach more people, and help

to maintain longer attention spans for people in the audience.

In addition to evaluation of the program by peer educators, program participants are asked to complete evaluation forms at the end of each program. These evaluation forms focus on the acquisition of knowledge, the likelihood of their taking action in medical emergency situations involving alcohol/other drugs, and the probability that they would now talk to a friend who has a problem with substances.

Peer educators can experience several different reactions to receiving feedback, though most find it beneficial for improving future presentations.

> *Peer J*: This term our peer coordinators will be coming to watch one or two of our programs, so we will get feedback from them. We also get feedback from each other. At programs there are two facilitators and they give each other feedback on a form that is filled out. Also, the participants in the audience give us written evaluations. Some feedback is uncomfortable. It's always hard to get feedback. I guess it's good in a way, too, because I'm always into improving performance, and so constructive criticism is good. Good feedback about the program is always a really good feeling, to know that you're getting to someone and making a difference.
>
> *Peer F*: It felt really good because at first I thought, "Well, maybe they're just going to come in, they'll listen to us and then it'll go in one ear and right out the other." Actually we got some feedback saying that they think about making more positive decisions about alcohol. Some people said the program really did affect them.
>
> *Peer J*: My first ADPEP program got great reviews. At the end of the program the RA who sponsored the program got our address and sent us a thank you card for coming in and doing the program. In doing a program on

alcohol where there are so many beliefs about it, and not many people want to learn about it because they think they know it all and they don't have a problem and all that, it's very rewarding to see that people actually appreciate it so much.

Peer D: At first it was scary to facilitate programs, but then it's kind of cool because you can figure out what they like about the program, which activities, too. I use the evaluations for later programs to figure out what I want to spend more time on.

Peer A: Actually it made me feel good. Most of the feedback was positive, mostly with my first program where I was a little nervous and to know that it actually did help them made me feel good. There are some good criticisms so I was able to change parts that I thought I needed work on.

Finally, some programs are evaluated and discussed by two peer facilitators and two observers. These observers are usually a health educator and/or the student coordinator, who provide immediate feedback to the peer educators following each program. Using these several levels of evaluation facilitates the development of a dynamic program that is continually modified to meet both the needs of program participants and the peer educators.

The Alcohol and Other Drug Peer Education Program has evolved from a program that relied heavily on didactic methods to deliver basic information about alcohol and other substances to a program that is interactive and emphasizes problem solving and skill development. This revised structure is consistent with the direction of other peer education programs around the country.

The students at the university level are sophisticated and have high levels of knowledge regarding the health impacts of substance abuse. The challenge is to help students think about their assumptions regarding the roles that alcohol and other substances play in their social lives and to make appropriate decisions about their own possible use of substances. A peer education program must enable students to determine when substance use becomes abuse, it must provide information about dealing with medical emergencies, it must suggest how one approaches someone who may have a substance abuse problem, and it needs to inform students on where to go for more information and assistance regarding alcohol and other drugs. Such information is often valuable to the peer educators themselves.

> *Peer A*: As a college student, I drank a little bit too much, like everybody else, I guess. And so being a peer educator helped me to make responsible decisions concerning alcohol. Being a peer educator taught me some things that I didn't know and that I guess I needed to know in order to be able to change and make different decisions.
>
> *Peer D*: Now I'm more likely to look for patterns in some of my friends if I think that maybe they're drinking too much, if they have signs of problem drinking. So I'm more likely to keep an eye out for those things.
>
> *Peer A*: I just notice things I didn't notice before about that. So when I interact with my peers socially, it's a little bit different than it used to be.
>
> *Peer J*: I guess now that I know a lot more about alcohol and other drugs and how people relate to them, I apply that to my role with residence staff a lot differently than I did last year. Last year I let my hall do pretty much anything they wanted, because I figured they are adults. But now I try to educate, I try to be a good role model for my residents. I never come home drunk or under the influence. I try to keep my hall under control as far as alcohol is concerned.
>
> *Peer I*: I know instances where I've been involved in a discussion about alcohol use, when people

didn't know my role in this program, and I was
able to contribute to the discussion moreso than
I would have otherwise. And so, in a sense, I
guess that affects the way I relate to people.
There was a hallmate of mine who was talking
to me about a friend who was drinking too
much, again not knowing my involvement in
the program, and I discussed with him that I
had these resources available, which we were
given as facilitators, and ways to confront
someone you are concerned about. He was
surprised that I had this information and that I
was knowledgeable. I just knew this person for
a short time, and it affected the relationship
that we had. A lot depends on the individual
who may need help. There's only so much that
a friend or a counselor can do if the person isn't
ready to accept that he or she has a problem. I
think the skills that we try to develop as
facilitators not only about alcohol but any sort
of one-on-one feedback pervades most of the
interactions and relationships that we have as
individuals. Just being aware of some of the
issues of how to give feedback such that it
doesn't dwell on the past but moves toward the
future can be applied in many other ways in
our lives.

While peer education programs are beneficial to the audiences receiving the information about the particular health issue being addressed, the training and skills acquired by the peer educators extend to many other aspects of their lives. For example, many of the educators feel that these facilitation skills have been applicable in other classes and have influenced their public speaking skills as well.

Peer A: I guess the basic thing I can see is that I
never used to speak in classes; I wasn't one of
the persons who raised my hand. And since I
get up in front of a group now, it's a lot easier
for me to be able to talk to people. So being a

peer educator has helped me kind of come out a little bit and develop my interpersonal skills.

Peer F: I have an organizational psychology class and my peer educator experience helps a lot in projects with groups and when we have to facilitate discussions. In my communications class, we have to facilitate discussion and it's not like the first time I've been up in front of a group, so I don't feel so terrified. It just makes me feel a lot more comfortable working with people.

Peer K: It helped me learn how to stand up in front of a group and talk and, even though I was nervous, it would go away within the first few minutes. If I was nervous, I just had to think back to the time that I did a workshop with a couple hundred people and I'd feel much better that there are only twenty in front of me now.

These applications extend from classroom situations to other interpersonal situations the peer educators face. The skills may also be helpful for teaching peers things about other people and, at the same time, teaching them new things about themselves.

Peer F: When my roommate and I have problems about something, we'll sit back and talk it out instead of yelling and screaming at each other or something.

Peer B: Probably just the general idea that I'm more aware of trying to use good listening skills, like in the middle of this one fight I said, "Wait! I learned in peer education I ought to be doing this!" and then I changed my strategy. Because of some of the other classes I'm taking and doing this peer education, at least I'm aware a little bit more of maybe how I'm interacting with other people, even if I don't always implement the most effective strategy at the time. At least I can recognize, "Okay, look. I'm not really following what I should be doing in terms of good communication here"; I'm just becoming more critically conscious of issues like that.

Peer I: My attitude has always been that everything I do is an opportunity to learn about myself. I think I do know more about myself, my skills and abilities in dealing with the situations, facilitating discussions, and my comfort level in discussions.

Peer F: I think any time you work with people you're going to learn something from working with them at the same time. You're going to learn something from them just by listening to their experiences. The more experience I have facilitating, I learn a little bit more about myself.

Peer educators noticed changes in problem-solving abilities, breaking down stereotypes, and negotiating the impact of group dynamics.

Peer E: As far as problem solving, I think I've just become more quick.

Peer B: It's also interesting to see that sometimes I have stereotypes about how a sorority or how a fraternity is going to react to a program. So, it's interesting to see how people actually react. It's also interesting to watch how peer dynamics play out and how the participants react, how much that can affect where the program goes. Like if someone says, "Oh, that's not cool," you can really see first-hand how peer pressure can influence people.

Peer K: Everybody has their own individual situation and you can make some generalizations about drinking behavior on campus, but everybody has their own experience through their family or friends or a sibling or whatever. You can't make assumptions about that.

> *Peer J*: This university is pretty diverse, and I think that's the key, everyone is different, and everybody brings with them different ideas, different values, and it's important to recognize this and incorporate that into your life, into your workshops. It's important to know that everybody's values and beliefs are valid, that no person is better or worse than another person.
>
> *Peer I*: I think each program I do is an opportunity for me as a group facilitator to learn about other people's attitudes, ideas, and perspectives, and I think one of the most rewarding aspects of the program is that opportunity to become aware of other people's perspectives, to understand the way the world works.

Furthermore, these experiences can influence career goals for some peer educators. Not only does the program give peer educators a chance to gain hands-on experience for considering careers involving a particular health issue, but certain aspects of the training may also be applicable to other fields.

> *Peer B*: At the School of Public Health you do a lot of classroom learning. And while we do have projects out in the community, there's not that many skill-building opportunities in terms of hands-on teaching. So, this is a really good supplement to the classroom learning we're getting. And I think it's important to actually get that "hands-on." So, I think it complemented very well what I was studying and my career goals.
>
> *Peer C*: The program didn't change or affect a career plan, but I think it's helping to develop a skill that I want. I'm going to be a doctor and a doctor is somebody who studies to become an expert and then goes and spreads that

knowledge to other people. That's how I feel as a peer educator.

Peer K: I already knew what I wanted to do, but the program helped me decide; it became one of my research interests. Now that I'm looking at schools that I want to go to, I'm interested in programs, like Washington, that do a lot of alcohol behavior research, like why people binge drink, how people respond to alcoholism. I'm interested in the whole socialization of alcohol, multiculturally.

While peer educating experiences make several valuable contributions to the personal lives of the peers, group facilitation can involve frustrating or challenging experiences as well. Some peer educators find facilitating groups to be particularly frustrating when the audience is not focused on the presentation.

Peer D: I have a big problem with the Greek system; I didn't want to do any programs with the Greek system but then I had to do them. But it was quite challenging to have to go in there and just do it, grin and bear it. The sorority women were rude. They kept talking through the whole thing, like even when their sorority sisters were talking. A group of them would sit in the corner and talk. And I'd have to sit there and be a teacher and say, "Guys, please, come on. Somebody's talking." And I felt like I had a room of kindergartners.

Peer I: I guess the most frustrating experience I had was the program that we had at a fraternity house. They were told by higher-ups in the university that they had to have this program in order to be taken off probation, and so we were invited in to do the program. But none of the members of the fraternity, except maybe one or two, really wanted us to be there. It was something they had to do; it wasn't because they wanted to really. So, it was difficult to keep the group focused; there were a lot of people who had their own discussions going on. In comparison with the other programs, I thought it went poorly because I didn't feel that we had really reached anybody. I guess that's how I judge how good a program is; whether we were able to get through to some people and have them think about these issues and become aware of the issues from other people's perspectives.

Peer B: I think personally the most frustrating thing for me is believing more in my skills instead of worrying, downplaying my abilities. I guess the other frustrating thing is when you can tell that people really aren't into it and you're really trying to draw them out and they're not necessarily being that responsive and you feel like, "I'm up here wasting my time." This hasn't happened all that often, but there are definitely certain individuals that can kind of put a damper on the whole program, and that's frustrating. The people that come maybe aren't the people who need to hear the message anyway. So maybe the person who's goofing off in the back and pretending not to pay attention is the one that needs to hear it the most and they're getting something from it.

Peer A: I wanted people to be able to just give it a chance because I think a lot of times people say, "Oh, these people are just going to lecture me about alcohol. I really don't want to hear it. I know everything I need to know anyway." I want people to just be able to have an open mind.

Since the peer educators present along with one other person, they welcome opportunities to reunite as a team.

Peer B: We did a lot of training in the beginning of the semester and then we have in-services, like two or three a semester. But a lot of times, unless you actually sign in for a program, you don't see the other peer educators all that often. We communicate over a computer conference, which is nice, so that helps us stay in touch. It's a supportive, helpful group and it's nice to be around people that you know are concerned about issues that you are and are also willing to do something about it. So, I find it encouraging; it's kind of like a nice camaraderie feeling when you go into your program together and you give each other feedback. So, I've enjoyed being a part of that group.

Substance abuse is still a stigmatized and sensitive topic, but it is a problem that permeates student life. This makes it critical to have an effective peer education program in place to provide a forum for honest discussion about an issue that weaves its way into almost every other social issue that students on university campuses encounter.

Peer G: I just like the fact that peer education is really valuable in a lot of ways. It's a good way for people to get talking about things. People feel like they're getting preached at sometimes, and we always get questions like, "Do you guys drink?"

Peer I: One of the issues that I began to think about throughout this semester is actually defining our role as facilitators. I think we come into a residence hall or Greek organization and they expect it to be a preachy program, and it's not. I think that's why people are unenthused at the beginning, because they expect us to tell them not to drink. It made me wonder about my role as peer educator/facilitator. Do we facilitate discussion and sort of help the group? If someone has a question about the physiological effects of marijuana, they expect you to have the answers. I guess they hold you with a certain degree of respect if you're a peer educator. If you can't answer the question, and the question is early in the program, they may not participate or listen, thinking, "What do these people know? They don't know more than I do." At the same time I think it's good to have information; I see my role as helping people through the process of learning about their experiences. If people can begin to think critically about these issues in the short time we have and to see things from a different perspective, to look at societal influences as well as individual influences, I think that's one of the most valuable points this program offers.

> *Peer C*: Sort of a philosophy I've heard about peer education is if you reach one person out there then you've made a difference. Once in awhile you'll reach people and tell them something that will affect their lives. I only expect the results to be small-scale.

> *Peer G*: I think being a peer educator gave me a bounce that I like.

Safer Sex Peer Education Program (SSPEP)

The Safer Sex Peer Education Program is a peer-facilitated workshop, also conducted by two or more peer educators. This program focuses primarily on imparting information about the prevention of sexually transmitted diseases (STDs), including HIV. Statistics on the rates of STDs among university students and national trends are shared. Referral resources regarding university and local STD and HIV anti-body testing sites are offered. Information on risk-reduction strategies, including demonstrations of products used during safer sexual activities, are also presented. Building skills in communication with current or potential sexual partners is achieved by facilitating roleplay exercises.

> *Peer B*: The Safer Sex program is geared toward informing people how they can practice safer sex *if they choose* to be sexually active. We deal with AIDS and HIV, of course, and then all of

the other STDs: gonorrhea, syphilis. The program really wouldn't be appropriate maybe for, like, high schoolers. It's definitely geared toward college students. And it's basically looking at the STDs—what causes them, what the symptoms are. The second half of the program is how you can help to protect yourself because you don't know what sexual activity is ever safe, just safer. So we go through all the prevention methods and then also try to encourage people to think that sex isn't just intercourse, that there's more to it than just what we see on TV. There are other ways to be intimate too.

Peer C: One of the purposes of the program is to show that safe sex can be enjoyable as well as safe.

Information is communicated through a series of interactive and experiential exercises as well as through a limited lecture format. An ice-breaker exercise demonstrates how a STD can travel through a sexually active population and the choices individuals can make to reduce their chance of infection. This is done by having the students randomly introduce themselves to each other while having certain pre-assigned behaviors representing exposed and protected sexual intercourse (e.g., shaking hands represents sexual intercourse; an individual wearing a rubber glove is protected). Before the exercise begins, one person is told that they "have an STD" like HIV and when enough people "shake hands" without rubber gloves, this demonstrates the speed at which an STD can be transmitted through a sexually active population. This type of exercise provides an experiential component to the program that makes a point more vividly than any lecture could. Evaluations often report that this exercise is one of the most meaningful parts of the program.

Another exercise used to get across factual information about STDs (transmission, prevention, incidence, testing, and treatment) is arranged in a *Jeopardy*-style format. Participants are divided into teams and a peer educator uses game boards with answers from the different categories. Points are assigned to each answer, with the more difficult ones having higher levels of points. To facilitate this game, participants consult with their group to come up with responses to each answer on the game board. During this process they learn from each other and, hopefully, retain some of the information covered during the activity, such as when to seek STD testing, how certain STDs are contracted through skin-to-skin contact, and so on. A fun part of this exercise occurs when the peer educator plays (or hums) the theme song from the television game show; this helps to create an upbeat mood as the exercise progresses. Such gentle humor helps keep participants relaxed and comfortable throughout the rest of the program.

The SSPEP educators strive to make the atmosphere upbeat, non-judgmental, and relaxed to help participants become more comfortable with publicly talking and learning about sexuality and safer sex behaviors. The SSPEP is one of the more popular peer education programs routinely offered on campus and is requested frequently by residence hall staff. Occasionally it is offered in sororities and cooperative housing units, rarely in fraternities. One vital marketing tool has been implemented with dramatic results. Any residence hall staffperson who wishes to provide condoms for his/her residents is required to bring the SSPEP or Contraceptive Education Program (CEP) to the hall prior to obtaining condoms for distribution to interested residents. This incentive plan continues to be very popular among residence hall staff.

The SSPEP is evaluated in several ways: through written evaluation by participants and by oral and written feedback from the peer educators. One special projected funded by an American College Health Association 1992 HIV/AIDS Prevention Mini-Grant put together focus groups to examine SSPEP's effectiveness concerning reaching students of color living in residence halls.

> *Peer B*: The best feedback I've gotten has been from the actual participants who come back after. They say, "I really liked this" or "That was kind of boring." Because then you can actually talk to them and you don't just get this thing on a paper. You can suggest, "Would this be better?"

> *Peer C:* I was doing a roleplay and the people that had volunteered to be actors in the roleplay didn't go anywhere with it. We had feedback discussions and that was good. It was really educational, both for me and for the people that were watching.

Ideas for program modifications are actively sought from the peer educators. Midway through and at the end of each academic year, the peer educators devote time to evaluate all aspects of the program. Tallies of the written evaluations completed by the participants are also compiled on a yearly basis. These give the "big picture" regarding how well program objectives are being met.

As with other peer education programs, the peer educators themselves benefit as well as the participants. Educators are given the opportunity to improve their public speaking skills, interpersonal skills, knowledge levels in this health content area, and opportunities to apply these skills to career development now and in the future. Other benefits involve the exposure to diverse perspectives and personal growth.

> *Peer A:* I've become a better organizer, facilitator, public speaker, which is really helpful. I started doing it my sophomore year, so it kind of threw me into the university and gave me a place to call my own.

> *Peer B:* When I'm giving the program and somebody calls me on something and they say, "Well, I heard that wasn't true!" I know I have been trained to come back with an answer or I can refer people. Just being up in front of people and being able to deal with that kind of intellectual conflict has really helped me.

> *Peer A:* With the Safer Sex program, I've learned a lot about STDs and HIV transmission and treatment. I get calls from my friends at home. I get calls from friends here. They're concerned and they know I know something, not a lot, not everything obviously, but enough. And I have tons of literature that I get from UHS about

new treatments for gonorrhea or warts or developments in HIV research.

Peer C: I guess being a peer educator has taught me that now I can become a source of information and that I do have valuable information.

Peer B: If I am someplace and I hear somebody talking about people who have AIDS or whatever, it really bothers me if they're misinformed or if they're just being sexist or whatever. So, I think being a peer educator has taught me that more people should come to our programs.

Peer B: I have a younger brother who's six years younger than me and so you can tell he's getting all those sexual feelings. So, even my mom asked me to take him aside and just tell him the whole thing because she couldn't do it. And so I think that being a peer health educator has changed me in the way that I'm more assertive and I feel more comfortable talking about safer sex. I mean, it doesn't bother me.

Peer C: I plan to go into hospital administration as a career and one of my goals is to become more of a healthcare communicator.

Peer B: I want to go into basic research in neuroscience. I think in terms of my career I would like to be a person who has lots of different interests, someone who can talk about sex education. Scientists are varied people like the rest of us, though sometimes they get this little stereotype that they're just looking at test tubes. So, I think it's very important that they have something else that they feel strongly about that's outside their research that they care about.

Peer A: People complement each other with really different ideas. Like, a lot of people think abstinence is the greatest thing; other people think there should be promiscuity, or monogamy, or whatever. There's all these different types of thoughts. Maybe what was the most interesting has been seeing people who had a more conservative viewpoint and seeing that as valid. Because of my parents, I grew up in this liberal community, and I didn't have much experience interacting with people whose views were radically different than mine.

Peer C: I guess being a peer educator has made me more aware of other sexual practices and activities and made me more sensitive to different types of lifestyles. It made me realize that a lot of people are really uneducated about this topic. I guess if somebody were to come to me and talk about it, like a friend of mine, it would be a lot easier to talk about it now that I've been more familiarized with it.

Peer B: Like, nothing really shocks me anymore. I mean, not a lot shocked me before, but it could. I may not have shown it, but it would, and I would say, "Ugh, I would never do that!" But, I guess, after dealing with other training that we get in the program in the year, it's kind of opened up my feelings and also kind of gotten me to see that these are people who have different viewpoints than mine, either more conservative or more liberal.

Future goals for the SSPEP include tailoring the program to be more effective in reaching students of color living in the residence halls. This will include training Minority Peer Advisors who work in the residence halls to co-facilitate SSPEP. Another goal is reaching larger numbers of varsity athletes through offering the combined SSPEP/Contraceptive Education Program for women athletes as well as reaching more men's teams with the basic program. Through working more closely with the Alcohol and Other Drug Peer Education Program (ADPEP), SSPEP hopes to meet another goal of linking the issues of alcohol/other drug consumption with sexual decision making and risk-taking behaviors.

Engaging students of color and men to become peer educators is an on-going challenge. Future advertising efforts during the recruiting phase will need to keep this important goal a high priority. The program planners must also continue to assess how our core messages are presented. For example, is the overriding tone of the program sexuality-negative or sexuality-positive? As safer sex educators, we must pay close attention to the use of scare tactics to promote behavior change at the expense of affirming positive feelings and norms about our sexuality and intimate relationships.

The SSPEP here differs from some comparable programs on other campuses in that it covers prevention information for all STDs and is not just looking at the HIV/AIDS issues alone. Frank discussion about latex and chemical barriers and sexual behaviors apart from vaginal intercourse as well as the availability of condoms during the program are attributes of the SSPEP that other colleges may not choose to offer for a variety of reasons. On the other hand, many other institutions offer peer-based safer sex education using similar strategies to reach their large and sexually active populations. The strategies of a program on safer sex can be adapted to some extent for the values and comfort of a particular institution.

Contraceptive Education Program (CEP)

In the mid 1970s, the Contraceptive Education Program (CEP) was the first peer education developed at the UM Health Service. The CEP program is designed to give students up-to-date information about contraceptive methods and contraceptive decision making. The program is intended to help students choose and use contraceptive methods effectively in order to avoid pregnancy and the transmission of sexually transmitted diseases.

The CEP is a one-and-a-half hour program facilitated by peer educators, usually in teams of two. The program covers the advantages and disadvantages of each method, their effectiveness in preventing pregnancy and sexually transmitted diseases, and the cost of each method. Information on personal decision making, gynecology clinic procedures, pregnancy testing, and male and female anatomy is also included in the program. The program is primarily didactic in nature, yet informal discussion is encouraged. An interactive communication exercise has been developed for use in programs presented outside the Health Service. The program is not a substitute for individual contraceptive counseling, which occurs during the clinician/patient interaction, nor is it assumed that participants are presently sexually active. Attendance at a contraceptive program is required in order to receive a prescription form of contraception at University Health Service (UHS). Programs are held twice a week during the academic year at UHS and upon request in residence halls, sororities, and fraternities.

> *Peer A*: It was becoming very time-consuming for a nurse practitioner or for a doctor to have to sit down with every single person and tell them everything about the pill or the diaphragm. So that's why this program was established. Anybody who wants to get prescription contraception at the Health Service has to go to our presentation; it's required. One purpose is to assist healthcare providers, but also we want to educate people on campus about different methods of contraception, different factors that may play into a woman's or a man's choice of contraception. Sometimes you don't know about particular methods, and you're kind of hesitant to go out and find out about them on your own.

> *Peer B*: CEP is out there to give information about all the contraceptive methods available in the United States. Because we are mainly informational, our program is not as interactive as some of the others. It's more getting up and talking in front of a group of people. We try and keep it to an hour and a half. We also provide examples of everything. We pass them

around if people want to become more comfortable with the subject.

Through demonstration and the use of handouts, information is provided on each method of contraception. First, each method is explained, followed by a discussion of the effectiveness rates in preventing pregnancy and sexually transmitted diseases. When appropriate, the contraceptive device is shown and passed around for participants to see. The possible advantages and disadvantages for each method are reviewed, which may include side effects, possible long-term complications, medical contraindications, lifestyle considerations, partner involvement, and cost.

The primary objectives of CEP are:

- to increase participants' knowledge of reproductive health
- to inform students about the contraceptive methods available to them, both prescription and non-prescription
- to increase students' awareness of how they might begin the process of contraceptive decision making
- to fulfill the prerequisite for receiving a prescription contraceptive method at UHS

Peer B: When I can talk to people about contraception issues I will often bring something personal into it, which will make them feel more comfortable. Because they don't know anything about me they may worry, "What is she going to think of me?"

Peer A: Some participants are just there because they have to be there. But it's really nice to see people genuinely interested in what we offer, to see that they are really enjoying what you are telling them or that they are actually learning something.

Participants come to these workshops for a variety of reasons, only one of which is to fulfill the gynecology requirement. Many attend for an overview of the subject rather

Peer Education at University Health Services

than for help in contraceptive decision making. The program reaches students at all class levels and, although graduate students are under-represented at the programs, one-third of the participants are over the age of twenty-one. Despite the program's position that contraception is the responsibility of both partners, only fifteen percent of the participants are males.

The CEP is evaluated by participants at the end of each program through written evaluations. The instrument includes questions related to method choice, satisfaction with the program content, and feedback for the program facilitators. Peer educators verbally share feedback with each other after the presentation and also complete an evaluation form describing what went well and what could be changed to improve the program. During monthly in-services with the peer educators and throughout the year, program modifications are discussed and new, updated contraceptive information is incorporated into the program. A final evaluation is completed by peer educators at the end of the year, which provides another opportunity for peers to make suggestions for improving the program. The peer education manual is revised each summer based on the above feedback. When available, selected peer coordinators for the upcoming year help with the manual revisions. The evaluations also allow the peer educators the chance to critique their own performances.

> *Peer A*: The big challenge for me was to learn the material well enough that I felt comfortable. I didn't want to stand up there and just read or be really dependent on our manual or notes. You have to talk with your co-facilitator beforehand to find out how they want to do the program, too. There are people who are not going to be compatible with my facilitating style and there are people I am not going to get along with. Also, being able to overcome your embarrassment about the subject matter and not feeling like you're going to offend somebody takes practice A lot of people have a problem saying words associated with

contraception; I totally understand that. But as an educator, if you express embarrassment about something, people might think, "Oh, there's something wrong with that" or "Why is the educator embarrassed about this?" Being able to put aside your own personal feelings and your biases about the material is a difficult thing to do. It takes time.

The CEP was developed to provide information and facilitate decision making for first-time gynecology patients. It is unique because it is the only peer program at UHS linked to clinical services at UHS, specifically the Gynecology Department. Over the years, the program has become more flexible by expanding the program outside of UHS into residence halls, sororities, and fraternities.

Most college health services offer some type of program on contraception. Using peer educators to present this information has proven itself to be a valuable and cost-effective strategy and something valuable for the peer educators themselves.

> *Peer B*: I'm pre-med. I am applying to medical schools this summer, and I think it will help me along as a doctor to be able to communicate with people on issues that could be kind of touchy subjects. I think to have been a peer educator who discusses contraception with other students really has an effect on my ability to have comfortable, personal, one-on-one discussions.

> *Peer A*: I really enjoyed being involved in the program because it gave me more contact with other students outside the field of public health. It was nice to get into something that I actually really enjoy doing. Some people just do extracurriculars so they can say they have done so, but I really enjoy doing this and I think that I learned a lot about education. It was a really good complement to my academic program. It gets you in touch with people like

you and it teaches you to relate to your peers in a more open and better way. A lot of the things that peer education deals with—counseling, alcohol and other drugs, safer sex, contraception, or stress—are things people don't always like to talk about. They may joke or just skim the surface of those topics. I think that when people become involved in peer education, it teaches you how to get people talking without making them feel really uncomfortable.

Body Image, Healthy and Disordered Eating[3]

The most recently initiated health education program in this series is designed for the prevention of eating disorders such as anorexia nervosa and bulimia—problems of almost epidemic proportions on many college campuses. Stated as its overriding goal, the "Body Image, Healthy and Disordered Eating" Peer Education Program aims to "reduce the incidence of restrictive dieting behavior within the university community."

> *Peer B*: The purpose of the program is to reduce the incidence of eating disorders and for prevention—to educate college students more on nutrition and things like that. I think we do a good job of it because we provide really concrete examples, like we have a menu plan for college students. We have roleplay scenarios like where a roommate has an eating disorder—situations that are really targeted to the college population.

Specific objectives of the program include encouraging students to accept their own body size and shape, i.e., to facilitate a positive body image both by recognizing potential

---

[3] Materials for this section were provided by Robin Nwankwo; text was written by Dr. Sherry Hatcher. The current coordinator of this program is Laurie Fortlage, a dietician at UHS.

sources of body image distortion and by assisting in encouraging those coping strategies that contradict our society's ad campaign: "You can't be too thin." Such slogans are thought to have particularly adverse effects on young, college-aged women.

> *Peer C*: The purpose of the program is to raise awareness on campus about the issues of eating disorders and body image concerns. The program was started around three years ago and then it stopped. We started it up again this year, so this was our very first year and it's been a real year for growing and developing. The peer educators have been able to help and give advice and criticize and redo different parts of the program. The purpose of the program is to do outreach and to make the campus aware of the issues of body image and eating disorders. We do programs in sorority houses and in residence halls. Generally the programs that we do in sorority houses are larger groups; sometimes they've gotten as big as sixty or seventy people, which makes it more difficult because people are less likely to talk. It becomes less interesting and it's more of a lecture, though it is still beneficial. You can still walk away with a list of resources and a list of symptoms and signs, knowing how to talk to a friend about it. I prefer to do programs in residence halls where its small, just ten to twelve people, where you can really talk to people and people really start to generate questions. That's where I think most of the learning comes in.

Healthy dietary and exercise goals are facilitated in this program by addressing fad diet myths, educating students about their caloric and nutritional needs, and encouraging students to examine their personal, food-related behaviors. When indicated, peer educators have available to them referral resources in the community for professional consultation, whether nutritional and/or psychological in nature.

Peer educators share information on how to recognize the signs and symptoms of those who may be "at risk" for an eating disorder. It is not an uncommon scenario that professors, RAs, and others in the university community are approached by a student who wants to know how to help a roommate or friend whom they suspect of having a serious eating disorder. This peer education program gives students tools both to identify such problems and to deal with those who are suffering with eating disorders in a caring, constructive, and supportive manner.

> *Peer A*: Part of what we're trying to do is also target people on campus who are not necessarily having a full-blown eating disorder but the eighty-five percent of people who have some kind of body-image-related problem. Those who are unhappy with their bodies are also people we can help in a preventative way.

> *Peer B*: We tell students that we are there to facilitate and provide information, answer any questions they have if we can answer them, and we tell them it's their program. They can feel free to ask questions at any time and if there are certain issues that they want to talk about that we haven't addressed or issues that they want to focus more on, we do that. Basically, we give them a broad overview of all the aspects of eating disorders— from unhealthy eating or restrictive eating to dieting; we discuss nutritional information and exercise, self-esteem, and body image concerns. We try to incorporate all those things.

Students who elect to participate in this peer education program are involved in twenty-five hours of training on issues specific to body image, nutrition counseling, and eating disorders. Peer facilitator training includes such topics as:

- Nutrition Services in the Residence Hall
- Body Image and the College Student

- Therapy Referrals for Eating Disorders
- A Medical Perspective on Eating Disorders: Explanation of Symptoms
- Nutrition: the Role of Food and Calories

They are presented by experts in each area; for example, a physician speaks about medical symptoms, a nutritionist about food and diet, and so on.

Peer B: We bring in speakers; a nutritionist may come in, therapists, maybe a social worker, medical doctors. With these encounters you get different aspects of information about eating disorders. You get factual information about medical problems.

Peer A: We spent a lot of time in our Body Image Program learning about eating disorders and treatment, information that was really specific to our topic. Then we spent some time with the whole group, which included all the other health education programs and did things like the group facilitation workshop, general information about being a peer educator, and resources.

Peer B: We have several supervisors in addition to our main supervisor; one is a graduate student in Public Health; the other person is a nutritionist from UHS. They set up meetings and they photocopy articles and give us assignments, and if we have any problems we can go talk to them. If a group requests our program, the supervisors call and set it up. The supervisors ask us how things are going; they provide feedback from our evaluations and so on.

Peer educators learn about genetic factors affecting body weight and build, such as those exemplified in recent studies of identical twins reared apart, which conclude that "genetic influences on body-mass index are substantial, whereas the childhood environment has little or no influence." Such studies estimate that genetic factors account for approximately eighty percent of metabolic rate, and therefore body weight variance, among people (Hewitt, et al., 1991; Tremblay, et al., 1990). Armed with this information, peer educators understand why the "ideal body weight" charts frequently cited by insurance companies are not always scientifically valid and why they need to attend more to the muscle/body fat ratio of an individual.

Peer educators are given a "caloric continuum chart," which illustrates the intake needs of individuals; they study various "daily food plans" for individuals' calorie needs. They learn about food substitutions and techniques for moderate and reasonable dieting. They also learn about varieties of exercise and its importance for a healthy lifestyle. Finally, peer educators learn why diets fail and why a severe restriction on caloric intake is counterindicated in that it can actually produce a drop in metabolic rate, stress, binge eating, and a sense of failure. Similarly, they study why extreme rather than prudent exercise can be counter-productive (Bennett & Gurin, 1982).

Peer facilitators in this program, as with the other University Health Service programs, present their program primarily in an outreach format: to classes, dormitories, fraternities and sororities, and so on. The program is skill-oriented and explores issues that impact personal body image and the lure of excessive dieting. Specific topics covered in the programs presented by peers include: meal planning for healthy eating, symptom recognition of eating disorders, referral information, and how to approach a friend whose eating habits concern you.

The tone of presentations is non-judgmental, as the title of the program suggests. The role of the peer educators is to facilitate discussions about body image and eating habits and to answer questions. Participants are encouraged to keep the content of discussions confidential so that people feel free to ask questions and share concerns.

> *Peer A*: We typically co-facilitate programs and they're either at residence halls or sororities. Our program is really interactive, although we do offer some didactic information about the

prevalence of eating disorders on campus, about healthy eating and nutrition. But I see it much more as a chance to invite people to discuss their own experiences.

Several interactive exercises are offered by the peer educators to their audiences in order to encourage self-exploration and active participation. One is a "Drawing Exercise," in which everyone is asked to "draw your body" and then identify which parts they like and don't like, which parts were difficult to draw and why. Facilitators write down common findings on a large newsprint pad for all to see. Following this exercise is a discussion of the factors that may affect body image and self-esteem; these include gender issues, the manipulation of advertising in our society vis-à-vis dieting and food, and the impact of the diet industry and how it may affect young women in particular.

> *Peer A*: In a way I guess we do have a message, which is not to tell people how to behave but really just to get them to be critical of what's going on around them, especially in the media. It's nice that we can help make that happen.

Workshop participants are given a "Self-Test" about eating habits and body image feelings. This questionnaire asks such questions as: "Do I hide my eating from others? How often to I think about food? Do I avoid meeting people because I feel self-conscious about my weight?" and so on. Respondents then discuss their answers with the peer facilitators in both small and larger group settings. Participants are encouraged to discuss those questions and/or answers that raise issues for them personally.

> *Peer B*: We just empathize; we try not to be judgmental but to let people know we are there for them. One of the girls, who was bulimic, shared her experiences and she became very emotional. She started crying and she said, "Just be there for your friends and don't ever leave them. Check on them everyday. Don't give up. You constantly have to be there." And then this other girl who was also bulimic

started crying and she related her experiences; they shared a common bond. They were great friends before, but they were hugging each other and crying. It was nice to see that they could relate to each other because they had each been through a common challenge.

Issues of particular concern to college peers are also addressed by the peer educators, including intra-group norms (e.g., athletes, co-workers, sorority members, etc.), perceptions of societal norms in relation to eating patterns, and messages that peer groups perpetuate. Coping strategies and eating habits are put forth as positive alternatives to excessive dieting and/or binging. The literature prepared by the "Body Image, Healthy and Disordered Eating" program states: "The first step is to acknowledge the messages that we receive from friends, family, advertising, etc., and then choose how we will deal with those messages."

> *Peer A*: I've learned something really interesting in this program and that's probably because I spend a lot of time thinking about this whole topic of body image stuff. I found out that a lot of people are really resistant to what we are talking about because what we're asking them to do is to challenge some things that they believe, messages that they get from media bombardment about thinness. I found that some people are actually a little bit hostile toward what we have to say. People seem to learn things a lot better if they relate to their own experience rather than just some random theoretical thing that you're talking about in a classroom setting.

Roleplays offer good opportunities for presenters to share information as to how one can help a friend in need of information about healthy eating. Written literature is also made available to workshop participants. All program presentations conclude with an evaluation, which is tabulated across similar programs for the year.

Peer C: It's kind of tricky to navigate both aspects of the program, because on one hand there's so much information we want to give them about nutrition, about exercise, about affirming themselves and improving their own body image. But then we also want them to talk among themselves so that they can hear how other people are feeling about these issues. We kind of try to navigate the difference between being a lecturer, a facilitator, and a group member.

Peer educators report many benefits from their work, including enhancing problem-solving skills, affirming career plans, improving interactions with others, and learning not to take responsibility for another person's problems.

Peer D: I personally have utilized a lot of resources that peer education training has introduced me to. I use a lot of skills from peer ed in other places. My friends may come to me and say, "This person has an eating disorder. What should I do?" I've been able to reach other people and teach them how to help others and themselves, which is nice. I've learned you can't change everyone and you can't get too upset if you don't touch everyone. You've got to learn to be happy with what you are and who you can affect.

Peer C: I definitely want to be in an educative role for the rest of my life, teaching people and talking about these things because body image and self-esteem are so close to my heart. Teaching women about self-esteem and helping women to feel good about themselves and their bodies and their experiences is what I really want to do.

Peer B: As far as career plans, I want to work with people with eating disorders and maybe go around giving lectures. That would be something I would enjoy doing, because I enjoy doing it now. I'd like to work in a college setting or give lectures in high schools.

Peer D: I'm planning on pursuing a career in medicine and I want to pursue something in gynecology, something to do with women's health. A big proportion of eating disorders is medically related, in addition to its being psychological. I want to explore something related to women's health.

Peer A: I hope that at some point I'm a health education coordinator, that I'll be involved with setting up or coordinating peer education programs like this one.

Peer C: With this program and also being a resident advisor, I've done a lot of work with individuals mediating conflicts. I feel like my skills with people have gotten a lot better this year. I also teach fitness. I think with these jobs you become a role model or a resource; a lot of people stay after class and ask you questions about exercise and even personal questions.

Peer B: Everyone is very different in their style of peer education. Some people are very rowdy and very loud and try to use humor a lot. Other people are more reserved. So there are different styles and sometimes these can conflict. You have to respect other people's opinions, even if you disagree with them. You just have to create an environment where everyone can be at ease and not go for each other's throats.

Peer B: This work helped me become more open-minded. Working with people, you have to give and take and compromise. I feel that I've become more open-minded in my personal relationships with other people.

Peer D: I have learned how to separate myself from these problems after the day is over. I can brood over things, but then I realize that's not going to change much if I didn't touch or really affect someone. I've learned I should be a professional and separate myself somewhat from the person I am trying to help.

Peer B: I really enjoy doing this work. I think it's fun and I learn a lot of stuff about other people. I feel it will help me in the future with my career. People always come up and say, "How do I get to be a peer educator?" Or I tell people that I'm doing this work and they say, "Wow, that's really cool" and they want to be involved in it.

Educators also benefit from the opportunity to reconsider their own eating issues.

Peer B: I think I learned what are my own biases about my body, too. I used to have more negative views of my body. After being in this program, you feel differently. I have become more accepting of myself. It would be dishonest to sit there and tell other people that they don't have to worry about their weight if I were to go home and work out for six hours a day. I feel that that would be a big contradiction, so I've learned to be more accepting of myself. I've learned more about how the media affects me and that I shouldn't let it bother me.

Peer C: I went into the program thinking that I was being hypocritical because I hadn't resolved all my own issues with food, yet there I was teaching other people about it. We eventually started talking about how other people felt, "Who am I to talk to people about this stuff when I just talk about it from an informational standpoint, but I don't take it into my own life all the time?" The point is that we're teaching people about healthy lifestyles, either through alcohol and other drugs, stress and time management, body image, even if we don't always do it ourselves. It feels so good to know that other people also face that kind of dichotomy.

Although peer educators greatly benefit from their work, there are also several accompanying challenges.

Peer D: The most challenging is trying to reach people who are very stubborn. One of the girls at a program said, "Well, I have been to the nutritionist and she told me that that's way too much fat for me. I know so because I put on too much weight." All you need is one person like that who makes you look a little discredited. I tried to explain to her that maybe hers was a special case and she kept trying to tell me, "No. I think those numbers are wrong. I think they're too high. I think you should check those over because I have been to a nutritionist;" this bothered me because a nutritionist is the one who designed our programs.

Peer C: I worry that people are seeing you as this person who is either coming into their hall or coming into their sorority house and saying, "Eat what you want, don't exercise, love your body, love your fat." That's been really frustrating. I don't want to come off as someone who's preaching to them or somebody who is way off target. It's been really frustrating coming up against such misconceptions.

Peer B: I think that because our program is not mandatory and because it's less formal, the people who attend are ready to participate. When we do some mandatory groups, people tell you that they want you to do a shorter program because they want to watch *Seinfeld*. I don't think people realize how much you put into the program.

Peer D: Maybe it's a personal thing, but when I hear someone who is more educated talk on a subject, sometimes other people say rude things like, "Oh! No! That is completely wrong. That's not what I read." So, I say, "Where did you read that?" and they say, "Oh, I read that in *Glamour*." Well, I got my information from the AMA. I've never met so many stubborn people. I always figured people would want to be polite as possible and that's not true. It's upsetting because it disrupts the whole flow of our presentation and it makes people doubt your credibility.

Peer C: Between my work with both aerobics and body image, I think there's definitely a perception that students have of me, that I'm very concerned with those issues. Once I was talking with some other students about self-esteem issues and how our body image is affected by the media and environmental factors. I mentioned something about how it's culturally unacceptable for a women to eat until she is full, that women are taught at a very young age that they should pick at their food, eat small amounts. I guess that's why women have a hard time filling up a plate full of food, sitting down, eating it, and enjoying it—enjoying the feeling of having a full belly afterward. One of the women in the group said, "How can you be saying this? I work at the cafeteria and I see that every day you eat a bagel and a light yogurt. How can you tell us that women don't know how to eat until they're full?" It was a challenge to my authority and it was really difficult.

Peer D: My friend and I gave a speech on eating disorders one day and the next day she was telling me how she was at a cafe and the people next to her recognized her as "the eating disorders woman." She was eating a salad with

> fat free dressing, and the girls across the table were watching her saying, "Well, how can she be eating that? How can she preach one thing and then practice another?" Because we do say, "You should eat some fat and you need this in your diet." For all they know, she could have had a lot of fat all day; they didn't know the whole story.

The "Body Image, Healthy and Disordered Eating" format nicely illustrates some of the differences in the way paraprofessional peer educators differ in their approach from professional psychologists. While peer educators in this program are taught the DSM IV symptoms of eating disorders, such as for anorexia and bulimia, they do not make psychological interpretations about the possible familial causes of an individual's eating disorders. For such a purpose, they would likely make a referral to a professional counselor. Peer educators are taught to recognize emergency situations, i.e., when an eating disorder can be a suicidal equivalent and/or when medical hospitalization may be necessary for an eating disorder. Referrals to professionals for the less serious variety of eating disorders are the more frequent outcome of the workshops.

Peer facilitators end each of their programs with a statement such as the one that follows, paraphrased from the Peer Program Manual for University Health Services:

> As a person learns to identify, value, and respond to his/her feelings and needs in a healthier way, the reason for an eating disorder diminishes. Unfortunately, once the behaviors become a way of life, they are difficult to break for both psychological and physical reasons. Eating disorders are curable if they are treated early by a group of trained professionals. Comprehensive treatment should involve collaboration between a physician, a therapist, a dietitian, and support persons. We will give you a referral list if you would like to seek assistance.

Thus, it is sometimes the peer educator who makes the first necessary intervention to help an eating-disordered peer to get back on track.

> *Peer A*: Going to a peer educator is less intimidating in some ways than going to a professional. I think a lot of times, when people go to professionals for help, like doctors, they're not given information. There's more of a weird power dynamic going on, but with peers it's just more of an equal relationship. Of course, sometimes people need to make use of both professionals and peers.
>
> *Peer C*: Sometimes when we do a program you can see all these little lights going on and people starting to see that things can be changing for the better. When you end on a positive note like that, it's really rewarding.
>
> *Peer D*: To actually touch someone, to actually make a difference, is the whole purpose in my life, to make lives better for other people. My view is, if I just touch one person, then that's satisfying.

Stress and Time Management Peer Education Program

The Stress and Time Management Peer Education Program, facilitated by two or more trained peer educators, provides stress-related health education for university students. The program focuses on sources of stress for college students, how stress affects a person physically, emotionally, and mentally, and exposes students to a variety of stress and time management strategies. Information is also presented regarding available campus and community resources for assisting individuals in managing stress.

> *Peer D*: Training was about six four-hour sessions, not only in this subject area but also in how to present and be an effective communicator. We had many speakers come in and talk, not only

> about our program itself but also about the other methods of dealing with stress—background information as well as practical information. In addition we had monthly in-services where we would invite a speaker who would give us an alternative view on stress management—another interesting perspective on how to approach it.
>
> *Peer B*: We have someone come to talk about how herbs and alternative medicines can work. We went to a floatation center to learn about floatation pods, which is for stress relief. There have been some interesting things, sort of different ways of dealing with stress.

While some information is communicated in a lecture format, the emphasis is on presenting information through interactive and experiential exercises. These include filling out worksheets to help participants identify their signs and sources of stress and organize their time more effectively. A continuum exercise encourages people to identify themselves as very stressed, somewhat stressed, or not stressed about a specific issue, to exchange information about why people respond differently, and to share managing strategies. Practicing relaxation exercises is a popular component of the program. These include visual or mental imagery, muscle tension relaxation, deep breathing, other short, stress-relieving exercises, and music.

> *Peer A*: In the beginning of the program, we start out by giving out a lot of information. So, the first part is kind of informative and it's basically just to direct the people participating in the program through exercises, getting them to interact and to explain to them all the stuff. We answer any questions; we are there as a resource for them about the actual information. We start out with an ice-breaker, which is just to get everyone talking, to identify where people's stress is, how much stress people have in their lives. Then we go through and define

stress. We talk about psychological, behavioral, and physiological stress and we give particular exercises and things to deal with each of the different kinds of effects of stress. Like for the psychological one, we actually have an exercise where we go through and talk about different aspects of stress they can and can't control. We actually teach some deep breathing exercises throughout the program. We end with a relaxation exercise.

Peer D: The purpose of our program is to raise consciousness about issues of stress and how it affects the body, as well as methods for coping with stress—we don't aim to totally remove it from our lives because a certain amount of stress is necessary for us to be productive individuals. In our program we use visual aids and audiotapes, and we practice stress-relieving exercises to music. We're there to raise consciousness because we realize, in an hour and a half, we can't solve the world's stress problems.

The Stress and Time Management Program is requested less often than other UHS peer education programs. This may be due to the fact that the program has only been offered for two years. We receive most requests for the stress program just prior to and during examination periods when academic pressures become acute. Most programs are presented in residence halls and sororities.

There are unique challenges to planning a one-time, one- or two-hour stress management peer program. Other programs, such as the Safer Sex Peer Education Program and Contraceptive Education Program, have a more clearly defined focus, such as reducing risk behaviors in the case of safer sex and informing participants of contraceptive choice in the case of contraceptive education. There is a generally agreed upon core of information students need and want to help them make wise decisions in these areas, and they often attend these programs for this specific purpose. Stress management seems to present a wider series of variables. There are a large number of stressors college students may experience, including academic pressures, relationships, finances, family problems, and issues related to identity. Individuals respond physically and emotionally to these stressors and stress management strategies in numerous ways. There seems to be no "one case" scenario. Given the large number of variables in how individuals experience and respond to stress, the challenge becomes one of finding a focus or common denominator that will be helpful and have meaning to a broad spectrum of students.

> *Peer D*: We've got a lot of interactive exercises. We try to keep people moving, having fun, and learning at the same time. We do exercises, games in which we ask each person to participate. We try and include everyone and get their different views, so as to better understand where our audience is coming from. We may have to target more academic interests; we may need to address more social interests, or even financial issues. It depends, in part, on the composition of the audience.

> *Peer C*: I think you can really help people, especially with time management. Sometimes you present the time management material and people say, "Oh, no! It looks like it takes a long time just to organize your time!" But then you say, "Oh, I tried this and it worked for me. Just try it out and take the part that works for you." And people will then say, "Oh, okay. She's under the same time constraints and she tried this and it works for her." With some of the more New Age stress management techniques, I found that people especially seem to like the deep breathing exercise that we teach. I think a lot of people would laugh or not take it seriously if it wasn't a peer showing them and saying, "That's okay, it's cool to breath deeply."

Because the programs are intended to meet the needs of the audience, specific training on the program format is primarily ongoing.

> *Peer A*: When we were trained, we were never really trained how to do a program. We learned about the issues so we could answer questions, but we were never trained how to facilitate the exercises. I thought that stress reduction was really interesting because I had done other peer work before and I expected to be spoon-fed how to do it and it was something that we pretty much had to learn on our own. In the beginning I was really angry about it, like "They didn't even teach me and I have to go do this program and I have no idea what to do." But I think that in the end I really benefited from it. You learn more to develop your own style instead of copying someone else's. It was something that stuck out. I remember when I did my evaluation on the training and I was really angry about it; now, five months later, I feel it was good that way.

> *Peer B*: I was very nervous to receive feedback. I was afraid that one of my peers was going to criticize me. But feedback was always presented in a very neutral way. It was never hurtful or in a form that would bother me. Actually it helped a lot just to learn things like to slow down when you talk.

In addition to the satisfactions, there are some frustrating elements to the work.

> *Peer A*: My first program ever, I was really nervous and my co-facilitator happened to be one of the peer coordinators, so that made things better because she had done the program all of last year. We had one participant who was extremely belligerent, questioning, "What are you doing this for? What are you gaining from this?" It really made the program difficult. He

attacked both of us, and it was really hard to deal with. The best thing about it was I had my co-facilitator. We just bounced off each other to keep the program going.

Peer B: If you get people whose RAs make them come to our program, they just kind of cool out and don't really pay attention. I think those are the people that as facilitators we struggle with to try to get involved and try to make them not be a distraction to other people, while hoping that they learn something.

Peer C: Toward the end of a program someone was asking a question and I remember not agreeing at all with how one of the peers responded to it. That made me think about co-facilitation and how to work with situations like that without undermining the program or making the other person feel horrible.

Peer B: It's very interesting to actually be working with peers. It's kind of nerve-racking too, especially the first time you get up there to do the program because you're talking to your peers who are having the same stresses as you are and you're supposed to be the expert on the topic.

Some of the benefits from peer education work include: maintaining close staff relationships, appreciating differences in others, affirming and enhancing career plans, assisting educators with their own time management, and having the chance to give back to their peers.

Peer A: I think we have a really good, solid team relationship. We're the smallest of all the peer education programs. There's only nine of us and we kind of think of the in-services every month as our own stress therapy get-together. I think we have a really good group and we're all really interested in what everyone else is doing, how everyone else's programs are going, and helping each other.

Peer D: I am not only learning things about myself but also about how I deal with other people, how I interact with them. I suppose one of my largest personal flaws is that I am a fairly judgmental person and I think that this program has helped me a little bit to understand people better and understand the different situations and circumstances surrounding their lives.

Peer B: The peer educators did a lot of telling about ourselves to each other and that was really helpful for me. It helped me open up. I found out some things about myself that I hadn't thought about.

Peer C: I know this program reinforced how much I like people and how much I like having contact with a variety of different people. I've been in this town a long time and have had a community of friends who are very nice, but who have kind of buffered me from all sorts of different people.

Peer B: I think being a stress management educator was one of the highlights of my year. It was so different than anything I've ever done before. So many of the other things that I do are academically oriented or don't have to do with anything I want to do with my life.

Peer C: One of the reasons I am doing this work is to really learn what it is like to give a program because I had just graduated with a health education degree. I'll be designing similar programs for my career. One day I said, "Wait a minute. I've never given a program so far." I wanted to do that for myself.

Peer D: I used to have a nasty tendency of not being able to say, "No." I'd say, "Sure I'll be there at four. I'll be there at six. Sure I can do that. Sure I can do that," and then I sat down and realized that there were only twenty-four hours in a day and you must choose how to spend those twenty-four hours. I realized you can't add any more hours to the day. Now I have definitely become a more effective manager of my time. I may say, "Yeah, sure I can fit this in if I can just shift this up a little bit." I'm a more effective user of my own time.

Peer C: The part of our program that has really affected me is when we describe what in our lives we have control over and the parts that we don't. I tend to get in a spiral of situations and just focus completely on the negatives and not separate this part I can control. And so it really helped me see that we have a lot more control in terms of the attitude with which we approach our lives.

Peer B: After our program people came up and talked to me one-on-one and said, "Yeah, I really learned a lot. I'm going to go try these things out when I get home tomorrow." That's very fulfilling and makes it all worthwhile.

Given that the Stress and Time Management Peer Education Program is only two years old, the present program format is bound to change over the coming years. Few peer-led stress management resources on campus are available for students. It would benefit students greatly if such programs became an expectable resource that students could access to help them deal with stress-related issues. If each campus unit could respond to a specific facet of stress management, thereby providing more comprehensive services to more students, it would be ideal.

Peer C: The main thing is to give people concrete ways that they could look at their stressors and their time constraints and work these through in order to live more stress-free, manage their stress better while they're on campus, and be happier and healthier.

REFERENCES

American College Health Association. (1992). *Healthy campus 2000: Making it happen*. Rockville, Maryland.

Baldwin, B. A., & Wilson, R. (1974). A campus peer counseling program in human sexuality. *Journal of the American College Health Association, 22* (5), 399-404.

Bennett, W., & Gurin, J. (1982). *The dieter's dilemma*. New York: Basic Books, Inc.

Bruch, H. (1973). *Eating disorders: Obesity, anorexia & the person within*. New York: Basic Books, Inc.

Hewitt, John K., Stunkard, Albert J., Carroll, D.; & Sims, J. (1991). A twin study approach towards understanding genetic contributions to body size and metabolic rate. *Acta Geneticae Medicae et Gemellologiae: Twin Research, 40* (2), 133-46.

Tremblay, Angelo, Despres, Jean-Pierre, & Bouchard, Claude. (1990). The response to long-term overfeeding in identical twins. *The New England Journal of Medicine, 322*, 1477-82.

Wallace, H., Patrick, K., Parcel, G., & Igoe, J. (Eds.) (1992). *Principles and Practices of Student Health*. (Vol. 3, 548). Oakland, California: Third Party Publishing Co.

Chapter 8

A Campus Peer Education and Counseling Line for Sexual Assault Prevention and Awareness

Kata Issari, MSW[1]

Editor's Note: Some programs such as this one combine a counseling service with peer education. Sexual Assault Prevention and Awareness Center (SAPAC) is also an example of a program that offers alternative peer helping options to those not accepted as peer educators or peer counselors.

Introduction

Years of work on the part of university students, staff, faculty, and community members spearheaded the implementation of anti-sexual assault programming on campus. A day-long sit-in staged by students in the office of a high-level university administrator was the catalyst for a series of events that led to the formation of SAPAC. This unique blend

---

[1] The University of Michigan Sexual Assault Prevention and Awareness Center opened in 1986. Many people have contributed to the design and development of SAPAC peer programs, among them Pam Kisch, Audrey Haberman, Maria Caballero-Valiente, Mary Bejian, David Lovinger, Julie Steiner, and, currently, Deborah Cain and Joyce Wright.

of students and administrators, community and campus, activists and academicians together planned what would grow into the largest campus-based sexual assault center in the country. SAPAC services and staff have historically been committed to providing assistance to the entire university community, with special attention to the needs and role of students.

> *Peer H:* I like the name of SAPAC, the Sexual Assault Prevention and Awareness Center. I think awareness is one of its big focuses. And that means putting on programs with the purpose of educating people, educating the community about issues involving sexual assault, sexual harassment, adult incest survivors, domestic violence, emotional abuse, and any of those sorts of issues. So that's one of the purposes: educating the community.

SAPAC's roots began with student activism, and SAPAC's programming has always sought to remain responsive to the experiences of student life. As a result, many of SAPAC's services are built upon peer involvement. The following discussion will describe two of SAPAC's largest peer programs, the Counseling Line and the Peer Educator Program. After a general overview of SAPAC philosophy and services, the common elements of the two programs are presented, followed by a discussion of the unique components of each.

The SAPAC Philosophy

The success of SAPAC over the years is due to many factors and many people, but its roots can be found in a philosophy that stresses the importance of comprehensive anti-sexual assault services with a grass roots, peer volunteer base. The mission of SAPAC is to work toward the eradication of sexual and physical violence on campus while working with the community to achieve a world where violence is no longer a reality. There are three areas of service at SAPAC: education/training, clinical safety, and physical safety. Each area employs professional staff, paraprofessional staff, and peer volunteers.

The SAPAC philosophy asserts that violence against women is the most extreme form of sexism, stemming from a culture that promotes physical and sexual violence. Sexual and physical violence are interconnected with other forms of oppression, so in order to end one form of sexism and its consequences, we must also work against other forms of oppression such as racism, classism, homophobia, anti-semitism, and ableism.

> *Peer E*: I've found that I'm not where I thought I was on the issues. I thought I was a lot more open-minded than I am and it made me realize where I stand in society. Like, I'm white, upper-middle class and my religion is not an oppressed religion. There's one woman in the group who's the complete opposite; everything that I'm privileged with, she's not. I never realized how lucky I was in the way I was treated.

Given that most sexual/physical violence is perpetrated by someone known to the survivor, SAPAC's primary focus is on acquaintance or "date" rape, sexual harassment, and battering. Survivors of sexual assault are not to be blamed for the violence that they have experienced. To end such violence, SAPAC works to establish an environment that facilitates the empowerment of survivors while challenging all forms of oppression and thus working to be culturally accessible to all. A key component of the SAPAC philosophy is that women and men must work together to eradicate sexual/physical violence and that such work necessitates approaches on many levels—education, clinical intervention, and safety services.

> *Peer H*: I've been really impressed with the extent of people's survival skills and the extent to which people really work hard to survive, even though they are hurting and going through really traumatic things.

At the heart of the SAPAC philosophy is a commitment to remain responsive to the needs of constituents while keeping violence against women issues visible on campus in a way that enhances university members' educational experiences. This mindset fosters an approach to service provision, which relies heavily on the involvement of peer volunteers. Peer involvement is crucial to the mission for several reasons. First of all, volunteer involvement is an extremely effective way to educate the community and promote awareness, both through the experience of volunteering as well as by volunteers talking with their peers about what they have learned.

> *Peer H*: When people know that I've been on the SAPAC phone line, that always makes them feel really comfortable talking to me. People say, "Yeah, I've heard you're on the line." And then maybe they'll say, "I'd like to talk to you about these issues sometime." So I think maybe that's changed my relationship with people, just people being aware of this work I do.

Secondly, this network of volunteers develops a broad base of support for SAPAC while also creating a community of people who can work together around issues of common concern. Third, service provision through peer volunteers helps to keep SAPAC in active communication with the constituency it serves. A large pool of volunteers allows SAPAC to accomplish extensive work on campus while—more importantly—ensuring that the quality and content of that work is directly accessible to all interested students.

Perhaps most significant of all is the personal growth volunteers experience as a result of their participating in SAPAC's peer programs. As with the other peer programs already described in this volume, SAPAC peer volunteers report that this work provides them with opportunities to learn in a holistic manner that enhances their educational experience and deeply impacts their life in many lasting ways. Over the years, SAPAC has worked with 1300-1500 volunteers, many of whom have continued their involvement with these issues in various capacities throughout the country.

> *Peer B*: It has affected my career plans in that I'm going to be a sociology professor and I already have a contract to teach at a university when I get my PhD, and I'm aware that at the university where I'm going there's no peer counseling and nowhere for people who have been sexually assaulted to go; so I've definitely been planning on doing that when I teach at a college. I've already talked to administrators there about that.

An Overview of Services

The largest of SAPAC's areas of service is the education program, which seeks to raise awareness on campus about the issues of sexual and physical violence while sensitizing the community to the needs of survivors of violence. These goals are accomplished in three ways:

1. professional training of service providers on campus (such as police, medical personnel, residence hall staff)
2. educational materials and campus-wide consciousness-raising activities, such as Rape Prevention Month and Sexual Assault Awareness Month[2]
3. educational workshops on sexual assault and related issues conducted by peer volunteers

Two volunteer groups work with the education program:

1. General Volunteer Program (GVP), forty to fifty volunteers who help with publicity, planning and implementation of the campus-wide events
2. Peer Educator (PE) Program, forty volunteers who conduct the educational workshops.

---

[2] Film series, guest speakers, and other special events are offered at these times.

More than six thousand people a year participate in or receive some kind of education from SAPAC.

> *Peer L*: I guess being more aware of what constitutes sexual assault and what doesn't and knowing where I was uncomfortable in situations just made me understand that it's really a problem that affects everyone. It can affect you and your friends and I guess I'm just surprised at how many people I know that it has affected, including myself.

The second component of SAPAC services, the clinical program, is designed to provide support, counseling, and advocacy services to members of the university community whose lives have been touched by sexual or physical violence. A professional counseling staff provides short- to medium-term therapy (individual and group) and advocacy to survivors of sexual/physical violence as well as to their family/friends. One aspect of the SAPAC clinical program is the Sexual Assault Counseling Line (CL). The CL is an evening and weekend phone line that operates during the academic year to provide phone support and emergency intervention to those who have experienced sexual or physical violence. The Counseling Line is also available to others who would like to talk about the impact of sexual or physical violence in their lives.

> *Peer C*: There are mainly two types of callers. One is controlled, like, "This happened to me and it's really upsetting me and this is what I think is going on." And the other one is just like, "Oh my god!" and they're really active and high pressure, real emotional. My first call was very controlled and it was really good because I could identify with this person and they got off the phone and they said, "This is the best place I've ever called, and you're the only one who's really ever listened, and you've helped me more than counseling ever has." And it was so nice to get this feedback from a caller.

This phone line is also available to friends or partners of survivors or anyone who needs some support around these issues. The Counseling Line is staffed by thirty-five volunteers who are available to answer the phone or to go to hospitals, police stations, or residence halls to provide face-to-face assistance immediately after an assault. Clinical services are provided to four or five hundred people a year by SAPAC staff and volunteers.

> *Peer J*: I've also realized that people who have been victimized are not necessarily weak; like, quite the contrary, these people are extremely strong with what they go through.

The safety component of SAPAC services includes:

1. coordinating physical safety concerns with the appropriate departments on campus
2. advocating on behalf of university members who have concerns about physical safety issues on campus
3. providing a night-time walking service for any individual who requests accompaniment within a twenty-minute radius of campus. This walking service, known as SAFEwalk/Northwalk, is a joint program of SAPAC and the university police department. SAFEwalk/Northwalk is run by four paid student coordinators and staffed by 250 volunteers. Safety services are provided to more than three thousand people a year.

The Counseling Line and Peer Educator Programs: Common Elements

SAPAC volunteer programs have fairly parallel operating structures. All require prospective volunteers to go through both an application process and an initial training. All programs maintain regular contact with their volunteers in order to provide information, supervision, on-going training, and evaluation and to involve volunteers in the development of SAPAC programs.

> *Peer C*: Peer education is preventative. The peer eds. go out and talk to people about making themselves aware of behaviors that are potentially sexist or harassing or scary to women. They're more in an educational type field. The peer counseling we do is more curative, to be there to let people who've been assaulted know that they have a voice and that someone is listening and that they're not a victim—but rather a survivor. We let them know that they're strong and that what happened was not their fault.

SAPAC volunteer programs value the experience and input of peers; peers are involved in as many aspects of SAPAC services as possible. In this spirit, "volunteer appreciation" events are held on a regular basis. In sum, all the volunteer peer programs seek to enhance the students' educational experience by fostering skill development, personal growth, and societal awareness. Peer helpers at all levels are encouraged to use their time at SAPAC as an opportunity to nurture their own development.

> *Peer C*: But there's just something I think that comes across from me that they can tell that I genuinely listen to others, that they have confidentiality with me. But, while I've always been really good at helping other people's problems, when it comes to my problems, I sometimes seem to hit a blank wall. So now I say to myself when I have a problem: "Now what would I say to somebody else needing help right now?"

The PE and CL programs are the most extensive of all the SAPAC peer activities. Peers in these programs go through a rigorous selection process and intensive training; they participate in demanding work—all with highly rewarding results. Both programs ask peer volunteers to make an eight-month commitment of ten to fifteen hours a month—although volunteers often devote considerably more time. Both programs recruit peers at the end of one academic year for involvement in the following academic year. When SA-PAC recruits for the CL and PE programs, information is advertised and distributed throughout the campus. Publicity takes place through advertisements in the campus newspaper, flyers posted around campus, public service announcements on radio and cable access television, letters sent to university and community organizations and by word of mouth. Current PE and CL volunteers visit classes and student groups to speak about their volunteer experience in hope of encouraging their peers to apply. They do a special presentation to the peer counseling class each semester (see chapter 3).

Each year about one-third to one-half of the PE and CL volunteers leave the program; this is mostly due to graduation, scheduling conflicts with academic programs, or a need to work more paid hours to support their educations. This means fifteen to twenty new volunteers are recruited for each program annually out of about seventy-five applications received per program. The selection process involves several steps, including an application and at least one interview conducted by the peers themselves. Once the final applicants have been selected, they are invited to an orientation meeting during the last week of classes in which returning peer volunteers have a chance to meet new incoming peers. During this orientation meeting, expectations of peer volunteers are reviewed and fall training is discussed.

The goals of the initial training for the CL and PE programs are many:

- To communicate the facts about sexual and physical violence
- To raise volunteer awareness about the role of sexism in perpetuating such violence
- To facilitate awareness of other forms of oppression and how these intersect with violence against women
- To promote sensitivity about the experiences of survivors in their healing from sexual or physical violence

- To communicate developmental issues of college-aged students as it impacts their work
- To teach the facilitation or counseling skills requisite for their work
- To build a sense of community among the volunteers
- To encourage personal reflection and growth
- To familiarize peer volunteers with their roles and responsibilities
- To acquaint volunteers with current SAPAC staff and SAPAC's history
- To continue the screening of prospective volunteers

Training

Training for the CL and PE programs is similar in format, but most of it takes place separately. Training sessions for both total forty to forty-five hours, each spanning evenings and weekends during the first weeks of the academic year. Most of the training segments are conducted by SAPAC staff, but sometimes returning volunteers or campus experts serve as guest speakers. A variety of techniques are employed throughout the training sessions—with a heavy emphasis on group participation, dialogue, skill development, and personal growth. Volunteers in both programs are continually encouraged to be alert to the ways in which training affects them on a personal level and to get support if they find themselves having difficulty.

> *Peer D*: It's been a bigger time commitment than I anticipated, particularly because if you have a beeper shift, you're supposed to be able to take the call from wherever you are, but in reality there aren't that many places that I would feel comfortable doing that, so I've spent a lot of extra duty sitting in my office in case the phone rings.

Peer H: I don't think that my involvement with SAPAC increased my interest in my original plan to go to graduate school in Social Work. If anything, my involvement probably should have warned me that I shouldn't go into social work because I could never do it full-time. And after even like an hour conversation with someone, I'm just totally wiped out. And so, I can't imagine doing that even twenty hours a week much less forty hours a week.

Since training is quite exhausting, attention to self-care is stressed repeatedly.

Although the specifics of training differ for the two programs, there are core elements that the two have in common, as follows:

- statistical information about sexual/physical violence
- rape laws and definitions
- discussions of sexism and rape culture
- anti-racism workshop
- anti-homophobia workshop
- how to get and give feedback
- the impact of violence on the survivor
- the healing process for survivors
- procedural and policy information
- domestic violence
- roleplays

Each volunteer is given a training manual that supplements the information they receive during training. They are expected to read the manual throughout training. The CL and PE programs have different manuals, but each covers the core topics outlined as follows:

- child sexual assault
- sexual harassment
- group facilitation skills
- peer counseling skills

- the criminal justice system
- the medical system
- alcohol and sexual assault
- sexual assault and people with disabilities
- cross-cultural issues
- relevant bibliographical examples

> *Peer K:* This program showed me that a lot of people were at different stages in their mental development about issues pertaining to rape or sex, gender, sexuality, all these issues. You kind of forget that other people aren't thinking the same way as you are. And in an organization, where you kind of expect to have this homogeneous group of people, you don't. And that's a great thing!

Volunteer response to the training sessions is a crucial element of the process. Every volunteer is asked to complete a written evaluation of each portion of training; feedback is continually elicited from the trainees throughout the year. The input of CL and PE volunteers throughout the initial forty hours and beyond helps to shape each subsequent year's training. In addition to communicating information and promoting group bonding, training serves an important purpose in that it sets a tone for the year. Themes are introduced during these initial forty hours that are reiterated as the year progresses. Training establishes the values of self-care, feedback, teamwork, dialogue, learning as an on-going process, and peer volunteer input as the foundation of successful CL and PE programs.

In addition to the initial training, both CL and PE programs conduct bimonthly mandatory "in-service" meetings in which on-going training continues. Thirty minutes of these two-hour meetings are typically spent with updates on current activities and with volunteers discussing the progress of their work. This is the time to exchange information and give and get support to and from one another. The remaining ninety minutes focus on a specific topic, often with a workshop or presentation by a guest speaker. Topics have included in-depth learning around anti-oppression issues, learning new skills or workshop formats, HIV/AIDS education in relation to sexual assault, sexual assault as regards people with disabilities, and the experiences of male survivors.

At the beginning of the second semester, a one-day training session is held for CL and PE volunteers. These sessions take place separately but concurrently. The CL workers, for instance, receive more in-depth discussion on the impact of alcohol on sexual assault, along with other relevant workshops. The January training day is also an opportunity for each group to spend some concentrated time together—for further group-building after four months of work as volunteers.

> *Peer I*: One of the things they emphasize for the counselors at SAPAC is to take care of yourself so you can do your job better—to get enough sleep and do things that are good for yourself and also, if you're having a problem, get support for yourself. People tend not to want to get support for themselves. But I find that since I've been working here I do. If I have a difficult call, I call one of the women who works the line with me.

Neither CL or PE volunteers are compensated for their work monetarily or through class credit.[3] Sometimes individual students will conduct an independent study with a professor and are able to obtain class credit, but this is arranged on a case-by-case basis. Nevertheless, both CL and PE volunteers display a tremendous amount of loyalty and commitment to SAPAC programs.

> *Peer E*: I'm also a member of the crew team, so that's approximately six days a week practice. I'm very committed to that. and that's number one priority and school is second. But when I'm

---

[3] Many of the other programs in this volume do offer a modest salary or course credit to their peer helpers. Some, like SAPAC, depend on volunteers.

on a beeper shift and we have to go on an outreach, that's number one.

SAPAC peer facilitators actively engage in program development and give of themselves wholeheartedly on all their SAPAC projects. The immense contributions of time and energy give peer volunteers a sense of true pride and ownership of their programs. Many develop lasting ties with one another that endure over time. The five hundred-plus women and men who have participated in the CL and PE programs over the years have created a strong community, across the country and even around the world.

Peer O: Working for SAPAC was great for my schooling because I was majoring in psychology. I have always been doing too many things. When I started volunteering I was also working two jobs. I've always been conscious about how busy I was going to be, adding this to my schedule each term, especially when I was student teaching. I chose SAPAC first because it's such a wonderful program, I just love it. It always fits in my schedule because I made it fit time-wise.

The Counseling Line Program

When SAPAC's Sexual Assault Counseling Line first opened, it operated twenty-four hours a day, 365 days a year, and was staffed by twenty-five volunteers. Weeknight and weekend phone shifts were staffed by SAPAC CL workers, with overnight shifts staffed by the female phone workers of 76-GUIDE (see chapter 4). Hours of operation were eventually reduced to evenings and weekends primarily because it became too difficult to maintain a consistent group of volunteers who could cover all hours on the phone line. Although there was, and is, tremendous peer volunteer enthusiasm, coverage during holidays and semester breaks and over the summer months often fell to staff and proved to be too much of a strain—given already large workloads.

Peer H: I have limits. Before I thought that you should drop everything for everybody all the time. And I think that after doing it for a couple years, I've just realized that some days you just can't handle it and that's okay that you have limits. So that's one thing and I think that's important because you've got to take care of yourself. Peer helping has also taught me how I'd like to stay active with helping other people because I feel like I'm a person that can do that and that for the most part I have grown up really healthy and supported and I would like to provide that environment for other people. So, I feel an affirmation of a responsibility that I feel to help other people because of the advantages that I've had.

When the Counseling Line was first conceptualized, it was agreed that it would be only answered by women. Since most sexual assault survivors are women and since at least half of all survivors prefer to obtain support or counseling from another woman, it was important to have an all-female staff for the phone line. Male peer counselors through 76-GUIDE (see chapter 4) are available to talk to any caller who requests to speak to a man.

Currently, the CL operates from five a.m. to eight p.m. during the week and twenty-four hours on weekends. CL workers answer the phone in the SAPAC offices from five p.m. to eleven p.m. After eleven p.m. and during the day on weekends, the CL is either answered by the female phone workers of 76-GUIDE or by a CL worker through a beeper and answering service. The phone is forwarded to an answering service that answers calls by explaining that the caller has reached the Sexual Assault Counseling Line and asking the caller to hold while a counselor is paged. When the CL worker is paged, she calls the answering service (usually within five minutes) and the two calls are connected.

Peer I: Over the phone, it's about twelve to fifteen hours a month; we do it in three-hour shifts. That's time we spend in the office, sitting by the phone waiting for it to ring. We do one or two beeper shifts a month; either during the week or over a weekend we wear the beeper so when the office is closed and people call and are in need of immediate counseling then we are beeped and we take the call from our dorm room or from wherever we are. The educational in-services are mandatory, so we're required to go to those. So, I sort of view my role in two parts. One is a counselor, but I also feel like I'm being educated about the issues. And I'm also friends with the women in the group now because we've been working together so closely.

CL workers are also available twenty-four hours a day to provide emergency assistance to survivors of sexual assault at hospitals, police stations, or residence halls. Such a visit is called an "outreach." The Counseling Line averages forty calls per month and one outreach per month.

> *Peer B*: It's taught me how much people who seem to have it all together may really be hurting. One of the most common things I hear on the line is, "Nobody knows that there's anything wrong with me." This has given me a lot of insight into the ways that society makes women feel about themselves and how much people just really don't understand how sexism and sexual assault work together.

All CL volunteers are at least in their sophomore year of college, with the majority being juniors and seniors. About fifteen percent are graduate students with typical concentrations being law, medicine, social work, and psychology.

> *Peer F*: Well, I think it will help my career in the long run. I don't plan on going into counseling or social work or anything like that. But, I plan on going into medicine and this will help me listen to people in a more active way. I've learned that I can help people even though I don't necessarily have experience in what they've experienced. And I've really been

impressed at how people can come together and volunteer their time in this way to help others.

Two or three volunteers each year are community members or staff members of other units within the university. On the average, forty to fifty percent of CL volunteers work on the line for the duration of their tenure at the university, with some staying as many as four years.

> *Peer B*: One of the things that we often do with people on the line is ask them to problem-solve about how they're going to relax and relieve stress. I've often used relaxation techniques on myself. Because I'm a graduate student I get really stressed out with work. And I tell myself, "Okay, what am I going to do to make sure I get some sleep tonight?" Those kind of things I can help others with, too.

The clinical coordinating staff who are involved with the CL are the SAPAC counselor and the SAPAC counseling line coordinator. Training sessions and in-services are jointly conducted by the counselor and coordinator, with most of the day-to-day supervision provided by the coordinator. The counselor supervises the work of the coordinator and together they supervise the work of the CL volunteers. A SAPAC clinical staff person is always available, by beeper, to provide support and supervision to CL workers. In SAPAC vernacular this is called "backup." CL volunteers are required to page backup in certain situations such as if there are technical problems with the phones, if a caller is suicidal or homicidal, if there is evidence of current child abuse, if someone does not show up for their shift, or if an outreach is requested. CL workers also will call backup if they want to check their plan for a call, if they cannot answer a caller's question, or if they need to discuss how they feel about a call.

> *Peer C*: I've had like one or two phone calls where I've just gotten off and been shaking. And I didn't think that was in me. It just kind of let me know how I sometimes function in an emotionally pressurized situation. I didn't

realize how helpless I could feel sometimes. It's because I wanted to jump in and start rescuing people and you can't do that. You have to just let them make their own decisions and stuff. I got off the phone and had to call my backup. Which is sort of funny. Like I was thinking about it—like the reason we work on the line is because the supervisor can't possibly be on the phone twenty-four hours. And I get off an hour phone call and call her for an hour.

CL volunteers have frequent contact with the CL coordinator and counselor. Each phone call or client contact is recorded on a form, which the backup reads. The CL coordinator follows up with each caller to offer further assistance and counseling. The CL coordinator and counselor also often follow-up with CL workers to discuss how they felt about the call and to give them feedback.

> *Peer H*: Generally, the most frustrating thing is not knowing what happens to your clients. When you see a client weekly or monthly, you get a sense of their life and you get to stay with that person; whereas by the time someone picks up the phone to call a crisis line, the person may be pretty desperate. It's a bizarre thing to pick up the phone and talk to a stranger in a pretty heavy crisis, whether it's about something that happened fifteen years ago or fifteen minutes ago. The frustrating thing is that you can never get a followup; you never know what happened to that person. Chances that somebody would call back when you're on the line are very slim. You can follow a writeup with someone who's called a couple of times. You can say, "Okay, X called last week and then they called two weeks later" and then compare writeups. Our coordinators try to keep us up-to-date. But a lot of people just call and then never call back. The challenge is having to trust yourself that you did the best that you could do for that night and say,

"Okay, this person called. I hope I helped."
And then leave it at that and just trust that you
did help.

CL workers are encouraged to call or come by the office in between shifts to discuss general concerns, ask questions, or share success stories. Each semester every CL volunteer meets individually with the CL coordinator in order to set goals for the semester, evaluate their own progress on the CL, give feedback about the CL or SAPAC, get feedback from the backups, and generally discuss how the work is progressing. These sessions have proved an invaluable time to provide support and conduct supervision around in-depth issues.

> *Peer K*: Basically the coordinators are your backup supervisors in case you have any problems dealing with a caller or when we go on outreaches, which means we would go and meet a survivor at the hospital or police station. Backup would be there to check in with if you're having problems, if you have questions, or even if you're scared. They review any transaction that has happened between a peer counselor and a client to make sure things are running smoothly. And they also do the training. So that's their main three roles.

The selection process for applicants to the Counseling Line involves three stages. The first is the written application. Once the application has been turned in, all applicants must participate in a group interview. These interviews consist of six to eight applicants who participate in several group exercises while observed by three to four current CL peer volunteers and SAPAC staff. The applicants are given instructions for each exercise, then told that they may not interact with the observers again until the end of the interview. The first task requires each applicant to explain why he/she wants to volunteer on the Counseling Line. Next, they are given a sheet of paper that lists ten possible "causes" of sexual assault (e.g., poor lighting, communication, violence in the media, sexism in advertising, racism, alcohol and other drugs) and they are asked to reach group consensus about the four most prevalent causes. Clearly there is no "right" answer here; it is, however, useful in observing the applicants' attitudes and knowledge base around sexual assault issues.

Participants are next given a scenario of a crisis call on the Counseling Line and asked to agree, as a group, how they would respond to this call if they were the phone worker. This scenario has become known as "the call from hell" among current CL workers, because it is a compilation of extremely difficult aspects of sexual assault phone counseling. Again, the purpose of this exercise is to ascertain the applicant's knowledge base and personal reactions to challenging crisis calls. The interview exercises conclude by asking participants to give feedback about the experience and to discuss what they will do after the interview to relax.

Observers have gone through a training before the interviews begin; this teaches them how to conduct the interview and what to look for in applicants. Once the exercises have begun, observers often act as time-keepers and quietly move around during the session in order to access the group from different vantage points. Each observer completes a standard rating and comment sheet on each applicant. These rating sheets are turned into the CL coordinator, who compiles them for use in screening out some applicants at this stage.

The third stage of the process involves an individual interview with the CL coordinator and counselor. The applicant pool is cut by fifty percent after the first interview; thirty to forty women are typically interviewed for the second round. This interview lasts about thirty minutes. The applicant is asked to discuss what she has to offer to the CL and what she hopes to gain from the experience of volunteering. She is asked to describe a crisis situation that she has experienced and what it is like for her. She is given a scenario of a situation involving police and hospital personnel and asked to explain how she would respond. Finally, she is asked to participate in two roleplays with the interviewers. These role plays are actual situations that come up on the CL.

After the second round of interviews, the CL coordinator and counselor assess all the ratings of the remaining thirty or so applicants in order to select the required number of volunteers. Applicants who are not selected are encouraged to participate in the General Volunteer Program and to try again next year.[4] Both those who are selected and those who are not are given careful feedback about their strengths and weaknesses during the interview process. This feedback is given in the hope of making the interview a constructive learning experience for all applicants, regardless of the outcome. This is a time-consuming process but has proved to provide an extremely accurate assessment of a student's ability to function successfully on the CL. Consistently, strengths and weaknesses of students noted during the interview process have successfully identified the areas in which they either excel or need extra support in developing new skills.

> *Peer M*: I was told by the supervisor that I have a tendency to get right to the heart of the matter instead of listening. It has helped my listening skills a lot. I had wanted to just cut through, you know, right to the quick. It's taught me a lot about myself. Although I knew some of it, I had to face that I was rather inflexible in my thinking. Most of the people that I talked to on the crisis line are a lot younger than me, and sometimes I wanted to take the mother role. I talked to a coordinator at SAPAC about my wanting to do that, and she helped me.

Counseling Line training begins the day before classes commence in the fall of the academic year. Training sessions are held two evenings a week and at least one weekend day for two-and-a-half weeks. New CL workers are required to attend all training sessions; returning workers are invited to all sessions, but only a portion are mandatory for them.

> *Peer F*: After I had successfully interviewed for the peer counseling line, we went through a forty-hour training period within two weeks in the beginning of the term. We went over basic information about statistics on rape, sexual assault, what the laws are, policies and

---

[4] See Editor's Note on the first page of this chapter.

procedures of the counseling line regarding interactions with clients, police, hospital interactions, stuff like that. They mostly guide us through what we should not say and what we should say. But they don't set down rules of, "Well, if this happens, then you do A; if this happens, then you do B." But they give us general guidelines. And they provide backup support for us at all times.

During training, only returning CL workers wear beepers in order to be available to do outreaches, since the CL does not begin full operation until training is over.

Peer B: In my role as a graduate student, sometimes my responsibilities clash. When I need to get something done in school, I have to put in my hours. But usually the confidence and positive feelings I get from working at SAPAC are carried over into my work as a graduate student.

In addition to the core elements of training outlined above, CL workers receive extensive information about peer counseling skills such as empathy and problem-solving as well as crisis and suicide intervention and preserving confidentiality.

Peer G: I have a boyfriend with whom I am close and I couldn't talk to him about my difficult call because it was confidential. I had this sense that he would never understand what this woman on the phone had been through or what I had been through. I sort of felt very apart from him and started to realize that there were a lot of ways in which life was different for me, that life was different for women and men, that he didn't really know what I meant when I was talking about issues about rape. It affected my relationship. I think the reason that what we do works at SAPAC is because we really have women who have been through a lot and other women who maybe haven't been raped but who have been well trained in listening skills and can understand. I think it's really hard to understand stuff if it's unlikely that it's going to happen to you. So I kind of developed more appreciation for family and friends—my own support system.

A considerable amount of time is spent doing roleplays to practice and develop these skills, including several times when the trainers (the CL coordinator and counselor) model roleplays for the group. Many discussions take place during training about the importance of self-care.

Peer G: I feel like I could always do more. I mean, you can always get more involved. There's a lot of times when the callers will try to get you to take care of them, and I resist doing that a lot. And whenever I resist that, I wonder, "Am I resisting rescuing them or am I being a drag? Am I being empathic or am I trying to take care of myself?" Survivors of sexual assault a lot of times can be very demanding and it's hard to keep boundaries. One of the things that's interesting is that I get these calls in which people basically tell me, "I was traumatized in this way," and it's a horrible thing. And they tell you these stories how they feel that they have no worth as human beings and they deserved the trauma. My role is to say, "I understand that you feel that way, but it sounds to me like you're a woman with a lot of courage." One of the things that I've realized about myself is that it's a lot easier for me to do that with other people than for myself. You know, I really believe it about other people too. And it's actually not that hard for me to hear support from other people about myself, but it's really hard for me to believe it. That's become more and more clear to me as time has gone on.

The direct impact of self-care on the effectiveness of their work as peer counselors is stressed repeatedly. Many ice-breakers are incorporated into training to give the volunteers an opportunity to relax together and to get to know each other. Ice-breakers include childhood favorites such as the Hokey-Pokey or relaxation exercises, or each person is asked to share something good that has happened to her since the last training session. Over the course of training and the year, CL workers often make jokes about how these opening or closing activities feel a little silly; nonetheless they serve an important role in group bonding—even if they all bond over how silly they are!

> *Peer K*: It's a very close group. Since you've trained for forty hours with people, you get to know them really well. And, it's all women—we only have women on the counseling line, although we do have men volunteers in other areas. We have in our group about twenty-five different women. Even though it's a big group, you feel pretty close to all of them because there are really intense emotional issues and you do a lot of really good, positive work.

A variety of techniques are employed throughout the training to relay information, though lecturing to the volunteers is avoided as much as possible. Trainers use "brainstorms," small-group discussions, and written exercises to vary learning methods while promoting as much participation as possible. The first day of training, CL workers are asked to generate a list of fears and expectations about working on the phone line. It has been very effective to identify these fears and expectations at the onset of training. Often volunteers are nervous about the responsibility of providing someone in crisis with peer counseling. They typically report that they are afraid they will not be able to help someone, that they will not know what to say, that a caller will hang up on them or that the caller will be suicidal. It is constructive to articulate these fears and for peer volunteers to hear that they are not alone in experiencing them. It also helps to have those fears validated by the trainers and returning workers.

Peer H: As a counselor I've changed a little bit. I'm a little more proactive in my counseling, trying to help people problem-solve a little bit more than just being a listener. I'm a listener, too. The people that talk to me don't even know who I am, and I find being a sort of nameless support a good role for me. That's sort of my role, being that nameless support that helps keep SAPAC running. It needs people to be there, putting in their time and their care about the program and about the people that call. I think as you go through the program, your first year you spend being really scared—"Oh my god, will the phone ring?"—and you're so afraid. And then after you've been in the program for a while, the phone rings and you know you can handle it and so you start to expand your role a little bit more, take on more responsibility.

This exercise provides an opportunity for returning workers to share their experiences and insights into the learning process that allowed them to overcome similar fears. Once these lists have been discussed, each worker is asked to write on a piece of paper their strengths and goals for training. This paper is put into an envelope and sealed. No one sees it but the individual worker. The envelopes are returned to them at the end of the training as a tool to assess their growth.

Peer E: It is challenging not to impress my opinion and beliefs on a caller. Like if they're saying, "I feel really frustrated about my boyfriend who can't understand how I feel about women's issues," it's hard for me not to say, "Well, you should dump him!" and just let them work it through themselves. It's hard to separate my beliefs from theirs, but I can do it.

Throughout training, all discussions are connected with issues of oppression. Racism, homophobia, and other oppression issues are not just discussed in those particular portions of training. Every issue presented is correlated with the impact of discrimination. In discussions of the legal and medical system, for example, the inherent racism of some of these institutions is identified.

> *Peer A*: We deal with a lot of really tough issues that are very difficult for people, including racism, sexual orientation, religion, that type of thing—they're difficult things that people don't deal with on a day-to-day basis, and those things have definitely brought us together as well as pointed out our differences.

> *Peer K*: I got called out on an outreach to the hospital and there was a survivor of sexual assault. Two of us go in a team, and the woman I went with chose to be with the survivor in the examining room. My job was to talk with the hospital personnel to make sure that the right thing was happening to this woman, to make sure that she wasn't being asked questions like, "What kind of clothes were you wearing?" or other victim-blaming questions like, "Did you provoke this? What did you do?" We also were checking on the hospital systems to make sure the woman was not waiting in there for three hours for somebody, feeling scared and alone.

In discussion of peer counseling techniques, the importance of being respectful of cultural difference in communication style is stressed. CL workers are taught to identify the ways in which they may promote racist or homophobic or sexist behavior in their peer counseling, and they are encouraged to change such behavior. CL volunteers who are themselves from non-dominant groups often share their experiences of prejudice—sometimes experienced within the CL group—which provides an excellent opportunity to stimulate both personal and group growth. Trainers challenge CL workers to think about the barriers to service that may be present for people of color, lesbians/gay men/bisexuals, people with disabilities, or other people from non-majority backgrounds. As a group, the CL volunteers work with the trainers to identify the strategies for providing successful service to people from these and other non-dominant groups. Throughout the academic year these issues are further explored during the course of in-service training sessions.

> *Peer A*: I found out about this as kind of a fluke and filled out the application for it and now I think this is the most rewarding, strengthening, empowering experience that I have ever experienced in my life. I've learned so much and I feel that I'm open to learning more. I think that I felt, when I first came to this university, by the end of my freshman year I was sick of hearing about issues of racism because I felt they were playing it to death and, "Hey, I'm aware." And I think that this has really changed my views on that. Now I think, "Okay, I'm aware, but there's still a lot of growing that I need to do." SAPAC has definitely put me on that road and has definitely helped me out with that.

Although CL workers provide an invaluable service to SAPAC by staffing the phone line, it is sometimes difficult for them to believe that they are making a contribution because the phone does not ring that often. Given that we receive an average of forty calls a month, many workers can go an entire shift and not receive a call. This tends to raise anxiety about how effective they will be once they finally receive a call—especially if that call occurs long after training.

> *Peer J*: "Wow! I got my first call!" It went really well; it's sort of a strange tension with the work. You feel great when you've gotten a call and it went really well, and then you realize, well, it's awful what this woman went through or what this man went through. [Interviewer responds: "I see what you're saying about the mixed emotion, kind of. You want someone to call, but you ultimately hope that no one will have to call."][5]

As with most peer activities, the CL workers realize that the best way for them to develop expertise as peer counselors is to have a chance to actually do the work. It can be frustrating when opportunities to peer counsel are not present as often as CL workers would like. To help alleviate this difficulty, the SAPAC staff continually remind them that their mere presence on the Counseling Line is what allows it to remain open. Cases are also discussed during in-services, so that all workers may learn from the calls that come. The CL workers have a log book in which to record all calls and keep a copy of each client contact form. They are requested to read each form, and many of them spend quite a bit of time studying these forms. They are also provided with opportunities to do roleplays throughout the year.

> *Peer F*: My role basically is to answer the phone line whenever there's a call. I'm there about ten or fifteen hours a month; I show up, just whenever I'm scheduled, and I take phone calls. Most of the time it just involves listening to people and telling them that what happened was not their fault, that they didn't deserve an assault, and offering them referrals if they need it for domestic violence therapists—anything needed to provide support for the caller.

In the last few years, SAPAC has been exploring ways that CL workers can be involved in other client support work. Workers have been trained to accompany clients to court when the need arises or to be ready to sit in with clients when they make police reports in the SAPAC office.

> *Peer D*: We also do outreaches in which we go on-site to someone who's been assaulted. Sometimes the officer calls and says someone needs support or someone to tell them what's going to be happening to them if they have to go to the hospital. Somebody who's familiar

---

[5] This exchange exemplifies the work of the peer interviewers on our research team and the empathic connections they made with those they interviewed across programs in this volume.

with the procedures tells the survivor exactly what's happening, and that is a comfort to them.

The hope is that SAPAC can continue to develop mechanisms that will respond to the enthusiasm and energy of CL workers' commitment to this work—without overtaxing the staff or the workers themselves.

Peer B: I had to go to court with an incest survivor and that was really challenging because I wasn't there as a witness; I was just there to support her. And I really didn't know what to expect even though I'd been fully briefed ahead of time and told that was the only thing I needed to do. It was really challenging to know here the line was between being supportive of her and telling her what to say or what to do because she kept asking me, "Should I have said that? Should I have done that?" And that wasn't really my role. It was a very emotional case but I had to stay detached so I could be supportive of her. That experience is the one that always comes to mind because at first I wasn't sure how much help I would be to her because most of the time I just sat next to her and held her hand while other people testified. But at the end she said, "I don't think I could have gone through it without you." And she also had lots of relatives there, her mother and aunts and uncles, and at the end, when it was all over, she wanted to talk to me privately about how it went. It was really rewarding that she felt that close to me. It's probably the best thing that I've done since I've been at college. I've learned so much about what it means to be a woman in America, as well as how these experiences happen to so many people, that it's not an isolated thing. I've just gained a lot of confidence in my abilities to really help.

The Peer Educator Program

Since the philosophy of SAPAC is that women and men must work together to address sexual and physical violence, the group of Peer Educators (PEs) is evenly composed of women and men. In co-ed teams, the PEs present workshops on acquaintance rape and other issues. It is believed that an audience's learning process is more dynamic when women and men hear from each other about these issues, so SAPAC prefers also to present to co-ed audiences. A female-male facilitation team offers an opportunity to model constructive anti-sexist behavior.

The PE program is supervised by two co-coordinators who are students—one female and one male, former Peer Educators—who work fifteen hours a week. They are in turn supervised by the SAPAC Director, who oversees the entire education program. The co-coordinators are selected from the group of PE volunteers and stay in their position for a (twelve-month) year. In this way, there is an opportunity for many Peer Educators to learn from serving in a supervisory role.

> *Peer J*: It makes the university smaller. It allows me to get into all these places in people's lives that I probably would never see or otherwise be involved in and to talk to lots of people that I wouldn't necessarily talk to.

> *Peer L*: It gave me a group of peers that did things other than get drunk all the time. It was a different part of the university that I hadn't seen. So it was nice to see a different cross-section of the type of students here where I could fit in. There are people on the line who I met last year working there who are now my best friends. I just think they're such wonderful people. They're so caring and open and they've become such an integral part of my life. I can't imagine what it would be like if I didn't know them. I always feel guilty because I feel like I get far more out of this counseling line than I put into it.

The workshop that the Peer Educators present the most often is on acquaintance rape. This workshop is two hours long and designed for college-aged, mixed-gender audiences. It can be modified for the fifty-minute length of a typical class, for all-male or all-female audiences, or for high-school-aged students. This workshop has also recently been modified for presentations to athletic groups. When the audience is all male, the presenters are both men; when the audience is all female, the presenters are both women. Other workshops that the PE volunteers are trained to present are: Sexism Awareness, Sexism in the Media, Rape Culture, Alcohol and Sexual Assault, and What Men Can Do to Stop Rape.

> *Peer E*: During Sexual Assault Awareness Week there is a "speak-out," which is when sexual assault survivors stand up in front of a group of people and just tell their story or say whatever they want. They just basically speak out or they tell their story—anything like that. This goes on for about four hours and it is very moving. I think that helped me considerably in peer counseling because I was able to see people's feelings and see different ways people cope with being assaulted, like the "aftershock" and things like that. I saw a lot of different aspects of this that I had learned about in books but not seen—people who have been through things, who are willing to stand up and say, "This happened to me."

The basic Acquaintance Rape workshop covers myths and facts about sexual assault, the elements of acquaintance rape (such as force, sex-role stereotypes, communication gone awry), prevention, and precaution issues. Scenarios of fictional acquaintance rape situations are shown on video. Most of the discussion is in a large co-ed group. During one section of the workshop, the group is divided by gender to allow discussion that focuses on the unique concerns of women and men. The workshop uses brainstorming the scenarios and targeted questions as a way of stimulating discussion among the participants. It has consistently proven extremely effective for students to hear from their peers about these difficult issues, particularly gripping when facilitators disclose their own personal growth around awareness of sexism and sexual assault.

> *Peer D*: Being a volunteer at SAPAC has definitely helped me in my own feelings as a sexual assault survivor. And that was one of my primary motivations for doing it.

Although there are always those who are not willing to listen to the information with an open mind, audiences generally respond well to the sincere, enthusiastic facilitation of the Peer Educators.

The Peer Educator selection process is very similar to that of the Counseling Line, but there is only one group interview. The group interview for PE applicants is almost identical to the CL interview, but the PE applicants are asked to complete different exercises. They are presented with a scenario of seven characters and asked to rank these characters from best to worst. They are asked to discuss their viewpoints in order to reach consensus as a group. The scenario describes a situation in which a woman is sexually harassed by her teaching assistant and the reactions of the people around her.

Peer Educator training is also very similar to Counseling Line training. The major difference between the two is that the PE volunteers go on a weekend retreat. This retreat is the first weekend of the academic year, usually at an indoor/outdoor camp thirty miles from campus. They leave on a Friday afternoon and return on a Sunday evening. Training takes place for most of the time that they are at the retreat, with breaks for meals and time to relax. This retreat is an excellent mechanism for team-building. Living, learning, and working in such close proximity—even for a few days—fosters a strong group sense. Although many PE volunteers grumble about being "in the woods" for a weekend, they consistently value the time they spend at the retreat.

> *Peer L*: There's a huge peer network here. I call them my warm-fuzzy friends.

In addition to the core elements of training outlined above, PE training focuses on in-depth understanding of the various components of the acquaintance rape script, coupled with skill development. The variety of techniques used by trainers during sessions are also examples of facilitation methods the Peer Educators themselves can employ. PE volunteers are taught to use inclusive language and techniques such as avoiding calling on men or white people more than women or people of color.

> *Peer M*: There are a lot of people at SAPAC from all different parts of the world. You get to learn a lot about different cultures, backgrounds, and even how views of the issue of sexual assault is quite different, depending on the person's culture or background.

> *Peer N*: I think it's helped me to be more aware of the compassionate side of myself and be more understanding with people. I also think since I'm older than most of the volunteers that it has been a challenge to work with people who are younger, and I've become more comfortable in saying things that reflect my additional years.

Conclusion

The peer counseling and education programs are some of the most successful components of SAPAC. They provide valuable service to a university community and an invaluable learning opportunity for the students involved.

> *Peer F*: The most rewarding thing is just at the end of the call when people are saying, "Thanks a lot for helping me. You've really made a difference." I guess in my own mind, I know I'm doing something. And it's not just something frivolous, you know, and it does make a difference in people's lives. It's just rewarding to myself.

Those who receive education or counseling from the peer volunteers greatly benefit from both the service received as well as from the process of receiving that service from someone who is pretty much like themselves. The peer programs are also a rewarding and gratifying experience for SAPAC staff. Peer programs are an exciting means of keeping SAPAC responsive to the community and to constituents while promoting an enhanced educational experience.

> *Peer I*: The biggest thing I've learned is that people can help themselves more than they think they can. I've been amazed by people who have called the line and have just done all the talking and all I've done is said, "Uh-huh" and "I'm so sorry" and "You must feel really frustrated." And then they launch into their own problem-solving and then they say, "Oh thank you so much; you've helped me so much." And I think, "I didn't do anything. All I did was listen." That's really amazing to me. I mean, that's sort of the purpose and the philosophy behind the line—for people to find it in themselves to solve their own problems, and I find that that really works.

Working so extensively with peers allows us not only to respond to the demands of today, but also to build for the future in a fashion that can constructively change the fabric and nature of our society.

Academic Peer Advising Practicum

Chapter 9

An Academic Peer Advising Program in Psychology

Sherry Hatcher, PhD, and Kate Fodor, BA[1]

Why Peer Advising?

For well over two decades, peer advising programs have been steadily gaining momentum across the country, and the evidence of their positive effect on the academic community is clear. As Layman (1981) points out, academic instruction alone is insufficient to meet the range of university students' needs, yet providing academic advising can easily consume a faculty member's time and energy. Academic peer advising programs expand resources by conserving university finances as student advisors generally work either on a volunteer basis or in return for earning credits (Harrington, 1983; Butcher, 1982; Layman, 1981).

> *Peer A*: Sometimes it's very hard to get an appointment with psych concentration counselors, like around the time of registration. So we're kind of there to listen and see what it is that they need to know: if they want to declare their major, we help them declare; we

---

[1] The psychology peer advising program was initiated in 1991 by Professor Pat Gurin, Chair of the Psychology Department, along with Professor James Hilton, Undergraduate Chair; Professor Sherry Hatcher, who designed the practicum course; and Ms. Sandra Vallie, Student Services Associate in the Undergraduate Psychology Office.

go over requirements for them; let them know about grad school; provide focus groups for them to help them pursue possible careers and let them know what kinds of careers they can get with a psych major—just anything that has to do with psychology. We're there to help.

Peer R: Sometimes it's hard to go to a concentration advisor in fifteen minutes and say, "I'm really not sure. Is it psychology or history or anthropology that I want to study?" Concentration advisors probably have five other kids they're going to see that day, and they don't have time to really sit and talk with you. So I think I've learned that there's a lot that goes beyond just declaring a major or asking about classes; people really have a need to talk. The Peer Advising Practicum has really taught me that people's issues aren't really as cut and dry as they seem. If we were just to offer students the psychology requirements, they could read that from a sheet. I think it's taught me that people really need contact with other people. Even more, they need reassurance, especially at a large university. They need someone to say, "You're doing okay; you're right on track."

Also significant are the unique benefits to students provided by such programs. Studies by Zunker and Brown (1966) have all shown peer advising to be comparable in many respects to professional advising. While professional advising clearly offers great expertise, ease of communication with advisors of their own approximate age and position means that the students are frequently more open to advice and exchange of information in peer advising programs than in other advising situations (Zunker & Brown, 1966; Botvin, et al., 1990). In addition, peer advisors tend to be available, accessible, and flexible (Habley, 1979); the fact that they work only for short periods of time means that they maintain a high level of enthusiasm for their task (Layman, 1981).

Peer N: I thought I was a really good listener before, but I'm a lot better now. I think that peer advising has emphasized certain things that I really wanted to be as a person, qualities that I wanted to portray like openness and helpfulness. When someone leaves and they know that their questions are answered and they feel good about what I've explained to them and how I've listened to them, it makes me feel really good that I could do that.

Peer B: Being a peer advisor has taught me that people really are very affected by how they're treated. If you interact with them in a positive way, give them positive feedback and make them feel good about themselves; if you are friendly and open with them, they're likely going to be that way with you. I think that the more you bring out in people, the more positively you want to respond to them.

Peer Q: It woke me up to peer advising as a counseling option for people who are having problems. It's not deep psychotherapy, but it's helping. It's friends helping friends. And I think it would be something I would like to set up if I ever work at a university or a club, even a church. To have more peer advising situations is really a good idea. Equals helping equals sounds good to me.

It should be noted that peer advisors come away with more than resume experience and academic credit in return for their participation. Peer advisors tend to learn about themselves through their service to their fellow students (Layman, 1981); in fact, objective tests such as the MMPI given to groups of student counselors before and after their training sessions show significant constructive personality changes, particularly in the areas of empathy and genuineness (Martin & Carkhuff, 1968; Hatcher, et al., 1994). Advising work helps undergraduates to gain interpersonal and communication skills useful in their personal lives and professional careers (Frisz, 1984).

> *Peer G:* This was one of my only clinically-oriented kinds of experience. I've had several research experiences and I think it really combines well with those as far as helping me realize what kind of opportunities exist in psychology. I think it's made me more well-rounded in that I've researched people's problems but I've never before really faced them one-on-one. I think this was a good stepping stone to my career.

> *Peer Q:* Being a peer advisor has taught me not to try to impose my view of the world onto others; that even my way of thinking about things may be very foreign to them. That made me realize that you do have to be a very open listener, to let other people tell their story, in their own words, and then to try to listen to them in their narrative style. If you're only looking at facts, you lose emotional charge behind them. So, I think I've learned that people think differently than I do and they feel differently or may have different goals than I do. Some others were just completely lost, had Ds and Cs on their report cards, and were changing majors for the fifth time. Yet, somehow they stayed in school, and this was a new sort of experience for me. I realized that you also have to respect other people, and you are not there to change their life; you're there to give them the tools to help them change if they want to. I think that everyone's sort of really struggling to make sense out of the world, and no one's really being malicious; everyone just wants to make peace of heart. Just because they're doing something different than you doesn't mean that they're a bad person. One shouldn't stereotype them like that—someone who comes in dressed a certain way, with an

aerobics outfit with neon all over or with tattoos or jeans—just try to look beyond that stuff and respect what they've got to say.

Peer L: I plan to go into social work after I graduate. And it's definitely very helpful to be able to sit down and listen to other people with empathy. To have someone come in all troubled and confused and leave somewhat satisfied and the problem somewhat solved gives you a warm, fuzzy feeling.

Psychology is one of the largest majors at many universities. This means that advisors in the psychology concentration are in such constant demand that students must sometimes wait to obtain an appointment, and then can often not be spared as much time as all involved would like. It is very important, then, that a peer advising program be an effective one if it is to meet the need that has been evidenced for it—a need both to aid in the handling of practical concerns and to promote the peer advisor's position as a positive role model. This arrangement can enhance the learning process while fostering camaraderie and a sense of community among the students (Lynn, 1986; Horton, 1992).

Peer R: The idea is to try to be able to see other students alone in a non-threatening environment, where they can really express their concerns. I had a lot of people who were caught in the med-school quandary. By that I mean that their families want them to be a physician and they want to be a psychologist. One poor kid was saying, "I want to be a psych major. How can I tell my dad?" We want them to be able to feel like they can talk about stuff like that.

Peer M: I really liked being in a situation where I got to interact with a lot of other psychology majors who liked psychology a lot. And it was a small class, so we got to know each other and I feel like that's really the only class that I made close friends that I'm going to have for a long while. And I think it was one of the classes that challenged me the most.

The work done by the Psychology Peer Advising Practicum is unique in that it is one of the first academic peer advising services in the country to be connected with an academic course and to combine training in peer counseling skills with the content of academic advising. In these respects, the program can serve as a model and guide for the creation of similar programs in other departments and universities wherever the need for them is felt.

> *Peer D*: The Peer Advising Practicum provides an alternative place for students to get information academically, specifically about psychology. What ends up happening is Academic Counseling Services send a lot of people to us because we're not as busy. We don't just deal with the person's academics because we're also trained in peer facilitative skills. Because we don't usually have as much clientele waiting at the door as professors do, we're able to spend more time with the students talking about a range of things. Maybe they're frustrated about how their parents feel about their switching majors, and we take time to talk to them about that, if they want to.

An Overview of the Peer Advising Program

The services of the Psychology Department's peer advising program are offered to undergraduate students at the university who are concentrating in psychology or are interested in psychology as a concentration. The program provides academic information and offers psychology students an avenue through which to discuss issues about the psychology concentration and an opportunity to problem-solve around those issues.

> *Peer G*: I think the purpose is to offer an alternative form of help for psychology concentrators, not only about the requirements to get one's

degree, which is an important part of our program, but also to offer students assistance on thinking about career goals or graduate school or what opportunities there are in psychology.

A typical class of peer advisors consists of twenty-two junior and senior undergraduate students. Students undergo ten to twelve hours of initial training in both peer counseling skills with the professor who teaches that class and in concentration information with the administration of the undergraduate office. On-going weekly training consists of the two-hour class taught by the professor, a licensed clinical psychologist, and a weekly meeting, as well as on-site consultation with undergraduate office staff. In the words of one student trained as a peer advisor:

Peer T: The peer advisor is a supportive listener to the student and is also able to understand the concerns and emotions of the client, give answers when specific questions are asked, or guide the client to find answers for him/herself by asking open-ended questions. The peer advisor has knowledge of the psychology program, is exposed to a wide variety of information and agencies, and anticipates common concerns students may have about classes, program requirements, information about professors, etc. The advisor is not just someone with a lot of answers to questions but an empathic listener to the client.

Specifically, the peer advising program is equipped to provide information regarding concentration requirements for the Bachelor of Arts in psychology. Peer advisors also help identify classes that meet the specific interests of a particular student and point students in the direction of professors who share common research interests, classes that are offered (including independent study options and advanced lab courses), and how to use them to best fulfill the requirements of the psychology major or concentration. The program can also help a student to work successfully with the psychology department and the larger university system. Students may declare a psychology concentration through the peer advising program; because of the responsible "track record" of the peer advisors over four years, they are now able to sign concentration declaration forms for their clients.

> *Peer M*: Clients come in seeking help or they have questions about the psychology major and want to talk about some aspect of the psychology department. And they're either seen by two counselors or by one, depending on how many counselors are available at the time. The counselee describes the problem and the counselor and counselee work together to try and figure out how to solve the problem. You don't really give advice—you kind of tell people about the options they have and from there they can choose what they think is best. And a lot of times I found that all I was really doing was being a good listener. People would come in and say, "Here's what I want to do and here's what I think that I'm going to do." And all I had to do was say, "Yeah, you're on the right track," and that was enough. There wasn't really anything more than just saying, "Yeah, you are going to be able to graduate doing it this way" or whatever.

In addition, the program provides publications about graduate school, the psychology major, and careers in psychology; it also organizes on-going seminar-sized focus groups about the process of applying to graduate school and other topics of concern to psychology majors. Over the years the peer advisors have selected focus group topics that range widely across all of the areas of psychology and include guests from all seven areas of psychology: Developmental, Social, Clinical, Organizational, Cognition and Perception, Biopsychology, and Personality. For their work with the focus groups, several sessions of the Peer Advising Practicum are devoted to learning group-facilitation skills: how to begin and lead a meeting, how to deal with challenging participants, and so on.

Peer R: I really like the small focus groups because we could sit around and talk about graduate school plans. And for me, it served as a great source of information about preparing for graduate school. "When do I have to take this test? What is this test like?" We put together a bunch of focus groups that were just phenomenally helpful on the subject of graduate school and what you could do with an A.B. in psych. I know how to plan better now, instead of only having a vague idea that I want to go to graduate school. Now I know how to get there.

The Peer Advising Program is dedicated to the service of psychology students. Although the program has thus far been very successful, suggestions from students and data collected on the responses of those who have used the program's services are taken seriously. The program remains open to whatever change is necessary to best meet the needs of the department and its students.

Peer C: So in opening the peer advising office here, we hope to show that we care for students and we have time for them when we can actually sit down and work through different issues they have instead of kind of rushing them. It's not only the time; it's helping plan their careers, the classes they're taking, and it's also to show them the Psychology Department really cares about their students.

Selection and Training of Student Advisors

Student advisors are selected through a careful procedure of application and interview in order to ensure that the Peer Advising Practicum will function successfully and that high ethical and accountability standards are met. As is standard procedure in peer program selection, there is a re-evaluation of the suitability of each student for his or her role as an academic counselor once that student's training has been completed. This allows for an opportunity to allocate alternative roles (such as that of an academic tutor) to those who seem unsuited to counseling. It is rare in this program that a student does not meet his/her commitment to confidentiality, professional reliability, and academic rigor.

> *Peer G*: I'd like to emphasize what you can get out of this experience in finding out more about your own character. I think this was an asset of the program that not many people were really expecting. You find out a lot about your strengths and weaknesses in helping people or listening to others and communicating. It's really valuable not only helping people out but helping yourself out too.

Since the success of the Peer Advising Practicum hinges in part on the structure, organization, and implementation of its training sessions, these must be thorough, informative, and engaging. Early semester training sessions for the Psychology Department's Peer Advising Program consist of two six-hour sessions on consecutive weekends. The sessions consist variously of introductory exercises to promote an open and responsive atmosphere within the training group, six hours of information on course requirements and academic procedures (presented by the Administrative Head of the Undergraduate Psychology Office), and approximately six hours of peer facilitation skills (presented by a licensed clinical psychologist and instructor of the course on peer counseling skills). To teach peer counseling skills, roleplays are used as practice for learning empathy, feedback, and decision-making models and are then played back on videotape and discussed by the group as a whole. The content of the roleplays are adapted for academic advising issues and related concerns. In addition, students read and discuss journal articles, ethics guidelines, and crisis intervention materials. Throughout the semester they have ongoing readings, journal assignments, and research work in addition to their advising commitments. For their final American Psychological Association-style papers, students study the training, advisee evaluations, and a variety of other program evaluative subjects.

Peer C: We had the professor train us in peer counseling skills, and then the administrator from the undergraduate psych office trained us in different workings in the psychology department. So, it was a dichotomy of the psych concentration information and the peer counseling skills.

Peer P: We were prepared with two six-hour sessions; they were on consecutive weekends. They dealt with both our advising and the counseling skills, such as correct body position and attentive listening, and how to recognize underlying emotions and issues that people bring in. We also learned how to make referrals. We read two books, we studied a series of roleplays, and we watched an instructional video. We also heard advice to us on a tape from previous peer advisors, which helped.

Peer R: We talked about different models of listening, empathic listening. We went over decision making models. We talked a lot about being non-judgmental. And we focused on the philosophy of what we were trying to do, that we were trying to get students to really think about what they themselves wanted to do, what classes they'd be interested in taking, while at the same time acknowledging the pressures that were there: their parents, their friends, the myths that they might have heard. You know, parents say, "You can't be a psych major; you have to take these particular classes," or their friends say, "Oh that professor's bad; oh I had that class and it was awful." Or just the misconceptions: "Statistics is horrible; I will fail," that kind of thing. So we're basically informed about what we would be up against and then given tools to get around it, to listen, impart information, and, if possible, correct the myths.

Many of the trainees felt enthusiastic about these training methods:

> *Peer O*: The videotaping that we did actually helped, even though I didn't want to be videotaped at first. But it was still interesting to see everybody on the tape in training. We really got to see other people's work and that was pretty good for learning to read body language, too.
>
> *Peer M*: Those who had been a peer advisor before mentored new trainees. For example, one of us would pretend we were a student coming in to declare the psychology major and the other roleplayer would go through the steps with the student in order to make sure he/she wanted to be a psychology major; to help the student gear the major toward his/her own interests; and to explain it to the student so he/she would understand exactly what to do to achieve the major. We also had some people come in who were having a problem with their parents or maybe a roommate or somebody they cared about and we went over roleplays like that.
>
> *Peer R*: We were often in the office in pairs. It was great to have somebody to consult, to fall back on. That's another thing I learned, that if you don't know an answer, you shouldn't fake it. It would be dishonest and would hurt the person that you're advising. So you just have to say, "I don't know, but we can ask somebody else." Other peers served as great referral resources. Like one woman, Laurie, was an organizational psychology major, so if somebody was asking me about that degree, and I said, "Well, you know, Laurie is one, and you can make an appointment with her if you want." We referred both to professionals and to each other, as we too had our "specialties."

Benefits of Participation for Student Advisors

Student advisors register for this practicum and earn two credits for two hours per week of practicum work or three credits for four hours per week of practicum work. All students are required to attend the same number of classes and training sessions and to complete the academic papers required regardless of the number of credits being earned. Academic credit, however, seems to be only a part of the over-all benefit that peer advisors receive for their participation and hard work.

> *Peer D*: I think one of the things that is most exciting is the paper that we're required to do. Not only are we counselors who are actively dealing with the students as they come in, improving our own facilitative skills and learning more about the concentrations in psychology, but we're also writing a paper on the program. We're either taking information from the evaluations or suggesting something to further enhance the program. So each student has a direct involvement in how the program is going to continue and what changes will be made, which I think is really good. We're actually doing research on the program.

The personal benefits for those who participate as advisors in a peer program include increased perception of self-competence, clarification of identity issues, and more flexible personality constructs (Gruver, 1971). Farley and Akridge (1986) found that participants in peer counseling training show "significantly higher levels of basic interpersonal skills" than do members of a comparison group with no peer counseling training or experience.

> *Peer A*: I can see, when discussing problems with people, when they're impatient or when they just don't want to discuss something anymore around which issues their stubbornness may be. This practicum helped me to read people more and it helped me to see what issues are

difficult for people to talk about and how they feel. Sometimes I can see if they're saying something totally different from what their body language is saying.

Peer N: The Peer Advising Practicum has really helped me offer feedback to others in a more constructive way. It's helped me talk about my feelings in a less offensive or condescending way. I think I kind of forgot that, because I'm really friendly and because I really like to make people feel comfortable, there are times the way I give advice or the way I explain things is probably patronizing to others. This work has really forced me to look at the way I'm talking about what I know. When I don't know something, it's not a problem. Or when I'm feeling a little bit vague on a subject, I'll say, "Oh, I'm not sure about this." But if I really think I know something, I think that I just forget to look at the way I talk to people. And peer advising supervision has really helped me to look at that.

Peer P: Some clients who come in want an answer right away and want to have everything solved in ten minutes. I now realize that things don't get solved like that, that it's the hard work and the diligence that pays off, and that solves your problems. I think I've learned not to immediately jump in with examples from my own life because sometimes when a person's talking, they just need to be listened to. I guess I've also learned that giving advice and solving problems is not the solution; it's brainstorming options, not giving advice.

Peer Q: This work has allowed me to realize there's a way to solve problems in a more open-minded and less hurried way, looking at different options. Sometimes looking at new options is harder because it makes you aware of different choices. But it's worth it.

In several student studies generated by the peer advising group, a majority of advisors reported that they carried over many of the listening skills acquired through their training and counseling into their everyday interactions. Specifically, they reported that they were more able to listen well and help effectively when others had problems; that their attention to the speaker's content, affect, or both, had increased; and that they also felt more able to listen non-judgmentally and without offering advice. More than three-fourths of the group reported that the effect of their advising experience on their everyday interactions had been "significant" or that it had affected them "very much." Not one member of the groups studied reported no change at all (Horton, 1992).

> *Peer M*: I definitely think this work has benefited me because in the peer advising training, I learned a lot, <u>such as not to give advice.</u> When I forget, I try to make a joke of it by saying, "I'm going to tell you how to live your life." I've learned how to try and put myself in somebody else's position and how to state how I'm feeling. This has really changed my argumentative tendencies. I think that now whenever I have a disagreement with somebody, it gets resolved quicker whereas before it would just escalate and escalate because I was feeling angry or upset or hurt and I couldn't say that and so instead I would try to hurt the person back. I really liked doing the counseling. It made me feel sure I want to go on in psychology and I want to continue to help people.

An open-ended questionnaire administered to the peer advisors found that all respondents felt that their peer advising training and practice had increased their empathy levels both in their advising work and in their outside lives. Advisors also generally reported feeling that their experience as focus group leaders had translated into increased interpersonal effectiveness and self-confidence.

> *Peer C*: One of the most interesting questions I've come across is: Can you be taught empathy? Some people say you can. If you're an empathic person, you just always kind of run that way. One of the things you could ask is whether you felt more empathic after the training program you went through. I wanted to know if people really were empathic before and didn't know it or if they really learned to be empathic. I don't think it's an easy thing to understand what other people are feeling and try to identify with them. This is what I studied in my term paper.

> *Peer L*: Peer advising has taught me that other people have their own various and sundry problems too. If you sit down with them, most people are very rational and can figure out what to do with just a little prodding from the outside. Most people can learn how to help themselves, given the right atmosphere and environment.

> *Peer O*: I think it's definitely benefited me as far as listening skills go and as far as picking up people's body language. I can now tell when I'm talking to a friend, family member, or client what they're looking for from me, what kind of response they want, whether they want me to be quiet, whether they want me to jump in with lots of advice, or whether they just want to talk.

> *Peer J*: As a peer advisor you have to be patient and listen carefully because what our clients say and their underlying reasons for saying things aren't always the same thing. You have to listen for both their verbal and non-verbal messages.

> *Peer A*: Being a psychology peer advisor made me better able to listen and more able to read peoples' feelings. I try to get to the root of the

problem—what it is students actually want to talk about—instead of just blowing them off or taking whatever they say at face value when there's something more going on.

Peer G: This work has really made me focus on how difficult it is to be a good listener. I think I'm a much better listener now and pay better attention to people, exactly what they're saying—not only what they're saying, but the emotional undertone of that they're saying. It's also just improved my confidence in being able to help people, which is something I want to do in my career. It's a good feeling when you think that you're helping others and they're telling you that you are. It helps your self-esteem a lot.

Peer D: Interestingly, this work has helped me primarily in my close relationships with my parents, with my close friends, with boyfriends. Just learning how to listen more, learning how to be more open to where others are coming from comes directly from listening. Before I was still open but it was a little harder to hear, whereas now I take more of an active role in listening. And with conflict too, I'm more likely to listen even if the other person is really upset, I try to stay calm and see what they're really getting at, what they're really upset about and try to talk about that.

Peer N: I've never done any crisis intervention type stuff, but I think that certain people, some friends of mine, don't think academic counseling is as important or as fulfilling as crisis intervention counseling. And while it may seem more important to save someone from incredible emotional turmoil or help someone out of it, I think this is a really important thing that I am doing and I think it's changed me a lot. I don't think there's a whole lot of difference in what you learn, it's just a question of intensity.

Other peer advisors mentioned feeling more at home on campus, being more aware of issues of diversity, noticing how others use effective listening skills, and experiencing a greater appreciation for the differences among their peers.

Peer R: Being an academic peer advisor has made me feel like I fit more in the Psychology Department. It makes me feel all warm and cozy inside when I run into someone later on and they say, "You know, you really helped me in explaining the requirements to me." Because it's such a big university, I really feel like it's a self-serve education and so what we do kind of makes it a kinder, gentler university.

Peer N: I think coming to such a huge university, especially first and second year when you're taking huge classes, I've sometimes felt like people weren't friendly. It was really nice to have people come in and say, "Hey, how are you doing? I just have a couple questions." People just don't seem to do that stuff in class. And it's just really nice to find out that everyone's friendly and shares the same questions and concerns.

Peer I: I did notice in my coming from a very sheltered background that by doing peer advising I meet other people. Learning about and understanding problems that different people face, I've gained a greater understanding of my own life, the childhood things. I have learned about myself and my values by comparing mine to other peoples'.

Peer E: I think that I learned a lot about diversity. We had a lot of discussions about the needs of people of various backgrounds and cultures. When people come in, you have no idea what background they're coming from, what problems they're dealing with, and I think I'm now more aware of that. I don't assume or expect anyone to behave or respond in any certain way now. I'm just more open to a wide range of experiences.

Peer G: I think I've learned about others and learned about other people's circumstances—different problems, different financial and social problems that come about in their lives—that I haven't had to deal with. Or academic problems—a lot of people have troubles in school that I've never really experienced directly. So it's made me understand how traumatic that can be—not being sure about what you want to do or being frustrated with your performances. Also, I've learned about people who don't listen as well as they like to think they do. People like to talk, engage in conversations, but it's rare that they're really listening to what you're saying and responding to the emotional aspects of the conversation.

Peer Q: One guy who was very uncomfortable and felt pressured by his parents to major in business or medicine but who had interests in other areas was feeling unsure. I tried to convey to him that his feelings were natural, normal, understandable, and probably healthy. I didn't push that much, because I thought that I would probably push my own ideas on him too much. But I said, basically, "It can be unhealthy to make a decision too early if you're not ready to make it. You've got a couple years left. You can keep exploring and try to explain to your parents just how your feeling." Another client, a woman probably in her mid-fifties, came in and she has a son who's mentally ill. She's a teacher in a high school but she wants to go back to school in psychology for a Social Work degree. She told us about her experiences with bureaucracy and the stigma of having a child who is mentally ill. She was interested in coming back to school and interested in taking classes. So it was very rewarding to try to help her and touching to hear her story.

Peer F: It's just fun to see how some people tick so differently than others. People walk into your office who are so high-strung about things and you get the idea that they're high-strung about things in general. I think the more you work with people, the more you realize how they function.

Peer D: I think that peer advising has taught me to be open to a lot of differences with the basic idea that we all feel the same way about many things. We all feel anger, we all feel frustration, we all feel happiness. And even if our situations are different, even if we have different life experiences, the range of feelings are the same. To me this work has been a real strength in terms of understanding other people and being more open to differences.

While being aware of and appreciating differences in others was an important benefit of their peer advisory work, some peer advisors also believed that this experience affected their understanding of themselves.

Peer Q: Through interacting with others and listening to what they had to say, I learned a lot about myself. Sometimes, in listening to other people, they articulate a feeling you've had but had never put it into words. When you interact with other people in a caring way, I think you become a more caring person or sensitive person thereafter. I've learned feedback models and I've used these in my interactions to sort of keep things cool and to the point. I get to the heart of the matter by not putting someone on the defensive or putting myself on the defensive. Identifying others' behavior, telling them how I feel really works well. It helps me stay more calm in interactions and more thoughtful. Now I am more mindful of the dynamics that might go on between people. But I think it's been helpful to me personally.

Another important benefit provided by this role was the opportunity to integrate skills and knowledge from other experiences and classes.

Peer B: I feel like it's a really good experience in terms of giving students the opportunity to practice being in a counseling role because so many of us want to go on in a counseling role.

Peer C: I guess you can't help but use the skills you're taught a little bit in everyday life. They just happen to pop up.

Peer R: I can actually speak in front of a group, which I never thought I could do before. You know, I don't feel like I'm going to throw up before I talk in front of a lot of people. I was in drama in high school, and I used to feel sick every time I went on stage; it was horrible! It was just a really wrenching experience, and now it's no big deal. Facilitating groups for the focus groups that we did wasn't a problem. This practicum has taught me how to slow down and to just listen to somebody else in a relaxed way. A lot of times when someone's talking to you, you want to jump in with information, but it's better to sit back and get the whole story. I've also watched other peers interacting with students, and a lot of times somebody will come in and say, "What's involved in concentrating in psychology?" and they pull out the sheet and they start going through the whole thing and the poor kid is like, "Uh, uh." I think you just have to slow down and check in with them and say, "Well, what do you know so far?" "What parts don't you understand?" Because if you just jump on them—like I used to do— they get really intimidated and overwhelmed.

The chance to help others was also considered very rewarding.

> *Peer F:* I think that a lot of times I walk out of the peer advising office thinking, "Wow! I helped someone." It was like helping a lady across the street or something. I feel good about it. It's reward enough for me to have helped somebody. It's a leadership role and that's definitely rewarding.

> *Peer R:* There was this pre-med guy, who I talked to for an hour. He came in and wanted to finish college in three years; he was a freshman. He was trying to decide between an A.B., a B.S., or a B.S. with a concentration in psych as a social science. He really wanted to go to medical school, and he felt like he wanted to crank though all these requirements in three years and then go. I talked to him for a while about why he wanted to rush—what was the hurry to get into medical school? And I think he felt like he couldn't begin to do anything, begin to live, until medical school happened. To him this was just a hoop he had to jump through. He really didn't plan on getting anything out of his undergraduate career. Med school was the mission. The reason he said he came in to see me was he wanted to schedule a lab and he was disgruntled because he didn't like any of the labs. I said, "But you know, you keep talking about wanting to do medical research. We have opportunities where you can do an independent study with someone." I got out the contract, and I got out the faculty's research interests, and his little eyes just lit up, and he said, "Oh gosh, this is great!" We talked for a long time about why he wanted to go to med school so quickly, how he felt about medical

school, and what would be the advantage/disadvantage about three versus four years. And you know, I got to give him an option that he hadn't really thought of. Before he left, he shook my hand and said, "I really appreciate your taking the time," and he gave me a really good evaluation. That's my most rewarding experience.

Inevitably, there are also some challenging elements of peer advising work. Some mentioned by the peer advisors include having clients who cross the line between counselor and counselee, not being able to form a connection with the peer, feeling pressured to reveal personal opinions about professors and classes, being second-guessed because they are a peer, having clients who do not put much effort into helping themselves, and having counselees raise issues that would be better addressed by other kinds of counselors. The counselor interviews provide some examples of clients who challenged them most particularly.

Peer N: Once there was a phone call and a woman was calling who was concerned about majoring in psychology. At first I didn't know this, but she was concerned about going to law school and finding internships, which is what I'm doing. It was just a fluke I think that I answered the phone. But it was good because we were on the same wavelength. But the most frustrating thing about it was that we talked for awhile, her call-waiting rang in, and she said, "Oh, I'll call you back. What's your name? What's your number?" And she never called me back. It was just really frustrating because I felt like I had all this great information to give her and she didn't call back. And so I think the phone call, because it was a phone call, was hard. You see so much from body language and from looking at someone's face and expressions that in a phone call it's really difficult. You have to be a lot more attentive, I think. I'm glad we mostly do advising face-to-face.

Peer M: My most frustrating and challenging experience was I had been to one of our focus group sessions one night and somebody had talked to me a lot afterward and then came in to see me for counseling later. And I didn't really want to counsel the person because I didn't feel comfortable with her, but there wasn't another counselor available. So I counseled her and I found myself getting irritated with her because it wasn't a situation I wanted to be in and I took my frustration out on her by not being as helpful or friendly or as supportive as I could have been. I gave her the answers but in a very short manner that pretty much said, "There's your answer, leave!" not like, "Can I help you with anything else?" So that was kind of frustrating because I knew that I was doing it. I should have referred the client to another advisor. I got the feeling that she wanted more contact with me than just as a counselor, that she wanted to become my friend. And in fact, she was saying, "Let's go for coffee. Let's do this. Let's do that." And I didn't feel comfortable. I wanted to keep a professional distinction there. This person kept trying to step over that barrier and that made me very uncomfortable. We talked about this in supervision.

Peer F: The most challenging is when you're trying to help someone whom you might not particularly like. You say to yourself,"Well, I'm in a professional position here and I should try to help her or him." And I think that brings up a lot of issues within an advisor. If someone walks in and has an attitude that you have a problem with, you know it's kind of up to you to ask yourself, "What was it about his/her attitude that bothers me so much and did I really help him/her as much as I helped someone that I like?"

Peer D: Most challenging is figuring out why something went wrong, taking a close look at myself to see where roadblocks come in, where I have trouble helping someone. That's the most challenging because it's not easy to find. I'm very willing to do that type of thing, but it's not always an easy answer—figuring out why this session didn't go as well, what the problem was here, or if this person really felt as uncomfortable as I did. I try and figure out where it's really coming from so I can help myself to improve!

Peer L: A student came into the office and asked me, "What do you think about this class and this professor?" One of the things about a peer counseling office is you're supposed to give honest advice, as a psychology major to a psychology major. We're peers, you know; we're not completely impartial. You can't bad-mouth any professor, but you can say something like, "This professor runs a very structured class." You can describe it somewhat objectively.

Peer C: I had a client a couple weeks ago who was very unwilling to work things out herself; she wanted me to do most of it. So we had one of the longest peer advising interactions in the history of the office. She was in there forever and she wanted help with everything. It's kind of frustrating when people don't take it upon themselves to try and work out some of it for themselves. I think the student just wanted someone to plan her whole schedule for the rest of her college career. And we basically did that. It felt really good because we got a lot accomplished and she went away satisfied. But on the other hand, it was sort of frustrating to keep going over the same issues and have her really not put much effort into understanding it for herself.

Peer P: One man who came in wanted me to tell him exactly what to do with his life, exactly what school to go to for a PhD program, of which there are three hundred or so out there. He wanted me to tell him exactly what school to apply to, he wanted me to tell him if he would get in, and he wanted me to do the work for him. It was really frustrating because his expectations were very different from what the program provides.

Peer R: A client came into the office when it was really busy, and I said, "Oh, I'll be with you in a second." She was a senior and she had one more term left. She wanted to stop by and check with us and just make sure that she was making good progress toward finishing her degree. And so I said, "Okay, no problem," pulled out the sheet of requirements, and started to go over these. She was really jumpy and she kept on talking about her old school, "Well in my old school, I took this course, but I don't know what it translates into." She didn't really know what psych classes she'd taken, at all. Like the names, the numbers, nothing. And I kept saying, "Well, was it social psychology? Did it have to do with how people acted in groups? Or was it more individualistic, like personality? Did it have to do with children—was it developmental?" And she just said, "I don't know, I don't know." I felt really frustrated because she couldn't provide the information I needed to be of help to her.

Peer B: This one guy came in and he said, "I'm not going to have any respect for you; you're just a peer. Who are you to know more than me?" It's not that I was saying, "Oh, look at how much I know." And to everything I would say, he would just act like, "Well, I knew that!" And then the more we talked, he totally changed and he started asking me lots of questions. The more comfortable he got, the more he realized that I wasn't trying to show him how much I knew. I sensed that he was initially feeling annoyed that he was talking with a peer and I said, "Well, you know, we're not here because we're some authority on everything. We're just here to help you out or maybe explain something that you need to know." So, he left and on his evaluation he was so positive. It was so funny because when he first walked in I would never ever have guessed that he would have said anything positive. Maybe he was scared.

Peer K: I think sometimes the most challenging sessions are of two kinds. There are the ones who won't believe anything you have to say because you're pretty much the same as them. And then there are others who think that everything you say is true to the word and you feel like, "Well, I'm not your real academic counselor." There are those two extremes. Those are the most difficult clients to work with because they don't have the sense that we're here to help them; though we have the knowledge, we're not the last step.

Peer H: One time someone came in and she was very anxious and she didn't really want to leave the office and she was bringing up a lot of very personal things. And it was a little uncomfortable. In my position as an academic peer advisor, I don't usually talk about such personal things with clients. It was challenging, but I think I handled it pretty well. I acknowledged her concerns and feelings about the situation she was going through as a single mother. But I didn't get too far into it because I just didn't think that was really my domain. I acknowledged that to the client and kind of just stuck to the academic concerns that she had. I think that same experience was also the most rewarding experience because I was so concerned about whether or not I was helping her out and she did come back again to see me and specifically said she was coming back. She knew when I would be working and said she would return because I was helping her out. For her personal concerns I made a referral to Counseling Services so she could meet with a professional counselor. This is part of how I was helpful.

Individual Advising Sessions

The work done in individual advising sessions constitutes the crux of the Peer Advising Program. A total of about six hundred students make use of the individual advising service during each academic year. The size of this number itself is testimony to the program's effectiveness and good utilization and to the fact that word-of-mouth feedback about the service constituted a frequent referral source.

> *Peer L:* We get a lot of people who say, "Oh, my friend came here and, you know, he/she really liked it. And so I decided to come also. I also know a friend of mine is the brother of one of the people who came in and she was just saying how much she liked it." So, you know, word-of-mouth feedback brings in a lot of new students.

Several student studies show that advisee response to the individual advising sessions have been overwhelmingly positive. In response to items on a questionnaire administered after their individual advising sessions, 99.4 percent of those who utilized the service reported that their advisor had listened to their needs "very well." Ninety-eight percent of advisees reported that their peer advisors had provided them with the information they desired "very well" or "somewhat well," with zero percent reporting that they had been provided with this information "not at all well" (Sedway & Sidell, 1992). Many of the peer advisors felt gratified by the positive feedback they received in these ways.

Peer F: I look at the evaluation form sometimes, but most of the time I pretty much know what they're going to say. I look at it in case someone writes something more or less negative, like I didn't help them with something, like maybe I didn't pick up on a question that they were asking me or I overlooked something. But for the most part, I always find the interactions to be positive. Usually the questions they come in with I can help them with. And usually I can tell when something's gone bad or something's just okay. Most often I feel very comfortable with my clients.

Peer O: Clients kind of let you know by body language whether they were really happy with you or not, which meant more to me than the piece of paper did.

Peer M: Well, one way we had feedback was after we saw each client, we asked them to fill out an evaluation form. Later on, we could look through the evaluations and see how we had done. And sometimes a few of them even referred to the person they had seen by name, so you could kind of think, "Wow, somebody else thought I was really good." We also had a weekly log in which we kept track of all our interactions, and we handed those in to our professor, who turned those back with feedback. When we talked to her about situations she gave us feedback on how we were doing. It felt really good because it was rare to get any negative feedback, and even when it was slightly negative, it was more constructive criticism than a personal attack. So it felt fine to hear.

Peer C: It feels really good because most of the feedback is always positive, and even if it's constructive, I guess the group is really tightly-knit now and if you get constructive feedback, you know they're doing it to help you out. It's just the atmosphere that we really care for each other and it seems that no one's really defensive about their feedback, so it's a really good atmosphere.

Peer E: I just want to reiterate my feeling about how much more comfortable I feel. The more I advise, the better my advising sessions are, the more I think the clients get out of it. And it just takes practice.

Evaluating the Success of the Peer Advising Program

Layman (1981) offered five "critical elements" against which the success of a peer advising program may be measured:

1. the formulation of meaningful peer counseling goals
2. the development of informed peer counseling support
3. a delineation of realistic peer counseling activities
4. the careful selection and training of peer counseling personnel
5. the evaluation and revision of peer counseling efforts

In the words of a student researcher:

All five of Layman's criteria were met by the University's Psychology Peer Advising program. Through the use of weekly supervision and daily support, informed peer counseling support, delineation of realistic peer counseling activities, and regular feedback were provided. Peer advisors discussed contacts on a regular basis and were provided with referral lists which were used when appropriate. Peers were selected through an application and interview process to ensure (suitability) for the program (Podolski, 1992).

The program has also been successful in terms of advisee response, as illustrated by feedback data on individual advising sessions and focus groups. In the most recent semester of 250 evaluations of individual peer advising, all but seven people cited their experience as highly successful. Forty percent of the respondents cited "friendly, open peers" as the most helpful factor in their experience, while another forty percent found the information imparted as quite valuable. Twenty percent of the evaluators spontaneously mentioned that having age-mates rather than professionals helped them to feel especially comfortable. Such comments as, "Peers are easy to talk to," "They had knowledge and insight," and "They understood because they'd had similar experiences" were typical. Suggestions for improvement included a number of suggestions for "better advertising" and a few jocular requests that there be a candy dish in the peer advising office.

The Future of the Peer Advising Program

From any perspective—that of the students served, the peer advisors, and the faculty—the Peer Advising Practicum in the Department of Psychology has been enthusiastically received. Most especially since the program is only four years old, its growth in volunteer peer advisors and clientele has been extraordinary. While there are some goals still to meet, such as increasing the number of freshpersons utilizing this service and increasing the clarity of advertising for those who may not spontaneously differentiate between academic peer advising and other peer counseling services on campus, on balance this program has been quite successful and will hopefully continue in order to serve students and faculty. It has also served as a model for other interested departments at the university. Indeed, a number of other programs have already consulted us about our training and services in an effort to develop similar programs for their departments and agencies.

Peer N: Not to downplay the professors or the advisors in the professional advising office, but a lot of times they're not sure of all the feelings going on behind the questions. So I think the peers provide such a great service because people are just so glad to finally be able to sit in one place and be there for more than two minutes and get their questions answered. They're just so thankful that the peers are there, that they don't have to go running around to thirty-five other offices again.

Peer A: It's something I definitely enjoy doing and I think it's very important to provide support systems to students here at the university. Each experience has been rewarding for me and each experience has helped me grow more as an individual and learn more about myself. I think all of them have made me a more well-rounded person and more aware of different issues that deal with the community.

REFERENCES

Botvin, G. J., Baker, E., Filazzola, A. D., & Botvin, E. M. (1990). A cognitive-behavioral approach to substance abuse prevention: One-year follow-up. *Addictive Behaviors, 15,* 47-63.

Butcher, E. (1982). Changing by choice: A process model for group career counseling. *The Vocational Quarterly, 30,* 20-209.

Clark, J. I. (1984) *Who, me lead a group?* Grand Rapids: Harper and Row.

Farley, R. C., & Akridge, R. L. (1986). The feasibility of peer counseling as a rehabilitation resource. *International Journal of Rehabilitation Research. 9* (1), 69-72.

Frisz, R. (1984). The perceived influence of a peer advisement program on a group of its former peer advisors. *Personnel and Guidance Journal, 62* (10), 616-9.

Gruver, G. (1971). College students as therapeutic agents. *Psychological Bulletin, 76,* 111-127.

Habley, W. R. (1979, Summer). The advantages and disadvantages of using students as academic advisors. *NASPA Journal, 17* (1), 46-51.

Harrington, D. (1983). Towards excellence: Developing high standards in youth programs. Report from National Commission of Resources for Youth, Inc., Boston, Mass. (ERIC: ED 240 187).

Hatcher, S., Nadeau, M., Walsh, L., Reynolds, M., Galea, J., & Marz, K. (1994). The teaching of empathy for high school and college students: Testing Rogerian methods with the Interpersonal Reactivity Index. *Adolescence 29* (116), 961-74.

Layman, R. (1981). The use of peers as college academic advisors: Reasons and evidence. (ERIC: ED 209 599).

Lynn, D. (1986). Peer helpers: Increasing positive student involvement in school. The School Counselor, *34*, 62-6.

Martin, J. C., & Carkuff, R. R. (1968). Changes in personality and interpersonal functioning of counselors-in-training. *Journal of Clinical Psychology, 24*, 109-10.

Zunker, V. G., & Brown, W. F. (1966, March). Comparative effectiveness of student and professional counselors. *Personnel and Guidance Journal, 66*, 738-43.

STUDENT WORKS

Bauer, A., & Sharfner, E. (1992). *The effects of peer advising on empathy and self-esteem.* Unpublished.

Feldman, J., & Reeker, J. (1992). *Year-end evaluation of peer advisors' responses regarding the effectiveness of training for a new psychology peer advising program.* Unpublished.

Foley, K. A., & Shafer, K. L. (1992). *Perceptions of peer helping programs: Misconception, awareness, and utilization.* Unpublished.

Horton, K. (1992). *Effects of a peer advising practicum on the student advisor's personality and perception of university resources.* Unpublished.

Podolski, C. (1992). An evaluation of the peer advising program: A practicum experience for group facilitators. Unpublished.

Sedway, J., & Sidell, C. (1992). *An analysis of the feedback from students using the peer advising program in the undergraduate Psychology Department at the University of Michigan during the Winter Term 1992.* Unpublished.

Standish, J. F. (1992). The peer advising program: A demographic analysis of its target population, a year in review. Unpublished.

Strimling, J. (1992). *Where have all the freshmen gone?* Unpublished.

Peer Teaching

Chapter 10

Peer Writing Tutors

*Phyllis Lassner, PhD, Helen Isaacson, PhD,
and Susan Marie Harrington, PhD*[1]

History

A Peer Tutoring Program is sponsored by the English Composition Board (ECB) at the university.[2] ECB is responsible for assessing incoming student writing, teaching intensive writing courses, overseeing upper-level writing courses offered in every department, and providing assistance to faculty using writing in their courses. To help students enrolled in any literature, science, or arts course requiring writing, the ECB's Writing Workshop provides thirty-minute appointments with an ECB faculty member. When the ECB was first established, its Writing Workshop was open only during regular business hours; more recently, Writing Workshop has begun to offer evening hours in selected residence halls and Sunday afternoon hours in the library.

In order to provide additional help for students, the ECB began a peer tutoring program in 1984, after two ECB faculty attended the first National Peer Tutoring Conference at Brown University. Ken Bruffee, the keynote speaker, who created the first such program at Brooklyn College of the City University of New York, spoke of the benefits of collaborative learning among undergraduates to a rapt audience of peer tutors and faculty from around the United States. As small discussion sessions convened, it became clear that

---

[1] Elizabeth Newman, a peer tutor, also contributed to this chapter.
[2] The ECB was established in 1978 at the University of Michigan.

there were as many different types of peer tutoring programs as there are different needs at four- and two-year colleges and universities in various parts of the country. With this array of models in hand, ECB faculty developed a plan for a peer tutoring program based on experiences in our Writing Workshop with a cross-section of undergraduates.

The Peer Tutoring Program was designed to fit the particular characteristics of the University of Michigan's student body and its institutional constraints. As a state university serving diverse American and international students, we could not assume a unified definition of excellence and achievement. On the other hand, as a highly selective research-oriented university, we could assume that our students would expect help writing academic papers. While some colleges and universities, like Brown, assign peer tutors to professors who train them to write comments on papers, we rejected this student-as-assistant-teacher model. Given the prior success of the ECB Writing Workshop, we decided that peer tutors would, like Writing Workshop faculty, meet one-on-one with students for collaborative discussions of papers. Although the primary methods of the faculty-staffed Writing Workshop and the Peer Tutoring Program are similar, we wanted the two programs to be distinct. We wanted students seeking help with their writing to have a choice between working with a faculty member and with a well-trained peer. We realized that some students might feel more comfortable working with another student.

> *Peer A*: A woman came to me with her law school application and we went over the whole thing. And in the law school application, she mentioned that she was a lesbian. I thought it was really cool that someone felt comfortable enough to come to me and share something for which she could possibly be attacked or discriminated against. But the sentence where she mentioned that didn't really fit into it and I had to explain to her how to better work it in. And I did.

In the first year of the Peer Tutoring Program, we experimented with placing peer tutors in courses within their own majors, assuming that the peer tutors would work most confidently with subject areas and faculty they knew best. For purposes of comparison, some peer tutors also set up a table in the undergraduate library while others worked at a station in one of the campus computing facilities. In weekly meetings the peer tutors registered their satisfactions and frustrations with these various settings.

> *Peer B*: I learned a lot about writing. I learned a lot about my own writing, too. I became a better writer because I was helping others. I was recommended for this by a professor who I really didn't think I did very good work for, but he recommended me for it anyway. If you wanted to and you find out about the Peer Tutoring Program, you can apply for it, but most people are recommended. I really don't feel like you need to be that good a writer to do it. Because all people really need is for someone to read their work for them; anybody who's reasonably competent at writing could do that.

Unfortunately, the all-too-gradual effects of advertising and word-of-mouth attention meant that many of the peer tutors were initially underutilized, especially those working with particular courses. Stepping up publicity and available tutors "on call" in their office seemed the best way to provide tutoring services to the greatest number of students and the best way to ensure that the tutors themselves could put their training into practice. The completion of a very large and centrally located computing center in a major classroom complex determined that the peer tutors would concentrate their efforts there. Peer tutors are currently available five nights a week, Sunday through Thursday, from seven until eleven in the evening.

Over time, the increasing number of students involved in the program has allowed us to consider other tutoring possibilities. Some senior peer tutors have requested that they be placed in junior-senior writing-intensive content courses taught by ECB faculty. Each semester for the last two years, two peer tutors have worked with students in a women's studies course entitled "Women, Culture, and Writing." The peer tutors have worked with the instructor in helping to shape writing assignments as well as working with students who need help with their writing. In this way, they have not only collaborated with students in the peer tutoring process but also with the instructor of the course. Other possibilities that have arisen with the expansion of the Peer Tutoring Program have included working with computer-assisted writing instruction in special education high school classrooms in local communities.

Those peer tutors who are still registered students after their second semester in the program have the opportunity to become paid peer tutors. This opportunity has developed from an emphasis original to the formation of the program that academic and intellectual opportunities be ongoing. The program offers academic credit: three credit hours for the first-semester seminar and from one to three credits for second-semester, depending on the number of hours spent as a peer tutor. Over time, peer tutors have evaluated their experiences as fulfilling in large part because of what they have learned.

> *Peer C*: Seeing how other people struggle with different things in writing makes it easier to spot the same things when I'm writing myself.

In presentations our peer tutors have offered at the National Peer Tutoring Conference over the last five years, many have also reported the importance of their peer tutoring to their work after graduation. Those who have gone on to the Peace Corps or *Teach for America* and to graduate and professional study in various fields emphasize the intellectual and social challenges of their work.

Future growth of the peer tutoring program is somewhat limited by the optimal class size for such training. Since a peer tutoring seminar cannot effectively function with more than fifteen to eighteen students, no more than thirty to thirty-six new students per year can enter the program.

Our peer tutoring program differs from other similar programs in that it is not housed in a single physical setting, although most peer tutors work in the computing site where a large "Peer Tutoring" sign hangs above their work station. Such a public location allows the tutors to go where the writers are and puts the tutors in an easily accessible place at times when students are working on papers. Yet, some students might prefer a quieter, homier writing center, so we are currently placing some of our peer tutors in the dormitories.

Program Philosophy

Although it shares many goals and purposes of the faculty-staffed ECB writing workshop, the ECB Peer Tutoring Program has its own setting and distinct aims. The Peer Tutoring Program was formed on the premise that undergraduates can offer peers who need help with their writing a special kind of assistance and support. After a semester-long training seminar, the peer tutors work autonomously while continuing to be supervised by ECB faculty. Their work in helping students with writing grows out of the belief that writing is a collaborative endeavor, that people learn most about their writing by sharing it with others. Thus, when working with students, tutors often read the work aloud so that the tutor and writer can hear inconsistencies in rhetoric, organization, logic, and grammar. Peer tutors are not editors; they teach students how to edit their own work. Their ultimate goal is to teach writers self-sufficiency.

> *Peer A*: I usually don't say that anything in particular is wrong with the writing. I usually say, "Well, this doesn't sound quite right. What's wrong?" I ask them. I ask them to make all the decisions. I make them figure out what's wrong with their writing because if I'm going to do it, I might as well just be checking the paper. They have to come to the conclusion that something's wrong or if they want to fix something. I help with commas and punctuation—you can't argue with a comma. I ask them to meet me half-way. I help them to realize what's wrong. I guide them, but it's their own work, their own decisions.

Peer tutors begin by focusing on the strengths in a student's essay. Whether it is a clever use of a metaphor or a strategic analysis of a societal issue, peer tutors encourage students to build on their writing strengths as well as to strengthen their weaknesses. The peer tutor's concern is not boosting the writer's grade but encouraging enthusiasm for the process of writing. Student-to-student interaction builds trust in the learning process, helping to alleviate feelings that "professors can be intimidating and are often busy," as reported by a junior Political Science major, who added: "That's why the ECB is a great place to get honest advice."

> *Peer B*: Well, once or twice I've gotten a story that I've liked a lot. When you read somebody's story, somebody's work of fiction, you can get a lot of insight into someone. I feel badly if I need to do a lot of cut-ups on it, like if someone makes a mistake or whenever someone does something stylistically that I wouldn't do. I believe that they should let their style come through. Why should I impose mine on it? So I really try not to say too much about it. I just like reading it and try to be of help.

Supervising the Program

The Peer Tutoring Program is supervised by three lecturers in the English Composition Board who also teach writing classes and serve other functions. As is the case with all ECB faculty, those lecturers who serve as program supervisors come with varied backgrounds; some have advanced degrees in literature, others in composition, linguistics, or education. All have had experience teaching a variety of college-level courses and in assessing the essays of incoming first-year students in order to help determine their placement in first-year composition classes. In addition, those who supervise the peer tutors have often had experience training graduate student teaching assistants and in conducting workshops on the creation and evaluation of writing assignments for a variety of university faculty.

One of the distinguishing features of our Peer Tutoring Program is the fact that it is based in a year-long sequence of courses. Writing tutors in some other institutions take courses in peer tutoring, but many receive less intensive training. Each institution designs a training program in accord with institutional resources and philosophies, and the variety of such programs is great. At ECB, supervisors take turns teaching the three-credit ECB seminar that aims to prepare students selected to participate in the tutoring program. Each semester the faculty member selected to teach the training seminar the following term sends letters to faculty members in different academic disciplines asking them to recommend students in their classes who have at least sophomore standing and who they believe have the necessary communication skills to help undergraduates with their writing. Recommended students are sent letters inviting them to become candidates for the program. Students who apply to join the program on their own are asked to provide a letter of recommendation from an instructor. All candidates are interviewed and asked to provide a sample of their writing for evaluation. The number of such candidates has increased dramatically since the program began; almost three times the number of students who can be accommodated sought a place in a recent peer tutoring seminar.

The aim of having a varied group of tutors helps to determine which candidates will be invited to join the seminar. Since students come for help with writing assignments in all disciplines, program supervisors make special efforts to ensure that students with concentrations in a range of disciplines enroll in the training course. Supervisors also aim to have a balance of male and female students and to include students with different racial and ethnic backgrounds. It is believed that a diverse community of tutors can learn from each other the full range of skills and special kinds of sensitivity necessary for serving a diverse student population.

> *Peer C*: For me, doing this work with a diverse student population confirms a lot of theories and totally trashes a lot of theories about composition. Seeing the work in practice is a lot different than talking about it in a classroom or even talking about it with a small group of homogeneous people. There is a huge diversity of writing styles across different people.

The instructor who conducts the seminar determines which material and training techniques will be the focus of the course. Since the three potential supervisors share a common philosophy of tutoring and often meet to exchange ideas, the seminar does not vary greatly from semester to semester. Students discuss a variety of reading materials on such subjects as collaborative learning, how to respond to student writing, philosophy of teaching, and the social construction of learning. Guest lecturers on topics such as how to teach international students and learning-disabled students provide expertise in these specialized areas. Writing assignments for the peer tutors usually include an essay in which students reflect on themselves as writers, as well as an essay in which they report on writing in their field of academic concentration. Practice peer tutoring is a major training element, and the ECB instructor supervises the seminar members as they begin to counsel students.

> *Peer A*: We had a class that met for four months. In that class we wrote three papers. One was about our experience as writers; another was about how we write in our discipline (I am a religion major or concentrator). Then the third assignment was to write about our experiences as peer tutors. We also tutored for the last half of the class, the last two months, as part of our training. And we talked about pedagogical techniques and had a coursepack of readings. We had a book that talked about tutoring techniques.

Seminar members who successfully complete the ECB class enroll the following semester in an advanced ECB course, "Directed Peer Tutoring."[3] Tutors may enroll for one to three credits hours in this advanced course, depending on the number of hours they are available for practicum work. A weekly planning and administrative meeting serves to further the students' professional development through reading and writing projects. The same ECB faculty member

---

[3] ECB 300 and 301 are the titles of the beginning and advanced classes, respectively.

teaches both courses so that students work with the same instructor for the full year of their training and tutoring.

After completing the advanced training course, those tutors who have not graduated are eligible to work as tutors for payment. The ECB has a small budget for this purpose. In addition, supervisors are always on the lookout for other types of related paid work, whether to facilitate discussions about writing among students taking introductory composition courses or to help teach a funded "electronic learning community," which connects fifty "special needs" high school juniors with university student tutors.

Supervisors clearly explore a variety of possibilities to help tutors further their professional development. ECB tutors have presented papers at conferences and published articles about tutoring. For many tutors, the tutoring experience has sparked or strengthened an interest in a teaching career. Former tutors have gone on to do graduate work in composition and education, to teach in a junior college, to join the Peace Corps, *Teach for America*, or other similar service organizations.

> *Peer A*: People have always told me that I should be a teacher of some sort but then sometimes they would say, "But you're too smart to be a teacher." So, I started out an engineer, but I decided through ECB that I'm going to major in English and that I am going to apply for *Teach for America* and maybe go on to teach English.

The Process of the Program

ECB peer tutors work one-on-one with students who are seeking help with a particular writing assignment. At any point in the writing process, a student may go to the peer tutoring area in the computing center and ask a tutor to discuss whether a rough draft seems to be fulfilling the assignment, to collaborate on developing an idea, to help determine whether an argument had sufficient evidence, or to offer feedback on whether a point has been clearly made. When students ask for help with grammar or punctuation, tutors look for patterns or problems and aim to enable students to recognize and correct their own errors.

> *Peer D*: Different people take advice different ways. Some people come just to get reassurance on their papers and some people really want changes. Other people were there just because they had to be there because their teacher told them to. Some people take my word like the word of God and for others whatever I say isn't even heard. Some people are really defensive.

Some tutors have also worked with students in dormitories; others have been attached to a particular class or participated in a special tutoring project. There is no set curriculum that the tutors seek to "teach" the students who come to them for assistance. Rather, each student receives help particular to his or her own needs and assignment. Since the tutors are mostly located at a computing site, it is possible to work with students at the computer; however, most students and tutors seem to prefer to use paper copies of the students' work. In some semesters, student-written guides to writing in particular disciplines have been available to tutees, but in general handouts are not used. The content of each tutoring session is determined by what help the student requests and by what needs the tutor perceives.

> *Peer D*: The best for me is when people come to me with a paper for a class that I've already taken. Then I can really help them with their papers. If they're in trouble I can see exactly what it is that they need to do. A lot of times what I'll do is make corrections and then they'll go off and they'll come back three hours later. Then I'll check it again and review the changes they have made.

Program Evaluation

Evaluation of any program is essential in order to ensure that the program meets the needs of the population it serves and to identify ways in which the program can continue to grow and evolve. Evaluation can occur both formally and informally and it can occur for summative and formative purposes. Given the flexible and collaborative structure of our Peer Tutoring Program, most evaluation has occurred informally with formative goals in mind. We have been interested in evaluating several different facets of the program: we need to evaluate the success of the peer tutoring seminar, the tutor's work with students, and the policies and procedures for the Peer Tutoring Program.

The committee of three faculty members meets regularly to discuss the questions, issues, and problems that arise in the course of teaching the program. Given that the ECB is a small program, this committee becomes a closely-knit group, ensuring amicable policy development and continuity over time. All three faculty attain at least some degree of familiarity with the training received by all students who have been involved with the program for more than one year. If students complete the coursework and are still enrolled as students the following year(s), they may be eligible to become paid peer tutors, in which case they would have contact with a greater number of faculty.

These committee meetings serve several purposes. First, they enable the faculty to identify policy issues that need to be shared and discussed with students before being finalized. For instance, at one point in the development of the program, the issues of accountability and evaluation of student tutors needed to be worked out; the program had no way of collecting data about what nights the tutors were most heavily used and there was no way to keep track of which tutors worked how many hours. We now know that the tutoring program is utilized more in the fall than in the winter term and more during the end of the term than in the beginning, as would be expected for any academic service. We do not offer services during the first three weeks of the term and Thursday evenings are traditionally slow.

In the early years of the peer tutoring program, students who saw the tutors were asked to fill out a complicated evaluation form that had been borrowed from the Writing Workshop. After discussions with the tutors about what they would like to know from the students they worked with, a streamlined evaluation form that provided room for open-ended comments was introduced. Furthermore, a tutoring log form was introduced, which allowed tutors to record the number of tutoring sessions they held and to make brief notes about those sessions. The logs can then be used to begin class discussions in either the peer tutoring seminar or the supervised weekly meetings of tutors. The process of developing these new forms helped increase the "on-time" tutoring performance as well as the tutor's involvement with policy decisions.

A second function of the committee meetings is to identify issues that need to be discussed at an administrative level. Several years ago, it became necessary to rethink the workload of faculty supervising the Peer Tutoring Program. The committee evaluated how much time it takes to teach and prepare for the tutoring seminars and met regularly with the appropriate administrator to ensure that release time for involvement with the program was provided for faculty. These policy procedures have advantages beyond a legalistic sense: meetings with the administrator and faculty members helped clarify the position of the tutoring program within the unit and ensured faculty that their work was valued by the unit.

Finally, and perhaps most importantly, the fundamental purpose of these meetings is to share information among instructors about the different assignments and issues discussed in different courses. Meetings of the committee enable all faculty involved in the program to have clearer expectations of what other instructors' students have experienced. Since all faculty involved in the program share a basic orientation toward the program, there is little overt conflict among the committee members.

Evaluation forms to date tell us that most students who see peer tutors are happy about the quality of tutoring. Students are asked to respond to the following statements: "I feel better about my writing than I did before this appointment," "The tutor is knowledgeable about writing," and "I would return again for help with my writing." The peer tutors receive uniformly positive evaluations in response to these questions; students who work with the peer tutors clearly believe that they receive effective assistance, as virtually all students who see a peer tutor once say that they would return for another session.

> *Peer A*: When the evaluation is positive I think, "Cool, I know I'm good," but one time I had this business student and he was an English as a Second Language student. I worked with him on his grammar and English and everything. He had a lot of problems with some of his English but they were workable problems and I worked on them with him. It was a marketing report, and I said, "Well, you know, I don't really know the form of a marketing report because I'm not a business student." And I said, "But, the way it works and the way it flows and the way you have it organized seems to work for me." I assumed that he had a form to follow. And then on the evaluation form I got two "Strongly Agrees," but on the one, "I feel the ECB tutor is knowledgeable on the subject," he wrote "Neutral." Well, "Neutral" isn't saying it's bad, but I just didn't know the form of a marketing report. I usually feel very good about feedback, but when it's bad, I'm one of those people that reacts strongly to positive feedback and very poorly to negative criticism.

> *Peer A*: Most of the time a lot of people just circle "Strongly Agree, Strongly Agree, Strongly Agree," like we're wonderful and god-like. We get that a lot and people just generally say, "Okay, cool, thanks." You get the little evaluation form and people usually say "thanks" and that's more than enough to feel gratified.

The peer tutoring seminars are also evaluated using the required university multiple choice forms as well as instructor-designed questionnaires. Peer tutoring faculty find self-designed questionnaires an even more useful way of gathering information about the students' experience in their courses. Since the class size is small, evaluation goes on continuously. Faculty and students can readily discuss the syllabus assignments and the tutors' needs for particular types of information as the need arises.

> *Peer C*: Well, it sounds cruel, but working with the second language students, I sympathize with their point of views but at the same time I think they kind of get dumped off on us a lot. We can help them with an actual paper, but we don't have the training to explain why they have a problem in our language as opposed to their language; that's a field in itself, and we don't have time to do more than touch on it; but we don't have training like an actual instructor.

In addition, the small class size makes it possible to respond on a weekly basis to tutors' needs. The tutoring seminar's curriculum covers issues that are generally considered basic to the experience of a peer tutor (i.e., collaborative learning, writing in the disciplines, the process approach to writing), but the tutors' needs and levels of confidence vary each term. One semester, for instance, tutors wanted particular extra attention to writing resumes and personal statements after a large number of business students came to tutors requesting help. Extra sessions in working with second- (or third- or fourth-) language students are regularly added at students' request. Often tutors will find that they have questions about particular types of grammatical structures or organizational issues relating to other cultures. These extra sessions are designed to help the tutors cope with some of the frustrations of peer work, which include not having enough information to help a student, not having enough time to spend with each student, and feeling as if students become too attached to their tutor, as well as difficulties with working with students for whom English is a second language.

> *Peer D*: I learned what to do in situations in which I'm expected to be an authority on something that I'm not and when I'm presenting something that I don't understand and

somebody wants an answer. You presume to make a guess. Either that or you'll be honest and say, "Look, I don't know."

Peer B: When we're busy, we only give half an hour to each person, so I'd have to sort of rush through sometimes. When there is one person right after another, my job is very frustrating.

Peer A: This one guy came in and we went over his paper for like two hours, and this guy thought I was great and said, "Oh, you're wonderful and I'll be back every week." Fortunately, he never was because I said, "You know, you should probably see other tutors; it will help you more in your writing because you only get one perspective with me." But he was going to be my best friend and I had fantasies of this guy trailing me everywhere.

Peer D: Probably the most frustrating is when I work with students when English is their second language. You say, "We say it this way," and it takes them a few times because they don't understand why you're correcting them. It is very frustrating to see a problem and understand how to change it but not be able to communicate it to the person.

Another issue of importance to us is assuring that students are satisfied with the assistance they receive from tutors and that the tutors find ways to reflect on their tutoring practices and grow into their potentials as writing tutors, thinkers, and writers. To that end, observations by faculty members have become a regular part of the course. The observations are informal and usually not scheduled in advance. The faculty member drops into the computing center, watches the tutors at work from as discreet a distance as possible, and is able to discuss the session with the tutor afterward. Because of the tutor selection process and the personalized nature of the curriculum, ECB tutors provide uniformly high quality assistance to students who seek their help. The observations by the faculty member thus serve not to monitor the quality of tutoring but rather to provide an occasion for tutors and faculty to talk together about tutoring and to give the faculty member added insight into the dynamics of the tutoring site. Late-night tutoring at the end of the semester is an adrenaline-packed experience worth seeing first-hand.

> *Peer A*: The purpose of the program is to have peer tutors on campus both for students who are uncomfortable with their writing and for students who are very comfortable with their writing but want to improve it—to have another student that they can go to for help with English and help writing a better paper. It's like having your own personal tutor without having to pay for it. When you tutor people, you try to give them the ability to revise their own papers rather than just revising it for them. We're not a spell-checker or anything. We don't just check spelling or grammar and say, "There you go." We try to work with them on how they can improve their writing. We empower them.

Chapter 11

Peer Facilitation in the Feminist Classroom: A Model for Peer Teaching an Introductory Course in Women's Studies

Jane Hassinger, MSW, Mildred Tirado, PhD, and Ruby Beale, PhD[1]

Editor's Note: The shift in supervisory format described in this peer teaching program emphasizes the need for professional consultation even in those peer programs with a quite democratic philosophy. The shift to more flexible and rational reliance on professional supervisory expertise reflects the increasing maturation of the peer counseling movement and those who set standards within it.

Peer counseling programs as well as certain social groupwork models (Glassman & Kates, 1990) promote an ethic of connection among people. This philosophy also recognizes the importance of equalizing power among people, of our essential interdependence, and of the value of being of service to others (D'Andrea, 1987). These values are appealing to feminist educators who have described how a classroom can help to reveal and make sense of complicated aspects of the

---

[1] Of the University of Michigan Departments of Psychology and Women's Studies.

gendered self and how it offers students a chance to ask the naive question or share beginning theories about their life experiences.

In this chapter, we will describe the development of a peer-led educational project composed of a series of three courses in our Women's Studies (WS) program. These courses[2] involve students in small group-learning experiences that include introductory readings on feminism and the circumstances of women's lives in North American societies, learning about the individual and social dynamics of prejudice, and an exploration of one's own gender-based experiences. The introductory course is taught in small groups facilitated by juniors and seniors who have completed relevant coursework and who are enrolled in an advanced class in which they receive supervision and education on teaching methods and group leadership skills.

> *Peer B*: The reason we specifically have peer facilitators goes along with the women's studies pedagogy that it's very important that women learn from each other and that there's a great wealth of resources within people that's often ignored. We always look to books and academics for all of our knowledge, but in reality we all have practical experiences that make us know our subject matter. It's especially important to have a peer facilitator because that breaks down some of the hierarchy and allows for a freer exchange of ideas. We're coming from the same perspective as our peers are and the same era generally. There's a commonality, a link between a peer facilitator and students. You gain a better knowledge of your subject matter if you're actually teaching it or at least facilitating a discussion of the issues. They're kind of cultivating leaders within the Women's Studies

---

[2] Women's Studies 100 ("Women's Issues"), Women's Studies 419/Psychology 411 ("Groups and Gender in Multicultural Contexts"), and Women's Studies 420 ("Group Facilitation").

> Department and they're making sure that graduates from the Women's Studies Department have organizational skills, leadership skills, and certain public speaking skills that are involved in facilitation.

From the beginning,[3] our Women's Studies Department faculty and students were inspired by a vision of education that enlivens the classroom, personalizes learning, gives voice to typically silent/silenced class members, and empowers students to participate in the construction of their learning agendas and to seek out connections among the theoretical and the practical so as to develop a critical perspective on our gendered world.

> One of the unique and inspiring features of women's studies is that it is a discipline which inherently appreciates and encourages the interrelationship between [the three components of education—the student, the teacher, and the material]. Because Women's Studies course material addresses the experiences of women in our society, women students have to strain *not* to identify. Instructors are often enthusiastic about the material because Women's Studies is a new and personally relevant discipline. Women's Studies is not an isolated study; it is intimately connected with the women's movement which is a dynamic and politically volatile social force. Appropriately, the principles of the movement are evident in the content and method of teaching Women's Studies. Feminist process (e.g., politicizing the personal, interacting cooperatively), manifested academically as Women's Studies, creates the potential for...a fulfilling learning experience (Rutenberg, 1983, 72).

As a basic part of the feminist critique of academia, feminist educators speak of learning that is grounded in theory informed by personal narrative. A fulfilling learning experience will necessarily encourage a student to examine the

---

[3] Women's Studies at the University of Michigan celebrated its twentieth anniversary in 1992. The current department chair is Professor Abigail Stewart.

"relationship between her intellect, her personal, and her politics" (ibid., 73). A critique of power relations in the construction of theory and dissemination of knowledge is central to the concerns of feminist scholars, and this same critique leads to particular pedagogical approaches in the classroom. Students are engaged by the challenge to critique their educational experience and the meaning and structure of authority and leadership in their classes. Guided in the feminist credo "the personal is political," Women's Studies faculty and students are concerned that a university education provide bridges, theoretical and practical, from the academy to the world outside and the real lives of students into the future.

> *Peer F*: Because I enjoy this class more than others, it ended up being the most important to me and taking up the most time. It generally fits in with a lot of the other things that I am doing because it's really interesting. Last semester I was peer teaching "Introductory Women's Studies" and I was taking a graduate-level feminist political theory class, and it was interesting to see the same issues talked about in radically different ways.

These bridges, traversing personal histories and cultural, racial, sexual, and class positions, also help to upset the illusion of a singular, unitary feminism. Feminist perspectives vary considerably as to their emphasis on economic factors, the domination of women by men, sexuality, race, the patriarchal family and its related forms in the workplace, and the construction of standards of gender normality (Stacey, 1993). Feminist theories attempt to describe the marginalized and disempowering conditions of women and to prescribe strategies and practices that empower women. In turn, these practices provide experience that grounds, informs, and enlivens feminist theory.

> *Peer F*: I was really shocked because several of the women in the class said, "Well, I've just never experienced sexism; I don't think that it really happens." I managed to explain to them what

sexism was and made them recognize it. I thought, "Okay, that's probably the hardest thing that I'll ever have to come up against in this group." Then at the beginning of this next semester I heard, "Well, yeah, we know what sexism is, but we basically think it's justified." And I thought, "Oo-ee, this is worse!" It's a much easier task to show someone and to explain to someone what sexism is and it's a totally different project to explain to them that it's wrong and they're worth a lot more than they think they are.

Women's studies courses aim to help students become culturally aware by illuminating areas of similarity and difference among women and men and by working to develop interpersonal skills in communicating across differences and under conditions of conflict. Our curriculum requires students to explicitly cross the bridge spanning theory and practice.

> *Peer A*: The whole experience of facilitating my own group was so overwhelming; I mean it changed my life in terms of learning about people and different ways to approach things, especially in feminist issues, because all the people in the class weren't like me: there were men in the class, there was an Indian woman in the class. It was a multicultural, very diverse group. I learned a lot.

The impact of the grassroots phenomenon of "consciousness-raising groups" in the mid-1960s was influential to the development of classroom innovations in women's studies, particularly with respect to group methods that were experientially based and that encouraged group members to develop an intellectually critical perspective on their experiences as women. Women's studies educators struggle to cultivate cohesive and supportive classroom climates in which students can feel safe and valued, learn from one another, and begin to identify with a cohort of women who share particular social circumstances. Personal experiences are seen as a source of legitimate data that contribute to explorations of prevailing gender ideology. Teaching is critiqued and re-envisioned as a form of feminist practice in which hierarchical distinctions between teacher and learner are analyzed and challenged. The teacher attempts to mobilize the resources of the entire class in the learning-teaching process.

> *Peer F*: In facilitating groups you try to make sure that everybody participates, that everybody teaches each other and pushes each other a little bit to challenge everyone into learning for themselves instead of just teaching them something.

Women's studies majors are required to participate in service activities that offer powerful experiential mentorships; they work in women's health and social service organizations, grassroots political groups, prisons, and classrooms. Our course is included in these service activities. The classroom boundary is flexibly constructed in that feminist pedagogy stresses multiple modes of learning. Teachers in women's studies are interested in helping the student develop a wide variety of intellectual and interpersonal competencies.

> *Peer E*: The class gave us as facilitators the experience of facilitating and helped us to become leaders and to better form our opinions about the issues. I think we all had our own personal reasons and our own purposes for doing this work, and we discussed that.

The introductory women's studies course covers topics such as women's socialization, health, body image, violence against women, sexuality and sexual orientation, family work, race and ethnicity, religion, and political action. Students discuss readings, keep personal journals, participate in the creation of positive group norms, learn effective group membership strategies, and work together on group presentations. Shuttling between "macro" and "micro" perspectives on women's experiences is emphasized. Students are encouraged to view their personal experiences through the lens of gender-race-class socialization processes. They are also offered opportunities for taking leadership in class and to work on the development of interpersonal competencies such as exploring authority dynamics, conflict resolution, and assertive communication skills.

> *Peer C*: The students who are facilitating or teaching develop group process skills for negotiation and conflict resolution. What I learned was applicable to my life experience. It opened up a lot of doors.

Women's studies courses use a structure that has also borrowed much from the blossoming peer counseling movement. Peer counseling, both as a method of service delivery and as a learning philosophy about empowerment and change, has been mapped onto the intellectual experiment in women's studies. Our women's studies project was envisioned as democratic groups where peers could learn from one another in a setting where authority struggles were minimized and collective responsibility for the group's directions and development could be maximized.

> *Peer G*: There were times when I found that maybe sometimes I just wanted to be too much a group member or other times I was a little too authoritative. When you've got different group members testing you, those are the times, I think, when you need to turn to other people and say, "Okay, how can I handle this situation in the best way for the group?" because ultimately that's what you're concerned with.

In the early days of the project, our facilitators were selected by those of the previous semester. This strategy was intended to relocate the center of power from faculty to student and reflected a value common to some of the early peer counseling programs blossoming in the late 1960s and 1970s. No prior experience in group leadership was required. Currently, faculty has increased input.

Applicants are selected at the end of a day-long workshop in which they meet in small groups and answer questions about their motivations for facilitating groups in women's studies, their personal views on feminism, and their experiences in small group learning. Communication and leadership skills are expressed through the use of structured roleplays and discussions. Exercises emphasizing conflict between group members or between a member and the facilitator are used to assess the applicant's competencies in confrontational situations. Considerable time is spent evaluating the performance of each applicant. The selection decisions are made by consensus, with emphasis placed on composing a group of peer facilitators who can work well together as a team. These students, for the most part untrained in peer counseling or group leadership skills, are selected for their personal attributes, feminist convictions, and comfort under fire.

> *Peer B*: I would have to say the most difficult for me was when I had a student who throughout the group was the most active group member—and in that sense very positive—but also the most disruptive. She presented constant challenges to authority, constant challenges to material, constant challenges to other group members. She was really dominating and manipulative to the rest of the group and it was hard for me to help other members of the group resist her attitude. So, that was probably the hardest thing for me: making sure that she was taken care of and that she wasn't excluded in any way from the group. That was tough to do because so many times I wanted to say, "I want you out. I don't want you in my group. We'd be so much happier without you." But I had to say, "Look, she has a lot to offer," and she really did. She had a lot of valuable viewpoints to bring out.

The students selected participate in a class for facilitators and function as leaders for the introductory course in women's studies. This class offers training experiences related to the tasks of facilitating and topics central to feminist teaching (Maher & Tetreault, 1994). The teaching staff are named "coordinators" and they work collaboratively with facilitators, who take responsibility for planning class sessions. Expertise of all participants is valued, and the student facilitators are empowered to set and implement much of the semester's intellectual and experiential agenda.

> *Peer G:* It seemed like so much of it was thinking about what went on in the group and thinking about our role in the group as facilitators. It really just took over my life, but I didn't resent it. You know, I loved it! I would do it again, definitely.

The agenda for the facilitator training class generally includes learning about group skills, dealing with conflict, understanding power and its relationship to gender and women's oppression, decision-making skills, and experiential learning methods. In order to illuminate, critique, and improve on the group dynamics for the class, some portion of each class meeting is devoted to functioning as a self-analytic group in which communication patterns and gender roles and authority are examined.

The training class meets for four hours a week and is the source of supervision for concurrent work of the students as they serve in their roles as facilitators for the introductory class. In addition, students meet in small peer supervision groups outside of class time with a coordinator, who comments on written weekly reports about the groups and gives feedback on the progress of the facilitator as a group leader.

The training course is a site of excitement, conflict, growth, pain, and hard work. Originally it was offered for four credit hours; students frequently spend many more hours in class, in group preparation, in consulting about and preparing each semester's coursepacks, in evaluating their experience, and in preparing reports on their groups' development. Coordinators are available to provide resources and guidance. However, relocating the center of responsibility and expertise to the student facilitators rather than the faculty may have inadvertently overburdened them.

> *Peer C:* When I got the job, I thought, "Oh my, what did I just get myself into? In a few weeks I'm going to have a bunch of freshmen and

sophomores asking me questions." There's an incredible amount of planning and organizing for this class. That was also super-overwhelming. I was spending easily fifteen to twenty hours in preparation for the first class, doing reading and planning lessons. I kind of over-did it, but it turned out okay. My over-preparing made me really prepared, and I think that my confidence in myself gave the students confidence in me.

Peer A: Yeah, it was overwhelming. I think we did like four credits, and the work was much, much more than four credits. It should have been a lab course. The sciences have lab courses and they get like five or six credits. That's what I think this should have been. But it blended perfectly with everything that I'm interested in. I'm a women's studies major, and I've worked at a women's shelter and I'm going to be working at SAPAC [Sexual Assault Prevention and Awareness Center; see chapter 8], so it just fits perfectly.

The training program and the syllabi are reinvented with each new cohort of facilitators. The emphasis on personal growth and self-discovery creates a heady, exciting atmosphere in which students and faculty feel themselves to be creating an educational alternative, an affirmative group culture within the Women's Studies Department. Facilitators are highly motivated and feel a deep responsibility for their students.

Peer G: It's structured around self-learning. We're supposed to think and reflect in our journals, come to class, and talk with each other. It's hard because you make a decision if you're going to participate and be a group member or if you're kind of going to sometimes watch the group dynamics a little bit more. Then the other times I felt really comfortable just throwing in a comment or two here and there.

Many faculty and students worry about the intellectual rigor of the course and how educational outcomes might be evaluated. Furthermore, concern about the minimal diversity of the facilitator group led many to speculate about the self-selection factors in the composition of the training course and the potential for exclusion of students of color. Women's studies, and the feminist movement in general, has been criticized by women of color for reflecting and favoring the circumstances of white, usually middle-class, women. Universities are confronted with the need to realize the goals of a learning environment in which there is optimal support and challenge for all students. Students must be helped to develop perspectives and skills that will enable them to participate fully in a multicultural, political, social, and occupational world.

> *Peer A*: After class on Wednesdays I would call my mom and just cry and cry because of all the things I learned about myself in terms of what my prejudices were and what my issues were. I had a really hard time dealing with issues of race within the class because I found that that's so foreign to me. Also, I found out that I wasn't so secure in some of my beliefs, that for the first time I was challenged by people in the group who would say, "I don't believe in something that you believe in very strongly." That was hard.

Cultivating culturally competent staff and peer leaders is a very difficult, yet essential, endeavor. In predominantly white institutions, there are few (if any) diverse people in positions of authority or who can provide adequate mentoring for students. Curricula frequently reflect European-American majority perspectives and white male biases. Attracting diverse faculty and students requires consistent outreach to student communities of color in order to avoid the damaging and regressive effects of tokenism on the quality of learning and experience of students (Higginbotham, 1992).

Currently, universities are experiencing storms of change as debates occur about the appropriate level of inclusiveness in curricula with respect to representation of difference. These debates, although invigorating and profoundly significant, are also often experienced as quite volatile, emotion-filled, and conflict-laden. For the most part, norms for acknowledging and engaging in conflict in academic settings reflect several strongly held values within the academic culture. Ideas may be debated within the parameters of rationality, civility, and academic freedom. Issues that inevitably elicit strong affect and intense disagreement may create anxiety, confusion, and fear.

Teachers and facilitators need to carefully prepare to surface and manage conflict and to develop group process that respectfully includes all voices and allows for diversity of emotional style. They must be able to protect against the marginalization, silencing, and punishing of difference. These are complex and sophisticated skills requiring a high level of self- and social-awareness. In addition, a teacher/facilitator should possess an appreciation for varying levels of developmental readiness in young adults for moving toward a perspective of relativity in thinking about such issues as authority, difference, and ethics (Chickering, 1981; Gilligan, 1982).

> *Peer B*: You kind of learn to sift through all the other things that come out when people get angered. There's so many outside forces that get involved and you really learn what the essential issues are. It's really helpful—when I have disagreements with anyone or when I observe disagreements with other people—that I've learned a lot more effective means of communication. People lose their heads and they stop thinking. You just need to get them to the point where they can make a rational argument with each other but not lose the passion that they feel for the issue.

> *Peer E*: When students don't respect each other and don't respect the group, it's very challenging and very frustrating. That happened to two members of my group. I was actually very lucky because I got a group of ten women and

eight of them it seemed really wanted to be there, which was really neat. Two of them didn't want to be there, and that was very challenging. It was also very challenging because they were all at different levels of understanding about women's issues. So, I had to find a level where they could all communicate about it and not just be really frustrated.

so true

In evaluating the student experience, use of faculty resources, support for the course's structure, and the feminist experiment in shared leadership and peer teaching have been strong. But some recycling concerns—the need to increase diversity among faculty and students in women's studies and the potential for over-burdening and under-training the student facilitators—motivated a review. This evaluation led to the recommendation that two new courses be created, in which teaching teams (one faculty member and one teaching assistant for each course) would be racially and ethnically balanced and in which efforts would be made to insure diversity by means of outreach to students of color across campus. The new courses proposed are vehicles for teaching about multiple lenses of feminism, perspectives on women and power, the dynamics of mixed-gender and multicultural groups. In these classes students are expected to demonstrate competencies in didactic presentation, in the use of experiential learning strategies, in developing a positive group climate, and in conflict management. The successful completion of the first course in the series becomes a prerequisite for enrolling in the second; this provides for on-going and greater skill training and supervision for facilitators of the introductory course.

Peer B: At the beginning of any facilitation experience there's always some anxiety. When others are experiencing that with you, you form a bond. There was conflict among some people because they had different facilitation styles and different ideas about the issues. Overall I would describe our relationship as a mutually beneficial, supportive one.

While maintaining an objective to share power and leadership skills among the participants in these courses, faculty have regained more typical reins of authority.[4] Student facilitators now receive weekly supervision and guidance from the faculty member and/or teaching assistant(s) as well as participate in peer problem-solving groups and discussions of reading assignments. Advanced skill training is organized by the faculty team at two workshops throughout the semester and in class, designed on the basis of an on-going assessment of facilitators' abilities and experiences in their sections. Peer group supervision has been incorporated into classroom meetings, and student facilitators share leadership of weekly planning discussions on the curriculum.

> *Peer B*: We would meet as a group of facilitators every week for two hours in addition to our two hours that we spent facilitating. We talked about the experiences that we had and shared ideas for the next week, that kind of stuff. We worked through some of the problems that we were having in our groups to get suggestions from others. The supervisor would offer suggestions as well. She would obviously intervene if there were any really serious issues with attendance or policy business-type stuff. She would also offer suggestions as another group member. We were required to send her a memo every week, recounting our experiences and talking about how we thought things were going and if we had any questions or comments and things like that, things she needed to be made aware of. We'd meet individually with her, and she also observed us throughout the semester.
>
> *Peer G*: It would have been a very different experience for me, and a very different group, I think, if I hadn't had such strong support from the other facilitators. I think I really leaned on

---

[4] See Editor's Note at the beginning of this chapter.

them a lot and tried to be there for them too. That was a lot of help.

The current model accommodates as many as twenty facilitators and 150 introductory students each semester. Outreach to students of color has increased diversity in the class; currently, approximately thirty percent of the students enrolled in the course are of color.

> *Peer C*: You see people's different styles of interacting. You see the person who is defensive, the person who is angry, the person who is withdrawn, those who include themselves in the conversation and those who exclude themselves, those who want to be heard and those who don't. You come up with different perspectives.

The focus on facilitator competency follows from our awareness of the developmental stresses and imperatives students face. College students experience a time of tremendous growth, conflict, and exploration. Developmentally, students must struggle with strengthening a coherent sense of self and experiment with new skills and interests. Compelling personal challenges absorb the student: exploring career pathways, solidifying skills in self-care and time management, expanding capacity for and seeking opportunities for intimacy (Chickering, 1981; Astin, 1993). These are also years in which students are introduced to unfamiliar theories about people and politics that may clash significantly with previously held convictions. Challenge must be balanced with support as students learn to stretch their thinking to accommodate competing modes of thought and perspectives.

> *Peer B*: I'm actually looking for a job where I'll be facilitating a group, and I see it as being really beneficial to me, really helping me grow. I think that speaks volumes and I wish there were more programs like this one. I wish that everyone had the opportunity to facilitate a group. I don't guess that everyone would want

to or that everyone should, but I think everyone should be given the opportunity.

Peer A: People would say to me, "Well, what are you going to do with a women's studies major? All you can really do is teach." At first I thought, "I don't want to teach," no way. Now that's a real option for me; this experience changed my whole perspective on teaching, and now I think, "I really could do this!"

Peer B: It's taught me that I'm very comfortable in the role of a leader, that I can be empathic yet strong. It's taught me when to compromise and when not to. Those were things that I think I already had within myself, but it exposed that side of me and helped me be public with it.

The structure of teaching and mentoring in the university is designed to emphasize the intellectual and cognitive development of students. Among others, feminist scholars have been critical of the extent to which quantitative modes of thought have obscured more affective and personal domains of student learning and growth (Light, 1990; Belenky, et al., 1986). Students' struggle to identify with course material, in which emotion and intellect are linked, is often inhibited by an overvaluation of the "rational." However, the notion that teaching must engage the whole person of the student and impact on her/his intellectual, ethical, and interpersonal development in a way that insures that she/he may become an enlightened and humane participant in the local and global community is central to the premises of a modern liberal arts education. In this sense, women's studies pedagogy attempts to realize these goals.

Peer F: I think this is the best thing that I've done with my university education. I really do. I mean, it's given me a way to give a lot of that back to other people and to the community.

Learning about participation in a small group as a stepping stone to larger and more complex settings is perhaps one of the main objectives of this program. Students in the introductory course are told that they will be expected to become active in the creation of a positive group climate in which all contribute to setting and achieving goals. Members learn about how to give and receive constructive feedback about their contributions, solve group problems, and make decisions in which all points of view are considered. They also take responsibility in the leadership of the group by facilitating a group discussion and/or presenting material to the group with collaboration of the group leader. Members are encouraged to approach their group experience as a sort of safe learning laboratory in which communication patterns among members, including women and men, may be illuminated and understood in light of the intellectual themes of the course.

Students are introduced to the structure and goals of the introductory course in a mass meeting at the beginning of each semester. Faculty and facilitators describe the course philosophy, attendance and grading policies, and events for the semester. Students are asked to express preferences for group composition (e.g., all women, mixed race, mixed gender, etc.), and wherever possible these preferences are honored. This initial mass meeting provides an opportunity for the peer facilitators to assume leadership and become involved in presenting didactic material on feminist pedagogy and course content. Facilitators are responsible for composing the groups, contacting group members, and planning the class experience for the following week.

> *Peer B*: We as peers facilitate Women's Studies 100, which is an introductory class entitled "Women's Issues." There is no lecture component to the class. It's solely discussion, so what we prepare for is meeting with a group. My group of eleven students met for two hours once a week. We had to create the experience entirely ourselves.
>
> Some of the things that we did as far as roleplays were to simulate a group in which we would all be assigned group member personas, and then someone would be assigned the position of facilitator. We would all kind of act out these

parts and then talk about how the facilitation went, how we could have all done things differently, how it felt to be a specific group member, how it was to empathize with everyone in the group, both the facilitator and all the members, in order to get different perspectives. If we did exercises, I was responsible for coming up with them. I was responsible for reading the journals and grading them. I was responsible for making all assignments and scheduling any kind of activities. I tried to leave it as open-ended with the group as I could and let them make the group what they wanted it to be, and that was one of the things I strived for throughout the semester. "What do you think about the way I'm facilitating? How can we make this group what you want to get out of it? Is there a movie that you particularly want to watch? Is there a topic that we haven't discussed that you really want to get into? What have I ignored?" So, I tried to make it as much as possible their group and let them guide my role. In addition to bringing things to the group and planning activities, I was also there as a mediator between students to make sure that all students were equally heard and were getting an equally valuable experience.

Typically, facilitators follow the framework provided by a coursepack of articles to which they contribute each semester. They enjoy considerable creative freedom in the design of class exercises and discussion strategies. Occasionally several groups plan to meet together in order to see a movie that supplements readings or to take part in an additional workshop offered by other peer education programs on campus.

Peer G: When you're the facilitator, you get so psyched up about the material and how the class is going to react. Then, if you've got even one person in a group that comes in and says, "I didn't do the readings" or "I thought it was boring," it really tears at you a little bit. And although you go into it knowing it's a class that

Peer Facilitation in the Feminist Classroom

they're taking pass/fail, it is disappointing when that happens. When I was first exposed to the material, I kind of grabbed onto it and wanted to read everything I could. I felt like a lot of other group members in our group were the same way, so every week there would be a really good, productive discussion. You want that for the students you teach, too. It takes time, but you see the light bulbs going on. But for the people who don't experience that, you feel their loss.

In order to contribute to the training of future facilitators, the groups are observed by students in the prerequisite course both early and late in the semester. Observers offer commentary only at the end of the class. In this way, we have attempted to form a "peer career ladder" in which more experienced peers help in the teaching of beginners while offering facilitators opportunities for feedback. Facilitators make weekly reports to faculty that describe teaching and facilitation objectives, group process events, group themes and areas of conflict, and observations about the progress of group development. Facilitators meet weekly as a group for discussing their sections, sharing resources, and planning for the future. Faculty give detailed weekly feedback to facilitators by means of an electronic mail conference system as well as in periodic meetings for assessing areas of growth and need for extra support.

> *Peer F*: The emphasis of the course is to prepare you to facilitate, but also it's about teaching you about group dynamics and about the way groups function. Roleplays give you more of a sense of hands-on experience. We observed introductory groups twice to get a sense of what the class actually looks like and what a facilitator does in that setting; this experience gave me a really good sense of what I would be experiencing the next semester.
>
> *Peer E*: I knew I needed feedback; it was important. We had been trained to appreciate feedback.

My faculty always gave it to me in a very nice way. If she had done it differently I might have felt less positive about it.

Peer F: Other peer facilitators came twice a semester to observe and give us feedback, both verbal and written. This is really helpful to get a sense of how other people see what's happening. The supervisor comes and observes once and usually gives verbal feedback, and then at the end of the semester you get written evaluations. Last semester, I did a verbal go-round to ask how everybody felt the class went. Reading over everybody's final journal from last semester, it's really exciting to "hear" people say thank you for making them more educated people.

As we reflect on the difference between our earlier model and our current structure, we observe that students emerge from the prerequisite course with far greater confidence, openness to on-going learning and supervision, and skill in facilitating and teaching. They have worked to become a collaborative and cohesive team with high morale, mutual respect, and an impressive collection of skills.

Facilitators develop an understanding of "group developmental phases." They realize that their most significant job is to "develop and tend the group" (Glassman & Kates, 1990) as it will be the vehicle for each individual member's growth and learning. In their sections of the course, they work to encourage participation and to deepen understandings of the cultural differences within the group. Slowly they observe that students, having initially depended on the facilitator for answers and for direction, begin to find their own voices, express their own opinions, and seek out the opinions of peers. They learn to utilize their analytical skills in response to the readings and to one another's commentary.

Peer A: I think the most rewarding was when the members of my facilitation group came up to me and would stay and talk to me after class. They had to hand in journals to us about things that they loved or didn't love about the class, so I received positive feedback and constructive feedback from them, which made me feel great because I felt like the lines of communication were open enough that they would say, "You know, I didn't like this when you did this in class." I felt like that said something about my facilitation skills; it felt really good. It was all very rewarding.

Peer C: There were days when you go in there and you feel like, "I just can't deal with it! I'm not going to learn anything; I'm not going to be pelted with everybody's emotional baggage." Toward the end I saw that people had come around and they had a new, heightened sense of awareness, seeing things that they hadn't seen before, starting to defend their rights, getting involved with socially active measures.

Peer G: One of the most rewarding times is when you don't have to do anything because the group is doing it all. What you want them to do is to teach themselves.

Currently, facilitators are evaluated using several strategies. Standard university course evaluation forms are distributed at the end of the semester. Facilitators also devise their own evaluation/feedback methods in which they receive both verbal and written feedback from students and from observers. Students are able to give anonymous or signed responses to questions about course content, readings, group discussions, facilitator skills, and the impact of the course on personal attitudes and outlooks.

Peer C: The feedback I received was in different forms. Mine came throughout the semester from students. I solicited consistent evaluations about what I could do better, what was working and what wasn't. The same thing occurred with my mentor. I would e-mail her and she would help suggest solutions to try to address certain problems. There were

> evaluations at the end from the students and from other peers who were facilitating. So, there were really two different group lives for me—my co-facilitators and students in the class.

Most frequently, students report finding their group experience to be enriching and unique. They see peer facilitation as particularly helpful in allowing discussion of new and controversial ideas in a relaxed and accepting atmosphere. We know of the power of the peer culture to influence and mediate attitudes among college students (Pascarella & Terenzini, 1991); this effect may be greatest when provided by persons who are only one or two developmental rungs beyond their students.

Our program relies on the positive impact peer facilitators can have on students in their groups. Commonly, students tell us that the first time they spoke in class was in their groups and/or that their participation helped them develop confidence in their ideas and self-expression. Students and facilitators speak of improving across a wide range of interpersonal skills—listening, engaging in debate, holding their own in discussions with men, accepting and participating in conflict situations in discussions, and contributing to solving group problems.

> *Peer C*: It made me a lot more open, a much more active listener. I'm a lot more confident because it was so successful. I have facilitated other groups since then because of this. I have a very different take now on experiential or peer learning as opposed to a more traditional lecture format. I really think experiential learning is a lot more effective.

> *Peer E*: I know in general that I'm probably more patient with lots of issues. I had to learn how to be non-judgmental and non-critical. I had to learn how to construct my feelings and thoughts so that it would be helpful to others.

> *Peer B*: I find myself slipping into the facilitator role in many situations academically and socially. It's positive and negative in that people

sometimes don't perceive that I'm also being myself when I'm being a facilitator. And sometimes, because as a facilitator I didn't want my personal views to enter our discussions and affect my presentation of the issues, I want to be as unbiased as possible. I am striving for that. Sometimes I find myself falling into a facilitator role in a conversation. I'm not getting my views across; I'm just mediating other people's views and making sure that they're heard and that they're comfortable talking. It happens a lot in my family.

Peer D: I think if you have a better understanding of yourself in terms of the issues you're facilitating, you're a step ahead going in, introducing students to these issues.

Young women, about seventy-five percent of the women's studies students, regularly refer to their feeling motivated by this group experience to further pursue personal and intellectual goals. They describe a deepening identification with other women as sources of learning and support; they talk about reconsidering roles and responsibilities in their personal relationships. Unsolicited commentary often reveals fortified self-esteem and increased identification with feminism. This connection may be more than serendipitous. A relationship between the cognitive centrality of gender schema and the experience of oneself as a member of a group whose members share a common fate has been linked to feminist consciousness, self-esteem, and a positive response to collective action (Gurin & Markus, 1989). In addition, recent evidence suggests that the benefits students derive in their women's studies classes—including increased confidence as students, greater assertiveness, and deeper engagement with the intellectual material—may generalize across their courses of study and be related to higher achievement in college (Bowles & Klein, 1983).

Peer E: I've become more clear in what I think, and also I've mellowed out; I think I've become more patient with other people. There were times when it was difficult as these students' peer to have to be the teacher, to have to make sure that they did their homework, and, when they didn't, to have to do something about it. When they weren't showing up it was my responsibility; there were times that this became a problem with a couple of students and I had to deal with it, and it was very difficult for me—in the middle of it I would get nervous. But I did it, and I did it in a way that I think was fair, and I think they thought was fair, and so it helped me a little bit with confronting with people well.

The facilitators share similarly positive reactions to their experiences in the training courses. They observe considerable personal growth in their capacity for assuming leadership, for creating learning experiences for others, for facilitating recognition of differences and resolution of conflict. They refer to a deepened understanding of the contributions of class, culture, sexual orientation, & ethnicity, & they claim a greater comfort in working with diverse groups. The facilitators speak movingly of their pleasure of assisting in someone else's growth and the unforgettable *esprit de corps* that inevitably develops in their groups. We must add that faculty happily share in this pleasure. And the students all comment on the wide applicability of the acquired perspectives and skills learned in their future educational and career goals.

Peer E: Facilitating was a wonderful experience. I learned so many valuable skills and I met some great people. It was just one step in dealing with people and dealing with groups. I think anybody who wants to and thinks that they are capable and is trained should do this kind of work because I think it helps people in their relationships with themselves and with others.

REFERENCES

Astin, A. (1993). *What matters in college? Four critical years revisited.* San Francisco: Jossey-Bass, Inc.

Belenky, M. F., Clinchy, B. M., & Golderberger, J. M. (1986). *Women's ways of knowing: The development of self, voice, and mind.* New York: Basic Books, Inc.

Blocher, D., & Rapoza, R. (1981). Professional and vocational preparation. In A. Chickering, *The modern American college* (212-31). San Francisco: Jossey-Bass, Inc.

Bowles, G., & Duelli Klein, R. (Eds.). (1983). *Theories of women's studies.* New York: Routledge Press.

Chickering, A. (1981). *The modern American college.* San Francisco: Jossey-Bass, Inc.

D'Andrea, V. (1987). Peer counseling in colleges and universities: A developmental approach. *Journal of College Student Psychotherapy, 1* (3), 39-55.

Gilligan, C. (1982). *In a different voice: Psychological theory and women's development.* Cambridge: Harvard University Press.

Glassman, U., & Kates, L. (1990). *Group work: A humanistic approach.* Newbury Park, CA: Sage.

Gurin, P., & Markus, H. (1989). Cognitive consequences of gender identity. In S. Skerrington and D. Baker (Eds.), *The social identity of women.* Newbury Park, California: Sage.

Higginbotham, E., & Weber, L. (1992). Moving up with kin and community: Upward social mobility for Black and White women. *Gender and Society, 6* (3), 416-40.

Light, R. (1990). *Harvard Assessment Seminars.* Cambridge: Harvard University Graduate School of Education.

Maher, F. A., & Thompson Tetreault, M. K. (1994). *The feminist classroom: An inside look at how professors and students are transforming higher education for a diverse society.* New York: Basic Books.

Pascarella, E. T., & Terenzini, P. T. (1991). *How college affects students.* New York: Jossey-Bass.

Rutenberg, Taly. (1983). Learning Women's Studies. In Gloria Bowles and Renate Duelli Klein (Eds.), *Theories of women's studies* (72-8). New York: Routledge Press.

Stacey, J. (1993). Untangling feminist theory. In Diane Richardson and Victoria Robinson (Eds.), *Thinking feminist: Key concepts in women's studies.* New York: Guildford Press.

Chapter 12

Reactions to Peer Teaching Assistants in the College-Level Peer Counseling Course[1]

Sherry Hatcher, PhD, and Brian Litzenberger, MA

Peer counseling courses in academic departments at the college level are relatively more rare than their secondary school counterparts. Yet the prospective college-level paraprofessional trainee has some developmental advantages over younger adolescent peer helpers. With most college students now solidly able to reason logically, having burgeoning introspective sensibilities and increased moral acumen, their capacity for mature paraprofessional work—including teaching—is considerable (Hatcher, et al., 1994; Benson, 1979).

While the use of peer tutors and academic peer advisors at the college level is sporadic but not novel (Titley & Titley, 1982; Carns, Carns, & Wright, 1993), the use of peer teaching assistants is little addressed in the literature.[2] Our findings (reported below) suggest that the use of undergraduate

---

[1] Reprinted with permission of *Peer Facilitator's Quarterly*, in which this chapter was originally published (vol. 11 [3], [March 1994].)

[2] At the University of Michigan, at the initial suggestion of the Department Chair, Profession Patricia Gurin, we have developed a curriculum and program for the peer teaching of the peer counseling course in the Department of Psychology.

teaching assistants, when carefully selected and supervised, can add a rich dimension to more conservative undergraduate education (Walker, 1987).

To contribute to the peer spirit of the class entitled "Peer Counseling for College Students" (see chapter 3 for course description), specially selected peer teachers who have successfully completed the course in a previous semester take a small group seminar with the graduate teaching assistant. Student TAs are selected by the professor on the basis of their grade/performance in the term they took the class on peer counseling and by their interpersonal and communication skills as these affect their potential for teaching. The process is quite selective as there are some sixty undergraduates per term in the peer counseling class and only one-tenth of these, at most, have the opportunity to go on to become peer instructors.

The Role and Duties of the Undergraduate TA

In addition to functioning as support staff within the class, the students meet for one-and-half hours weekly outside of class to learn and discuss both skills of "advanced" peer counseling and those related to college teaching. They take a seminar with the graduate TA, in which their own assignments run parallel to those assigned in the larger class, i.e., they write weekly journals on their experiences (now, not as a class member but as a teacher), learn how to facilitate discussions, grade journals, critique writing, and construct and demonstrate roleplays. They are assigned readings from such sources as W. J. McKeachie's (1986) *Teaching Tips* and professional journals, most particularly *Teaching of Psychology*. Altogether they learn, both academically and experientially, how to function as a member of a supervised teaching team.

Undergraduate peer TAs are present at classroom sections and are active participants in a course they have once taken—and now help to teach. They learn about the logistics of running a course, including taking attendance; ordering films, books, and coursepacks; operating video equipment to film student roleplays; and confirming guest speakers. Often they are surprised at these "less glamorous" aspects of teaching that professors and graduate teaching assistants routinely negotiate as part of their jobs.

In addition, undergraduate TAs discuss both their own journal entries and their reactions to the journals produced by students taking the course. They also write a final paper addressing the nature of their role as a peer teaching assistant and the ways in which this work may have contributed to their educational and career plans. As with the students enrolled in the course, their final paper is also in the format suggested by the American Psychological Association with the requisite literature review, method, results, discussion, and references. Undergraduate TAs are graded on their attendance and participation in the seminar, the quality and depth of their grading of peer journals, the quality of their discussions, and their final paper.

Some of the weekly journal topics suggested to them by the graduate teaching assistants were:

- the experience of their change in roles from being a student to being a TA
- how they have learned to give feedback on journals
- how they have learned to facilitate class discussion
- what has surprised them in the role of teacher
- in what ways they respond to the different personalities of their students; how they avoid favoritism
- what biases and prejudices they think they bring to the class; what limitations their identity gives them
- how they have learned to facilitate small groups; what trends they have noticed in their leading of discussions
- how they evaluate themselves
- what has/has not worked in roleplay demonstrations and why they believe this is the case

- their evaluation of the special peer-led class on issues of identity and diversity

Data on the Response of Students to Undergraduate Teachers

In surveying the current class of sixty peer counseling students, the following optional and anonymous evaluation was obtained from the students, addressing the function and work of the undergraduate TAs. For each of the following items, the undergraduates had to respond from "Strongly Agree" to "Strongly Disagree" on a five-point scale:

1. In general, I like having undergraduate TAs for the Peer Counseling Class.
2. I found their roleplay demonstrations valuable.
3. I approve of their grading journals under the supervision of the graduate TA.
4. The undergraduate TAs did a good job of leading discussion.
5. This feature of the course is in the spirit of peer work.
6. I would like to see the undergraduate TAs continue in this role.
7. I would like to be an undergraduate TA in the future.

Survey Results

Two thirds of the class "strongly agreed" that they liked having the undergraduate teaching assistants for the peer counseling class; only one student rated this item lower than "agree."

Approximately four fifths of the class "strongly agreed" that the roleplay demonstrations of the undergraduate TAs were valuable. Only one student disagreed with this item.

Slightly more than one half of the class "strongly agreed" that the undergraduate TAs did a good job of leading discussions when they had the opportunity to do so; one-third "agreed" with this item. Again, only one student "disagreed." All but one sixth of the class (who "agreed" with this item) "strongly agreed" that "this feature of the course is in the spirit of peer work."

All but one of the students responded that having undergraduate TAs for the class should continue.

Indeed, the only item on which there was notable controversy was in the reaction of the undergraduates in the peer counseling course to having their peers read and comment upon their journals. Our finding here is consistent with that of Kotkke (1988); that is, even though students were given the option of having their peers not read their journals, and even though all but two students chose to have their journals read by the undergraduate TAs for half of the semester (the professor reads them during the other half), only half of the students "strongly agreed" that the undergraduate TAs did a good job in evaluating and commenting on journals. One additional third of the class "agreed" that the undergraduate TAs did an adequate job of commenting on journals and assigning a check, check-minus, check-plus to each journal; one-fifth "disagreed" that they did an adequate job of grading and commenting upon the weekly journals. This resulted despite the fact that the students were aware that the final grade on each journal was reviewed by either the graduate TA or the professor of the class and that they also added comments to each journal as they saw fit.

Typical complaints in this regard were that the undergraduate TAs were too judgmental in their comments, "graded too harshly," expected too much or even more than the professor, etc. Thus, this was the only component of peer teaching that received negative feedback from the class.

Open-Ended Feedback

The evaluation questionnaire had an open-ended component as well, in which the students were asked about positive and constructive feedback in relation to the undergraduate teaching assistants. Here feedback was mostly positive except, once again, for comments opposed to student grading.

Some examples of typical feedback in response to the open-ended questions were as follows:

Student A: The undergraduate TAs are very easy to relate to since they are more or less peers to us. They do a great job in modeling appropriate peer counseling skills and give me the confidence that I too can use skills appropriately.

Student B: The undergraduate TAs are valuable in that they are in the exact same positions many of us are in school, our social lives, etc. This helps to keep the focus geared toward our level. I thought that having UGTAs for this course was really important. They served as a link between the student and the professor. It was also helpful because it made the section more comfortable because we could relate and identify with them.

Student C: They provide a sense of equality. They make me feel like I can learn as much as they know in a short time—and they seem very knowledgeable.

Student D: They are more experienced with peer work and because we are so close in age, I saw how I could apply what I have learned.

Student E: It made me more comfortable discussing certain issues because I felt that they could relate to me.

Student F: Their roleplays were great—they really added to the class and provided good role models of peer counselors.

Student G: It brought the spirit to a lot of our teachings with the roleplays and the presence of "our peers" to help.

> *Student H:* They were my peers, which helped me to better understand the concepts in the class.
>
> *Student I:* The UGTAs made me feel as though there are others like me who feel this work is important enough to dedicate time to.
>
> *Student J:* They seemed less like teachers and more like just a part of the class (who knew what they were talking about).
>
> *Student K:* Having someone our age be motivated to TA in this class motivated me to listen and be involved.
>
> *Student L:* It's a great idea—definitely in the spirit of peer work since this class is about working with peers.

The comments above were typical of those produced by the fifty-five respondents in our survey.

Response of the Undergraduate TAs to their Jobs

For their part, all but one of the undergraduate teaching assistants over the four semesters this feature of the course has existed report this as a quite positive experience, noting that it boosts their confidence and augments their resumes for graduate school or the job market (they are primarily college seniors with an occasional junior). They feel they come to appreciate the complexities of teaching. The one dissenter was fearful that her job would supplant opportunities for graduate TAs, which is, in fact, not the case.

Some typical comments from the undergraduate TAs include:

> *UGTA A:* I think that the purpose of having undergraduate TAs (UGTAs) for the class is really in keeping with the subject of the class. Because the class is about peer counseling and peer facilitators and the impact that peers have on each other, it's really kind of crucial that in

our class we use undergraduates to help facilitate other undergraduates.

Undergraduate TAs also believe they refine and improve their own, now more advanced, peer counseling skills by preparing additional roleplays and getting feedback from the graduate teaching assistant and the course instructor. Said one undergraduate TA in this regard:

> UGTA B: I find myself using peer counseling techniques more and more of the time and being careful about the way I attend, especially when I'm with new people who aren't my friends and fall under the criteria for the difference between a peer and a friend. It has positively affected my relationships with others.

Said another:

> UGTA C: It made me see how seriously students take the things that their peers are modeling and that their teachers are lecturing about. There are some people who really took everything the professor said to heart and the examples we set in our roleplay demonstrations.

The only complaints UGTAs sometimes register is that they want to do even more teaching and leading of discussions; the professor and graduate TA have been responsive to this request and, to some extent, increased both their leading of discussions and administrative responsibilities. For example, they were invited to originate and conduct a workshop on multicultural peer counseling, and this has become a regular and quite important feature of the course.

At times, too, the UGTAs report that it is difficult to feel like a "professional" in relation to one's peers. As one peer TA said: "There was really that line between having fun with people and being their TA."

Not insignificantly, undergraduate TAs feel this experience can impact their career plans. Said one typical respondent:

> UGTA D: It hasn't changed my career plans to be a clinical psychologist; it has solidified my career plans. I know that along the way to fund my education I will be a TA. It has made me feel more at ease with what I know is coming along.

The Response of the Graduate TA

The graduate TA gets experience learning how to run a small seminar in addition to the usual larger sections of undergraduates assigned to the graduate teaching assistants. The graduate student serves as a mentor to students about to graduate from college in a very small setting, as there are only six to eight UGTAs each semester.

In addition to the added support in the teaching of peer counseling, the graduate TA reports that working with the UGTAs has been a rewarding experience in many regards. Teaching a smaller seminar has allowed more contact with these students and provided the opportunity to interact in quite specific ways, such as observing and commenting formally and informally and providing frequent feedback. In this way, being more involved in these students' development, the graduate TA has worked to help them understand themselves as they grow to understand and learn through their jobs as assistants in the teaching process. In addition, the graduate TA has found it helpful to have other perspectives on the course of the class. Not only do the UGTAs provide the graduate TA with an additional set of eyes and ears but they are also available to undergraduates, some of whom feel more comfortable speaking with a peer than with a graduate student. The relationships established between the graduate TA and the UGTAs and the professor have made the teaching of peer counseling a more fulfilling and rewarding experience.

The Response of the Professor

The professor gets much-needed assistance with the course and has the opportunity to demonstrate through these layers of peer-based teaching assignments an augmented peer spirit for the class. The professor reports a sense of reward in supervising the students, the undergraduate TAs, and the graduate TA at their increasingly sophisticated levels of ability: "It is gratifying to see people who once took the course able to facilitate creative and productive discussion, i.e., help *teach* the course."

In sum, this appears to be a "win-win-win-win" situation at all four levels: for the professor, for the graduate teaching assistant, for the undergraduate teaching assistants, and for the students enrolled in "Peer Counseling for College Students."

REFERENCES

Benson, J. (1979). A comparison of peer and professional trainers in teaching basic counseling skills to undergraduate residence hall assistants. *Dissertation Abstracts International, 40* (2-A), 669.

Carns, A., Carns, M., & Wright, J. (1993). Students as paraprofessionals in four-year colleges and universities: Current practice compared to prior practice. *Journal of College Student Development, 34,* 358-363.

Hatcher, S., Nadeau, M., Walsh, L., Reynolds, M., Galea, J., & Marz, K. (1994). The teaching of empathy for high school and college students: Testing Rogerian methods with the Interpersonal Reactivity Index. *Adolescence, 29* (116), 961-74.

Kotkke, J. (1988). Students as peer critics of writing in a psychology course. *Psychological Reports, 62* (1), 337-8.

McKeachie, W. (1986). *Teaching Tips.* Lexington, MA: D. C. Heath & Company.

Titley, R., & Titley, B. (1982). Academic advising: The neglected dimension in design for undergraduate education. *Teaching of Psychology, 9*(1), 45-9.

Walker, W. (1987). A model for curriculum evaluation and revision in undergraduate psychology programs. *Teaching Psychology* 14(4), 198-202.

Multicultural Peer Facilitation

Chapter 13

Addressing Ethnicity within Peer Helping Programs

Calvin Chin, BA,[1] *and Jena Baker, BA*

As today's society becomes increasingly multicultural, it becomes even more important that cultural differences be recognized and respected. Awareness of cultural differences may be especially important in the helping fields, as biases and stereotypes may interfere with the successful helping relationship. The peer helping field has not ignored this imperative, attempting to address ethnicity in largely two ways. One way has been to create peer programs targeted at specific ethnic groups. Archer and Turner (1976) describe one such program geared toward African-American university students. The other way has been to include aspects of cultural awareness within traditional peer programs not necessarily targeting a particular population. A good example of this approach is a peer program for a diverse group of foreign students at the University of Guam (Miller, 1989). It is the second way of addressing ethnicity that will be the focus of this chapter.

Approaches to addressing ethnicity within peer programs will be informed by the literature on cross-cultural counseling. Just as techniques form Carl Rogers' client-centered

---

[1] These data were collected as part of a University of Michigan Summer Research Opportunities Program (SROP) grant awarded to Mr. Chin in the summer of 1992 under the supervision of Dr. Sherry Hatcher. SROP awards are funded by the Rackham School of Graduate Studies.

therapy have been modified as the basis for individual peer counseling, the techniques and approaches used in the literature on cross-cultural counseling may be applied to work with peer groups.

This chapter is divided into two parts. The first part will address the theoretical issues on ethnicity and peer counseling, a discussion of the pros and cons in addressing ethnicity through education about specific ethnic groups, and how peer counseling naturally lends itself to cross-cultural learning.

The second part of the chapter deals with more practical issues. How does one address ethnicity in an applied program? How can sensitivity to multicultural issues be encouraged throughout all aspects of the program, from training to practice?

Theoretical Issues

How should peer counselors deal with ethnicity? There are several answers to this question, which has been the topic of much debate. The preliminary issue that is usually first decided upon is whether to take an *emic* or an *etic* approach as one's framework for viewing human behavior (Draguns, 1989). An etic approach concentrates on the universal patterns across all human behavior, while an emic approach highlights human behavior in a cultural context. If one takes a purely etic approach with peer counseling, one would focus on the universal themes of problems that cut across all individuals. A peer counselor using an emic approach would try to focus on how the culture of the individual makes his/her problem unique: focus on the individual as a member of a specific social group. There is no clear answer in the literature as to which approach is better suited to effective peer counseling; some of it becomes a matter of choice.

Problems exist with both the etic and emic approaches to understanding human behavior if each approach is used in isolation from the other. Klineburg (1985) points out several dangers of a too narrow focus on the cultural particulars of a situation. The danger exists when the counselor, whether it be a peer or a professional, loses sight of the client as an individual and instead focuses upon him or her as merely a symbol of that cultural group. Klineburg (1985) stresses the importance of determining the veracity of a cultural pattern for an individual. Campbell (1967) goes as far as to warn that the highlighting of differences between ethnic groups may lead to exaggerated stereotypes of these differences. For example, one of the peer counselors in our group told of a time when she assumed that her "client," also African-American, was going to be just like herself. She discovered that she and her client were from very different social classes and that this issue was really the focus of her client's concerns, not race.

There also exist problems with a strict etic view. Devore (1985) reports that historically counselors have ignored ethnicity in an effort to develop a general understanding of human behavior, believing that attention to ethnicity betrayed the commitment to the equality and uniqueness of the individual. However, since the uniqueness of the individual is due in a large part to his/her ethnicity and background, addressing such issues is vital.

Perhaps the real answer to the question of how to address ethnicity lies in combining the two approaches. Throughout the literature on cross-cultural counseling, the necessity of focusing on both the universals of behavior (etic) and the cultural specifics of behavior (emic) is stressed. The effect of a person's ethnicity and its resulting social consequences are vital to the makeup and development of the individual. At the same time, however, it is essential that the peer counselor not lose sight of the individual differences within ethnic, racial, or religious groups. Just as two Caucasian clients' experiences can be extremely different, two people of color of the same ethnic or racial background can have quite different experiences, behaviors, and attitudes.

How then can both universal themes and cultural specifics be taught to peer counselors? Green (1982) suggests that "the avenues for cultural awareness...have to do with important qualities for effective social work, openness, alertness, and, most particularly, flexibility in relations with others" (Devore, 1985). It is interesting to note that the qualities Green cites are among the same skills that form the basis of peer counseling (see chapters 1-3); peer counseling inherently lends itself to a sensitivity to multicultural groups. Difficulties that might come up for peer programs in dealing with issues of ethnicity may also be rooted in the cross-cultural application of specific microskills.

One of the most important principles of peer counseling is remaining non-judgmental of the counselee. A peer counselor may have different values than his/her client but must keep those personal values from interfering with the counseling relationship. The peer counselor must not impose his/her own value system upon the counselee. Being non-judgmental is extremely important in all peer counseling interactions, but it is especially so when dealing with someone of a different race, culture, religion, or ethnicity. Cultures carry with them different value systems, which may be different from the counselor's own. The principle of being non-judgmental is very important when dealing with a person of color because of the social dynamics of the situation. A person of color must deal on a daily basis with pressure from the dominant culture. Any environment with institutionalized racism also leads to further marginalization by the dominant culture and a further invalidation of cultural differences in values and beliefs. People of color may already come into the counseling session with the frustration of feeling judged and may therefore be especially sensitive to judgment from another figure with more apparent power. The principle of remaining non-judgmental is one that clearly lends itself to multicultural situations and also is vital to a successful multicultural interaction.

Perhaps the major principle upon which peer counseling is based is the principle of empathic listening. D'Andrea and Salovey (1983) define empathy as "the ability to see a problem from the counselee's point of view and, accordingly, to be warm and supportive" (5). The question that naturally arises is whether a counselor of a different ethnicity can truly see things from the perspective of the counselee. Is it possible for a Caucasian counselor to empathize with the experience of a person of color?

To answer this question, one must examine what is involved when a person attempts to empathize with another. It is generally accepted that a person does not need to have the same experience as another to empathize, as it is impossible for two people to really experience a situation identically. Empathy can be viewed as a process by which an individual takes something from his/her own personal experience and uses it to relate to the other person. One must use much information, both verbal and non-verbal, to determine as closely as possible the counselee's feelings. Are there limits to empathy? Are there situations in which counselors simply have no way of connecting emotionally? Of course there are. These situations just sometimes happen, and they do not occur only in cross-cultural counseling. Just as with most issues in peer counseling, whether or not a peer counselor's ethnicity differs from that of his/her client, the outcome depends on the individuals involved. For example, in a case where the issue being presented is procrastination, a college peer counselor of a different ethnicity could likely empathize. But where the counselee presents a problem dealing with institutionalized racism at the university, it is possible that a Caucasian counselor may not be able to empathize as well as a person of color who has faced similar problems.

The experience of a person of color in this society where racism still exists is a very powerful one. Because this experience is almost impossible to perceive from a position outside of the non-dominant group, there may be situations in which empathy is difficult to maintain. There exists a definite need for people of color who work as peer counselors not only to fill the gap in services for people of color but also to increase and improve the quality of multiculturally sensitive programs. An exploratory study (Chin, 1992) gives anecdotal evidence that peer counselors of color felt better able to empathize with all groups of people because of their challenging experiences as members of a non-dominant group.

> Peer A: As a person of color, I can appreciate how much it hurts when something racist or discriminating happens. I think a lot of my Caucasian counterparts may not understand how serious even the slightest racist comment can be. I know how invalidating it is because I have experienced it. I can use my experience to better empathize with the person. That is

something I can understand better because I am a person of color.

There are people who believe that empathy is possible even between people who come from very different backgrounds. Jones (1985) describes empathy based on differences that would "focus the imagination in a way that would transpose oneself into another, rather than upon one's own feelings, and in this way achieve a more complete understanding of culturally varied predispositions, personal constructs, and experience" (178). Jones' construct of empathy serves as another example of how well peer counseling may fit with multicultural awareness.

Peer B: I guess, maybe in some ways, peer counseling can help you to be more aware of your own culture and how it has affected you and to feel proud of that too, realizing that it's not a bad thing. I realized that everyone has different perspectives and cultures and everyone is really proud of where they are coming from, so it kind of strengthens our uniqueness, strengthens our group. Does that sound cliché? It's true though: our diversity strengthens the group.

While good "attending" skills are necessary for effective peer counseling, it is important to recognize, that there exist cultural differences in acceptable "body language." In the dominant culture, good attending skills include facing front, eye contact, leaning forward, open posture, and responsive facial expression. These five elements do not hold true for some cultures in which, for example, it is impolite to maintain eye contact. In such situations, it may appear that the counselee is not listening when, in fact, he/she is really being attentive. The amount of personal space, or proxemics, is another characteristic that varies among different cultures (Hall, 1969). It is important to be aware of such differences and not to make conclusions about the individual or the interaction based on cultural misinterpretation.

How does one make sure that he/she is not violating the personal space of a counselee or making a misinterpretation of body language? Feedback can be used throughout the peer counseling interaction by both the counselor and counselee. The counselor might solicit feedback about whether he/she understands the counselee correctly, or the counselor may provide positive feedback about the number of personal goals that have been met by the counselee. The counselor can also use feedback to ensure that the counselor does not misinterpret something said or done by the counselee; this is especially important in a cross-cultural interaction. The counselor needs to "check in" with the counselee frequently to ensure that they are both understood. Counselors should be encouraged to solicit a good deal of feedback, as some cultures (e.g., the Japanese) might not see providing unsolicited feedback to an authority figure as appropriate. Counselors should also be encouraged to ask questions when they do not understand something that the counselee does or says so they will not run into "roadblocks."

Roadblocks are personal beliefs, values, or behaviors that might get in the way of a helpful counseling relationship. If a counselor feels strongly about a certain issue (for example, freedom of choice in abortion cases) and must work with a counselee who is pregnant and who believes abortion is wrong, the counselor might not feel able to provide good help. The abortion issue would be a roadblock and the counselor would have to refer the counselee to someone else. It is important that counselors be aware of their own roadblocks concerning people of different ethnicities and/or values. Counselors should be encouraged to be aware of and acknowledge their personal cultural biases. If a counselor does not feel comfortable speaking to a counselee of a different ethnicity, he/she should refer the counselee to someone else because if the counselor feels uncomfortable, the interaction probably will not turn out well.

Devore and Schlesinger (1981) point out that it is important to keep in mind the history of different cultural groups and its impact upon the individual within a group. It is also useful to consider the different roles ethnicity can play for a person. Ethnicity can be a source of "cohesion, identity, and strength as well as a source of strain, discordance, and strife" (Devore, 1985). Although peer counseling is primarily concerned with the present, it is important to note that the past, including ethnic history, can affect the present.

> *Student C*: We had a session in which we all said where we were coming from—not just where we were originally from, but how our culture affected us. That was a really good session because it made us realize, "This person's coming from a really small town and that's why she thinks like that and this person's coming from inner-city Detroit and that's why he might think a certain way." That really helped out a lot because I realized how different people's culture and environment totally affect how they think and how certain problems are out there that they may be more likely to run into.

Practical Issues

It is important to address the practical issues of how to incorporate sensitivity to ethnicity, race, religion, and culture within peer programs. To effectively deal with people of color, a safe atmosphere must be created. Multiculturalism needs to be addressed by peer programs throughout the outreach, training, and implementation of the program. Many times this is effectively accomplished in peer group facilitation settings (see chapters 11, 12, and 14).

Outreach to communities of people of color is important since it is often the case that groups that most need the support of peer helping programs are those that include people of color. Outreach needs to be active in nature. Peer programs must include educational presentations to members of communities where they are located. This may mean going into churches or other community meeting places and facilitating groups of diverse participants.

A way to demonstrate this commitment is to ensure that there is fair representation from the different communities among the peers who actually work for the program. Not only does this display a willingness to work with people of color, but it also provides potential users of the peer program with the opportunity to seek help from someone of a similar background. Harrison (1975) concluded in his research with African-American and Caucasian subjects that many counselees tend to prefer counselors of the same race.

> *Student D*: I think being a person of color comes in handy because you can kind of empathize better with certain callers who feel really different from everyone. Sometimes, for whatever reason, they feel like not a part of things. I think I can better empathize because being a woman and being Indian, both of these combined, help me understand people who are coming from different backgrounds and find that no one can relate to them because they are from this different kind of background.

A commitment to diversity should be made within the training of the peers in the program. Pedersen (1983) proposed a training model that makes use of a counselor and a culturally different client accompanied by an "anti-counselor" and a "pro-counselor" of the same cultural background as the client. The purpose of the anti-counselor is to point out the cultural differences between the counselor's and client's expectations and values, while the pro-counselor points out the similarities between the counselor's and client's expectations. The immediate and continuous feedback provides the counselor with an opportunity to increase skill in four areas:

1. perceiving the problem from the client's viewpoint

2. recognizing specific sources of resistance

3. reducing counselor defensiveness

4. rehearsing recovery skills for "getting out of trouble"

One of the best aspects to Pedersen's Triad model is that it enables the counselor to learn about a culture through direct contact in a safe context.

Nevertheless, there are some practical problems in implementing Pedersen's training model. The first is the necessity of providing two trainers for each counselor. This may be impractical for smaller peer programs to engage in such an individualized training, in part because of the sheer lack of numbers of people of color in some peer programs. Another problem with Pedersen's model is that it places the burden of educating on people of color. In this model, people of color are the ones whose job it is to point out cultural similarities and differences. They may not want to carry this burden of educating because they are forced into playing this role in society every day.

Among the various multicultural student programs at the University of Michigan, three make use of traditional peer mentoring formats in addressing multicultural differences.[2] Large numbers of students of color enroll in these programs' research and practica offerings. As part of their training, peers view a standard videotape on peer counseling and point out cultural differences that may occur with the skills presented. Eye contact, for example, is a skill highlighted by the videotape that may differ in its cultural relevance. The richness of experiences within the group of peers allows for productive discussion of cultural differences as they relate specifically to peer counseling situations. The peers are in effect educating each other during training.

> *Student E*: I believe there are some things that you can never understand without actually living through the experience. A lot of people of color that come for help simply will not go to someone who is not of color. I can totally understand where they are coming from. In doing peer work, I can be there for those people when they come in. Everything seems geared toward white middle-class people, and by doing peer work, maybe that can be changed. I

---

[2] The Summer Research Opportunities Program (SROP) is sponsored by the Rackham Graduate School and directed by Associate Dean Warren Whatley. The Undergraduate Research Opportunities Program (UROP) is sponsored by the College of Literature, Science and Arts and is directed by Sandra Gregerman, MS. A third peer-oriented multicultural program, Intergroup Relations and Conflict (IGRC), is discussed in detail in chapter 14.

don't mean being a counselor will stop institutionalized racism, but I do think that providing a place for non-dominant groups is a decent start.

There are still other ways in which training can address multicultural issues. Peers can brainstorm together about how each peer counseling microskill could be especially important when dealing with someone of a different ethnicity. Peers in training might engage in some of the exercises used in the intergroup relations program described in the next chapter.

Peers also need to be trained on what to do when they make a mistake, as in Pedersen's (1983) model in which peers rehearse recovery skills for "getting out of trouble." It is important to stress the need for acknowledging a mistake based upon a cultural value or stereotype. Peers need to know that it is okay to make mistakes, that it is part of the learning process. During training, roleplays could be carried out that would lead the peer to practice strategies for acknowledging mistakes.

It is also important to teach peer helpers how to decide when to refer a client to another counselor if the problem is that the client is of a different ethnicity. The usual guideline is that a referral should be made if the differences in cultural backgrounds get in the way of effectively helping the client deal with his/her problem.

One can see that training does not have to be drastically altered in order to promote cross-cultural understanding. Along with the usual roleplays used to teach peer counseling skills, one can incorporate some that deal with a cross-cultural interaction. Counselors could be asked questions like, "How could the client's ethnicity have affected the interaction? the progress of the interaction? the way you perceived the interaction?" When peers practice different skills in pairs or groups, encourage them to seek out partners of a different background. Bring in a variety of community leaders to discuss concerns that are of special importance to their group. All of these approaches can be implemented with little disturbance of the usual training schedule (see chapters 2-3).

Each month could be devoted to a different cultural group, and the uniqueness and beauty of that culture could be highlighted and celebrated in events during that month (see McGoldrick, Pearce, & Giordano, 1982). Multicultural peer counseling is effectively taught in group facilitation settings; the following chapter illustrates this point in compelling fashion.

REFERENCES

Archer J., & Turner, A. L. (1976). A Black peer counseling program. *Journal of College Student Personnel, 17,* 155.

Campbell, D. T. (1967). Stereotypes and the perception of group differences. *American Psychologist, 37,* 780-7.

Chin, C. (1992). UROP Research Grant—Summer 1992. The University of Michigan.

D'Andrea, V., & Salovey, P. (1983). *Peer Counseling.* Palo Alto: Science and Behavior Books.

Devore, W. (1985). Developing ethnic sensitivity for the counseling process: A social-work perspective. In P. Pedersen (Ed.), *Handbook of cross-cultural counseling and therapy* (93-8). London: Greenwood Press.

Devore, W., & Schlesinger, E. G. (1981). *Ethnic sensitive social work practice.* St. Louis: Mosby.

Draguns, J. G. (1989). Dilemmas and choices in cross-cultural counseling: The universal versus the culturally distinctive. In P. Pedersen, J. D. Draguns, W. J. Lonner, & J. E. Trimble (Eds.), *Counseling across cultures* (3-21). Honolulu: University Press of Hawaii.

Green, J. W. (1982). *Cultural awareness in the human services.* Englewood Cliffs, NJ: Prentice-Hall.

Hall, E. T. (1969). *The silent language.* Garden City, NY: Anchor Press.

Harrison, D. (1975). Race as a counselor-client variable in counseling and psychotherapy: A review of the research. *Counseling Psychologist,* 5 (1), 124-33.

Jones, E. E. (1985). Psychotherapy and counseling with Black clients. In P. Pedersen (Ed.), *Handbook of cross-cultural counseling and therapy* (173-9). London: Greenwood Press.

Klineburg, O. (1985). The social psychology of cross-cultural counseling. In P. Pedersen (Ed.), *Handbook of cross-cultural counseling and therapy* (29-35). London: Greenwood.

McGoldrick, M., Pearce, J., & Giordano, J. (1982) *Ethnicity and family therapy*. New York: Guilford.

Miller, K. L. (1989). Training peer counselors to work on a multicultural campus. *Journal of College Student Development, 30,* 561.

Pedersen, P. (1983). The cultural complexity of counseling. *International Journal for the Advancement of Counselling, 6* (3), 177-92.

Pedersen, P. (Ed.). (1985). *Handbook of cross-cultural counseling and therapy*. London: Greenwood Press.

Pedersen, P., Lonner, W. J., & Draguns, J. D. (Eds.) (1976). *Counseling across cultures*. Honolulu: The University Press of Hawaii.

Chapter 14

Bridging Differences through Peer-Facilitated Intergroup Dialogues

Biren A. Nagda, MSW, Ximena Zúñiga, PhD, and Todd Sevig, PhD[1]

As a democratic relationship,
dialogue is the opportunity available
to me to open up the thinking of others,
and thereby not wither away in isolation
(Paulo Freire, 1994).

Introduction

Changes in national demographics as represented on college campuses pose extraordinary challenges and opportunities for students. Students are faced with greater possibilities of contact with people whose experiences and cultural contexts are distinct from their own. Even though students come to campus with great excitement about interacting with people different from themselves, they quickly discover that their expectations about diversity are markedly divergent from others (Duster, 1993; Holliman, Jenkins, &

---

[1] We would like to thank Sherry Hatcher and Al Spuler for their comments and assistance on earlier drafts of this chapter. We also appreciate the continued commitment and energy of the intergroup dialogue peer facilitators.

Wade, 1994).[2] They find it puzzling and difficult to "make sense" of these differences. To their dismay, students experience a climate that provides few opportunities for positive intergroup contact and inquiry. It is not surprising then that students revert to the familiar homogeneous social networks in their academic and social lives—in classrooms, study groups, residence halls, and student organizations (see Hurtado, Dey, & Treviño, 1994, for a discussion of campus segregation). Ironically, college students are at one of "few times in life when individuals are as open to new experiences and change" (Dalton, 1991b).

To further complicate a college environment already in flux, the explicit focus on diversity and inclusion is marked by increasing incidents of bias and hate crimes. The unfolding institutional context is often contradictory and confusing (Chesler & Crowfoot, 1989; Dalton, 1991a; Duster, 1993). Although institutions have commonly responded through changes in the curriculum, student codes of conduct, and "Diversity 101" workshops, many students find themselves unfulfilled. Students are increasingly looking for options where they can openly ask questions, compare perspectives, learn from peers, and begin to bridge the "us/them" divide. They are interested in exploring "what they can do" to take personal and collective responsibility for the need to strive for justice.

> *Peer I:* I think a real challenge is trying to get people to see that racism isn't something that can change overnight, that you really have to work at it. Even after making a list of ways you can combat racism, a lot of them are unrealistic or will only make a small dent in a big issue. And I want to help people realize this but still try to

---

[2] For example, Duster (1993) reports that White students coming to the University of California at Berkeley define diversity as opportunities to become friends with students of color. Students of color, on the other hand, are more concerned about institutional support for diversity efforts. Holliman, Jenkins, and Wade (1994) report comparable findings from the Michigan study, a longitudinal four-year study of the Class of 1994 at the University of Michigan, Ann Arbor.

give them hope that even they can make their corner of the world a little better.

We describe here a unique program that appeals to students' desires to communicate with one another while making sense of the complexities of intergroup relations on college campuses through peer-facilitated intergroup dialogues. We discuss the framework of these peer-facilitated dialogues and their programmatic structure, content, and processes. We elaborate on the challenges that peers face in engaging themselves and fellow students in these multicultural learning situations.

Peer-Facilitated Intergroup Dialogues

The peer-facilitated intergroup dialogue activities described in this chapter are offered through the Program on Intergroup Relations and Conflict (IGRC).[3] The IGRC mission is to educate undergraduates about intergroup relations and various forms of social conflicts between social groups—focusing explicitly on the relationship between social conflict and social justice. Other program activities include four undergraduate courses and several mini-courses aimed at linking academic course work to the living and social experiences of students on campus. The program is based on the premise that only through systematic instruction, interaction, and dialogue among social groups are we going to create multicultural educational communities (Schoem, 1991b).

---

[3] Located at the University of Michigan, the IGRC program originated in 1988 as part of a presidential initiative and was awarded to the Pilot Program (a living-learning program for first-year and sophomore undergraduates) and the Program on Conflict Management Alternatives (an interdisciplinary research and development center based in the College of Literature, Science, and Arts). Most recently, the program has been institutionalized under the Division of Student Affairs with the academic courses and mini-courses offered through the College of LS&A and the Sociology Department.

The program reflects a growing emphasis at the university level on the study of social and intergroup conflict, multicultural perspectives, social justice, and social change (Collins & Andersen, 1987; Schoem, et al., 1993; Takaki, 1989; Wehr, 1979). IGRC also demonstrates a growing commitment of student affairs divisions to provide effective leadership and service from a multicultural perspective (McEwen & Roper, 1994) and to encourage dialogue with the goal of helping students in their own development and understanding of others (Pomerantz, 1993).

> *Peer C*: It's a great program and luckily we are funded by the university now. I think these are the type of things that the university needs to fund. This is what the campus needs and what the whole country needs.

An *intergroup dialogue* is a face-to-face meeting between members of two social identity groups who have a history of conflict or potential conflict (Schoem, 1991b; Zúñiga & Nagda, 1993). These dialogues constitute a unique forum for students from different backgrounds and cultural identities to discuss commonalties, learn about differences, and address issues of conflict. Through the use of a semi-structured format, students learn about each other's histories and experiences, challenge stereotypes and misinformation, explore and understand some of the sources of intergroup conflict, and identify ways of addressing institutional and individual forms of discrimination.

> *Peer D*: I think that this has probably been the most exciting and rewarding experience that I've had at the university. I got involved with IGRC at a time I probably shouldn't have because I was involved in too many other things already. But it was one of the few things that I actively participated in and got as much of a reward in return—as much as I put out and more. It's taught me about myself: I thought that I was almost really immune to the same stereotypes that other people had, and I was wrong. It has helped me understand the effects of racism and

> helped me to understand a lot of the impressions I grew up with. I formed opinions about others that were totally unfounded. It was almost impossible to be able to distinguish between something that society was telling me about other people or something that was actually coming from another person. So that's a revelation for me because I thought that I was seeing things so clearly and I wasn't.

Intergroup dialogues are broadly defined by ethnicity, race, gender, sexual orientation, ability, status, religion, socio-economic class, geographical origin, and other characteristics. The dialogues are facilitated by two trained student peer facilitators—one from each of the participating groups. These facilitators receive training, ongoing consultation, and close supervision from the program staff. The groups typically meet on a weekly basis for about two hours for three, six, or twelve sessions. Some intergroup dialogues are scheduled as a full-semester course, while other dialogues are affiliated with courses that address diversity issues.[4] In addition, other intergroup dialogues are organized specifically to meet the needs of student organizations and residence halls.

Dialogue groups typically enroll twelve to fourteen students. Deliberate recruitment efforts are made to secure a balanced group composition, particularly as it attends to the social identity group category(-ies) around which the intergroup dialogue is structured; gender balance is also desired in most groups. Short readings and experientially based activities are incorporated to encourage dialogue and discussion of pertinent issues. In some instances, students can receive academic credit, and attendance at all sessions is required. In other cases, participation is voluntary.

---

[4] Semester-long intergroup dialogues are offered for credit through Sociology 389 ("Practicum in Sociology"). Other dialogues have been linked to courses in the Pilot Program (see, for example, Sfeir-Younis, 1993, and Gurin, Nagda, Lopez, & Sfeir-Younis, 1993), Sociology, and Women's Studies.

Peer B: The purpose is to get different groups together on campus—groups that are often isolated from one another: white people/people of color, men/women—groups that have issues between each other. We get together in a dialogue setting where facilitators have specific exercises that they bring to get people talking about their concerns with the other group, what they get from the other group, to promote understanding. Sometimes it's hard to hear; especially after facilitating, you just want to kind of let everything down and relax. Sometimes it can be hard but it's also really good. It definitely helps me grow, but sometimes I don't want to hear it all.

Every semester IGRC plans and implements about ten intergroup dialogues. Past offerings have included:

- Men and Women
- People of Color and White People
- Women of Color and White Women
- Blacks and Whites
- Blacks and Jews
- Latino(a)s and Blacks
- Christians and Jews
- Muslims, Christians, and Jews
- Latinos and Latinas
- Asians and Asian Americans
- Gay, Lesbians, Bisexuals, and Heterosexuals
- People with Disabilities and People without Disabilities
- International Students and US students

Since the first dialogues were implemented five years ago, peer facilitators have co-led more than 120 dialogues, reaching about 1500 participants.

Working Framework

There are two broad goals of intergroup dialogues: 1) "to foster deeper understanding among groups by exploring attitudes, feelings and perceptions of one another;" and 2) "to create a setting in which students will engage with each other's intellectual and emotional selves in open and constructive dialogue, learning and exploration (Program on Intergroup Relations and Conflict [IGRC], 1994). The following principles provide a working framework for intergroup dialogues (Zúñiga & Sevig, 1994):

- We are all members of several social identity groups—e.g., race, gender, ethnicity, socio-economic class, age, ability status, sexual orientation, religion.
- Our positionality[5] across social identity groups influences our intra- and inter-group experiences and perspectives.
- Dialogic communication and intergroup learning are necessary to work constructively with conflict and build multicultural educational communities.
- Awareness, knowledge, skills, and passion are required to effectively work with the contradictions, dilemmas, and paradoxes involved in intergroup work.[6]
- Engaging in intergroup/multicultural learning entails a complex and multilayered learning and "unlearning" process.

This framework recognizes the impact of social group identities—gender, race, ethnicity, age, socio-economic class,

---

[5] For a discussion of "positionality," see chapter 15 in Hooks and Bell (1991), *Yearnings: Race, Gender, and Cultural Politics* (Boston: South End Press).

[6] For this framework, we are indebted to Bailey Jackson, Dean of the School of Education at the University of Massachusetts, and the trainers facilitating at the National Training Laboratories Diversity Work Conference, Washington, DC, January 17-22, 1993.

ability status, religion, and sexual orientation—as dialogue participants explore their experiences on campus and in society at large. Within the dialogues, we encourage students to recognize their own multiple social group identities—that is their own multiculturality—while we simultaneously keep "some of the lines still" (Zúñiga, 1994) to intentionally explore a particular relationship. For example, in men/women dialogues, participants primarily focus on the gender relationship in different contexts, while acknowledging the influence of other social group identities in participants' lives, such as race/ethnicity or sexual orientation. Such an approach is by definition multidimensional and complex. It demands working at multiple levels of analyses—personal, interpersonal, intragroup, intergroup, and societal/institutional. It requires learning the history of "my social identity groups" in relation to the history of "other's social identity groups"; that is, unpacking the intergroup relationship within a particular socio-historical context. Moreover, it involves taking responsibility for one's group's socio-cultural history. This learning task also requires acknowledging the unearned privileges granted by virtue of our membership(s) in relatively powerful or dominant groups (McIntosh, 1992). Similarly, it involves acknowledging some of the ways in which "my group(s)" actively or passively participate in systems of oppression—either in oppressor or oppressed roles (Hardiman & Jackson, 1994).

Dialogue provides a conceptually simple process, yet one that requires genuine openness and readiness to learn on the part of all participants (Isaacs, 1992). This process is particularly delicate with college-aged participants who are spending most of their energy trying to define who they are. Learning how to listen and ask questions before responding to what is being said is often a challenging task. Similarly, refraining from simply telling "my story" is also quite a challenge. In dialogue, students engage in critically examining personal experiences and institutional dynamics to clarify some of the sources of intergroup conflict. As such, dialogues also provide students with opportunities for collectively understanding social actions and impacting the world around them.

Peer I: We try to just give people an open space where they feel comfortable to talk to each other, understand each other, and possibly resolve conflict. Our motto is: "Conflict is okay"—it's okay to disagree; just try to understand and respect each other for the opinions you hold. My role is to make sure that students follow the ground rules and don't attack each other verbally—or physically, for that matter. I try to tie in comments people make, clarify misunderstandings, and challenge misinformation. Basically, we provide a format to students with activities and exercises to open up discussion.

Peer B: I think I'm much more willing, when someone says something I don't agree with, to really look at the context of what they're saying and why they're saying what they're saying. Instead of just assuming the whole person is someone that I disagree with and I don't want to talk with, I'm much more willing to engage with people like that.

Given the dearth of in-depth discussions among students of different social backgrounds on college campuses, intergroup dialogues provide a critical forum for students to learn about each other and discuss issues that are often avoided in diverse group settings. Such climate issues are not unique to any particular college or university; in fact, they are common across institutions of higher education. Although many efforts have arisen on campuses that attempt to address issues of social diversity, IGRC's peer-facilitated intergroup dialogues are unique in a number of ways.

Coalition Approach to Facilitation

Intergroup dialogues involve sustained contact between students from two different social identity groups. The dialogues are facilitated by two peers; this model values the skills, experiences, and interests that peer facilitators bring to create discussions about the impact of social issues on student life. The "peer-ness" allows for a connection among students and facilitators that is more grounded and closer to each other's experiences as their lives overlap in friendships, classrooms, libraries, cafés, and student organizations; they share a student culture and language.

> *Peer I*: I think that peer helping is one of the best ways to help people come together to understand differences and work through these. Because a teacher lecturing, "Yes, you should be nice to someone who's Black, who's White, who's Gay, or whatever," is not the same thing as sitting down with these people and hearing from a peer what's going on and finding your commonalties and working through your differences together. And I think if the program got more money, then we would be able to have more peer helpers and we'd have more facilitators and more dialogues and more understanding and more diversity acceptance on campus and in the world.

The coalition approach to a facilitation relationship is a critical resource in affecting the multilayered learning experiences. Each of the peer facilitators is a member of one of the groups participating in the dialogue. For example, in a White People/People of Color dialogue, we would have a White student and a Student of Color as co-facilitators. Wherever possible, we also strive to have the teams balanced in terms of gender and other relevant characteristics. Balanced co-facilitation shows members of the groups in dialogues that they are "represented in leadership," that they are validated in the dialogue. Moreover, such facilitation partnerships model how groups can collaborate across differences.

> *Peer A*: It's taught me to value different ways of thinking and different ways of interacting. I've especially been thinking about different cultural styles of interacting and how clear that was in the Black-White dialogue. How the White people were working on one set of rules

and the Black people seemed to be working under a different set of conversation rules just became really fascinating to me. And I really learned how to see all of those as good and valuable in and of themselves; what's really bad is when one style or cultural way of interacting is set up as the norm that everyone else has to follow.

The intergroup contact with its coalition/co-facilitation also enables members of different social groups to take responsibility in effecting multicultural communities. Dialogue groups allow for an exchange of misinformation and misunderstandings as well as an understanding of the role of individuals and institutions in perpetuating these gaps in the relationships. Participants struggle with the paradoxes of power in their separate and joint roles and responsibilities in enacting more just societies.

Peer E: For awhile, I felt very much like a dominating man in the group even though I try not to come across as being a stereotypical sexist man and I wasn't being sexist with respect to women in the group. One of the issues we explored in staff meetings was "passive control"—where you have a group divided along a power dynamic continuum, one group at either end, and the minority group, the group at the low end of the power dynamic, takes on an "educational role," i.e., "I'm going to educate this ignorant oppressor and therefore they're not going to oppress me anymore." So, it's really easy for the other people in the group to kind of sit back and take on this aspect: "Oh, I'm learning about these people that I know nothing about" and never have to take any risks and never have to put anything on the line. They keep thinking: "Oh, I don't want to offend anybody," so they sit back. If you don't say anything and you take no risks, it's a very safe, comfortable position, but, on the other hand, you have the minority group people talking and talking, trying to preach to the somewhat converted. It is best when everyone can take risks.

Peer J: We encourage a lot of soul-searching on the part of the White students, like, "White is a race too; stop thinking of race as only people of color." It definitely makes you explore your own identity and your attitudes around various social issues, ranging from everything like affirmative action to multicultural issues at the university.

Dialogic Education

The notion of dialogue to explore issues of cultural identities and power relations is articulated by Paulo Freire (1972) in *Pedagogy of the Oppressed*. Freire's work teaches us that through dialogue, students can learn to recognize their position in the world and begin to change the world around them as they critically examine their perceptions of the world and themselves. In dialogue, facilitators and participants are in a cooperative format. The learning process is organic in that it works closely with participants and their "here and now" experiences; personal experiences are valid sources of knowledge and co-learning.

Experiential activities then become one way to engage students in critically reflecting on their experience in light of the experience of others. As these activities simulate parts of social realities, they allow students to hear about a shared experience from different perspectives. Typical questions that students struggle with include: Where do our experiences converge? Where do they diverge? What forces impact us similarly and differently? How do these activities resonate with our realities? Kolb (1984) says that such conceptualizations enable students to actively experiment and expand their learning across a variety of situations.

Peer D: Now I can put myself in somebody else's shoes and be able to look at things from somebody else's perspective. I think that as a result of this I'm able to see things a bit more objectively than I had in the past. I'm majoring in cellular molecular biology and my intent is to become a research scientist, but I have a really broad scope of interests, and working in this group is something that is a personal fulfillment for me—not necessarily something I would get involved in as a career, but something I think is extremely important. If I weren't doing it I would be relatively unhappy with my college career because I wasn't able to fulfill all I wanted to fulfill.

Peer G: I find myself using a lot of "intergroup terminology," which is, I think, using "I statements" and talking about how something has affected me: "This has hurt me or this is how I feel." In terms of problem-solving, I think that has helped me to get closer to the root of the problem. Then we can work through, "This is where I'm coming from and this is where the other person is coming from," instead of bashing it out. Starting there you can work toward saying: "Okay, well this is the problem. This is what we need to do to solve it."

Peer I: I think that the compensation or the reward, if you will, is really internal; it's been a learning experience for me all along. Through the dialogues and working with other peer helpers, it helps me see how I interact with others in my own life. And when things come up with my roommates or my boyfriend or my family, I can understand a little more where my reactions are coming from and I have better ways of dealing with conflict.

The striving for shared understanding makes it imperative that we work with conflict in ways that are collaborative and constructive. We hope that in addressing conflict constructively through dialogue, new ways of understanding the relationship between groups and new ways of actually relating will ensue. It is in settings outside the dialogue that the students continue to expand their learning.

Linking the Individual and the Institutional

As students begin to expand their understandings beyond the dialogue group, the links between individual/interpersonal experiences and institutional/societal structures become clearer—historically contextualized and more complex. This aspect of our pedagogy draws heavily from feminist (see chapter 11) and multicultural pedagogies and Wright Mills' "sociological imagination"—understanding "private troubles" in terms of "public issues"; our pedagogical approach highlights the exploration of societal forces that influence intergroup tensions and enables critical thinking and problem solving.

This "personal as political" connection highlights ways in which privilege, power, and oppression impact students. Societal stratifications and differences are made overt in the dialogue format. Consideration of the relationship between one group's privilege to another's oppression can evoke anger, guilt, and emotionality; when the level of conflict is high, so can be the concern for safety. Our pedagogy of dialogue offers an opportunity for all participants to gain clarity about the nature of conflict and the differences between participating groups. It is not a forum to fight for the "right view" or to debate one's group perspective over another's.

> *Peer B*: It's really taught me to look at each person as a valuable person; we all grow up and form our opinions and the way we look at things because of our life circumstances, things that have happened in our lives. I think I've learned to judge others much less harshly and therefore to realize that each person is an important person.

Intergroup dialogues strive to create spaces that acknowledge participants' rich experiences by combining a participative and pluralistic diversity. The effort involves a "hard look" not only at issues of racial diversity but also those based on ethnicity, gender, sexual orientation, socio-economic class, ability, religion, geographic origin, and others. Within the dialogues, we push for students to recognize their own multiculturality, that is, to explore their multiple identities.

> *Peer H*: I moved a lot in terms of the way I saw race relations, in terms of the way I saw myself as White. That was the big thing that came of this for me was that I always thought of myself as Jewish, but I didn't think of myself as a White woman in America. So that did a lot for how I see myself in relation to people of different races and ethnicities, how I view myself externally. I've learned that it's really important to talk about how you're going to come to a solution instead of just saying, "Okay, here's the solution"; it's important to compromise. I guess one thing I've learned is that you really have to understand where everyone is coming from in terms of reaching a solution to a problem and understanding different backgrounds and different life experiences.

Training and Resources

IGRC incorporates a number of different resources for peers to draw on as they facilitate intergroup dialogues: initial training and bi-weekly staff in-services, a facilitator manual, consultations with peer and professional consultants, and the richness of a diverse team of facilitators, consultants, and trainers. We tap into these various resources to support and challenge ourselves—facilitators, trainers, and consultants—as we engage in intergroup dialogue work.

Training and Staff In-Services: The working framework and unique features of intergroup dialogues inform facilitator training and staff development activities. The goal of training is to develop the tools necessary to facilitate intergroup dialogues. Facilitator training takes fifty hours at the beginning of the academic year, including a twenty-five-hour weekend retreat. Following the training, facilitators and program staff meet bi-weekly for in-services.

> *Peer B*: We go through an intensive training period in the fall, which includes a weekend retreat. You go through about fifty hours of training in the fall and after that bi-weekly meetings two hours every two weeks to do in-services and to keep challenging the staff as a group. Some of it is learning group facilitation skills, things like active listening—real skill-oriented. Other stuff is more issues-oriented, like race and gender. We really work within the group to think about those things ourselves and how our own identity has shaped the way we think about different issues.

Following Bailey Jackson's (1993) model of multicultural competencies (see footnote 5), our training emphasizes the development of awareness, knowledge, skills, and passion. Awareness work includes self-awareness of the impact of social group identities on one's communication, conflict, and facilitation styles; experiences of power; expectations of intergroup work; "blind spots"; and "hot buttons." The knowledge aspect includes conceptual frameworks of intergroup relations—both of overall intergroup dynamics and more specific relationships—statistics around inequalities; social justice issues; education about different social groups' histories; the role of power and oppression in society; models of communication and conflict; knowledge of group development and processes; etc. The skill areas are included in the multifaceted role of the facilitator: co-facilitation, setting the tone in multicultural groups, active listening, feedback, workshop planning/design issues to plan agendas relevant to different intergroup dialogues, among others. Passion involves helping facilitators understand their personal motivation for doing this work, nurturing a personal commitment and a vision of multicultural work.

> *Peer A*: I realized that I like to work with people and that working in this program has felt very exciting and exhilarating. I started to think that

> it would be really great to have a job that felt like this all the time, where I was always learning from other people and always learning new things about myself and other people.

We utilize multiple training "formats" to address the different needs of the facilitators. For example, we encourage "personal time" for trainees to reflect on their feelings and thoughts through journal writing. Writing breaks are taken after each long exercise to provide a space for self-reflection and awareness. Small groups work on tasks to compare their experiences in understanding the impact of social identities on their perspectives and styles. Large group discussions are useful in examining intergroup issues and patterns within the whole group. Experiential exercises are used in conjunction with didactic presentations to integrate awareness and knowledge. Learning partners, pairs of trainees, help each other in exploring difficult and sensitive issues in a safe format. Videotaped vignettes and case scenarios dealing with intergroup issues are useful in skill development, as in clarifying personal reactions, conceptualizing the situational dynamics, and generating facilitator interventions. Role-playing intergroup situations allows for actual practice.

> *Peer B*: Another peer who is on staff and I were simulating co-facilitating a group between people of color and white people for our fall training. There were about six people from the group actually talking and everyone else was watching and this was supposed to be kind of a demonstration of co-facilitation. We were co-facilitating and everyone else had a role they were supposed to play, and people really played their roles well. But we didn't have roles as co-facilitators; we were supposed to facilitate the discussion. Afterward, what happened was that everyone in the room went around and talked about our job as co-facilitators and what we could have done better and what would have been worse. And it went on for about two-and-a-half hours! It was hard simply because it was one of our first

training sessions. I feel a lot more confident now that I know how to facilitate and knowing myself better. I have grown personally and in terms of my identity and how comfortable I feel doing this kind of work.

Peer C: I had one case where there was a man in one of my male/female dialogue groups, and he was just obviously disgusted by the dialogue. He was angry, he was very hostile, and my first reaction would probably be to get back at him emotionally and be combative. But because I was facilitating and I had been taught to be a facilitator, I took a step back, discussed with him what he was feeling, asked for participation from my co-facilitator to let her help me. So the training definitely helped me, just to anticipate that something like this might happen. I learn something new every time I facilitate and I think I become a better facilitator. It's an ongoing thing; you can always improve and there are times when you make mistakes and you go back and talk about it and you realize that you made a mistake so you won't do it again.

Training is continued throughout the year at the bi-weekly staff meetings. The topics of these meetings include administrative tasks, in-services on such issues as affirmative action, comparison of facilitation experiences and consultations, troubleshooting with other facilitators, co-facilitator team-building, and planning for dialogues. These meetings also allow for continued exploration of intergroup issues within the whole team through intensive explorations in "race-like," "gender-like," or "mixed" groups.

Peer L: When I was facilitating the dialogue, I deliberately chose to do it during weeks when I had nothing else to do. It is extremely demanding. I was constantly having to come to meetings, and then if you do a two-hour dialogue, you have to come an hour early and

> stay an hour later. I was also an RA and I still had classes; that is why I didn't do a twelve-week dialogue group. It's a really big time commitment. Staff meetings are two hours and sometimes three hours if the topic runs over. Because of the type of work that it is, it can be extremely emotionally draining. You can get tired of talking about cultural issues because you start to look at the world—and the task can feel overwhelming.

Intergroup Dialogue Team: The dialogue group team includes part-time professional staff, faculty, peer consultants, and facilitators. The team is diverse in terms of race, ethnicity, gender, sexual orientation, physical ability, and socioeconomic class as well as interests and facilitation abilities. The professional staff is composed of about four part-time program associates (student affairs professionals, faculty, and graduate students) who team up to facilitate the initial training, ongoing consultation, and in-service staff meetings. The "peer consultants" are experienced facilitators who help with training facilitators, consulting, and supporting the implementation of dialogues.

In building our own community—a sense of "we"—across differences and commonalties, we embark upon and nurture a journey of "self" and "other" discovery by working on intergroup dynamics that emerge within the team and giving personal and group feedback.

> *Peer J:* We have a really, really diverse staff. A lot of what we do at our staff meetings is talk about these same issues that come up in our groups and learn to listen to other points of view and backgrounds/ identities within our own staff.

> *Peer G:* Feedback is not meant to denigrate me or hurt my feelings. It's something to make me a better peer consultant, to help me to be better able to do my job. We all have roles; our lines of authority are like dotted lines. It's very easy, if I have a problem or disagree with someone, to bring that up and say: "You know, I disagree

with that." There is definitely a hierarchy for organizational purposes, but it's easy for me to get feedback as well as to give it, just because the lines of communication are very open.

This serves as a model for facilitators' work in the dialogues. In a sense, we are using our whole team—facilitators, peer consultants, and professional staff—as data (i.e., feelings, thoughts, behaviors, opinions, and so on) to explore issues. We utilize the talents, knowledge, and experiences of the whole staff (trainers and facilitators) to examine our own development as a multicultural group. In fact, a large part of the experience is learning to interact in a diverse group (in terms of social identities, knowledge, skills, awareness, commitment, and other variables) while working on intergroup issues.

Peer G: I think my peer consultant training has mostly come from just doing the job and learning about it and working with others who are in the same program. Getting feedback and helping each other out is a team-oriented approach. We talk, we share, whether it's good or bad, conflictual or not. Hopefully there's some kind of conflict because I think it's a good opportunity to learn about yourself and all the barriers on common issues that you share.

Peer I: We all kind of work together and it's really helpful, even though some are undergraduates and some are graduate students. It's good to get feedback from someone your own age and who's going through what you're going through now and can identify with you.

Manual for Intergroup Dialogue Facilitation: We have developed a facilitator manual (IGRC, 1992) that includes resources for facilitators to use in dialogue groups. First, there is administrative material, which includes the facilitator job description, guidelines for writing reports, and descriptions of an intergroup dialogue. Second, there is a process/content outline for intergroup dialogues (Zúñiga & Nagda, 1992). Third, there are sample exercises for intergroup dialogues.

These are categorized by appropriateness for dialogues dealing with race/ethnicity, gender, or sexual orientation. Fourth, there are readings pertaining to the same topic areas listed above. Supplementary readings and exercises are available in the IGRC Resource Library.

The process/content outline builds on a group development model of intergroup dialogues. The diagram on the next page shows a typical intergroup dialogue process that is divided into four stages and six weekly sessions (Zúñiga & Nagda, 1992). The stages progress from group beginnings, to learning about the issues between the two groups, to exploring the individual and institutional manifestations of the intergroup relationship, to an action-oriented stage to identify ways to deal with issues raised in the dialogue group.

> *Peer A*: You're dealing with hard issues. You're dealing with things like racism and people's feelings about this. And it's not like if they don't read a chapter in anthropology class, they'll get that next year, or they won't learn it—so what? But if a dialogue group goes badly, it makes a big difference. It might mean that this person comes away with an awful feeling about talking about these things, that they would feel really emotionally hurt, they could feel really silenced. When things are going well and people are engaging, you're dealing with very intense stuff. And you've got a bunch of people like us—peers— who aren't therapists, who are working through their own issues, and we're all just doing the best we can. And in some ways I think that's good because you don't have these professional people who have "all the answers" being in charge. But in some ways it can feel uncertain in its outcome.

This model is a helpful tool for facilitators in developing a sustained and long-term plan of learning activities. It helps facilitators to assess the development of their groups and make decisions on appropriate exercises and interventions.

STAGES OF INTERGROUP DIALOGUE

Stage One: Group Beginnings

Session 1: Getting acquainted and setting norms

Stage Two: Learning about Commonalities, Differences, and Conflict

Session 2: Beginning to listen to your own group and the "other" group

Session 3: Identifying existing or potential conflicts with the "other" group alliance-building around continuing dialogue about difficult issues

---

Stage Three: Linking Individual Experiences to Institutional and Social Structures

Session 4: Bringing stereotypes and prejudices out into the open

Session 5: Linking the personal to the institutional

Stage Four: Working Together "With and Across" Differences

Session 6: "Where do we go from here?"; alliance-building around taking action

> *Peer E*: I found the whole thing enlightening, just because I've never done this kind of group before and I was kind of nervous and apprehensive and curious about just what it would be like for me. It's sort of like doing a roller coaster; you do it once and it seems, "Oh, I know what it's like," and then you do it with another group and it feels like: "Are we doing the right thing? Is the group falling apart?" That feeling of anxiety goes away after a while.

The model is designed to be modular, that is, sessions build upon previous ones and set the stage for the succeeding ones. For example, in Session 5, facilitators may do the "Take a Stand" exercise (The Lesbian-Gay Male Programs Office, 1993). This is an effective tool for examining differences in values and opinions around topics that directly impact the intergroup relationship. In an interracial/ethnic dialogue, for example, topics range from racism to reverse discrimination to affirmative action to monoculturalism. In a Men/Women dialogue, such issues as reproductive rights and sexual harassment typically arise. This session builds on Session 4, in which students have examined the stereotypes and prejudices they carry about other groups and how these beliefs are perpetuated (Katz, 1978). In Session 5, then, the activities aim to clarify the link between the pervasiveness of stereotypes, societal values, inequities, and institutional policies.

> *Peer L*: The facilitator role involves planning and asking: "What exercises are we going to do?"; "What discussion topics are we going to talk about?" It's a very "on your feet" type of job. There is a co-facilitator. I'm a Black person and my co-facilitator is an Asian person. So we would meet and we would say: "How did the last dialogue go?" We would say what issues we had been thinking about from our own personal experiences. We had two consultants, an Afro-American woman and an Asian woman, who were teaching a course on African-American and Asian relationships. I

say it's an "on your feet" job because you wonder: "What happens if three Afro-Americans show up and fifteen Asians, or even twenty Asians?"; "How do we make these people feel comfortable?" When we start with the exercise called "Take a Stand" and we throw out a statement and then people agree or disagree, we get people to talk about why they agree or disagree. If you don't think that they're talking about all the issues, or if you don't think that they're hearing each other, you may probe them: "What do you mean by that?"; "Can you elaborate further on that?" You do a lot of rephrasing and redirecting questions to people in the group. Sometimes just throwing in a few comments like, "Well, in my experience, I think this; what do you all think about that?" gets the discussion flowing.

Toward the end of Session 5, the facilitators may have members in their dialogue group state one action to address an inequality or issue of conflict between the groups. The students are asked to try out this action in the week between Sessions 5 and 6. In a men/women dialogue, a man may say that he will confront his male friends who read pornographic magazines and explain to them how such media contribute to the degradation of their mothers, sisters, and women friends. A woman in the same dialogue may state the same or different action. When the students return for Session 6, they compare notes on their actions, others' responses to their actions, and their own learning. They identify further actions that are necessary in addressing the issues and delineate those that they can engage in individually, jointly, and in their separate groups. Finally, implications of these actions are discussed.

The model is only a guide; the planning of each session is tied to the life of the group. In some cases, certain stages may take longer than others while some groups may take action more readily than others.[7]

---

[7] Zúñiga and Nagda (1993) elaborate more on student learning

Consultation and Supervision

Consultation involves helping facilitators with agenda planning, troubleshooting, paying attention to group dynamics, flow of the sessions, and co-facilitation issues. Supervision involves evaluation of facilitators, ensuring facilitators are following through on tasks and planning, and checking the quality of the process. The facilitators usually meet with two consultants. The goal of the consultation remains constant—to achieve a working environment in which there is continuity from the training and a built-in format for facilitators to receive support, be challenged, give and receive feedback, or to "troubleshoot" during the course of a dialogue group. Much of the teaching and support for peers while they are facilitating a group is lent by a peer or professional consultants. Consultation meetings are scheduled weekly for the duration of the dialogue. These meetings are especially valuable in addressing issues of co-facilitation, group development, agenda planning/design issues, and intergroup communication.

> *Peer B*: I think sometimes it's really hard to do dialogues. I work with two other peers and my relationship with them is pretty supportive and affirming. We all do the same thing and so we can give each other support. And then for the other peers who are volunteers with the program, I need to do some consulting. Sometimes, if they're not fulfilling their responsibility, I have to challenge them. That one's harder for me to play that kind of tough person role.

For example, co-facilitation issues often arise, which have an impact on how the group is developing (e.g., one facilita-

---

outcomes in intergroup dialogues. They give an example of an African-American/Latino(a) dialogue group wherein students emphasized a need for reeducation about their respective histories because of distorted education. We have found that they also readily engaged in actions such as writing letters and organizing more joint activities through their student organizations.

tor might be having a hard time connecting with the "other group" and with his or her co-facilitator); this can be worked through in consultation with the goal of using this experience constructively in the dialogue.

Facilitation Challenges

Zúñiga and Nagda (1993) have identified challenges that are involved in sustaining a multicultural pedagogy of dialogue—"facilitating dialogue not debate," "confronting conflict constructively," "examining the multiple layers of identity," and "linking the micro- and macro-levels of analysis." Below, we focus on issues that are particularly challenging for the facilitators and some ways in which we, as trainers and consultants, address these.

The role of the facilitator calls for the "wearing of many different hats" and "walking fine lines." Facilitators often report being caught between roles of participant/co-learner and facilitator or between that of educator/teacher and facilitator. They are often intrigued by the complexity of their roles—guides, planners, organizers, designers, observers, interveners, and activists, among others.

> *Peer H:* I guess it's by choice how much you choose to be active in the program. You can facilitate a three-week dialogue and that's it, or do a longer one. The first time I enrolled in the program, it met twice a week for two hours a week, so it was four hours in the classroom and I worked there with another woman. We had to plan different exercises that would get the participants talking about issues related to their communities or their identities. And then for the second two hours we had to put together an action project, some sort of campus-wide activity that would reflect what we were doing in the classroom, and take it out to the broader community. So we did that. That was more of an organizational role. As a facilitator, you have to not only plan the exercise but you have to keep it moving and keep it on track. You

have to balance between participating yourself and letting others know that you're not only a facilitator but also that you have feelings and you have similar issues to struggle with as they do.

While participants are able to freely share their personal experiences in the dialogue groups, facilitators may feel they need to be more neutral in directing the discussion. There is a fine line between directing a dialogue among peers without being domineering and "telling it like it is." Facilitators are encouraged to share their views when these will enhance the dialogue. Since it is often the case that facilitators are still themselves learning about intergroup issues, their use of "self" is important so long as it does not overpower other students' own explorations.

Peer E: As a facilitator, I shouldn't be directing the conversation of the group continuously, but at the same time, I can't hang too far back. I think the group needs some direction. One thing that was bothersome in the first couple of groups was I got terrified by silence. I thought: "Oh no! They're not talking. I'm not doing my job! The group's falling apart!" So I was saying a lot and I was giving examples and I was giving anecdotes of my own life and that's when people started saying that I was talking too much. So, I started to back off a little bit. And I realized that it was okay for them to be silent because sometimes silence is good. So, I went back and forth on how much I should participate and finally came to a nice middle ground.

We encourage facilitators to try out new styles and to learn from using these in the group. We believe that facilitators are also learners and we attempt to look for "teachable moments" whether they arise in direct facilitation of a group, in reactions to group processes, or in the co-facilitation relationship. We ask facilitators to discuss student reactions openly, using student feedback as a learning opportunity. For example, in mid-dialogue evaluations, we often find that women facilitators in men/women dialogues receive less positive feedback than their male co-facilitators. We have encouraged facilitators to "feed" such information back to the group: What expectations did the group have in regard to the gender of the facilitators? Whose style is more appealing and why? How might students' stereotypes about gender roles affect their evaluation of the facilitators?

> *Peer A*: In the male-female dialogue group I did, I realized that I'm much too angry at men; the anger at being treated in what I consider an unjust way was too close for me to deal with constructively. It was too hard for me to care about the men in the dialogue group and that's what you really need to do in order to be a good facilitator, in order to help them see and overcome whatever is stopping them from growing. I think I still have trouble being a woman in a leadership role because I want people to like me and I don't want to bowl people over. I've found that it's very hard for a lot of people to accept women in leadership positions. You either have to be teasing and cute or you have to be really hard-line. Facilitator evaluations show that the women facilitators across the board—and we're all very different people with different styles of relating—get lower evaluations than the men.

The facilitators are thus challenged to be aware of how their social group identities influence their communication, conflict, facilitation, and collaboration styles. Co-facilitators develop an intercultural awareness that examines the reciprocal impact of their styles on each other and the participants. These are all important considerations in using the "self" in the group and developing a collaborative working relationship that can serve as a model process for participants.

> *Peer A*: I'm a very outspoken person and assertive. And a lot of times I just never notice quiet people at all and that's really bad because when

you're the facilitator you have to notice everyone. Because I was working with people who had very different styles from me, I now notice that being quiet or not participating in a conversation is a way of participating. I'm more aware of how my way of interacting affects other people.

Peer C: Well, first of all, everybody's different; even facilitators are different. My co-facilitator, who I ended up getting along with very well, was very quiet and sometimes frustrated me but then there were other times that she would have insight into things that I'd never seen before because I was too busy talking and she was quiet and observing things. I realized that just because people may be quiet doesn't mean that they're not interacting with the group.

Given the complexity of their role and different styles, the co-facilitators are also encouraged to be aware of their strengths and limitations and to recognize their needs for personal support. In a sense, co-facilitators find themselves engaged in a "mini-dialogue," that is, working on the intergroup issues reflected between them in their partnership. The quality and depth of the parallel process that unfolds between co-facilitators before, during, and after the duration of the dialogue group is often reflective of what is going on in the dialogue itself. An ability to examine these issues, in many instances, sets the stage for each team's ability to effectively co-facilitate and support each other throughout the intergroup dialogue process. Understanding the parallel processes (see chapter 3) is an important challenge in sensitizing the co-facilitators to issues that are latent or manifest in their group(s). It is also useful in analyzing intergroup dynamics and how these are perceived similarly and/or differently by the co-facilitators. The challenge comes in working on issues both within the group and between the facilitators while continuing the co-facilitation relationship. It is to be expected that co-facilitators need personal support as well as team support in order to maintain a productive working relationship—one that is mutually beneficial. The questions that co-facilitator pairs must examine include: How do the issues being discussed inform the co-facilitation relationship? How does the understanding at the intergroup level enrich the understanding at an interpersonal level?

> *Peer J*: The closest relationship we have is with our co-facilitator. I have had the same co-facilitator for both of my groups because I've been in the same group this year as I did last term. A lot of other people do a Black and White group one semester and then Jews and Christians the next semester. Then they can't very well have the same co-facilitator. You are really forced to develop a close relationship with someone who is very different from you. And, the closer the relationship, the better it goes. The better my co-facilitator and I get to know each other, the better the level of our group and how we facilitate it.

> *Peer L*: I've always been interested in culture, so I'm kind of wavering between doing clinical psychology, multicultural psychotherapy, and organizational behavior within multicultural organizations. That's just because through my work in intergroup relations I have become much more aware of the significant effect that people's backgrounds have upon the way they look at the world, their behavior, their attitudes, everything. It's really interesting to me now because before, in high school, I thought that we're all the same underneath, and we're not. There are some people that have different experiences because of their cultural background. And, I don't think that's bad. I think it does have serious implications for working with people with different backgrounds; I think it has a lot of serious implications for treating people in psychotherapy.

Working with peers defines a second "fine line," that of challenging and confronting ignorance without invalidating and silencing participants. For the dialogue process to go beyond simply acquiring information about the "other," it needs to have creative tension that encourages, urges, and challenges students to think critically and reflectively; students must examine their ignorance and biases and ways in which these impact upon intergroup relationships. Some stereotypic images, prejudicial ideas, and discriminatory behaviors may come up in the ways that the students frame the issues; others may arise from their communication patterns.

Challenging and confronting such issues and dynamics has to be done in a way that the emergent "data" can be used as a learning tool. Although the need for safety is crucial both in facilitating a dialogic mode of communication and in constructively addressing issues of conflict, it is important that the facilitators not create a safety that fosters ignorance and apathy and perpetuates the intergroup inequities within the dialogue setting.

> *Peer E*: One group I facilitated was frustrating in the sense that it was so low-key and non-confrontational that people weren't taking risks and we had a very "safe" group. The interaction and the dynamics of the people themselves just weren't very high key. I fault the facilitators because we didn't actively press and push the confrontation. Probably we didn't want it; probably subconsciously I didn't know how to deal with it.

The process of *planning dialogue sessions* represents a unique challenge for co-facilitators largely because of the many skills involved in workshop design—articulating learning goals and objectives, selecting/designing appropriate learning activities, anticipating the impact of the agenda on the group, and planning an agenda that balances content and process. Additionally, facilitators also identify who will lead different segments of the session and what segments they will facilitate together. The process/content outline, described earlier, provides facilitators with guiding modules to plan each of the sessions. The modules are particularly useful in the early stages of a group to lay the groundwork for more difficult dialogue. The facilitation team works to establish an environment conducive to dialogue, sharing, and intensive explorations of social identities, conflicts, and issues in the intergroup relationship.

Design issues and decisions become more complex after the third or fourth session of an intergroup dialogue. It is at this point that we encourage facilitators to be more creative in their planning rather than "mechanically" rely on the process/content outline. As participants raise new questions and unexpected issues, we encourage facilitators to revisit the original goals and articulate more specific ones tied to the needs of the group.

> *Peer G*: This job creates an environment to work on important issues, but sometimes it's very hard to do to overcome some of the barriers—not only being able to work with the group and keep that group going but also trying to work through your own stuff as well as other peoples'. I feel pride when everything's going okay and people are getting something out of it, when I see that all this work has not been in vain, the many hours of planning and organizing. I find that rewarding.

In consultation sessions, we ask facilitators to take a close look at "where the group is at": What issues have come up? How are they talked about? Was there conflict in the group? How is conflict worked through? What are the levels of participation of the different individuals and groups in dialogue? In what ways do the emergent dynamics—communication and participation patterns—reflect larger societal arrangements? What kind of rapport exists between the parties in dialogue and between facilitators and the participants? Mid-dialogue written evaluations are also helpful at this stage in providing facilitators with feedback to help with future planning.

The planning process is further complicated as the facilitators unravel the dynamics in their co-facilitation relationship. For instance, working on joint goals and interests while at the same time asserting individual needs and styles is "tricky" especially since the relationship has to be sustained over time. Other challenges include balancing short- and long-term learning goals, developing a sense of timing for introducing an issue or particular activity, and identifying the best "flow" for a given session.

Devoting enough time to ensure a quality planning and preparation process remains a continual challenge for co-facilitation teams. In our experience, co-facilitation teams need at least two hours per week to effectively address the complexity of planning and implementing an agenda while remaining cognizant of the "big picture." Such a time commitment is, in some instances, difficult for facilitators to manage, given their school schedule and extracurricular involvements. Their "spirit" and passion for the work remains strong throughout.

> *Peer C*: One problem the peers have is that we are all very busy. We are students and we are working, so we don't get a chance to interact all the time. When we had our staff meetings, we were always very friendly and very family-like; we all care about one another. The people who get into this type of work are very feeling-oriented and it was particularly helpful for me because I could throw something out and I could be assured that somebody was going to give me their opinion back, give me feedback on how I was doing. On the flip-side of that, it can feel negative because sometimes you have a tendency to overanalyze what you did in the dialogue group.

Conclusion

Peer-facilitated intergroup dialogues are a cherished forum in which students examine their perceptions and experiences of intergroup relations in an institutional climate often characterized by lack of positive intergroup interactions. The peer facilitators provide an intentional structure for students from different backgrounds to "think aloud" about their social, cultural, and political realities and visions in changing times. Through dialogues, students learn to value others' opinions and have the opportunities to challenge each other without being threatened by or threatening others. This pedagogy affords participants insights into how institutional injustices impact their relationships with each other and opportunities to struggle with issues that arise in the "here and now" of intergroup dialogue. Additionally, facilitators gain experience in leadership, workshop design, and facilitation in the context of multicultural issues in diverse groups. These skills go beyond the specific context of dialogues; many facilitators integrate their learnings into their academic specializations.

> *Peer G:* Sometimes I have felt almost in conflict being a part of intergroup relations and being in the business school. At this point I have decided to study organizational behavior, which is looking at the relationships between groups and how organizations work. So I am wanting to combine my major with my extracurricular activity for the future because I think that this is what I want to do with my career.

Finally, in intergroup dialogues, students are able to take responsibility for each others' learning and to uncover some of the roots of intergroup conflict. In many instances, students make a commitment to each other to continue working within and outside their communities on the issues raised in the dialogue. With the support and encouragement of trained peer facilitators, student-centered approaches to learning are structured to promote co-learning and multicultural educational empowerment:

> *Peer B:* I definitely want to do this kind of work in the future. I see this work that IGRC does as creating places where people talk to each other about what they need as people in society, and I think social justice policy is challenged. We need to have this type of work where people are talking and people are building communities together, so when the policy is

formulated we don't have a bunch of people who don't know how to talk to each other. I want to continue to do social action work and I also like working with peers and really trying to get at the heart of our feelings.

REFERENCES

Chesler, M. A., & Crowfoot, J. (1989). *Racism in higher education I: An organizational analysis. Working Paper Series.* Ann Arbor, MI: The Program on Conflict Management Alternatives.

Collins, P. H., & Anderson, M. (1987). *Towards an inclusive sociology: Race, class, and gender in the curriculum.* Washington, DC: American Psychological Association.

Dalton, J. (1991a). Racial and ethnic backlash in college peer culture. *New Directions for Student Services, 56,* 3-12.

Dalton, J. (1991b). Racism on campus: Confronting racial bias through peer interventions [Editor's note]. *New Directions for Student Services, 56,* 1-2.

Duster, T. (1993). The diversity of the University of California at Berkeley: An emerging reformulation of competence in an increasingly multicultural world. In Thompson and Tyagi (Eds.), *Beyond a dream deferred: Multicultural education and the politics of excellence* (238-255). Minneapolis: University of Minnesota Press.

Freire, P. (1972). *Pedagogy of the oppressed.* New York: Seabury Press.

Freire, P. (1994). *Pedagogy of hope.* New York: Continuum.

Gurin, P., Nagda, B. A., Lopez, G. E., & Sfeir-Younis, L. F. (1993). Diversity and multicultural curriculum: Understanding social causation. *The Michigan Journal of Political Science,* Issue 16, 1-22.

Hardiman, R., & Jackson, B. (1994). *Social oppression: An operational definition.* Amherst, MA: New Perspectives.

Holliman, D. A., Jenkins, S. Y., & Wade, K. C. (1994, June 2-7). *The multiple meanings of diversity: Assessing the multiculturalism expectations and experiences of African American, Latino, Asian American, and White students on campus.* Presentation at the 7th Annual National Conference on Race & Ethnicity in American Higher Education, Atlanta, GA.

Hurtado, S., Dey, E. L., & Treviño, J. G. (1994, April). *Exclusion or self-segregation? Interaction across racial/ethnic groups on college campuses.* Paper presented at the Annual Meeting of the American Education Research Association. New Orleans, Louisiana.

Isaacs, W. N. (1992). *The dialogue project. The diversity factor*. Cambridge: Massachusetts Institute of Technology.

Katz, J. (1978). *White awareness: Handbook for anti-racism training*. Norman: University of Oklahoma Press.

Kolb, D. A. (1984). *Experiential learning: Experience as the source of learning and development*. New York: Prentice Hall.

The Lesbian-Gay Male Programs Office. (1993). Classroom and workshop exercises: Take-a-stand exercise. In Schoem, Frankel, Zúñiga, & Lewis (Eds.), *Multicultural teaching in the university* (323-324). Westport, CT: Praeger.

McEwen, M. K., & Roper, L. D. (1994). Incorporating multiculturalism into student affairs preparation programs: Suggestions from the literature. *Journal of College Student Development, 35*, 46-53.

McIntosh, P. (1992). White privilege and male privilege: A personal account of coming to see correspondences through work in women's studies. In Andersen and Collins (Eds.), *Race, class and gender: An anthology* (70-81). Belmont, CA: Wadsworth.

Pomerantz, N. K. (1993). Dialogue and the ethic of responsibility: A new perspective on racial harassment and free speech. *NASPA Journal, 31*(1), 30-35.

The Program on Intergroup Relations and Conflict. (1994). *What is an Intergroup Dialogue?* University of Michigan. Unpublished program manual.

Schoem, D. (1991a). *Inside separate worlds: Life stories of young Blacks, Jews, and Latinos*. Ann Arbor: University of Michigan Press.

Schoem, D. (1991b). College students need thoughtful, in-depth study of race relations. *Chronicle of Higher Education*, A48.

Schoem, D., Frankel, L., Zúñiga, X., & Lewis, E. (Eds.). (1993). *Multicultural teaching in the university*. Westport, CT: Praeger.

Sfeir-Younis, L. F. (1993). Reflections on the teaching of multicultural courses. In Schoem, Frankel, Zúñiga, & Lewis (Eds.), *Multicultural teaching in the university* (61-75). Westport, CT: Praeger.

Takaki, R. (1989). An educated and culturally literate person must study America's multi-cultural reality. *Chronicle of Higher Education*, B1-2.

Wehr, P. (1979). *Conflict regulation*. Boulder, CO: Westview Press.

Zúñiga, X., & Nagda, B. A. (1992). *A process/content outline for intergroup dialogues*. Ann Arbor: University of Michigan Program on Intergroup Relations and Conflict.

Zúñiga, X., & Nagda, B. A. (1993). Dialogue groups: An innovative approach to multicultural learning. In Schoem, Frankel, Zúñiga, & Lewis (Eds.). *Multicultural teaching in the university* (232-248). Westport, CT: Praeger.

Zúñiga, X., & Sevig, T. D. (1994, June 2-7). *Incorporating multiple learning goals to facilitate multicultural learning.* Presentation at the 7th Annual National Conference on Race & Ethnicity in American Higher Education. Atlanta, GA.

Zúñiga, X. (1994). Opportunities and challenges in coalition learning: Women of color and white women in the community. (Reprinted in *Praxis III: A faculty case study on community service learning* by J. Galcera & J. Howard, Eds., [in press], University of Michigan Office of Community Learning.)

Discussion and Conclusions

Chapter 15

Peer Helping for Prevention on the College Campus

Sherry Hatcher, PhD

Our college peer counselors have spoken for themselves. The enthusiastic chorus of "the voice of the peers," which we have presented throughout these chapters, is replete with statements of the value of their work to those they help, the challenges inherent in being a peer facilitator, and the enormous personal benefits they derived from learning to help their agemates. There are probably no more compelling prevention programs than these involving the theory, training, and research in peer helping. If there were such a phenomenon as "preventive psychotherapy," training in empathy, self-observation, and communication skills would be a viable approach to such a goal.

On some college campuses where peer helping exists, we know that it is categorized as a non-academic "club" activity. This is of concern for at least two important reasons:

1. To view peer facilitation as a recreational activity removes it from the more respectable forum of academic scrutiny, readings, research papers, and faculty/staff input.

2. Of even greater concern, proper professional supervision cannot often be provided in such settings.

Peers supervising peers without professional guidance flies in the face of ethical guidelines of all varieties (APA, 1992;

NPHA, 1990). The course we have offered here, as well as the various applications of peer helping on campus, are all properly supervised and comply with high ethical standards; we recommend such "quality control" for any college or university that sets up peer helping services.

As is clear by now, the primary format of this volume has been to look *within programs* for the experiential reactions of peer facilitators to the training, philosophy, and practice inherent in each of their respective programs.

It is also of value to have looked at the commonalities and differences *across our twelve peer programs and the 110 interviewees* (see Appendix C for interview schedules) for demographic and survey data. This was achieved by coding (see Appendix D) both the demographic interview schedules and the semi-structured interviews that were administered and analyzed by our research team (see Appendix E for tables.) Rater reliabilities for the coding of all data was eighty-two percent; in noting the following findings, bear in mind that we interviewed only a subsample of about fifty percent of the peers in each program in a specific timeframe. Nonetheless, the data is consistent enough that we feel confident that the findings presented below are valid.

For each of the 110 peer facilitators we interviewed, their comments were tape recorded, transcribed, and then analyzed in accordance with our coding schema by our research team of undergraduate and graduate students. Our sample was comprised of four percent sophomores, eighteen percent juniors, forty-five percent seniors, six percent graduate students, and eight percent geriatric peer counselors; the members of our peer counseling class, however, were not identified by year in school. It is not surprising that there were no first-year students in our sample as peer facilitators are usually required to be upperclassmen/women.

Seventy percent of our sample were women and only thirty percent men, a split that is increasingly typical in the helping professions. This is about the same gender distribution that currently occurs in applications to graduate programs in clinical psychology. In age, eighty percent of all the peer facilitators were between the ages of twenty and twenty-two, as one might expect in a college population. The rest were younger (four percent) or older, non-traditional undergraduate students (twelve percent); our geriatric peer counselors were clearly well over the age of twenty-four!

There is ethnic diversity in our sample in about the same proportions as in the university itself: 11.8% of the peer counselors are African-American; 7.2% are Asian-American; 68% are European-American; 3% are Hispanic-American; and 9% are Native-American. The greatest percentage of European-American participants are in the elderly group. Thus, were we to remove these from our statistics, the percentages of ethnic diversity in the traditional college sample would rise. It is not surprising that IGRC has the highest percentage of students of color, but all of the college-aged programs were multicultural in composition.

Most of the participants in our study were majoring in the social sciences (fifty-seven percent); six percent were students of natural science; nine percent were studying the humanities, and another four percent of those who were decided were in the School of Education. Not surprisingly, career plans tended to run in about the same percentages, with a slight increase toward fourteen percent in education and as many in public health. Most of the peer facilitators in our sample plan a career in one of the "helping professions." It is clear from their narratives that their peer work has, for most of them, convinced them of the correctness of this career plan.

The vast majority of peers (sixty-six percent) report having had an "Excellent" experience with their peer work on campus; this is the highest rating on a scale of five. Another thirty-six percent report having had an "Above Average" experience, and amazingly *no students selected the lowest two categories* of either "Poor" or "Below Average" experience.

Almost all the peer facilitators reported that their paraprofessional work had affected their sense of themselves and career plans "quite a lot"—and in positive ways. Seventy-four percent reported great personal maturation as a result of this work; eighty percent reported improved relationships with others. This personal benefit in being a peer helper is consistent with the increasing research on this subject (Hahn & LeCapitaine, 1990). Most had worked for their programs six months or more at the time they were interviewed for this project, and forty percent of those interviewed had been in their programs for more than a year, which means that, in most cases, they applied for a second or third year.

About one fifth of the students we interviewed were paraprofessionals in more than one program—we have called them "dual peer helpers" (Richman & Bench, 1993). These versatile paraprofessionals made distinctions between those programs they worked in that addressed a fairly uniform set of issues (e.g., SAPAC; UHS) and those that worked with a wide and sometimes unexpected variety of problems (e.g., GUIDE; Resident Advisors). All of the "dual peer helpers" reported that their participation in the first program led to their interest in the second. From their accounts it would seem that such peer "cross training" accelerates and ameliorates the maturity of peer facilitation skills.

> *Peer A (from Women's Studies):* I would say that my peer facilitator role is complementary to any other role that a person could have. I mean, you're learning how to better relate to people and pretty much every role you have is relating to other people somehow. Specifically in the volunteer work I do, it helps me communicate more effectively, not only with the other people I'm working with as other volunteers but also with the clients there. I work in the middle of the night with crisis intervention, often entering a really hostile environment. I think that my ability to facilitate all of what's going on—to kind of be a moderator to make sure that everyone is heard, everyone's saying what they need to say, everyone's to some extent taken care of as much as they can be at that point—has been really helped by that role.

Dual peers seemed particularly committed to career choices in one of the "helping professions." This group seemed especially cognizant of not wanting to take the problems of other students "home with them." This may be because of their exposure to a large number and wide variety of clients.

In the course of their work, most peer facilitators in our sample had worked with at least twenty clients; some, such as Resident Advisors, had worked with sixty or more. Clearly the "dual peers" had worked with at least twice the number of "clients" per year as most of the other paraprofessionals in our sample.

Peers across all the programs report that they received overwhelmingly positive feedback from the populations they served. As the chapters frequently state, they are all continually evaluating their training and service, seeking ways to improve. ==The serendipitous gain for most of the peer helpers is their self-improvement in psychological-mindedness, empathy, relationships, self-esteem, and self-observational skills.== For this reason, it is clear that the "voice of the peers" tells us that this experience in their college lives, in which they are simultaneously able to help others and themselves, is one of the most profoundly rewarding.

It would seem fitting to end with the voice of a peer:

> *Peer B (from the Peer Advising Program in Psychology)*: This has been a tremendous experience. I have matured and grown in so many ways. Being in a position of responsibility like this has given me a new perspective and gives me an inkling of all the empathy I am capable of; my sense of pride has developed because I realize that my peers really value my services.

REFERENCES

American Psychological Association (1992, December). Ethical principles of psychologists and conduct. *The American Psychologist*, 1597-1611.

Hahn, J., & LeCapitaine, J. (1990). Impact of peer counseling upon emotional development and self-concept of peer counselors. *College Student Journal*, 4, 410-20.

Richman, W., & Bench, S. (1993). Dual Peer Helpers. Unpublished manuscript, University of Michigan.

Toole, J. (1990). National peer helpers association programmatic standards. *Peer Facilitator Quarterly*, 7 (4), 6-29.

Appendices

Appendix A

Presenting Concerns to College Peer Counselors: Roleplay Scenarios[1]

Cultural/Religious Issues

- A student of color believes that her professors and other students do not consider her as an individual but as "the minority" of the group; she is further distressed by other students' insinuations that she is only in the university because of affirmative action policies and not her merit.
- A student believes she is being made to choose between observing religious holidays and attending sorority house functions, as the sorority does not take her religious holidays into account when planning parties.
- A student is upset by her boyfriend's lack of respect for her deeply held religious beliefs.

---

[1] Appendix A was compiled by Jennifer Stevens, EdM, from actual college student peer counseling roleplays done as part of a course assignment in Dr. Sherry Hatcher's class. All identifying information has been removed or disguised to protect the anonymity of the students. Please see chapter 3 for discussion of peer counseling techniques (i.e., empathic listening, reflecting back, clarifying, and appropriate open- and closed-ended questioning) and their creative and flexible uses.

- A student worries about telling her ethnically identified parents about her serious relationship with a classmate who is of a different ethnicity for fear they will not understand; however, if she does not tell them soon, she fears they will no longer trust her.

School Related/Academic Concerns

- After spending a lot of time and energy on a campus comedy show, a student begins to have difficulties concentrating on and being interested in schoolwork she once found exciting but now finds boring in comparison.
- A student feels overwhelmed by pressures to participate socially with her friends, work a part-time job, and do her schoolwork; she is worried because it is her schoolwork that suffers most.
- After recently deciding to pursue organizational psychology at the graduate level, a junior psychology student wonders whether he should change his major from general to organizational psychology so late in his undergraduate career.
- A student feels frustrated and like she is wasting her time in class because her teaching assistant is not doing what the student perceives to be an adequate job.
- A student on the women's varsity softball team believes that her coach singles her out and harasses her with sarcastic remarks for no apparent reason despite the student's efforts to minimize conflict.

Issues of Independence/Dependence Involving Parents

- A graduating senior wants to live with her boyfriend after graduation and knows her

parents will be against the arrangement; she feels bound by their values and does not know how to tell them of her plans.
- A student is afraid she will disappoint and hurt her parents by telling them she does not want to live with them during the upcoming summer break.
- A student's parents forbid her to go away for a weekend with her long-term boyfriend after he wins a trip for two at a fraternity event. The student is perplexed and upset, as she is in a long-distance relationship and her parents know she has visited her boyfriend many times at his university.
- A graduating senior is offered a job by the firm at which her father works and where she held an internship for three consecutive summers. Although the job is her most promising offer, the student's father does not want her to take the job; she believes that honoring her father's wishes will be at her own expense.
- A student feels confused about what to do after graduation because of what he perceives to be outside pressures; while he feels the need to please his parents and go to graduate school, he also knows that he wants to take at least a one-year break between undergraduate and graduate school.

Other Issues of Dependence/Independence

- Although her boyfriend urges her to do so, the student feels uncomfortable discussing problems concerning her relationship with her mother with him. She feels guilty about her need for privacy and is afraid her boyfriend will interpret her privacy needs as a negative comment on their relationship.

- A student feels stuck because she does not want to be completely apart from her now ex-boyfriend but cannot be with him without them both feeling too dependent on each other.
- A student believes that in order to preserve her friendship with her roommate she needs to spend less time with her and does not know how to tell her she no longer wants to live with her for fear of alienating her.
- A friend is interfering in a new, potentially romantic relationship and making the student feel very uncomfortable; the student wants to focus on the friendship part of the new relationship and is afraid her friend will frighten him away by pushing him toward something more seriously committed.

Loyalty Issues

- A student feels obligated to live with her friend but knows it is not in her own best interest; she is afraid to do what she believes would be best for her for fear of hurting her friend and destroying their friendship.
- A student feels betrayed by her trusted friend after overhearing her ask the student's boyfriend out on date while at a birthday party.
- Her two best friends from high school have become much closer with each other and the student feels left out and uncared for by her friends.
- A student feels betrayed by a good friend and ex-boyfriend who are now dating each other.
- A student feels responsible and guilty because she testified against her violent ex-boyfriend, who is now in prison for one year; she wants to be supportive yet needs to distance herself from him.

- A student feels betrayed and hurt when an old friend, for whom the student has always provided support, is perceived as not reciprocating concern.
- While briefly broken up, the student and her boyfriend both asked other people to attend two upcoming dances. They are together again and the student made arrangements for her significant other to accompany her to the dance at her school; however, he was unable to explain the situation to his date, leaving the student feeling betrayed by him.
- A student feels uncared for when her younger sister, with whom she is very close, does not seem receptive to discussing the student's difficulties with her significant other; the student is always there for her sister and feels let down.

Parental Divorce

- Since the student's parents recently divorced, he feels that his father has been treating him like a ten year old and putting down his intelligence; he feels shut out by his father, who becomes angered whenever his son tries to talk about their relationship.
- During a recent holiday break, a student was stunned to be told her parents are separating; she is worried about her younger sister and unable to focus on her schoolwork.

Social/Peer Pressure

- A male student believes that one should be friends with someone before dating her, yet feels torn between the comfort of friendships with women and the desire to take risks to see if they can be more than friends.

- A student is being pressured by her friends to quit dating her new boyfriend because they have heard he has a bad reputation; she does not understand why her friends don't respect her judgment.
- A student does not know how to maintain friendships since she has quit drinking alcohol. Her friends spend a lot of time in bars on the weekend and are not supportive of her decision not to drink; she fears that if she does not participate in weekend activities with them, she will lose their friendship.

Loss Issues

- At the time of the four-year anniversary of her mother's death, a student begins to feel angry at her friends and sad and unable to concentrate on her schoolwork; she tries to act as if nothing is wrong but feels frustrated, alone, and dishonest toward her friends.
- After his grandfather was recently diagnosed with terminal cancer, a student cannot quit thinking about his grandfather's imminent death to the point where he can no longer concentrate on his schoolwork.
- A student wonders how he may be helpful to his stoical grandfather after his wife's death. While the student knows his grandfather is lonely and wants to be supportive, he fears any gesture of support will be poorly received.

Intervention in a Perceived Potential Crisis

- A student is worried, but does not know what to do, about the health and well-being of her roommate with a long-standing and worsening drug abuse problem. While once close friends,

- the two no longer speak, which hurts and causes the student further concern.
- A student feels helpless and frustrated as to how to help her roommate, who is suffering from an eating disorder that is obviously getting worse.
- After receiving an angry response to confronting her roommate about her severe weight loss, the student is debating whether or not to tell her roommate's doctor and parents. She feels torn between her concern for her friend's health and her desire to respect her autonomy.
- A student fears her close friend is bulimic and does not know how to help her. The situation is further complicated by her friend's recent withdrawal of trust and communication, leaving the student feeling hurt and shut out.
- Following a sexual assault prevention presentation, a female student experiences wakened feelings of anger associated with being date-raped one year ago and feels the urgent need to talk with someone after putting it out of her mind and having kept quiet about it for so long.[2]

Roommate/Housemate Conflicts

- A roommate is often loud and sloppy and comes home drunk, making it difficult for the student to do his best work. However, the student feels guilty confronting his roommate because he provides a lot of resources (e.g., TV and VCR), which the student enjoys.
- The student is angry and frustrated because, although she has broached the subject of what she perceives to be her roommate's lack of respect for her, her roommate does not listen

---

[2] Witnessing or discussing a present crisis may often trigger the memory of past traumatic experience.

and continues to come in late at night with friends on weeknights, waking the student up.
- A third housemate feels her privacy has been invaded and her feelings not taken into account because her two housemates' boyfriends are very frequently at their home. Not only has she gained two extra "housemates" that she did not bargain for, the student also misses time alone with her housemates; she hesitates to talk with them about this matter for fear of creating a greater distance between them.
- A female student feels angry and inconvenienced because her housemate invited her brother and a male friend of his to stay with her for four days. The student is used to living only with women and believes she is unfairly being made to feel uncomfortable in her own home.
- A student feels frustrated at his housemate for not doing his fair share of housework around the apartment. He resents having to tell him to clean the stove and does not know if it is worth the hostile reaction he may receive in return if he confronts his roommate.

Financial Concerns

- After having made plans to move out of state with his girlfriend following graduation, a student is confronted with the problem of being unable to sublet his apartment for the summer. He is short on funds and does not know if he should risk moving where there are better job opportunities and he may be able to afford losing one thousand dollars in rent, or stay in town where he is less confident about finding a job to cover his expenses.
- A student feels helpless and frustrated by a family court battle that has been going on for

some time and will be decided within the week; the outcome of the trial will determine whether or not her father will be able to afford to pay her tuition next year.

Planning for Life after College

- A student is overwhelmed and intimidated by the choices she must make after graduation from college; it is the first time in her life she will have to make decisions on her own, and she does not know what to do.
- A student seeks direction in making a difficult decision between two equally appealing graduate schools to which she has been accepted.
- Not having done a lot of preparation for life after graduation, a student is experiencing difficulty deciding whether or not to accept a job offer that would take him back to his hometown, where he does not care to return, or moving alone to an unknown area of the country without a job. He is torn between the security of having a job in a location he does not want to live and the excitement of starting fresh socially but without a job.
- Although she has been advised to get some work experience, a student fears that if she gets a serious job after graduation she will get caught up in her work and having an income and will never fulfill her plans to get an MBA.
- A student has been involved with her much older boyfriend for five years and, in the face of graduation, is concerned that she will "settle down" and forego exploration of life possibilities; she does not, however, want to lose the relationship.
- A student, who for years assumed he would continue his education at the graduate level and get a PhD in psychology, has recently begun to

question his commitment to the amount of work required of a psychologist and the lifestyle the profession affords.
- A student cannot choose one of the three graduate schools to which she has been accepted; one is in her homestate, and the other two are out of state and in large cities. The prospect of being in a city where she does not know anyone is unnerving, yet the school in her homestate does not offer her financial aid and as appealing a program.
- A student feels increasingly anxious and overwhelmed as graduation draws near; she has not made any definitive plans for the near future yet has several options (e.g., move out of town and live with a friend; stay in town and get a job), one of which she must commit to soon.

Appendix B

Sample Exercises to Practice Peer Counseling Skills[1]

Introduction Exercises

1. *Class Introductions*: Each student gets to know another classmate by interviewing the person next to him/her for three minutes (asking, for example, "Where are you from? What are your career plans?" etc.), paying particular attention to the feelings this person expresses. After five to ten minutes, the students switch roles and then introduce each other to the rest of the class, *being sure to identify where they heard their partner express the most feeling* (see page 35).

2. *Qualities of a Good Counselor*: Students list the qualities they look for in a confidante. The class generates a long, inclusive list; students note which of these qualities they already possess and which they want to work on. On the last day of class or when they complete the program, they review this list and reflect on the progress they have made.

Behavioral Attending Exercise

In Dyads: One student is counselee, the other counselor. The counselee talks about a personal problem/experience while the counselor practices *poor* behavioral attending skills (e.g.,

---

[1] Compiled by Meredith Reynolds, MA, and Brie Jeweler, BA. For each of the following skill-building exercises, discussion and "debriefing" are always part of one experience for the purpose of sharing views and for closure.

435

does not maintain eye contact, sits with closed posture, etc.). The students then switch roles and the new counselor practices good behavioral attending skills or FELOR. Students evaluate each of the roleplays, discussing how it felt to be/not be attended to by the counselor (Carr & Saunders, 1980, 47).

Empathy Exercises

1. *In Dyads*: The counselee describes a personal problem/experience while the counselor listens empathically. The counselor responds to the counselee by saying, "The most important thing I heard you say was...." In this response the peer counselor includes the content of what the counselee said but also identifies the affect or feeling he/she heard (based on Carr & Saunders [1980], 5).

2. *Jungle Exercise (used by SAPAC)*: To get an idea of how to empathize with a rape survivor, students close their eyes and imagine what it is like to be chased by a tiger through a jungle (see chapter 8).

Paraphrasing Exercise

In Dyads: The counselee describes a personal problem/experience and the counselor responds by paraphrasing and summarizing the counselee's own words, using such phrases as: "What I hear you saying is..." or "So it sounds like...." The counselor checks with the counselee to make sure the summary is correct (Myrick & Erney, 1978, 84).

Roadblocks to Communication

In Small Groups: One student is given a topic to discuss with the group while the remaining group members receive a card with a specific (destructive) role to play in the conversation (e.g., "Don't talk," "Preach or give advice," "Judge or criticize others," etc.) The student with the topic starts a conversation with the group, and each member acts out his/her particular role. Afterward, the group evaluates how the conversation went, particularly how it felt to do this exercise, and discusses the various "roadblocks" to communication (Carr & Saunders, 1980, 51).

Values Exercises

1. *Intergenerational Exercise*: Students make a list of the three most important values for him/herself, his/her parents, and his/her grandparents. Students then share their personal and family values with the class, discussing any differences, similarities, or trends they notice (Lewis, 1993, 327-8).

2. *Taking a Stand*: One end of the room is labeled "Strongly Agree," the middle of the room is labeled "Neutral," and the other end is labeled "Strongly Disagree." Various controversial topics are presented to the class (e.g., "Alcohol should not be served on campus" or "I would work with a client even if he/she were prejudiced against my religion, ethnicity, or sexual preference"). Students must physically place themselves on a continuum of where "they stand" on these issues (The Lesbian-Gay Male Programs Office, 1993, 323).

Identity Exercise

Students pick three different stickers representing the three main ways they define themselves (e.g., blue sticker = gender, red = race, yellow = religion, etc.). The students wear their stickers and explain their choices to the rest of the class, including what these choices mean to them personally (Zúñiga & Nagda, 1993, 323).

Nonjudgmental Listening

1. *In Dyads*: The counselee receives a card containing a controversial scenario on it, one that would normally elicit judgmental responses from people (e.g., the counselee cheated on an exam, shoplifted, used drugs, etc.). The goal of the counselor is to practice non-judgmental listening.

2. The counselor clarifies and summarizes a political point of view very different from his/her own in an objective and nonjudgmental way. The counselee indicates if he/she believed the counselor's statements were biased or judgmental (Myrick & Erney, 1978, 55).

Affect Exercise

A few students make statements to the class while expressing various emotions with their voices, which may or may not correspond to the content of the sentence (e.g., "I won a free trip to Hawaii" in a disappointed tone; "I was fired from my job" in a happy tone, etc.). The class tries to identify the emotions that are expressed in the students' voices, which requires students' expectations based on the content of the sentences to be suspended (Carr & Saunders, 1980, 60).

Circle Counseling

One student plays the role of the counselee while the other students all play the role of the counselor. The counselors form a circle around the counselee, who begins to talk about a personal problem/experience. The counselors go around the circle, taking turns asking a question or making a comment to the counselee. Each counselor can only ask one question or make one comment (Litzenberger, 1993).

Open- and Closed-Ended Questions

1. Students sit in a circle and must each ask an open-ended question to the person on his/her right. (Note: Questions may not begin with "Why.") Periodically, the students reverse direction and ask the person on the left a closed question. At the end of the exercise, students discuss which types of questions were more difficult to ask and what it was like to answer the two types of questions.

2. *Ask the Professor*: The professor tells the class of a personal situation, giving minimal information. Students first ask only closed questions and then switch to asking open ques-

tions. Students compare the amount and type of information each type of questioning tends to elicit. This exercise offers an opportunity for the professor to share something selected from his/her life (see chapter 3).

Tag-Team Counseling

One student volunteers to be the counselee and another the counselor. Both students sit in the middle of the room and start a counseling session while the rest of the class observes. When the counselor gets tired or stuck, he/she raises his/her hand and another student replaces him/her. If at any time another student wants to replace the counselor, he/she places his/her hands on the counselor's shoulders. The counselor is allowed to finish his/her line of questioning before being replaced.

"I" Versus "You" Statements ✓

Shoes on the Coffee Table: Two students play the role of someone whose parents just bought a brand new and very expensive coffee table (an actual table/prop can be used). When the instructor puts his/her feel on this table, one student must respond using only "You" statements (e.g., "You are so rude!"). The other student must use only "I" statements (e.g., "I would feel horrible if something happened to this coffee table") (Carr & Saunders, 1980, 83).

Positive/Constructive Feedback Model

In Dyads: Counselee, counselor, and observer practice using the feedback model both for positive and constructive feedback (see chapter 3). After a ten minute conversation, each participant gives the other specific "positive feedback." Constructive feedback can be practiced by imagining in a role-play format that the other person is someone you have been wanting to confront about an unresolved issue.

Decision Making Exercise

In Dyads: Students think about a few good decisions and a few bad decisions that they have made in their lives and try to evaluate what criteria they used to evaluate the decision as either good or bad. Students then practice the decision-making model (see chapter 3) by applying it to a decision they are currently trying to make (Carr & Saunders, 1980).

Double Circle Exercise

Part of the Identity/Multicultural Exercise: Students sit in two circles, one inside the other, and face each other so that each person in the outer circle is facing a partner in the inner circle. Students are given a few minutes to discuss an important identity or multicultural issue (e.g., the first set of partners might choose to discuss their religious affiliations/views). When they are finished, the outer circle rotates one position so that each student now has a new partner (e.g., this second pair might discuss gender issues) (based on Myers & Zúñiga, 1993, 318).

Relaxation Exercise

Used by Stress Management to Show Students How They Can Relax Themselves: Students practice deep breathing to music and relaxing by first tensing then relaxing each muscle group, starting at the head and working down to the toes (see chapter 7).

"Countertransference" Roleplay

A counselor who is talkative and favors talkative others works with and reflects upon this work with a rather silent client. Students roleplay, observe, and then discuss the process of working with a client about whom they may have personal feelings and/or reactions.

Supervisor Exercises

1. *In Dyads*: A counselor shares his/her feelings about another roleplay (e.g., midterm; see chapter 3) with a student who practices the role of a supervisor.

2. *Parallel Process Roleplay*: Three students prepare a roleplay in which the interaction between a client and a peer counselor is replicated with the counselor's supervisor. For example, in the client/counselor "session," the client displaces (previously unexpressed) anger he/she has felt toward a boss by directing it toward the peer counselor. In a subsequent counselor/supervisor meeting, the peer counselor (who did not understand the client's anger) finds her/himself (inadvertently) "repeating" an angry outburst toward the supervisor. Suspecting the anger may have something to do with the client/counselor session, the supervisor inquires as to this possibility. The audience is then asked to describe and discuss what they have observed. The concept of parallel process is useful because it offers the supervisor an additional source of information about the affective tone of the peer counseling session.

REFERENCES

Carr, R., & Saunders, G. (1980). *Peer counseling starter kit*. University of Victoria: Peer Counseling Project.

D'Andrea, V., & Salovey, P. (1983). *Peer counseling skills and perspectives*. Palo Alto: Science and Behavior Books.

Ivey, A. E., & Authier, J. (1978). *Microcounseling*. Springfield, Illinois: Charles C. Thomas.

The Lesbian-Gay Male Programs Office (1993). Classroom & workshop exercises: "Take a Stand" exercise. In D. Schoem, et al. (Eds.), *Multicultural teaching in the university* (323-4).

Lewis, E. (1993). Classroom & workshop exercises: "Ethnographic Charting" exercise. In D. Schoem, et al. (Eds.), *Multicultural teaching in the university* (327-8).

Litzenberger, B. (1993). Personal communication to the author.

Myers, P., & Zúñiga, X. Classroom & workshop exercises: "Concentric Circles" exercise. In D. Schoem, et al., (Eds.), *Multicultural teaching in the university* (318).

Myrick, R., & Erney T. (1978). *Caring and sharing: Becoming a peer facilitator*. Minneapolis: Educational Media Corp.

Schoem, D., Frankel, L., Zúñiga, X., & Lewis, E. (Eds.) (1993). *Multicultural teaching in the university*. Westport, Connecticut: Praeger.

Zúñiga, X., & Nagda, B. (1993). Classroom & workshop exercises: "Identity Group" exercise. In D. Schoem, et al. (Eds.), *Multicultural teaching in the university* (323).

Appendix C

Interview Schedules for Research Protocol

Please complete this questionnaire. For each item, check the answer that most closely applies to you. Thanks for your time!

Part I: General Information

1. Year in School:
   - ☐ Freshperson
   - ☐ Sophomore
   - ☐ Junior
   - ☐ Senior
   - ☐ Graduate
   - ☐ Other (specify) _____

2. Gender:
   - ☐ Female
   - ☐ Male

3. Age:_____

4. Ethnicity (optional):
   - ☐ African-American
   - ☐ Hispanic-American
   - ☐ Asian-American
   - ☐ Native American
   - ☐ European-American

5. How long (in months) have you been active in this program? _____

6. How long was your training period?
   - ☐ Less than 1 week
   - ☐ 1-2 weeks
   - ☐ 2-4 weeks
   - ☐ 4 or more weeks

APPENDIX C

7. On a scale from 1 to 5, how well did your training prepare you for your job (5 being excellent)?   1 2 3 4 5

8. Approximately how many clients have you had since beginning the program? ____

9. How did you find out about the program?

10. How did you get the job?

11. Are you
    - ☐ paid
    - ☐ working for academic credit
    - ☐ volunteer
    - ☐ other (explain) _____

12. How many hours do you work per week? _____

13. On a scale from 1 to 5, how would you rate your overall experience with the program (5 being excellent)?   1 2 3 4 5

14. On a scale from 1 to 5, how much do you think the program has affected your personality (5 being greatly affected)?   1 2 3 4 5

15. What is/are your concentration(s) and interests?

16. What are your career plans?

Part II: Oral Interview
("The Program and the Peer Counselor")[1]

1. How were you trained or prepared for your peer facilitating position?

2. a) Is there a supervisor for the program? b) What role does the supervisor play?

3. Describe the purpose of the program.

4. As a peer facilitator, describe your role in the program.

5. If you received feedback of your work, a) in what form did you get it? b) How did it feel?

6. Some people report that peer helping has affected their relationships with others. Is this true for you?

7. Some people report that peer helping has affected their own problem solving abilities. Do you have any personal examples of this?

8. Experiences with peer helping affects career plans for some people. Have you had a similar experience? If so, how?

9. Peer helping sometimes teaches people new things about themselves. Is this true for you? If so, how?

10. Peer helping can also teach people things about others. Has this occurred through your experiences? If so, how?

11. Describe your relationship with other peer helpers.

---

[1] The wording for this part of the Interview Schedule was adapted for relevance to each program; here we present the generic version. All interviews were taped and transcribed. Interviewers were trained in the administration of a "semi-structured interview," which means they may ask followup questions, elicit examples, and encourage elaboration.

12. How did your role as a peer helper fit in with your other roles and commitments?

13. Describe the most challenging or frustrating experience that you have had in peer counseling work.

14. Describe the most rewarding or interesting experience that you have had in peer counseling work.

15. Describe anything else that was not already mentioned that would tell us how you feel about your experiences in peer helping.

Appendix D

Coding Schema for Analyzing the Data[1]

Files were created for each peer program in a uniform format so as to facilitate the coding of the interview schedule. Since questions 1-5a (see Appendix C) yielded similar responses from members within a program (e.g., all participants received the same training and supervision), these particular responses were compiled as an exhaustive list rather than coded individually. Questions 5b-12 were coded using the Likert scales as follows:

Question 5b explored how it felt to receive feedback as a peer helper. Responses were coded as:

1 Very Uncomfortable

2 Uncomfortable

3 Neutral

4 Helpful or Good

5 Very Good

Questions 6-10 explored the effects of peer work on relationships with others, problem solving abilities, career plans, self-knowledge, and insight in relation to other people. Responses were coded according to the number and quality of examples given as follows:

---

[1] Prepared by Jill Sullivan and Sherry Hatcher.

APPENDIX D

1 Not at All

- Explicitly stated by the respondent, e.g., "Not really," "No, I don't think so"

2 Some

- Uses tentative language, e.g., "I guess so"
- Seems vague
- No examples given

3 Moderately

- Uses statements such as, "Well, yeah," "Sort of," "A little"
- Seems neutral
- Gives only one example, not described in depth

4 A Lot

- Explicitly stated as "A lot"
- At least one clear example, described in depth
- Example, though clearly explained, doesn't pertain to other experiences (e.g., only describes relationships with others within the program, problem solving with program topics and issues, and taught him/her things about others who have participated in the program rather than people in general)

5 Very Much

- Uses declarative descriptions, e.g., "Very much," "Really," "Totally," "Definitely"
- Includes many examples
- Examples generalize to other experiences as well (e.g., describes effects on several relationships, problem solving with other topics and issues, self-knowledge, etc.)

For Question 11, the peer workers' relationships with co-workers were coded using the following scale:

1 Contentious

- Describes friction or animosity
- Has chosen to work on his/her own rather than with the group
- Is unhappy with the quality of the relationships

2 Somewhat Tense

- Concentrates on disparities
- Explicitly states that relationships with some are positive or neutral but the majority are negative

3 Neutral

- No specific friendships, but expresses no disappointment in the quality of the relationships
- States that relationships revolve around peer work with no outside activities

4 Good

- Focuses on the positive
- Describes friendships above and beyond working relationships
- Sometimes associates with co-workers outside of the work setting

5 Excellent

- Uses positive tone
- Is very close to several co-workers
- Engages in activities outside of work
- Chooses to continue to do work/enjoys work more because of these relationships

Question 12 explored how well the role as a peer worker fit in with other roles and commitments, using the following criteria:

1 Not at All

- Explicitly states that the peer worker experiences role conflicts
- Time strain
- No longer fits with career or personal interests

2 Slightly

- States that it is hard to balance with other roles
- Is not very connected to other interests
- Still enjoys peer work despite these factors

3 Moderately

- Is not necessarily connected to other roles and interests, but is able to balance peer work with other commitments
- No time strain
- Uses tentative language, e.g., "I guess it fits in okay."
- Gives only one example, if any, to illustrate

4 Well

- Uses language such as "Somewhat," "Pretty well," "Well with some, though not with others"
- Gives clear example of how peer work is balanced with/connected to other interests and commitments

5 Very Well

- Uses declarative statements, e.g., "It's great," "There isn't any problem," "Excellent"
- Gives multiple examples of how peer work is balanced with/connected to other interests and commitments
- Became involved in related issues/other peer work

The remainder of the questionnaire pertained to challenges or frustrations with peer work, rewarding and interesting aspects of the experience, and the opportunity to mention

Coding Schema for Analyzing the Data

anything else that the participant believed would help describe his/her peer helping work. Exhaustive lists of these responses were maintained and added to the file as a tool for noting themes that emerged both within and across programs. Files were completed with salient quotes, which were later inserted into the chapters as "the voice of the peers."

Appendix E

Demographic and Survey Findings[1]

Table I: Subjects' Years in School

Table I displays the subjects' years in school. Note that this question does not apply to Turner Clinic peer counselors, who were not students (all TC subjects chose "Other"). Across all groups there were a total of zero freshpersons, four sophomores, twenty juniors, fifty seniors, eighteen graduates, and eighteen "others."

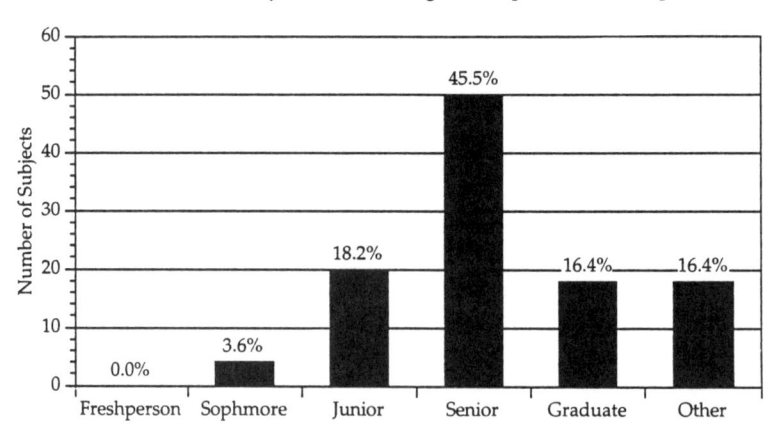

Total Number of Subjects and Percentage of Sample (Across Groups)

Year	Number	Percentage
Freshperson	0	0.0%
Sophomore	4	3.6%
Junior	20	18.2%
Senior	50	45.5%
Graduate	18	16.4%
Other	18	16.4%

---

[1] Contributors to Appendix E include Brie Jeweler, Gregory Marion, Renee Tikkanen, Meredith Reynolds, and Sherry Hatcher.

Table II: Subjects' Genders

Table II displays subject's gender. Across all groups in the sample, there were seventy-seven females (70.6%) and thirty-two males (29.4%).

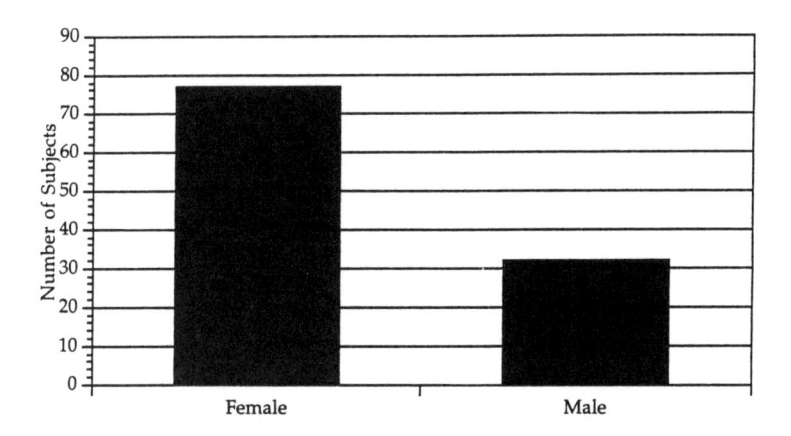

Table III: Subjects' Ages

Table III represents the ages of the subjects. Across groups, there were four subjects between seventeen and nineteen, eighty subjects between twenty and twenty-two, eleven subjects between twenty-two and twenty-four, and fifteen geriatric subjects.

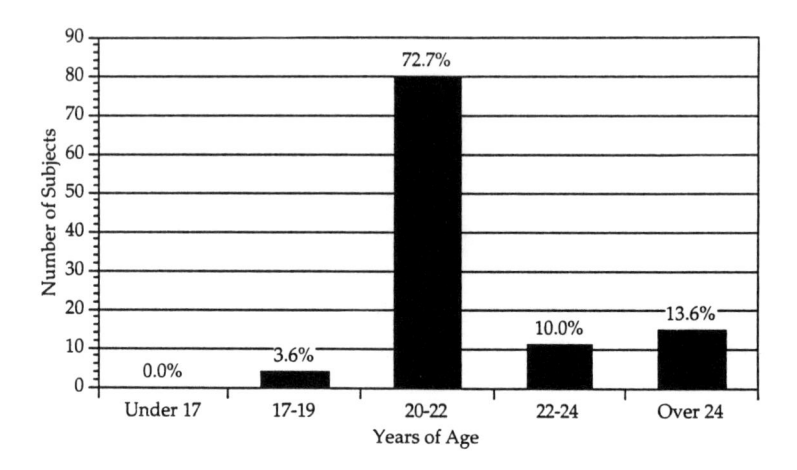

Table IV: Subjects' Ethnicity

Table IV represents subjects' ethnicity. Across groups, there were a total of thirteen African-Americans, eight Asian-Americans, seventy-five European-Americans, three Hispanic-Americans, one Native-American, and ten subjects with missing data for this (optional) item.

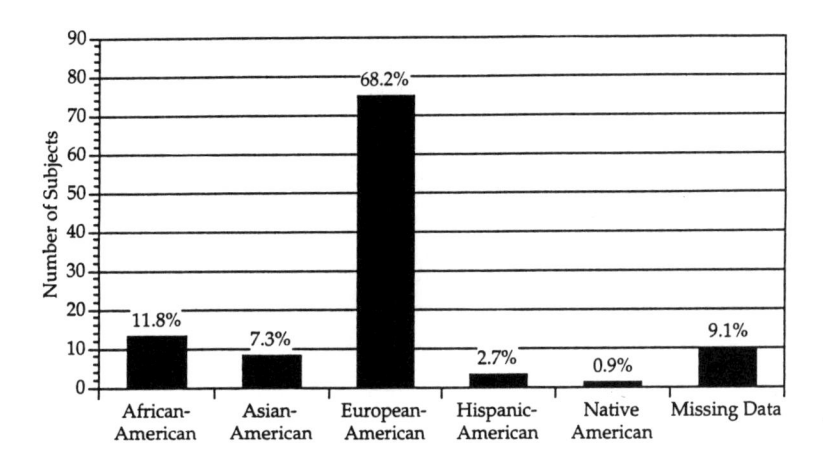

Ethnicity	Percentage
African-American	11.8%
Asian-American	7.3%
European-American	68.2%
Hispanic-American	2.7%
Native American	0.9%
Missing Data	9.1%

Table V: Subjects' Ratings of Their Experience

Table V displays subjects' ratings of their overall experience in their respective programs. No subjects rated their experience as "Poor" or "Below Average." Across groups, four subjects rated their experience as "Average." Thirty-nine subjects rated their experience as "Above Average" and sixty-six subjects rated their experience as "Excellent." One subject did not respond to this question.

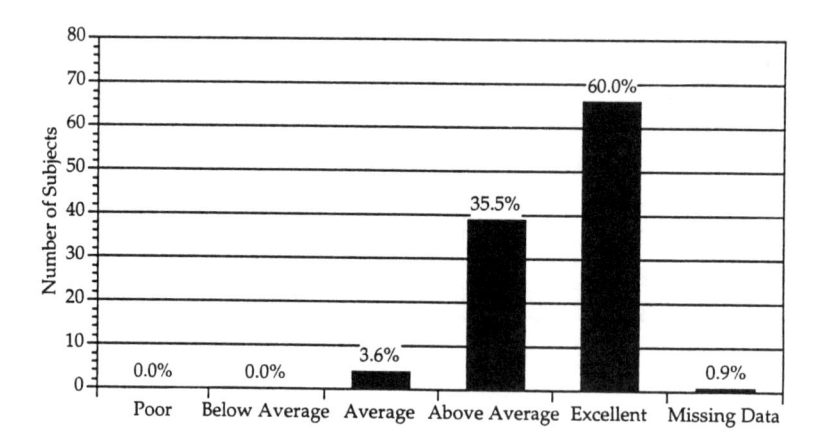

Rating	Percentage
Poor	0.0%
Below Average	0.0%
Average	3.6%
Above Average	35.5%
Excellent	60.0%
Missing Data	0.9%

Table VI: The Effect of the Programs on Subjects' Personalities

Table VI displays subjects' perceptions of how their participation in their respective programs affected their personalities. Across groups, four subjects indicated that their personality had been affected "Extremely Little" or "Not at All" and thirteen rated their personality as having not been affected "A Great Deal." Twenty-one subjects rated their personality as having been affected "Somewhat" by their participation. The majority of subjects believed their personalities were strongly affected. Sixty-eight of the 110 subjects (sixty-nine percent), forty-four, and twenty-four, respectively, rated their personalities as having been affected either "Quite a Bit" or "Quite a Lot." Four subjects had missing data for this item.

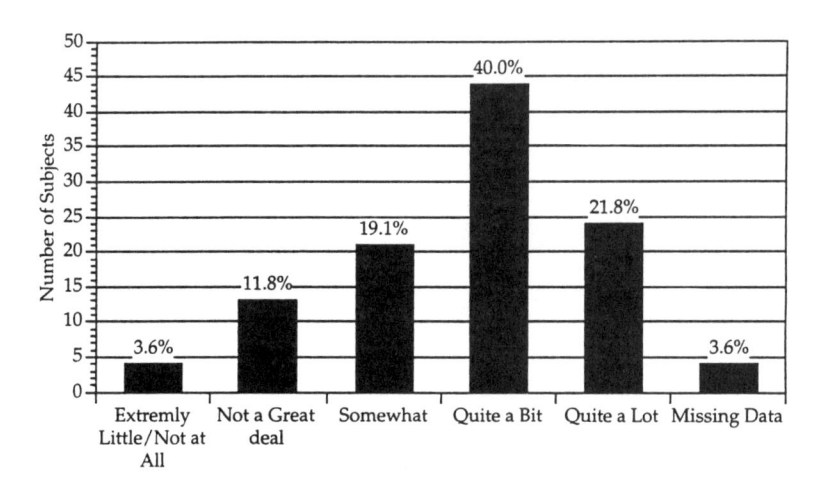

Category	Percentage
Extremly Little/Not at All	3.6%
Not a Great deal	11.8%
Somewhat	19.1%
Quite a Bit	40.0%
Quite a Lot	21.8%
Missing Data	3.6%

Table VII: Subjects' Academic Concentration and Interests

Table VII displays subjects' areas of academic concentration and interests. The majority of subjects, sixty-three (57.8%), rated the social sciences as their main interest or concentration. Seven subjects rated the natural sciences as their primary interest, and ten subjects chose the humanities. "Education" was selected by four subjects, and fifteen subjects chose "Other." Ten subjects did not supply data for this item; some of these may not yet be sure of their area of concentration.

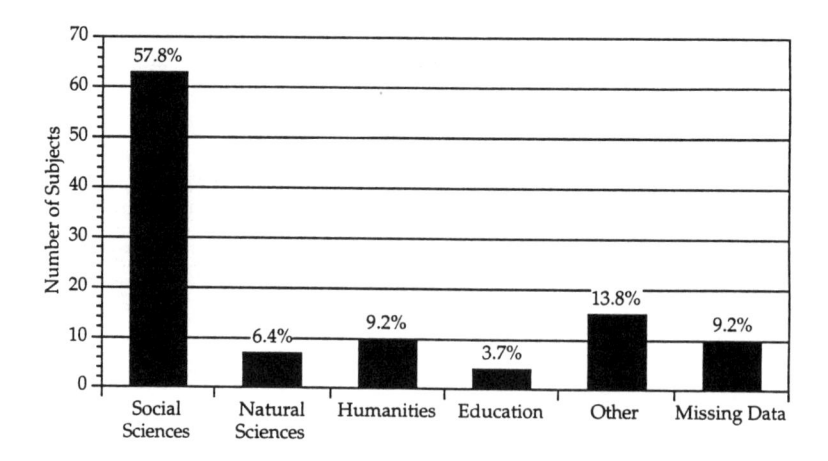

Category	Percentage
Social Sciences	57.8%
Natural Sciences	6.4%
Humanities	9.2%
Education	3.7%
Other	13.8%
Missing Data	9.2%

Table VIII: Subjects' Career Plans

Table VIII displays the discipline areas in which subjects planned to pursue careers. Across the subject groups, forty subjects rated social sciences (including social work), four rated natural sciences, two rated humanities, and fifteen selected education as their intended career field. Thirty-seven subjects selected "Other"; many of these may be undecided. Twelve (elderly) subjects indicated this question was "Not Applicable."

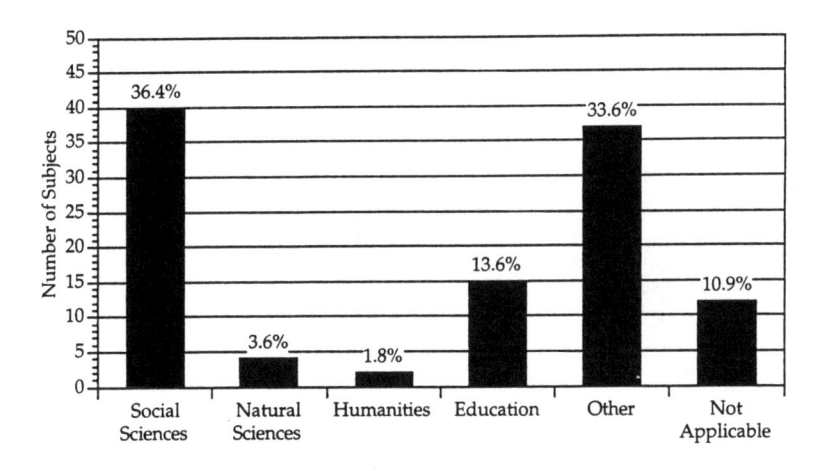

Category	Percentage
Social Sciences	36.4%
Natural Sciences	3.6%
Humanities	1.8%
Education	13.6%
Other	33.6%
Not Applicable	10.9%

Table IX: Months Active in Program

Table IX shows the number of months subjects participated in their programs. Across subject groups, twenty-four subjects were active for less than six months. The majority of subjects (seventy-six percent) were involved in their program for six or more months. Thirty-nine subjects participated between six and ten months, seventeen subjects were active for eleven to fifteen months, and seven for sixteen to twenty months. Twenty subjects were involved in their program for more than twenty months. One subject did not respond to this question.

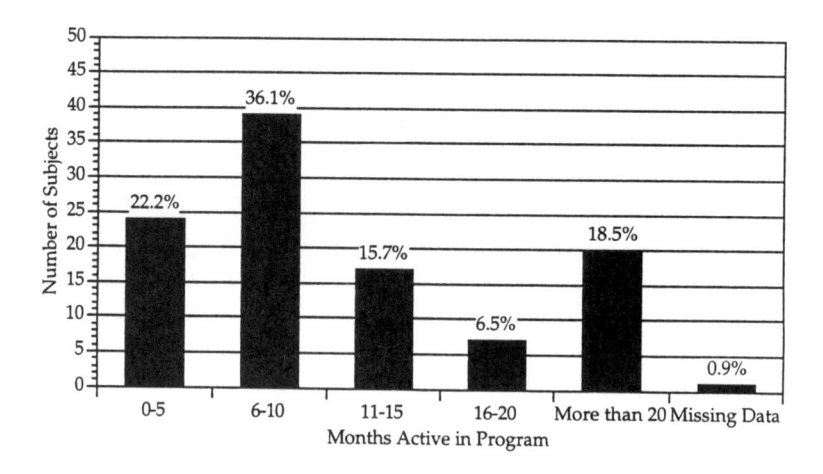

Table X: Length of Training

Table X displays the length of training subjects experienced. Across groups, thirty subjects trained for less than one week. Thirty subjects also received one to two weeks of training. Twenty-two subjects had two to four training weeks, and twenty-four subjects trained for more than four weeks. Eight subjects did not provide data for this question. This question was rated "Not Applicable" by two subjects.

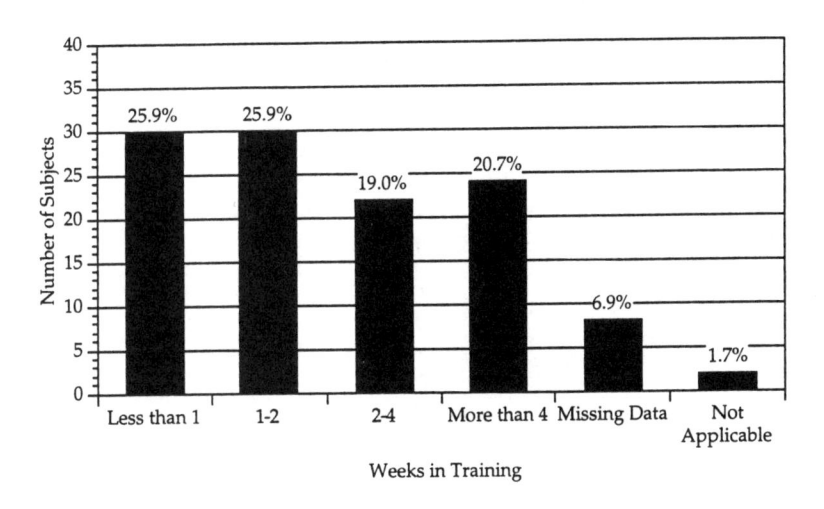

Weeks in Training	Number of Subjects	Percentage
Less than 1	30	25.9%
1-2	30	25.9%
2-4	22	19.0%
More than 4	24	20.7%
Missing Data	8	6.9%
Not Applicable	2	1.7%

Table XI: How Subjects Were Selected for Their Positions

Table XI represents subjects' responses to the open-ended question, "How did you get the job?" Across groups, six subjects got their jobs by application only, and thirty got their jobs by interview only. Almost half of the subjects, fifty-two (forty-seven percent) were selected for their programs based on an application and an interview. A class provided seven subjects with their jobs, and eleven subjects got their jobs by some other method. Four subjects did not answer this question.

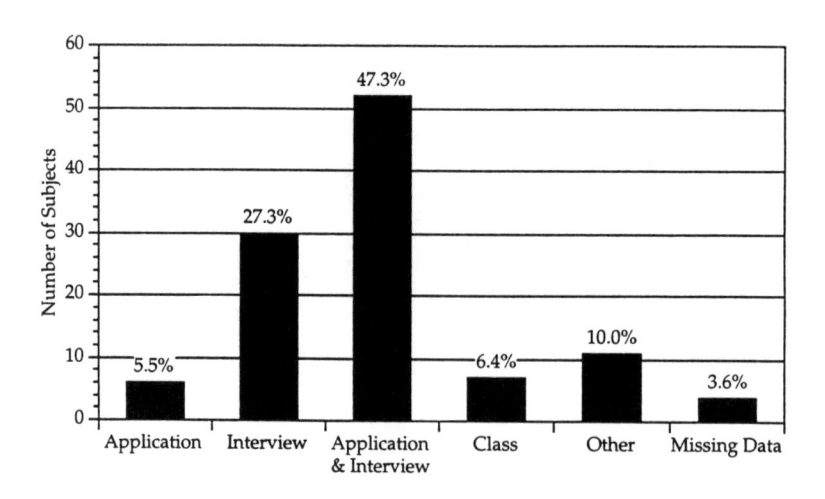

Method	Percentage
Application	5.5%
Interview	27.3%
Application & Interview	47.3%
Class	6.4%
Other	10.0%
Missing Data	3.6%

Table XII: Subjects' Compensation for Their Participation

Table XII presents the type of compensation subjects received for participating in their programs. Across groups, thirty-five subjects were paid and thirty-five subjects volunteered and did not receive compensation. Thirty-two subjects earned academic credit and five subjects were paid in addition to receiving credit. Three subjects received some other form of compensation (e.g., a "title").

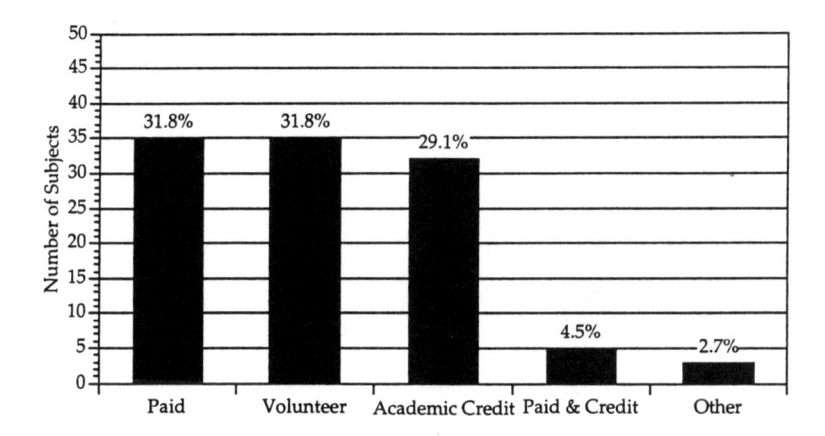

Table XIII: Number of Clients Served

Table XIII shows the number of clients subjects served in their programs. Across groups, forty-five subjects saw fewer than twenty-one clients. Sixteen subjects served between twenty-one and forty clients, and seventeen subjects saw forty-one to sixty clients. Twenty subjects served more than sixty clients. Five subjects facilitated one to five *groups* of clients. One person replied "Other" to this question and eight subjects did not respond.

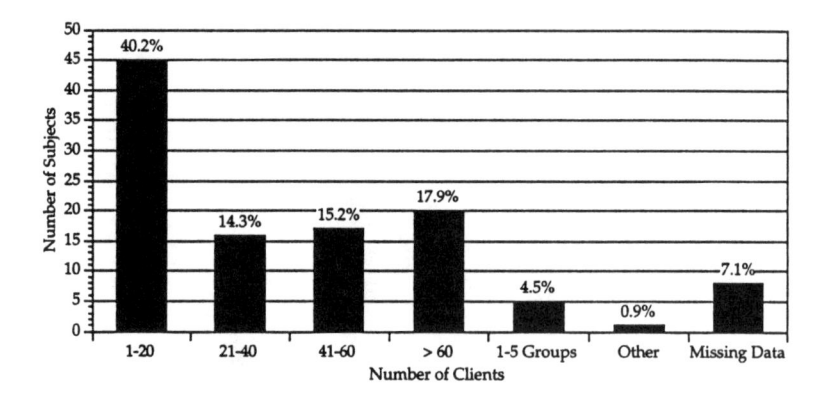

Table XIV: How Subjects Heard about Their Programs

Table XIV shows how subjects found out about their respective programs. Across groups, six subjects heard of their programs through previous participants or clients. Twenty-two subjects were told about their program by friends, and twenty-seven subjects heard about their programs in a class. The most frequent method of learning about programs was through advertisements and newspapers; thirty-five subjects were introduced to their programs this way. Nineteen people heard about their programs from some other source. Only one person did not respond.

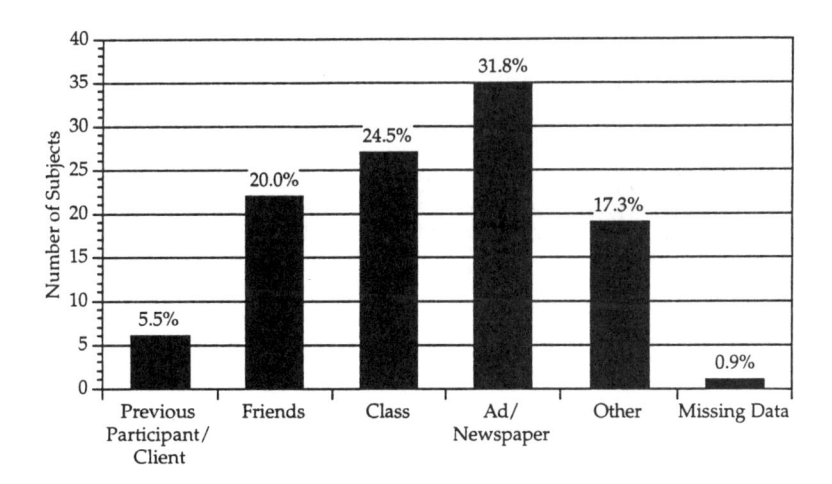

APPENDIX E

Table XV: Hours Worked Per Week

Table XV displays the hours subjects worked each week in their programs. Across groups, the majority of subjects, fifty-seven (51.8%) worked between one and five hours per week. Fourteen people worked six to ten hours, eighteen worked eleven to fifteen hours, and eight worked sixteen to twenty hours per week. Eight people worked more than twenty hours per week. Four subjects answered "Other" in response to this question, and one subject did not respond at all.

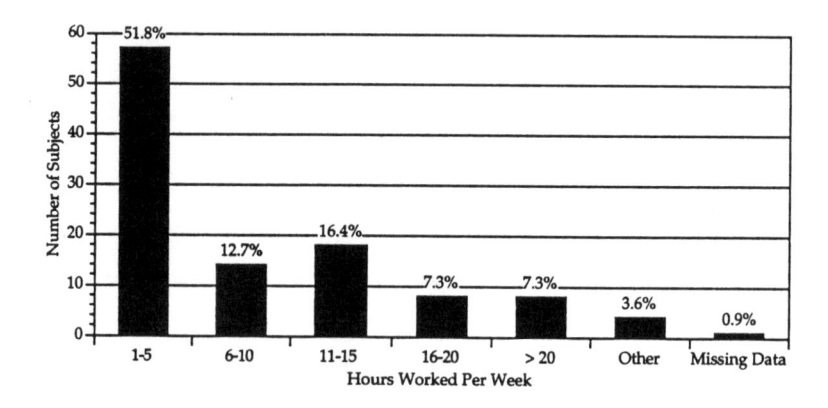